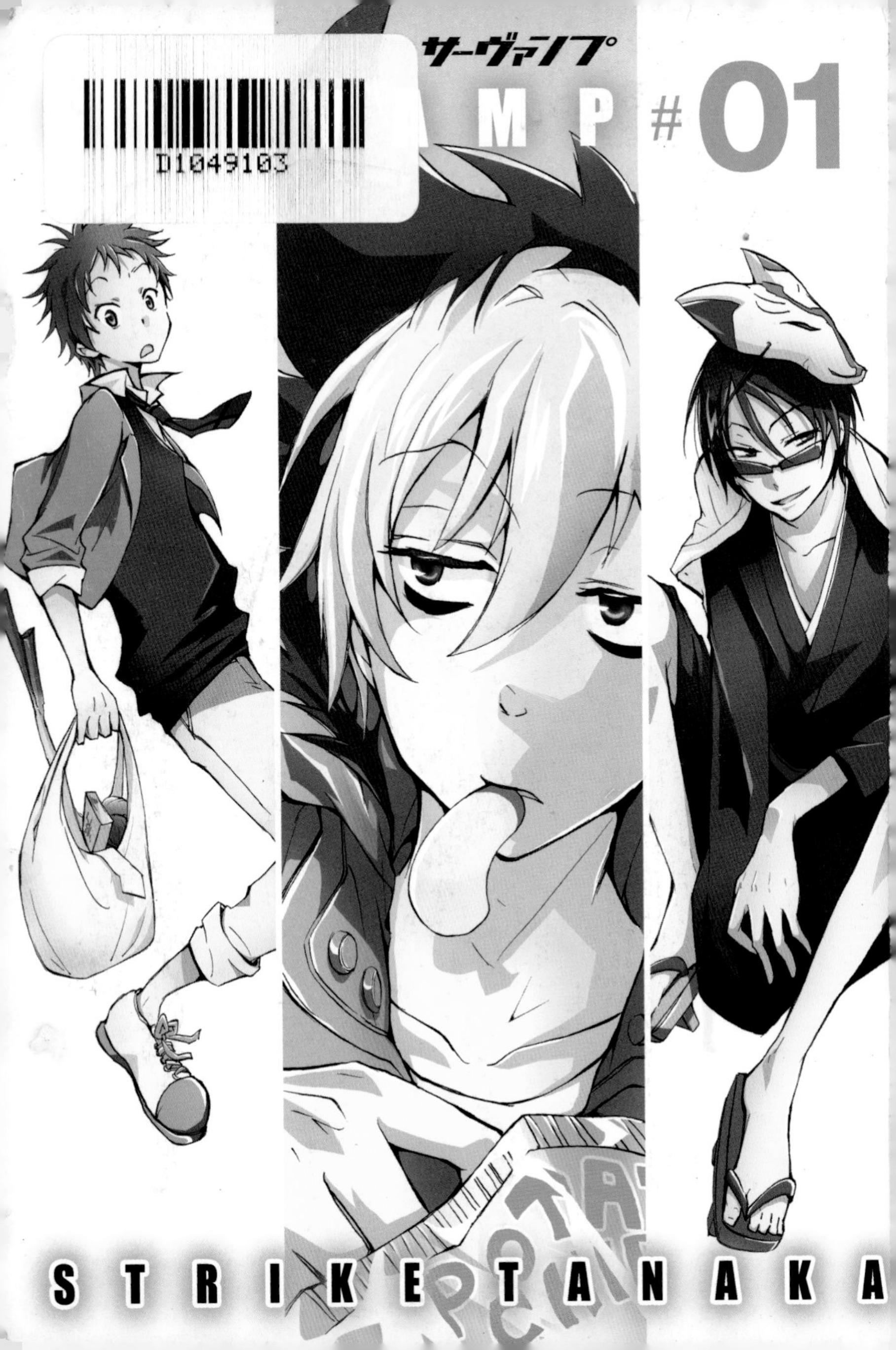
サーヴァンプ
AMP
#01
STRIKE TANAKA

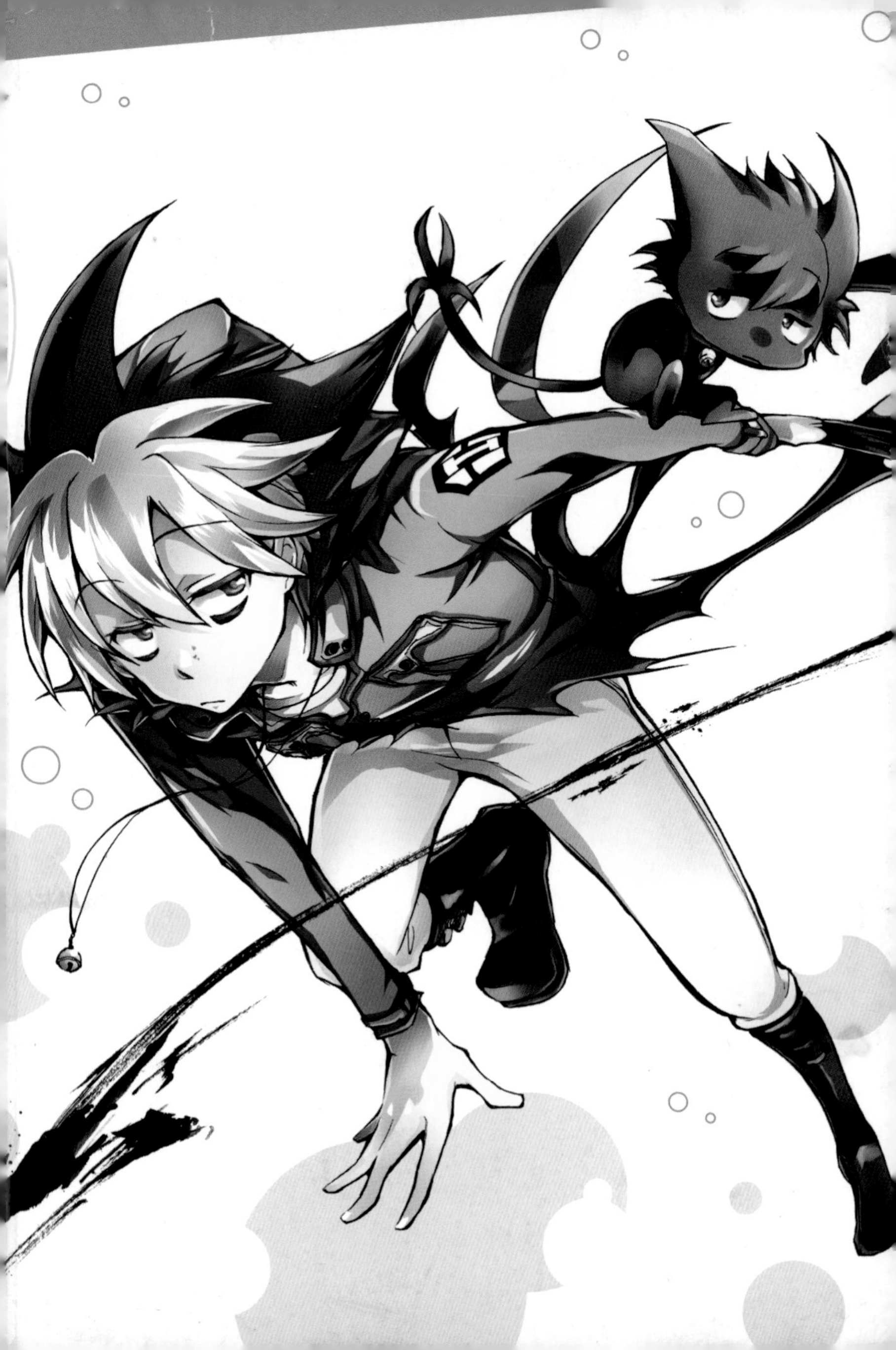

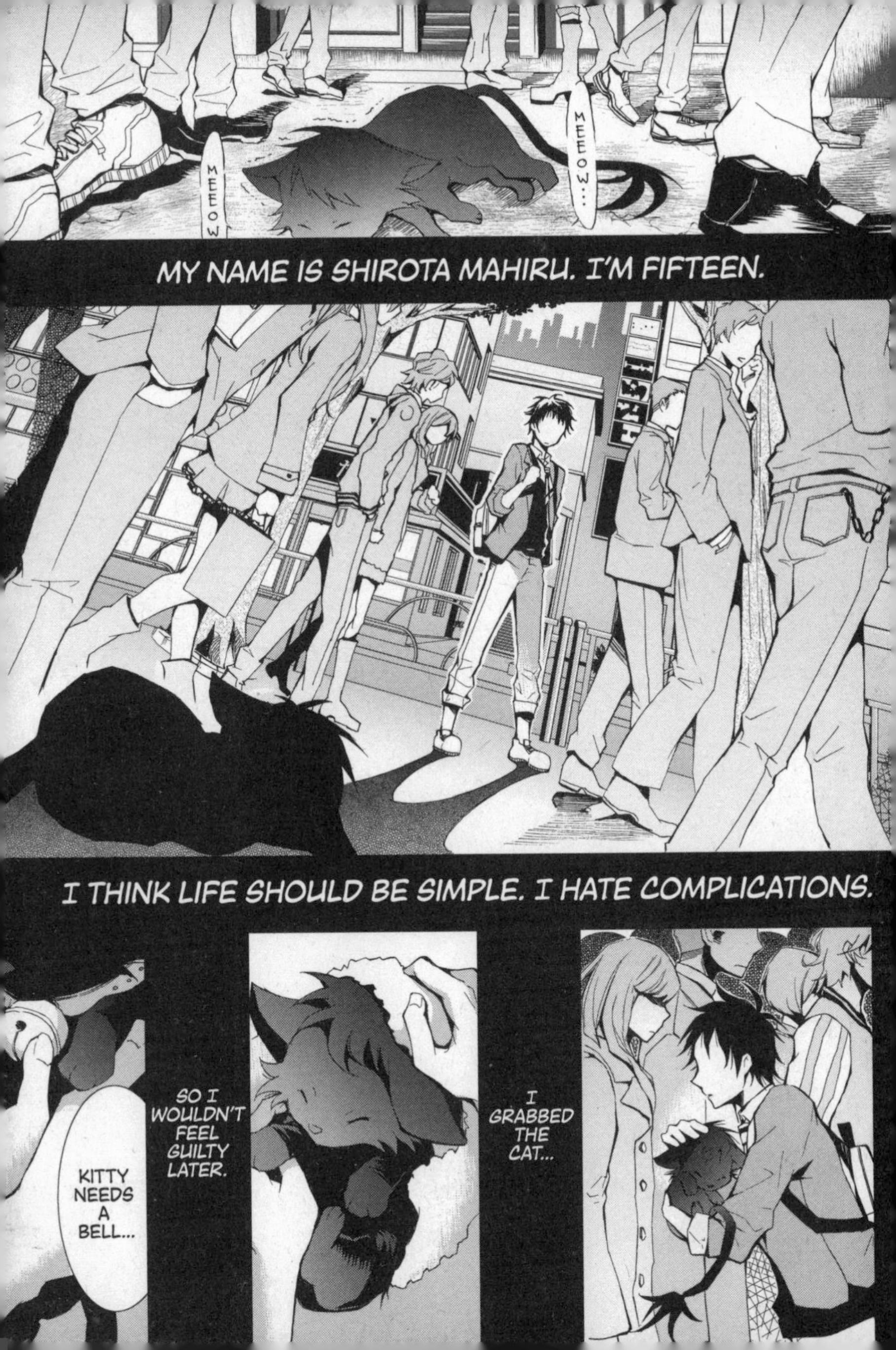
MEEOW...
MEEOW
MY NAME IS SHIROTA MAHIRU. I'M FIFTEEN.
I THINK LIFE SHOULD BE SIMPLE. I HATE COMPLICATIONS.
I GRABBED THE CAT...
SO I WOULDN'T FEEL GUILTY LATER.
KITTY NEEDS A BELL...

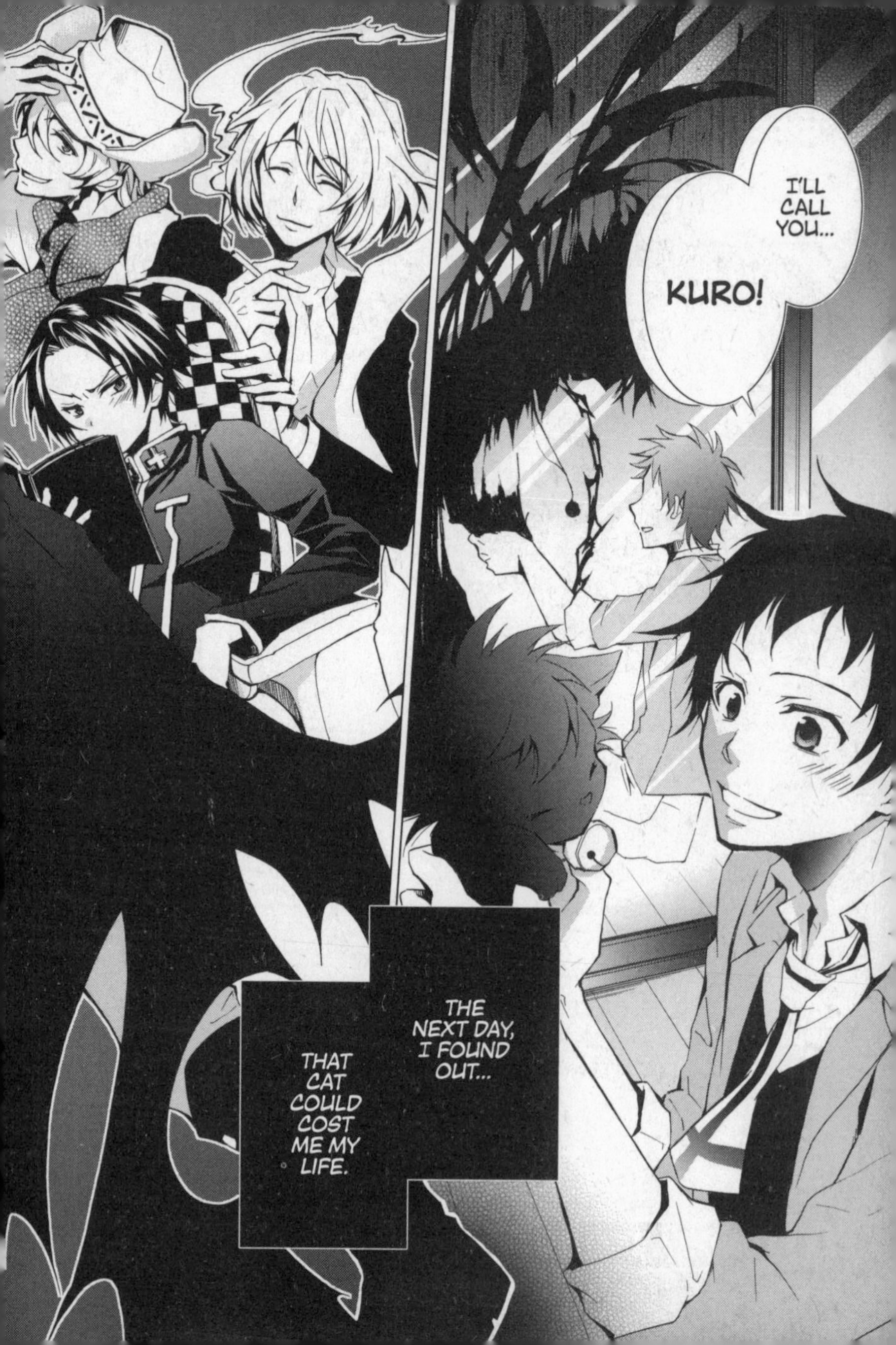
I'LL CALL YOU...
KURO!
THE NEXT DAY, I FOUND OUT...
THAT CAT COULD COST ME MY LIFE.

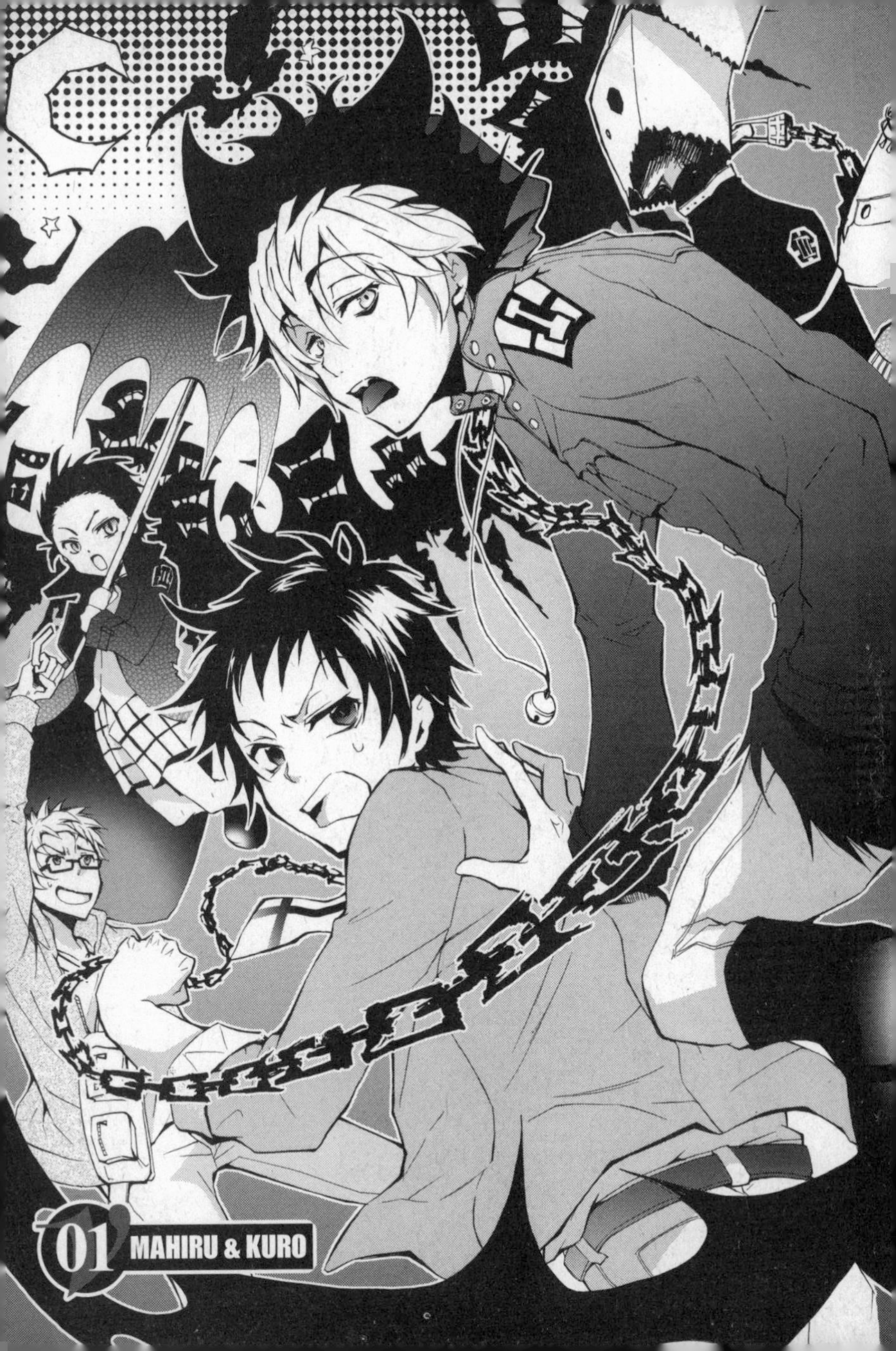

01
MAHIRU & KURO

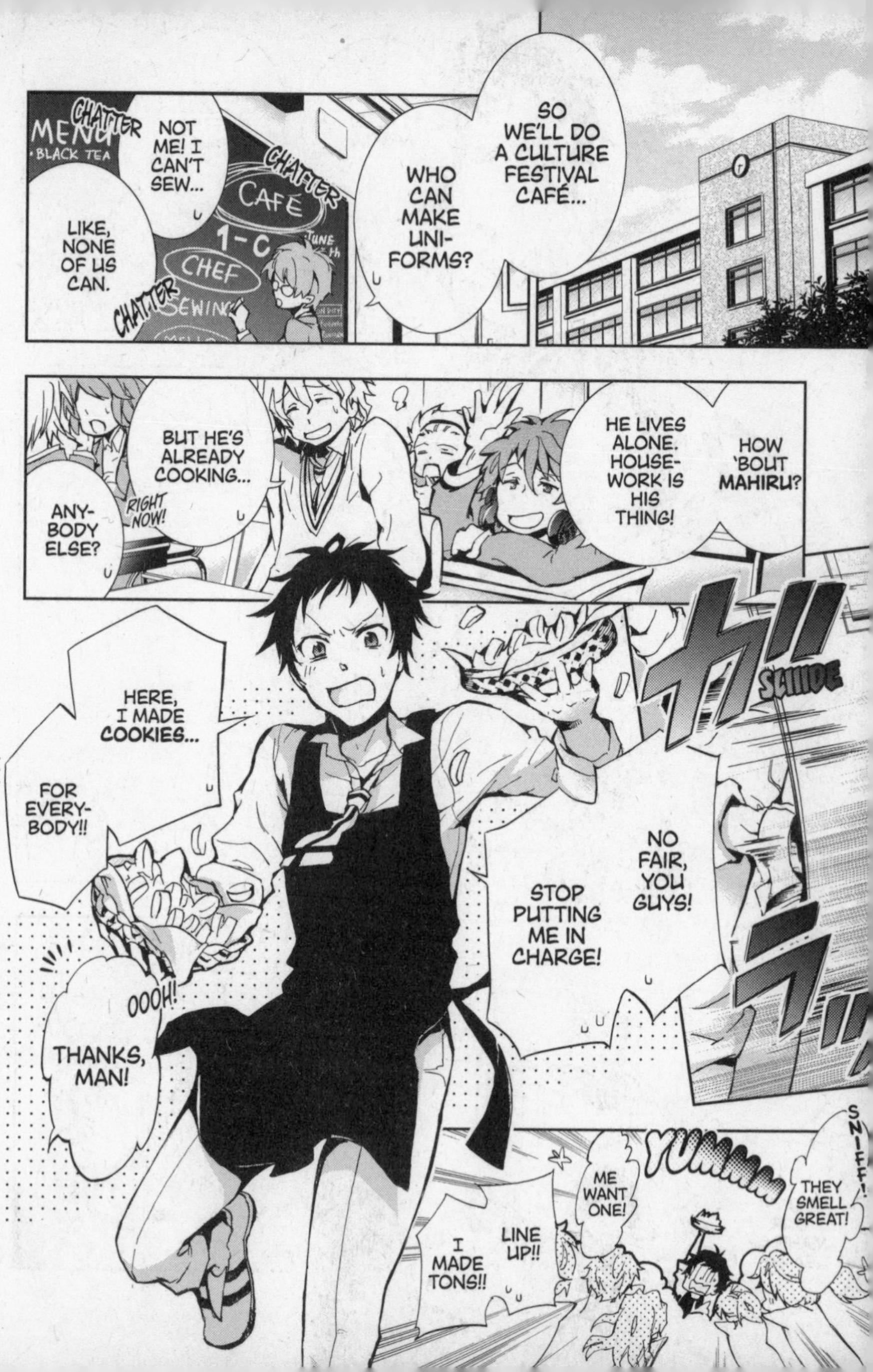
SO WE'LL DO A CULTURE FESTIVAL CAFÉ...
WHO CAN MAKE UNI-FORMS?
CHATTER
CHATTER
CHATTER
MENU
• BLACK TEA
CAFÉ
1-C
CHEF
NOT ME! I CAN'T SEW...
LIKE, NONE OF US CAN.
HOW 'BOUT MAHIRU?
HE LIVES ALONE. HOUSE-WORK IS HIS THING!
BUT HE'S ALREADY COOKING...
RIGHT NOW!
ANY-BODY ELSE?
SLIIIDE
NO FAIR, YOU GUYS!
STOP PUTTING ME IN CHARGE!
HERE, I MADE COOKIES...
FOR EVERY-BODY!!
OOOH!
THANKS, MAN!
SNIFF!
THEY SMELL GREAT!
YUMMM
ME WANT ONE!
LINE UP!!
I MADE TONS!!

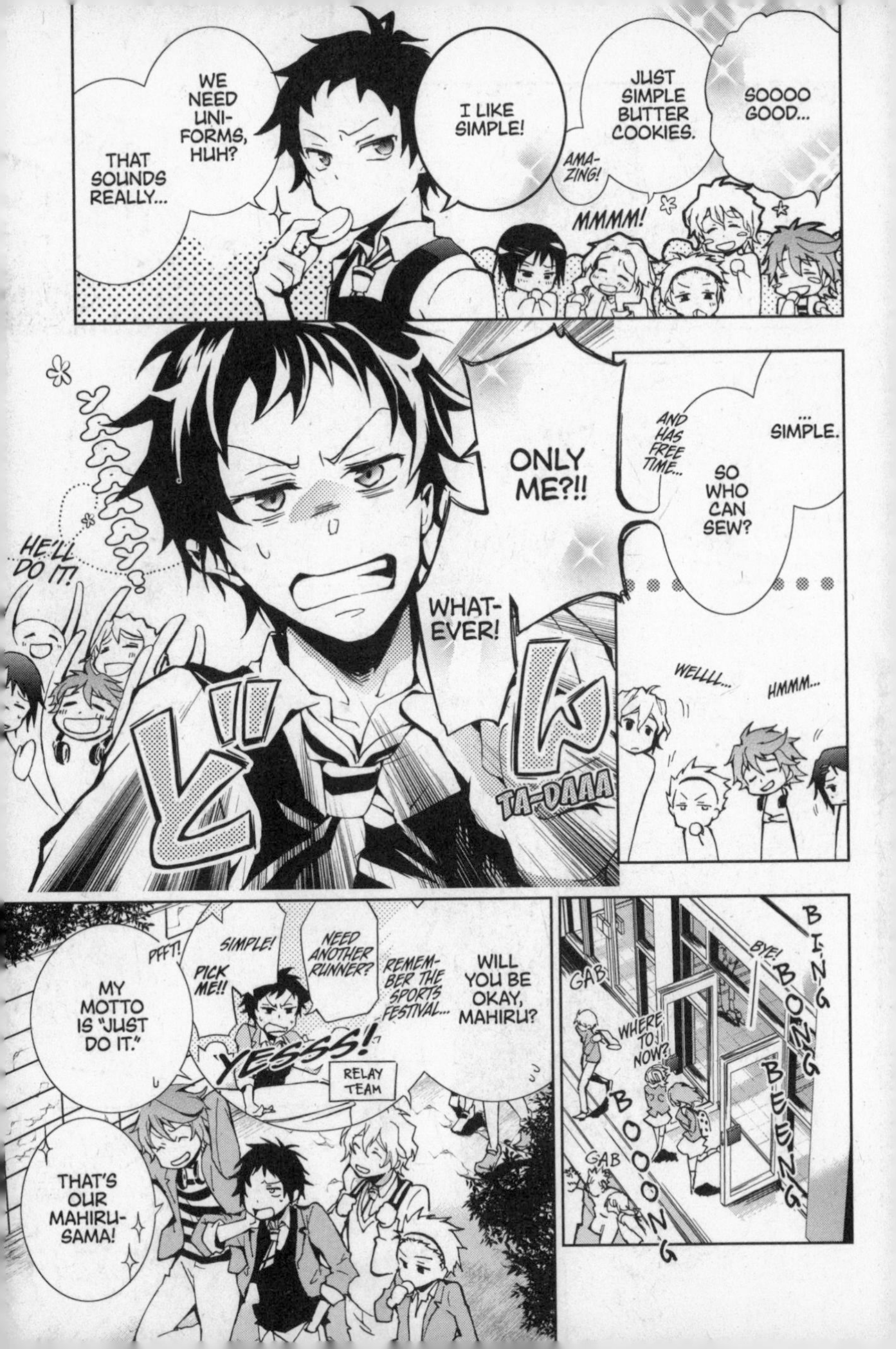
SOOOO GOOD...
JUST SIMPLE BUTTER COOKIES.
AMA-ZING!
MMMM!
I LIKE SIMPLE!
WE NEED UNI-FORMS, HUH?
THAT SOUNDS REALLY...
... SIMPLE.
AND HAS FREE TIME...
SO WHO CAN SEW?
HMMM...
WELLLL...
ONLY ME?!!
WHAT-EVER!
ん
TA-DAAA
ど
HE'LL DO IT!
BING
BONG
BEENG
BYE!
WHERE TO NOW?
GAB
BOOONG
GAB
WILL YOU BE OKAY, MAHIRU?
REMEM-BER THE SPORTS FESTIVAL...
NEED ANOTHER RUNNER?
SIMPLE!
PICK ME!!
PFFT!
MY MOTTO IS "JUST DO IT."
YESSS!
RELAY TEAM
THAT'S OUR MAHIRU-SAMA!

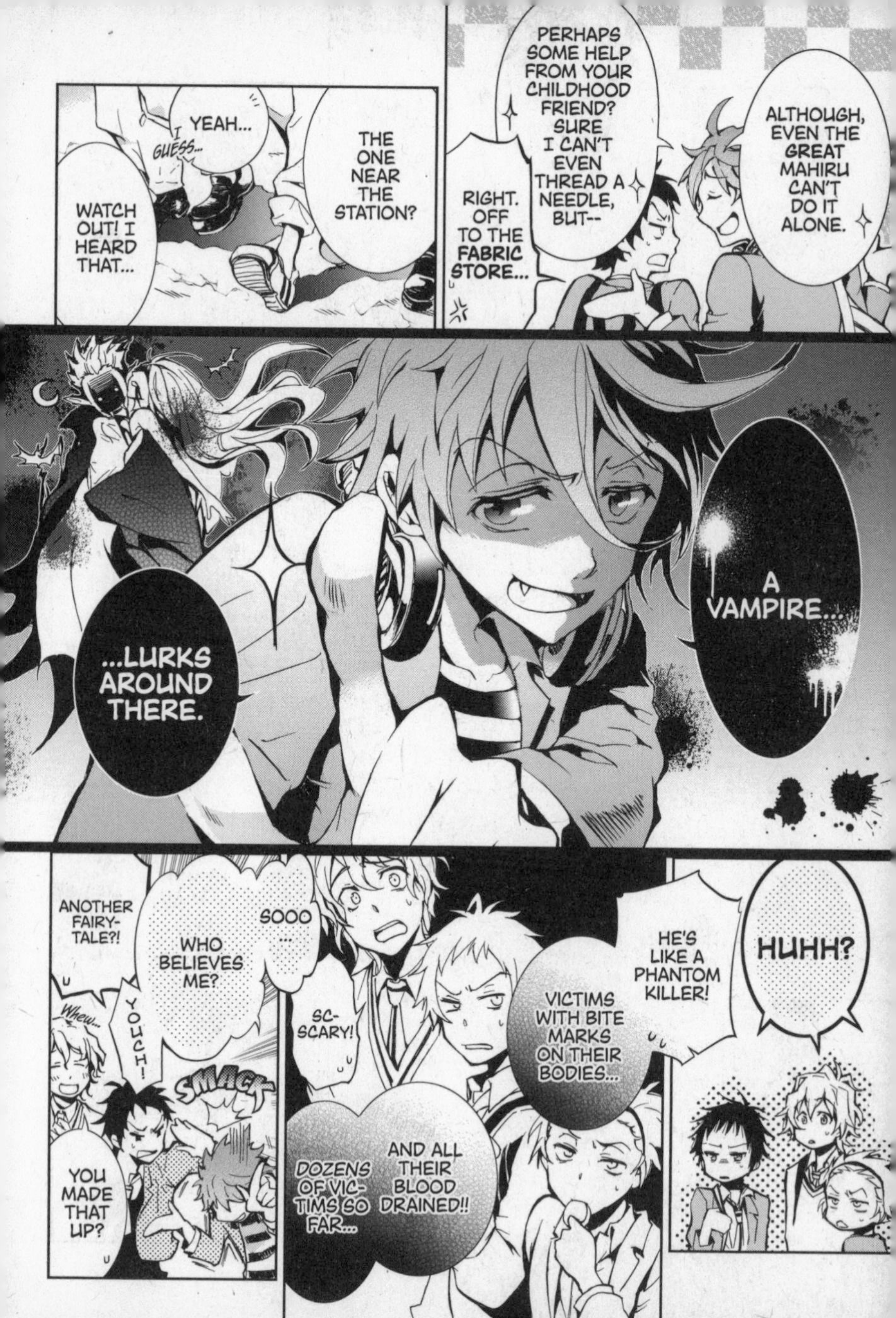
ALTHOUGH, EVEN THE GREAT MAHIRU CAN'T DO IT ALONE.
PERHAPS SOME HELP FROM YOUR CHILDHOOD FRIEND? SURE I CAN'T EVEN THREAD A NEEDLE, BUT--
RIGHT. OFF TO THE FABRIC STORE...
THE ONE NEAR THE STATION?
YEAH...
I GUESS...
WATCH OUT! I HEARD THAT...
A VAMPIRE...
...LURKS AROUND THERE.
HUHH?
HE'S LIKE A PHANTOM KILLER!
VICTIMS WITH BITE MARKS ON THEIR BODIES...
AND ALL THEIR BLOOD DRAINED!!
DOZENS OF VIC-TIMS SO FAR...
SC-SCARY!
SOOO ...
WHO BELIEVES ME?
ANOTHER FAIRY-TALE?!
YOUCH!
SMACK
Whew...
YOU MADE THAT UP?

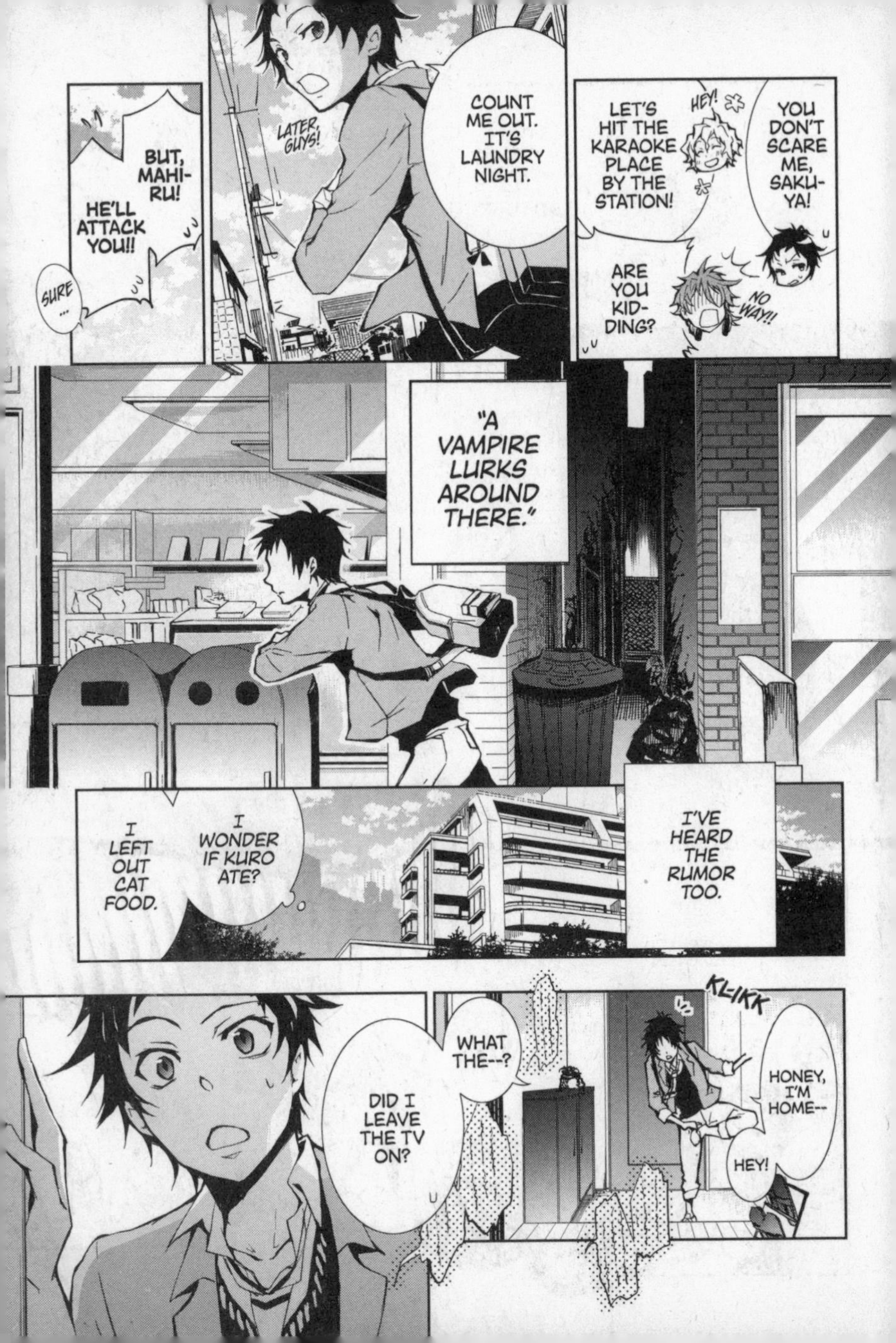
YOU DON'T SCARE ME, SAKU-YA!
HEY!
LET'S HIT THE KARAOKE PLACE BY THE STATION!
NO WAY!!
ARE YOU KID-DING?
COUNT ME OUT. IT'S LAUNDRY NIGHT.
LATER, GUYS!
BUT, MAHI-RU!
HE'LL ATTACK YOU!!
SURE...
"A VAMPIRE LURKS AROUND THERE."
I'VE HEARD THE RUMOR TOO.
I WONDER IF KURO ATE?
I LEFT OUT CAT FOOD.
KL-IKK
HONEY, I'M HOME--
HEY!
WHAT THE--?
DID I LEAVE THE TV ON?

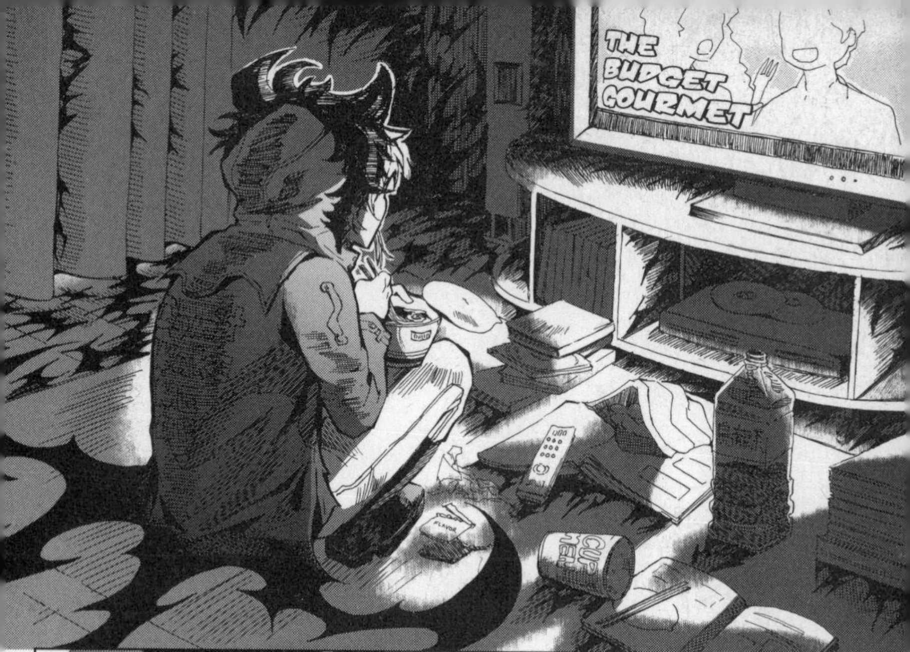
THE BUDGET GOURMET
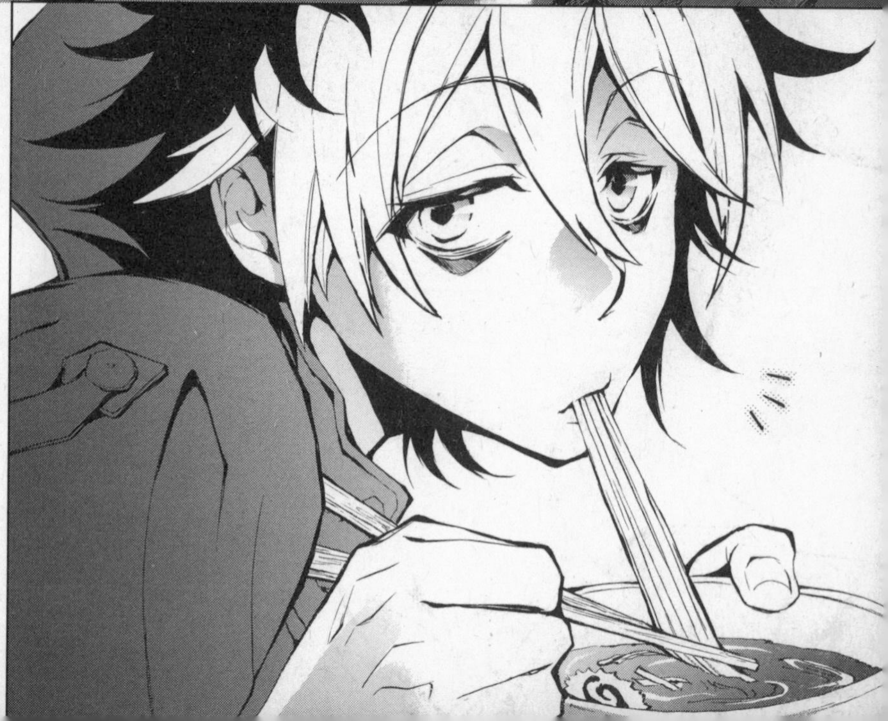

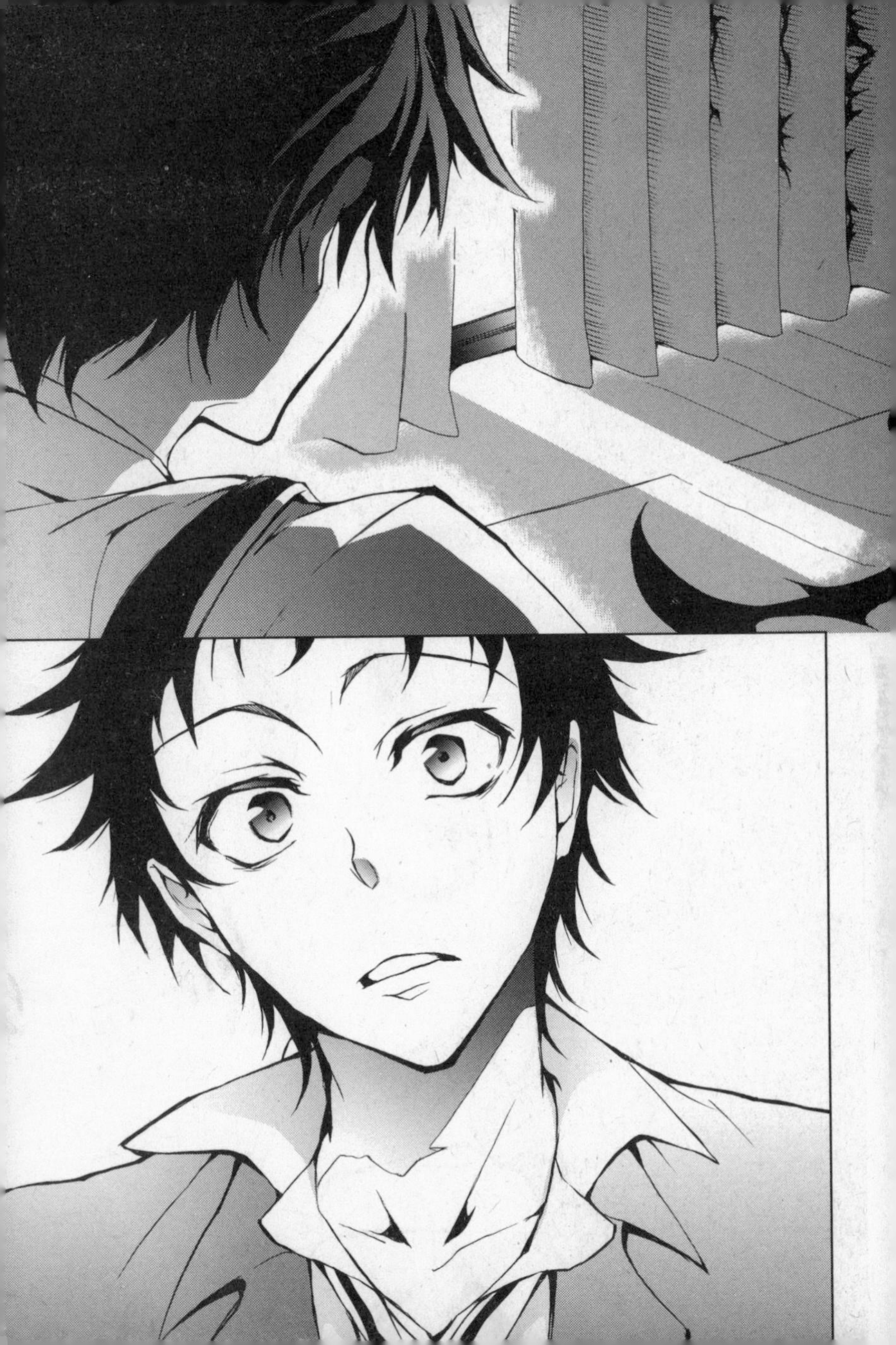

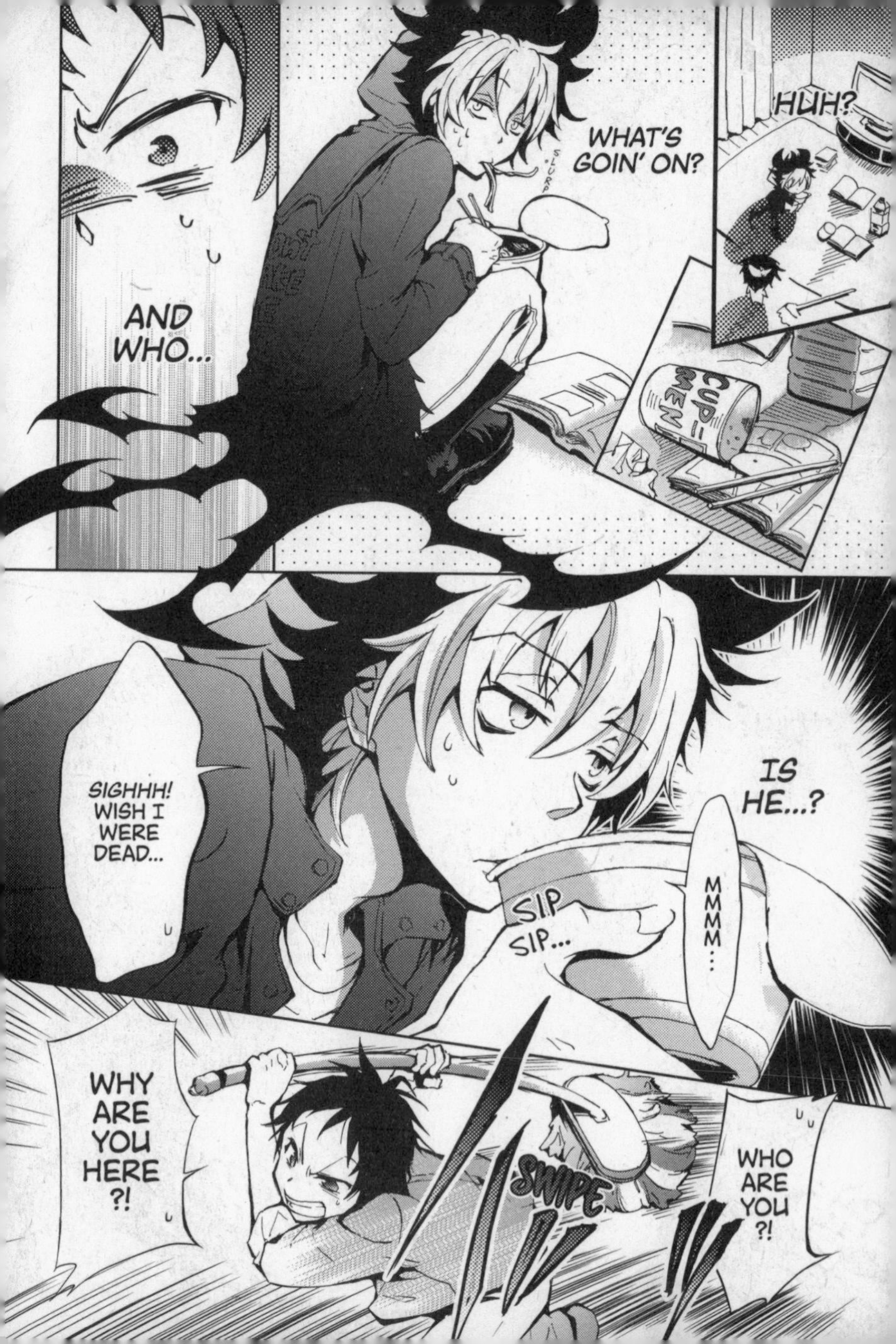
HUH?
CUP MEN
WHAT'S GOIN' ON?
SLURP
AND WHO...
IS HE...?
MMMM...
SIP SIP...
SIGHHH! WISH I WERE DEAD...
WHO ARE YOU ?!
SWIPE
WHY ARE YOU HERE ?!

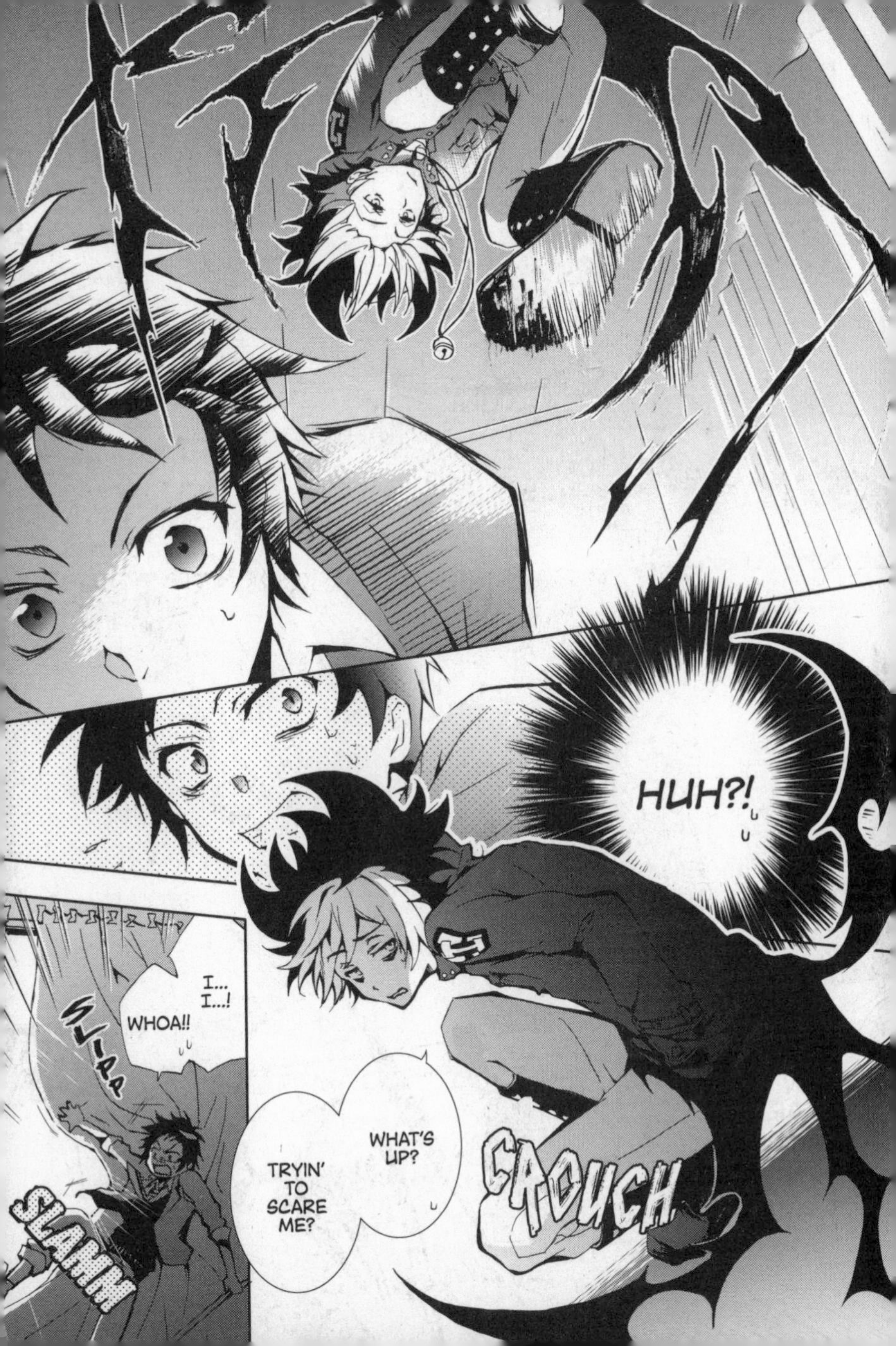
HUH?!
WHAT'S UP?
TRYIN' TO SCARE ME?
CROUCH
I... I...!
WHOA!!
SLIPP
SLAMM

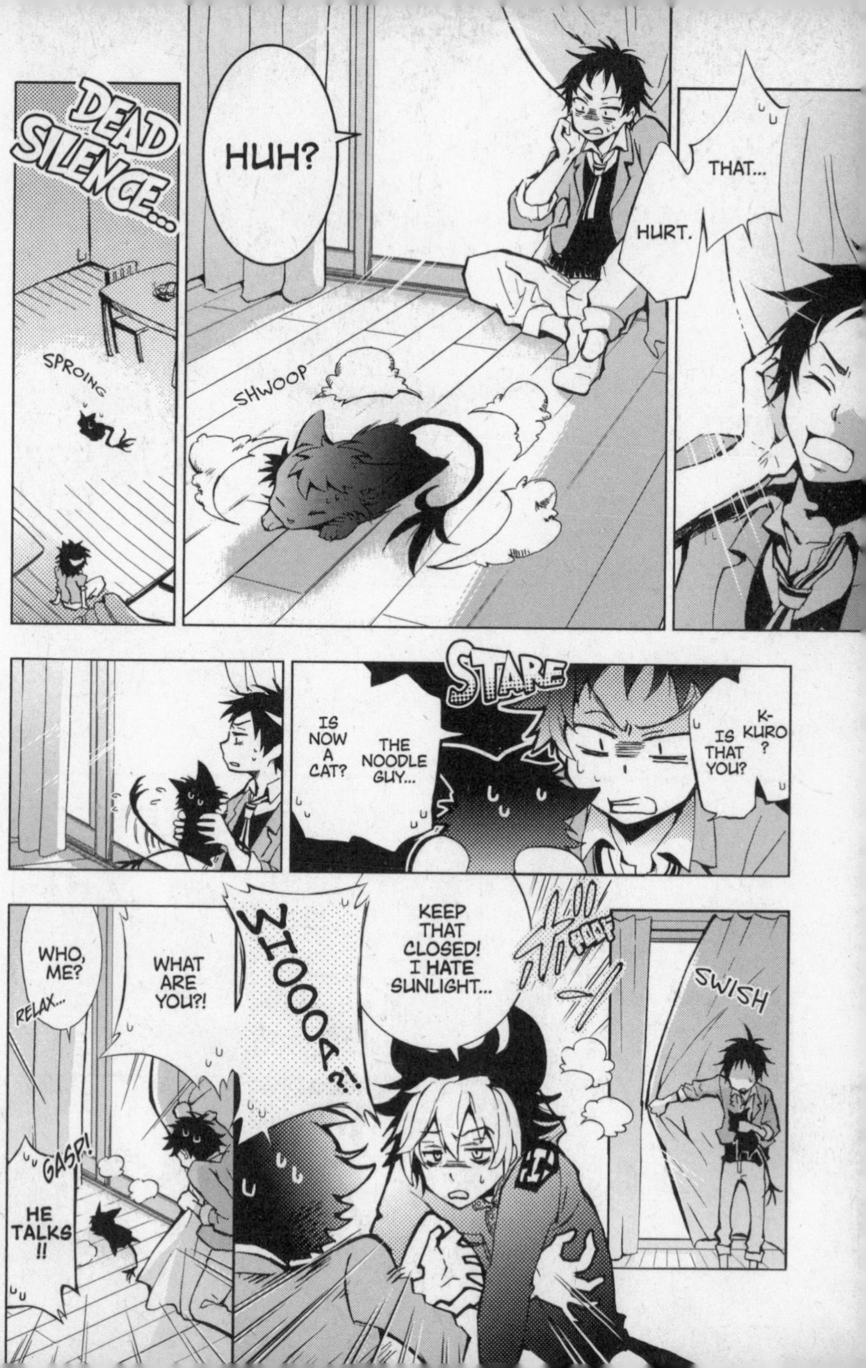

THAT...
HURT.
HUH?
SHWOOP
DEAD SILENCE...
SPROING
STARE
K-KURO? IS THAT YOU?
THE NOODLE GUY...
IS NOW A CAT?
SWISH
KEEP THAT CLOSED! I HATE SUNLIGHT...
WHOOOA?!
WHAT ARE YOU?!
WHO, ME?
RELAX...
GASP!
HE TALKS!!

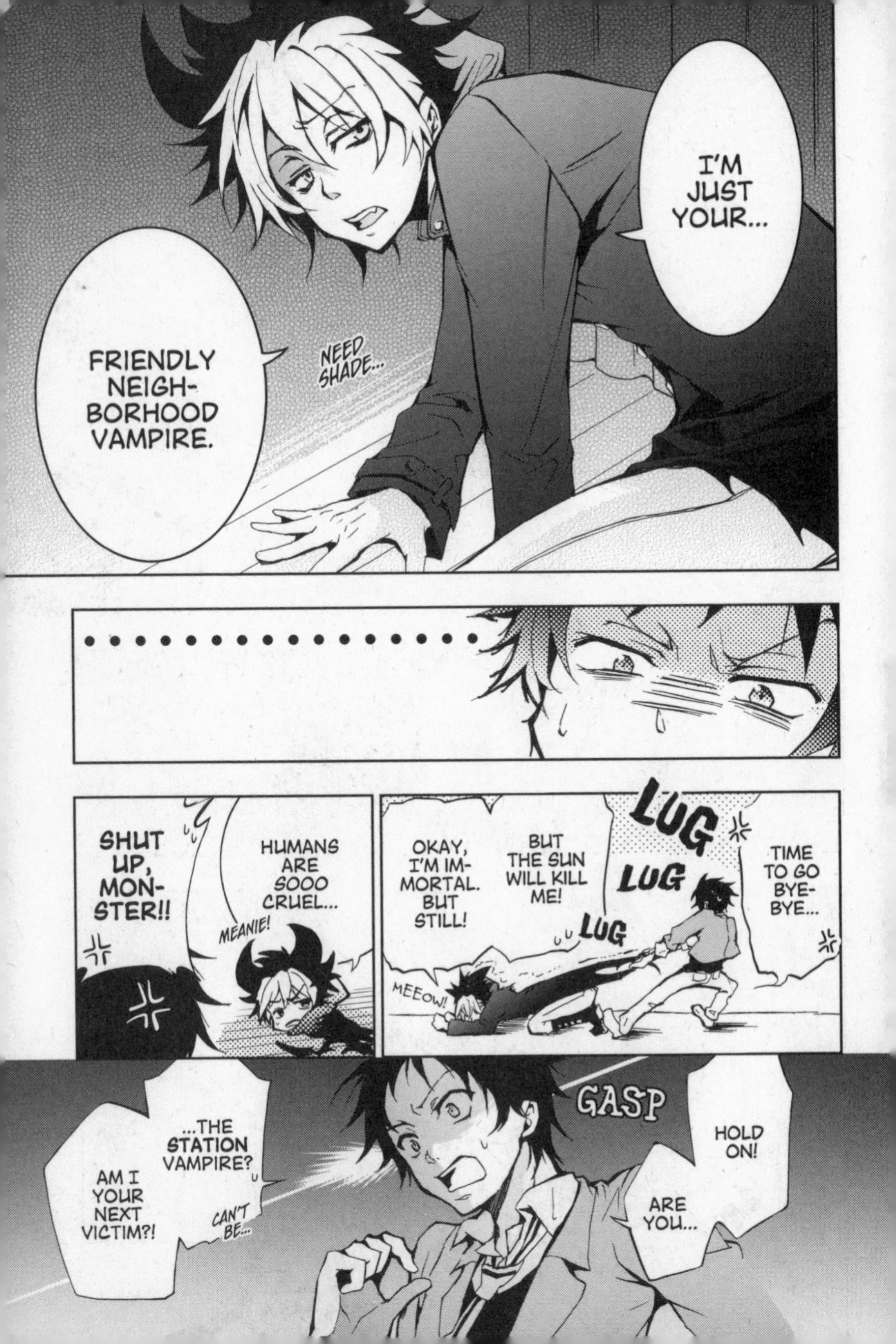
I'M JUST YOUR...
NEED SHADE...
FRIENDLY NEIGH-BORHOOD VAMPIRE.
....
TIME TO GO BYE-BYE...
LUG
LUG
LUG
BUT THE SUN WILL KILL ME!
OKAY, I'M IM-MORTAL. BUT STILL!
MEEOW!
HUMANS ARE SOOO CRUEL...
MEANIE!
SHUT UP, MON-STER!!
GASP
HOLD ON!
ARE YOU...
...THE STATION VAMPIRE?
CAN'T BE...
AM I YOUR NEXT VICTIM?!

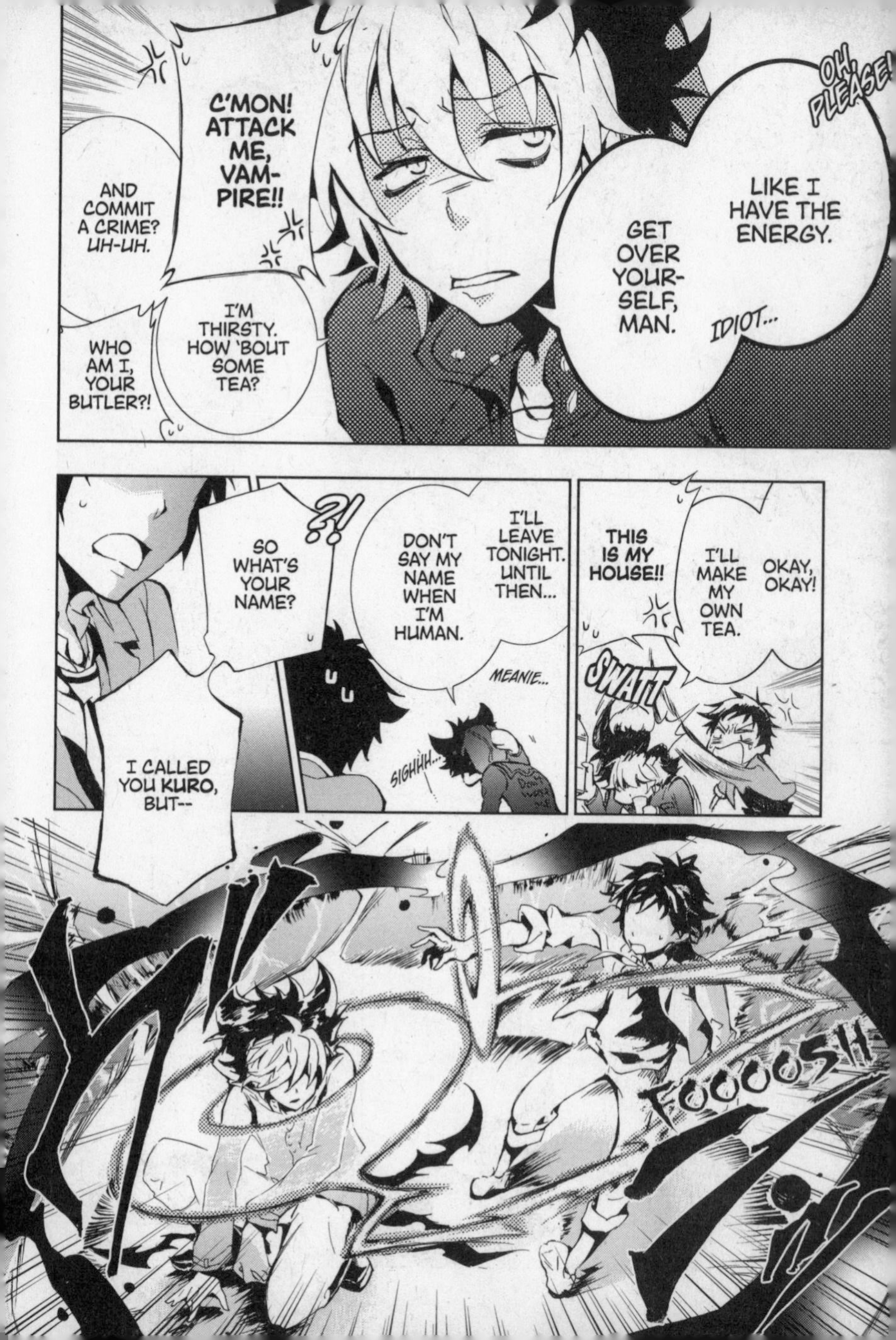
OH, PLEASE!
LIKE I HAVE THE ENERGY.
GET OVER YOURSELF, MAN.
IDIOT...
C'MON! ATTACK ME, VAMPIRE!!
AND COMMIT A CRIME? UH-UH.
I'M THIRSTY. HOW 'BOUT SOME TEA?
WHO AM I, YOUR BUTLER?!
OKAY, OKAY!
I'LL MAKE MY OWN TEA.
THIS IS MY HOUSE!!
SWATT
I'LL LEAVE TONIGHT. UNTIL THEN...
DON'T SAY MY NAME WHEN I'M HUMAN.
MEANIE...
SIGHHH...
?!
SO WHAT'S YOUR NAME?
I CALLED YOU KURO, BUT--
FOOOOOSH!!

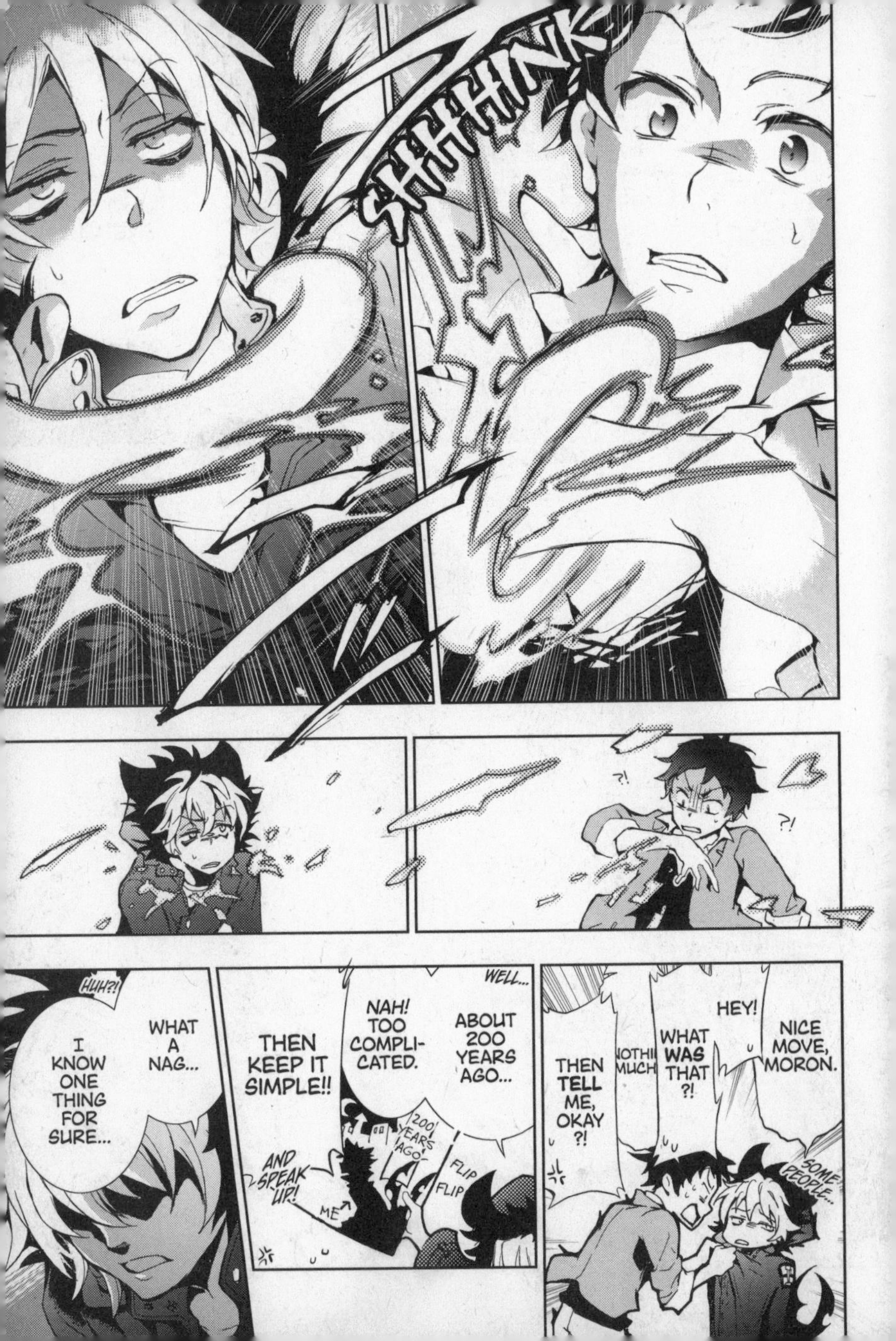
SHHHHINK
?!
?!
NICE MOVE, MORON.
HEY!
WHAT WAS THAT?!
NOTHI MUCH
THEN TELL ME, OKAY?!
SOME PEOPLE...
WELL...
ABOUT 200 YEARS AGO...
NAH! TOO COMPLI-CATED.
THEN KEEP IT SIMPLE!!
200 YEARS AGO
FLIP FLIP
AND SPEAK UP!
ME
HUH?!
WHAT A NAG...
I KNOW ONE THING FOR SURE...

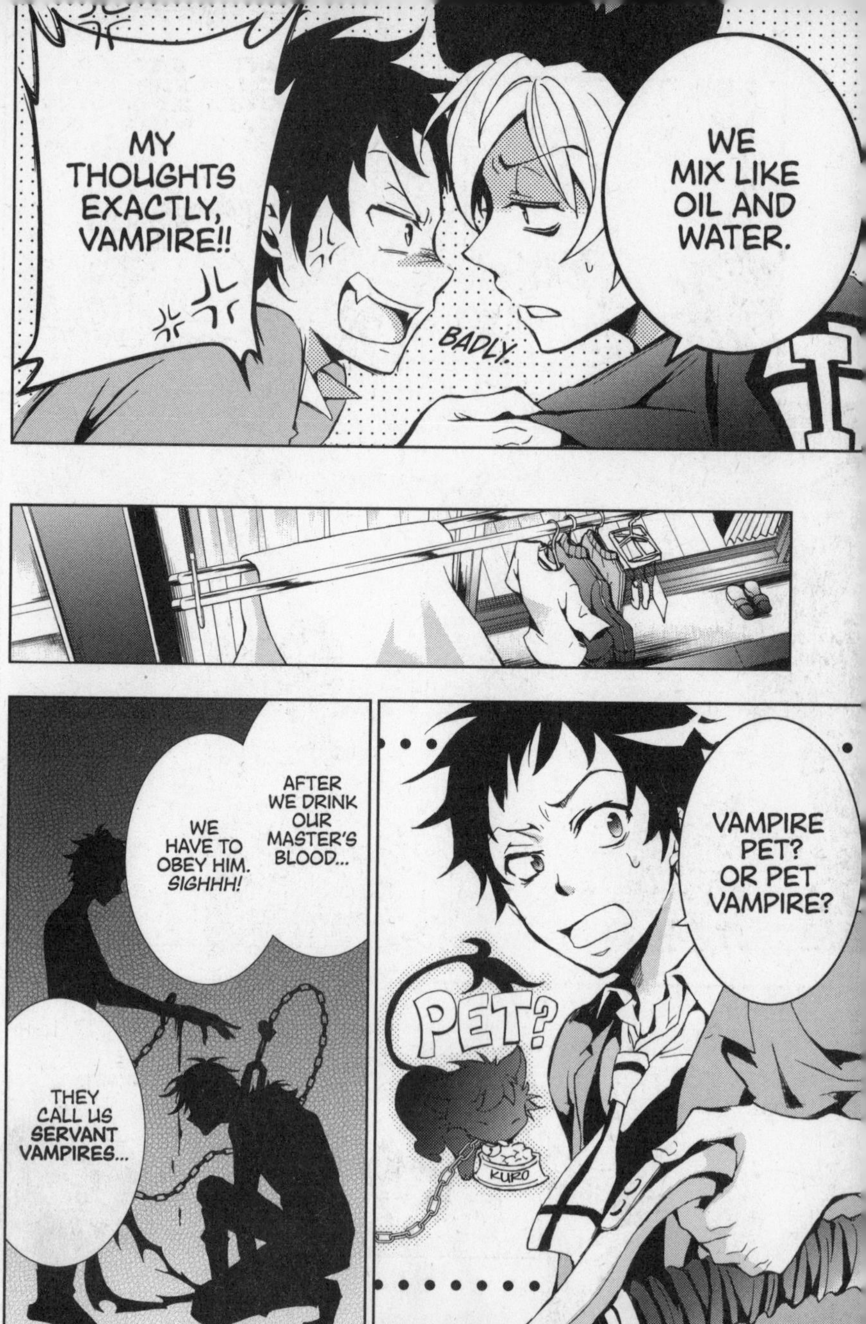
WE MIX LIKE OIL AND WATER.
BADLY.
MY THOUGHTS EXACTLY, VAMPIRE!!
VAMPIRE PET? OR PET VAMPIRE?
PET?
KURO
AFTER WE DRINK OUR MASTER'S BLOOD...
WE HAVE TO OBEY HIM. *SIGHHH!*
THEY CALL US SERVANT VAMPIRES...

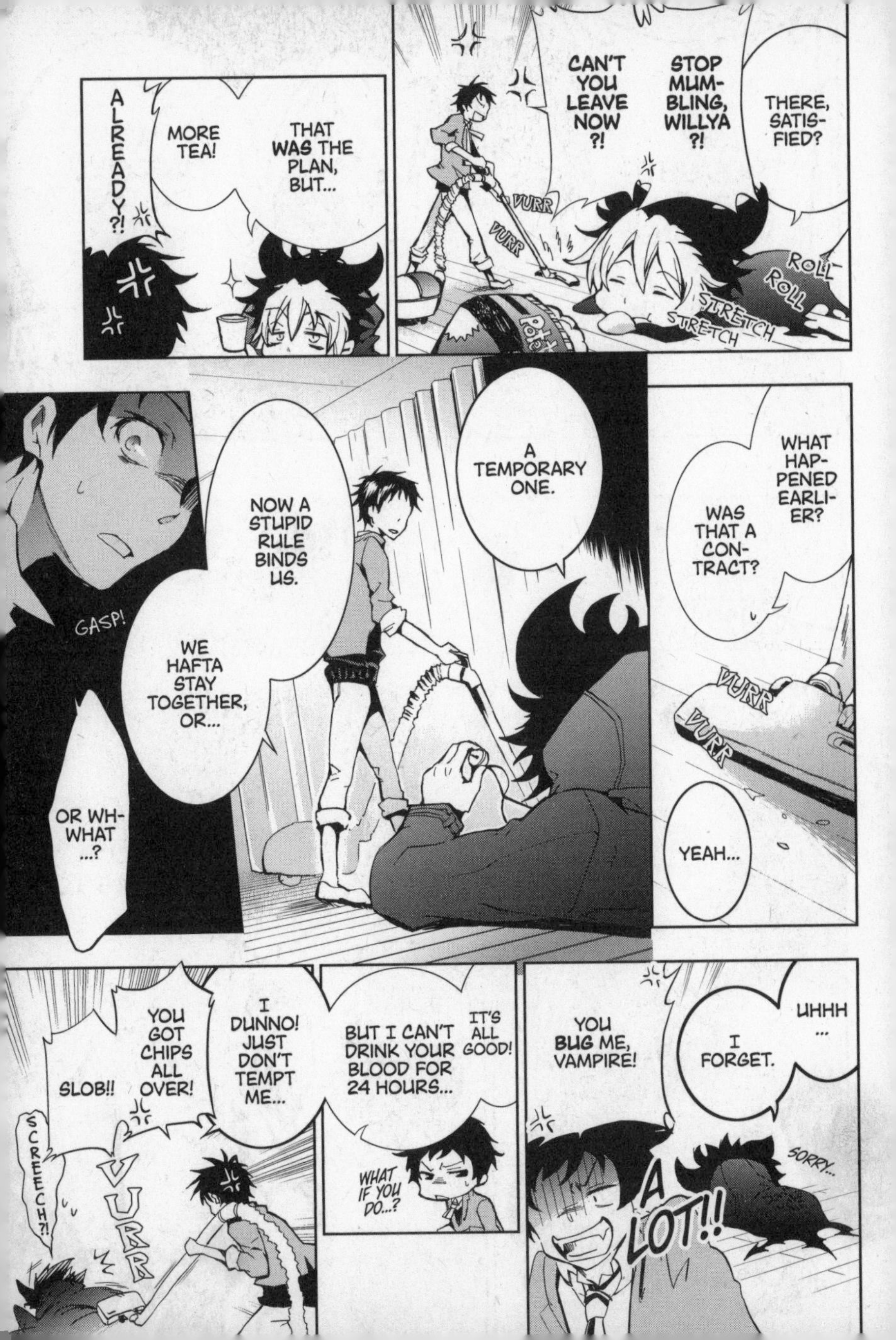
THERE, SATIS-FIED?
STOP MUM-BLING, WILLYA ?!
CAN'T YOU LEAVE NOW ?!
VURR
VURR
ROLL
ROLL
STRETCH
STRETCH
THAT WAS THE PLAN, BUT...
MORE TEA!
ALREADY?!
WHAT HAP-PENED EARLI-ER?
WAS THAT A CON-TRACT?
VURR
VURR
YEAH...
A TEMPORARY ONE.
NOW A STUPID RULE BINDS US.
WE HAFTA STAY TOGETHER, OR...
GASP!
OR WH-WHAT ...?
UHHH ...
I FORGET.
YOU BUG ME, VAMPIRE!
A LOT!!
SORRY...
IT'S ALL GOOD!
BUT I CAN'T DRINK YOUR BLOOD FOR 24 HOURS...
WHAT IF YOU DO...?
I DUNNO! JUST DON'T TEMPT ME...
YOU GOT CHIPS ALL OVER!
SLOB!!
VURR
SCRECH?!

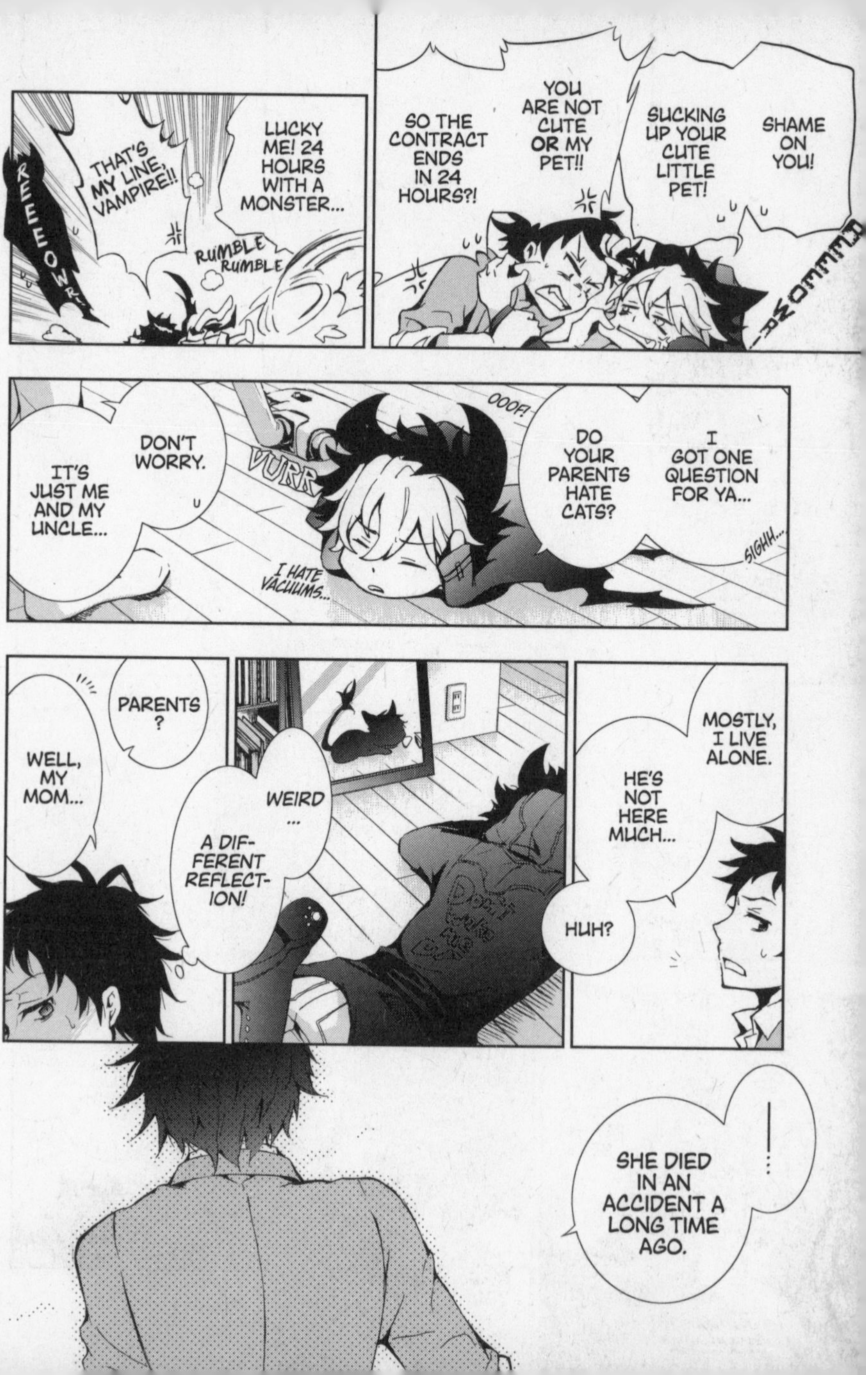
SHAME ON YOU!
SUCKING UP YOUR CUTE LITTLE PET!
YOU ARE NOT CUTE OR MY PET!!
SO THE CONTRACT ENDS IN 24 HOURS?!
LUCKY ME! 24 HOURS WITH A MONSTER...
THAT'S MY LINE, VAMPIRE!!
RUMBLE RUMBLE
REEEOWR!
I GOT ONE QUESTION FOR YA...
SIGHH...
DO YOUR PARENTS HATE CATS?
OOOF!
VURR
I HATE VACUUMS...
DON'T WORRY.
IT'S JUST ME AND MY UNCLE...
MOSTLY, I LIVE ALONE.
HE'S NOT HERE MUCH...
HUH?
WEIRD...
A DIF-FERENT REFLECT-ION!
PARENTS?
WELL, MY MOM...
—...
SHE DIED IN AN ACCIDENT A LONG TIME AGO.

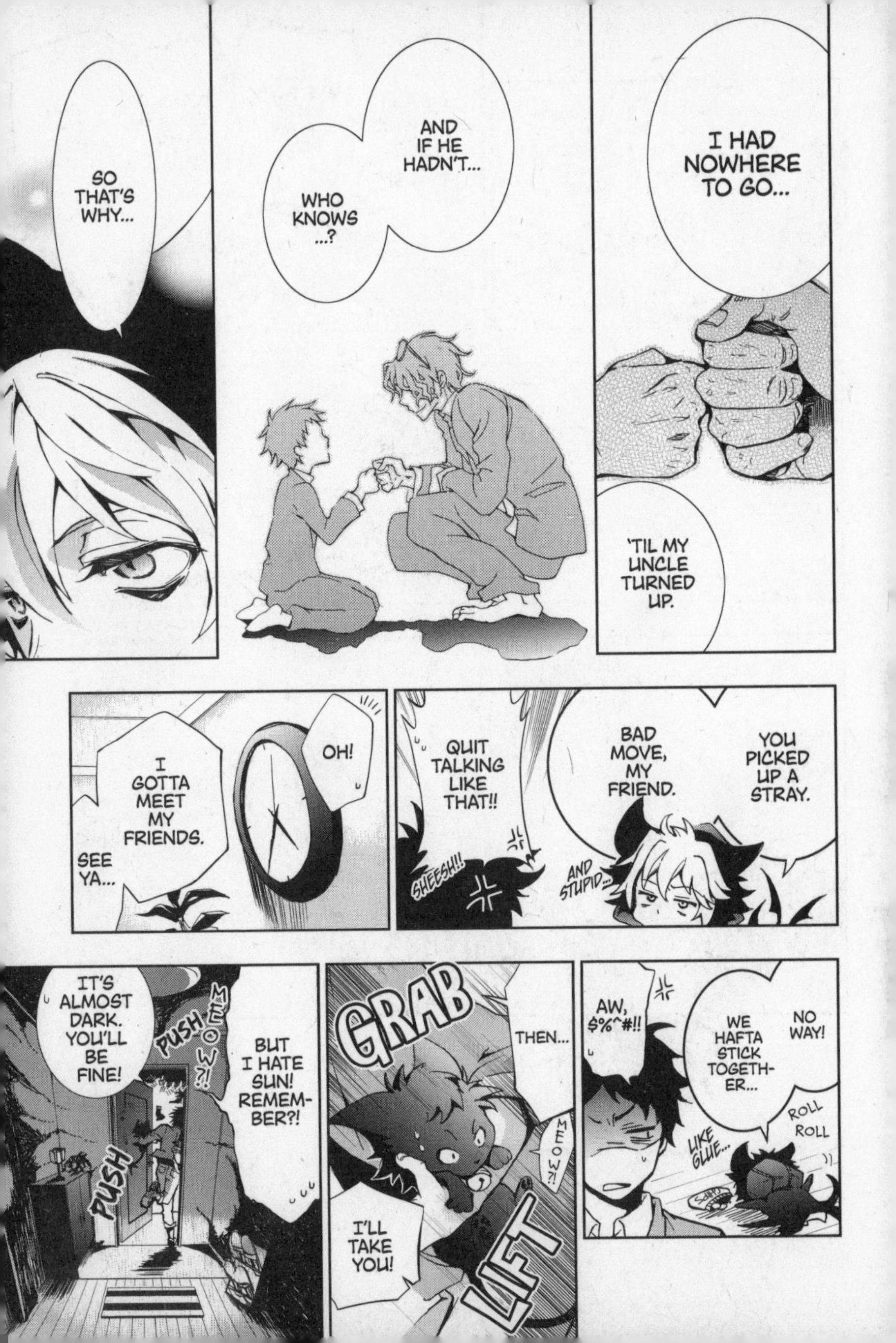
I HAD NOWHERE TO GO...
'TIL MY UNCLE TURNED UP.
AND IF HE HADN'T...
WHO KNOWS ...?
SO THAT'S WHY...
YOU PICKED UP A STRAY.
BAD MOVE, MY FRIEND.
AND STUPID...
QUIT TALKING LIKE THAT!!
SHEESH!!
OH!
I GOTTA MEET MY FRIENDS.
SEE YA...
NO WAY!
WE HAFTA STICK TOGETH-ER...
AW, $%^#!!
LIKE GLUE...
ROLL
ROLL
GRAB
THEN...
MEOW?!
I'LL TAKE YOU!
LIFT
BUT I HATE SUN! REMEMBER?!
MEOW?!
IT'S ALMOST DARK. YOU'LL BE FINE!
PUSH
PUSH

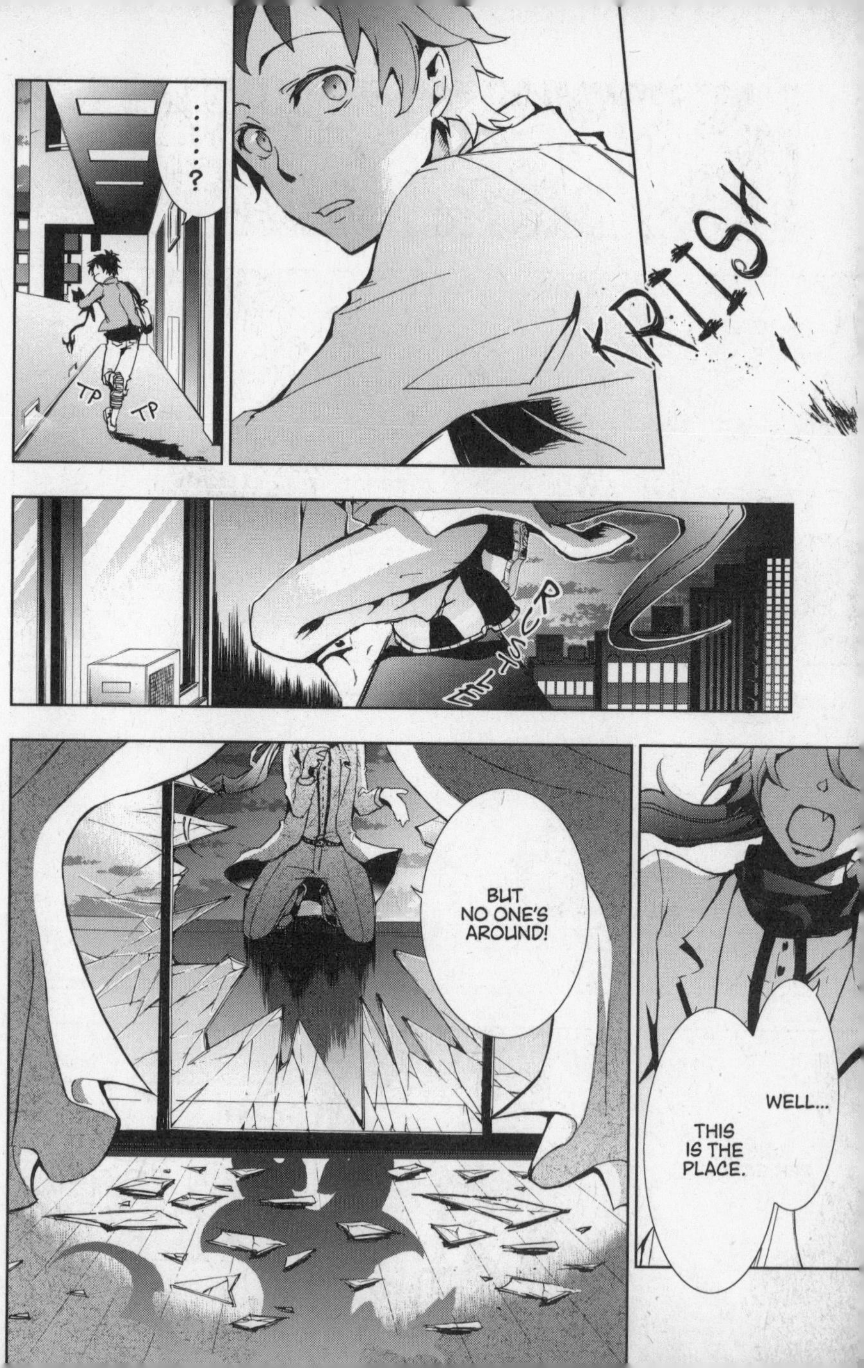
KRIISH
......?
TP TP
WELL...
THIS IS THE PLACE.
BUT NO ONE'S AROUND!

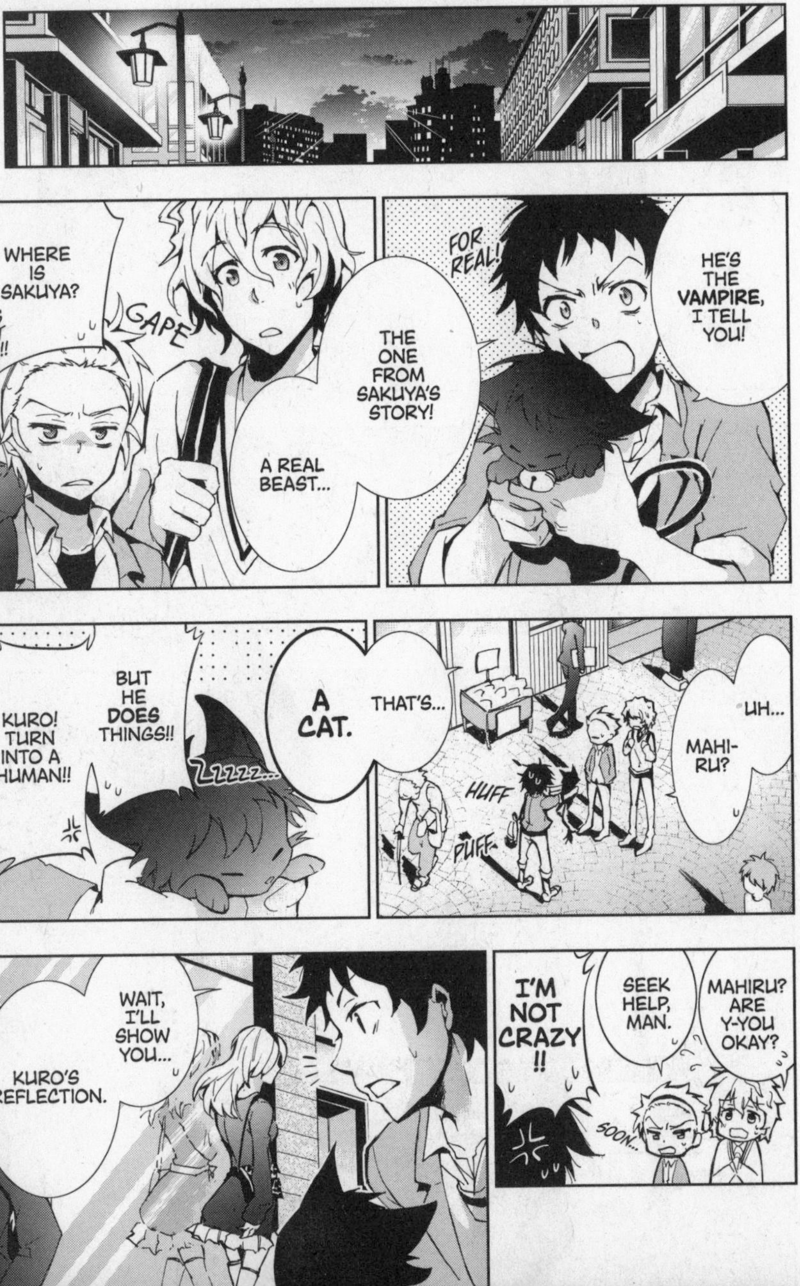
HE'S THE VAMPIRE, I TELL YOU!
FOR REAL!
THE ONE FROM SAKUYA'S STORY!
A REAL BEAST...
GAPE
WHERE IS SAKUYA?
HE NEEDS A CAT BITE!!
UH... MAHIRU?
HUFF
PUFF
THAT'S... A CAT.
BUT HE DOES THINGS!!
KURO! TURN INTO A HUMAN!!
ZZZZZ...
MAHIRU? ARE Y-YOU OKAY?
SEEK HELP, MAN.
SOON...
I'M NOT CRAZY!!
WAIT, I'LL SHOW YOU...
KURO'S REFLECTION.

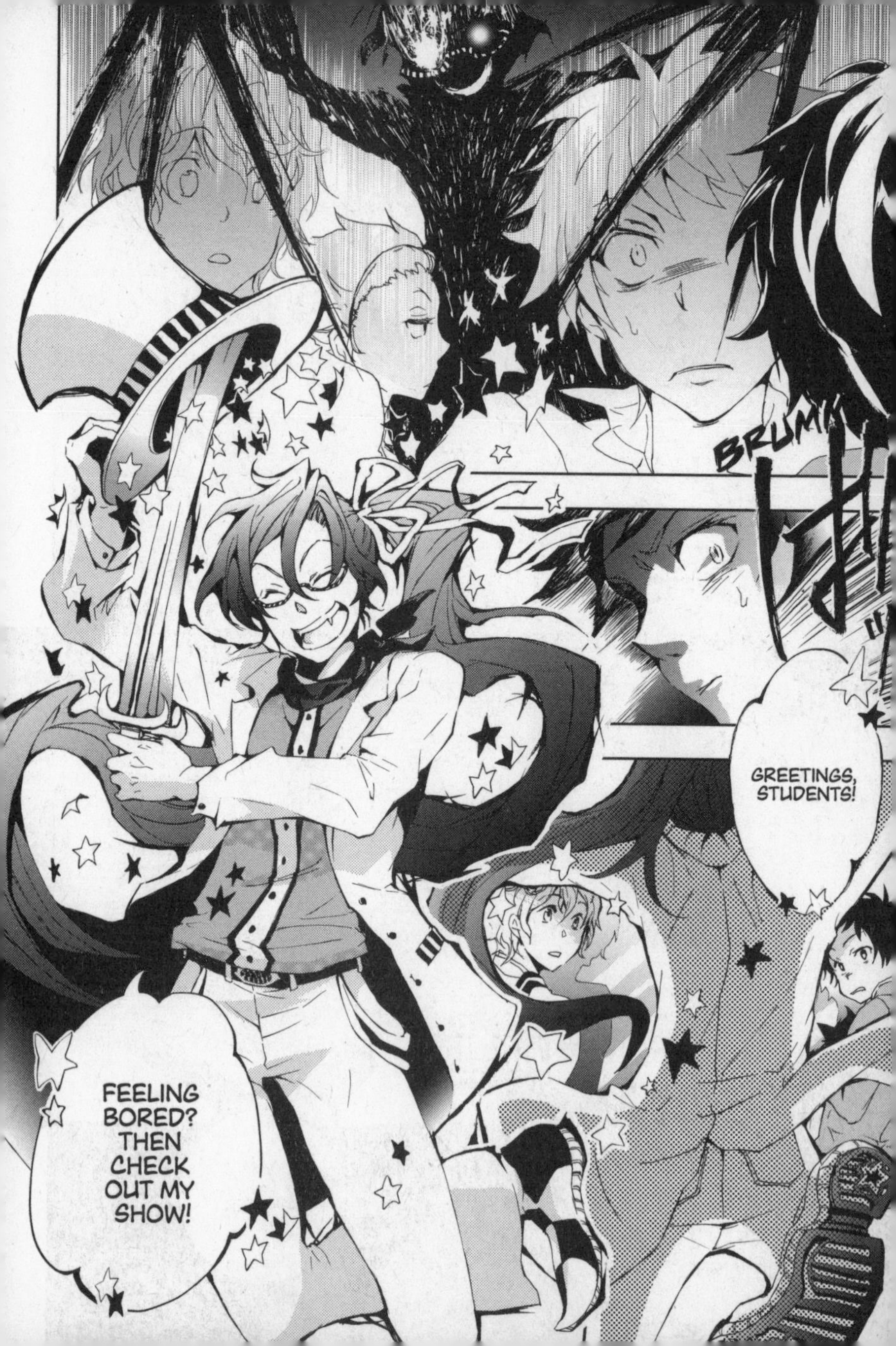
BRUM
GREETINGS, STUDENTS!
FEELING BORED? THEN CHECK OUT MY SHOW!

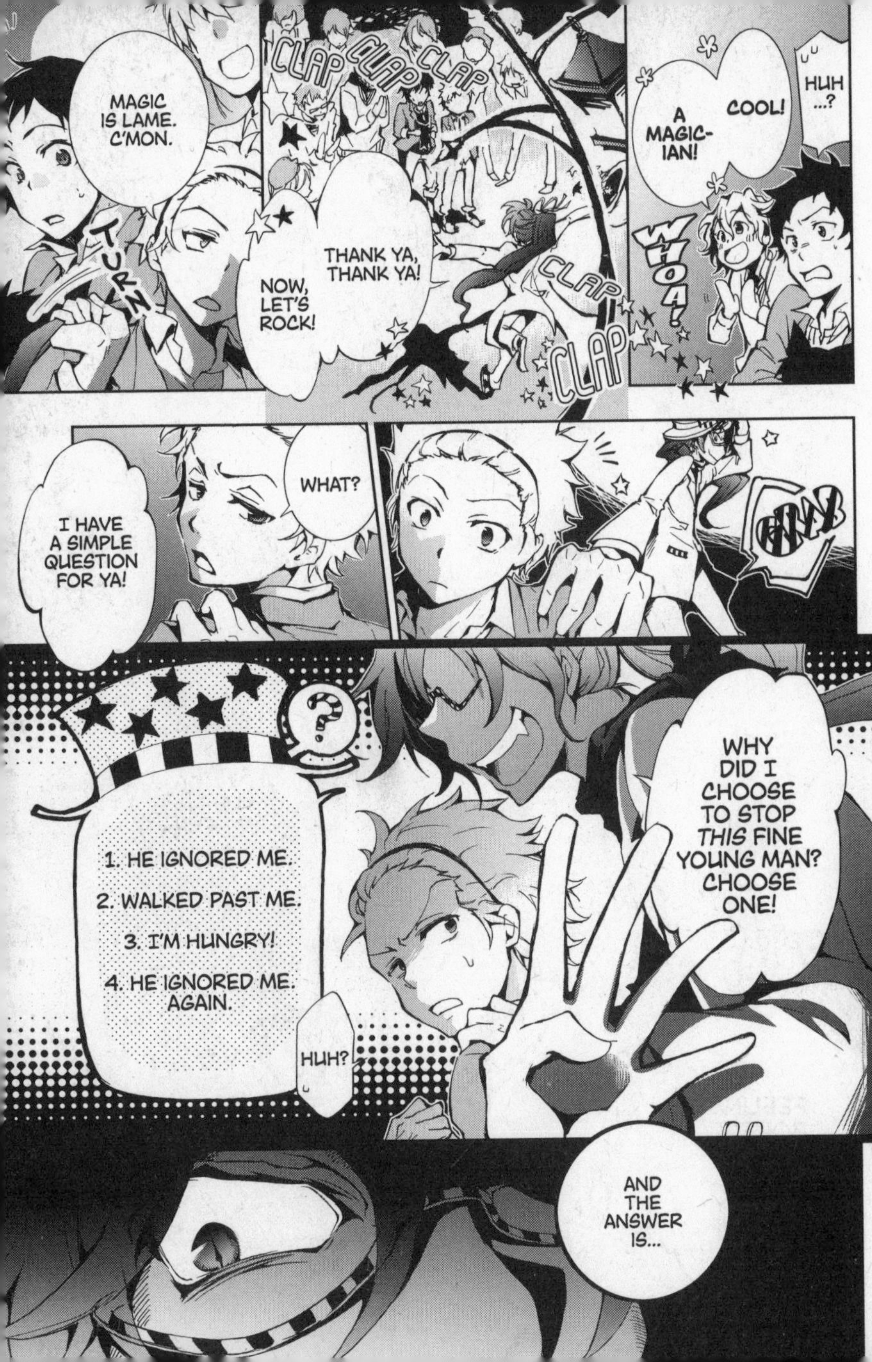
HUH ...?
COOL!
A MAGIC-IAN!
WHOA!
CLAP CLAP CLAP
THANK YA, THANK YA!
NOW, LET'S ROCK!
CLAP
CLAP
MAGIC IS LAME. C'MON.
TURN
WHAT?
I HAVE A SIMPLE QUESTION FOR YA!
WHY DID I CHOOSE TO STOP *THIS* FINE YOUNG MAN? CHOOSE ONE!
1. HE IGNORED ME.
2. WALKED PAST ME.
3. I'M HUNGRY!
4. HE IGNORED ME. AGAIN.
HUH?
AND THE ANSWER IS...

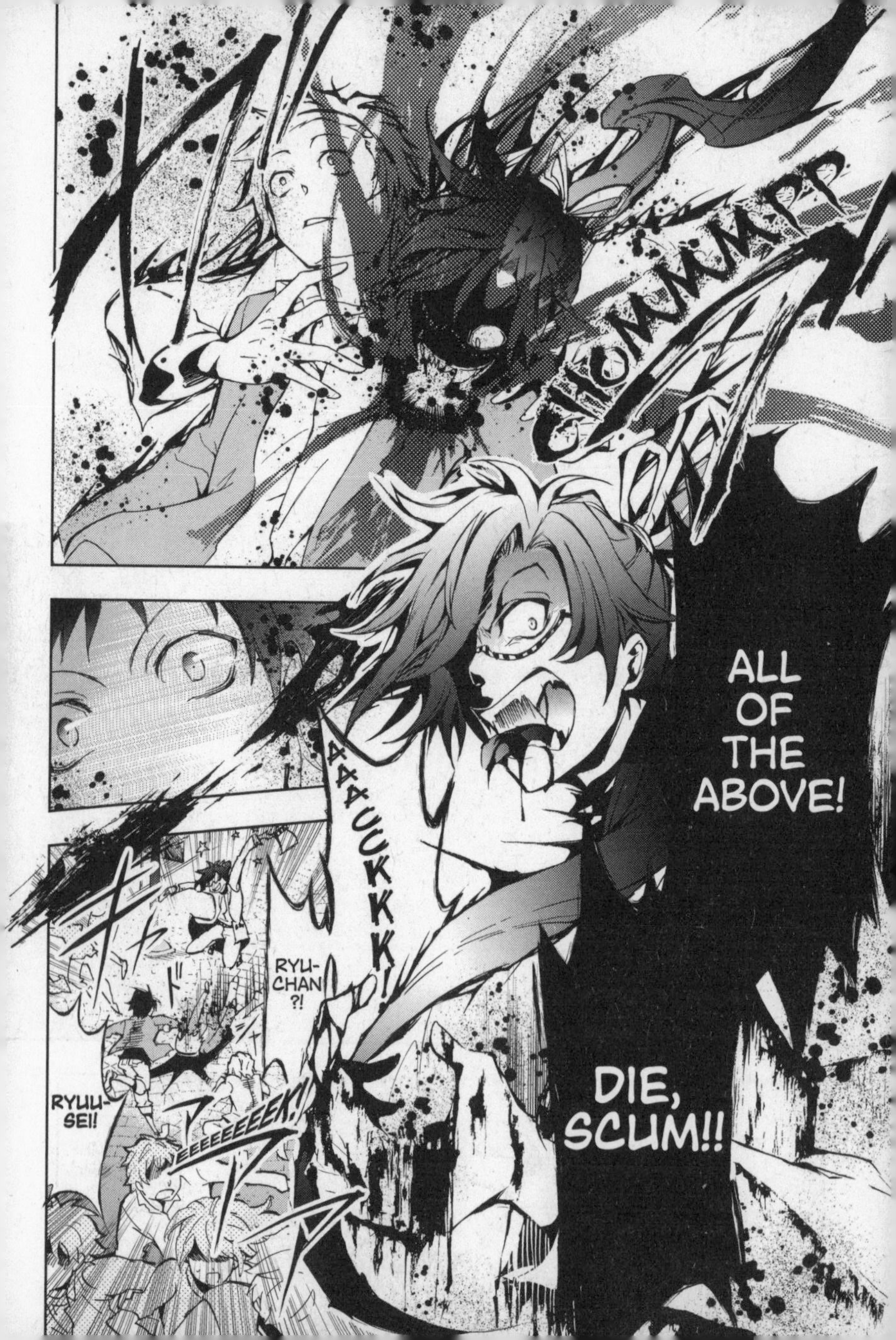
CHOMMMPP
ALL OF THE ABOVE!
DIE, SCUM!!
AAAUCKKKK!
RYU-CHAN ?!
RYUU-SEI!
EEEEEEEEK!

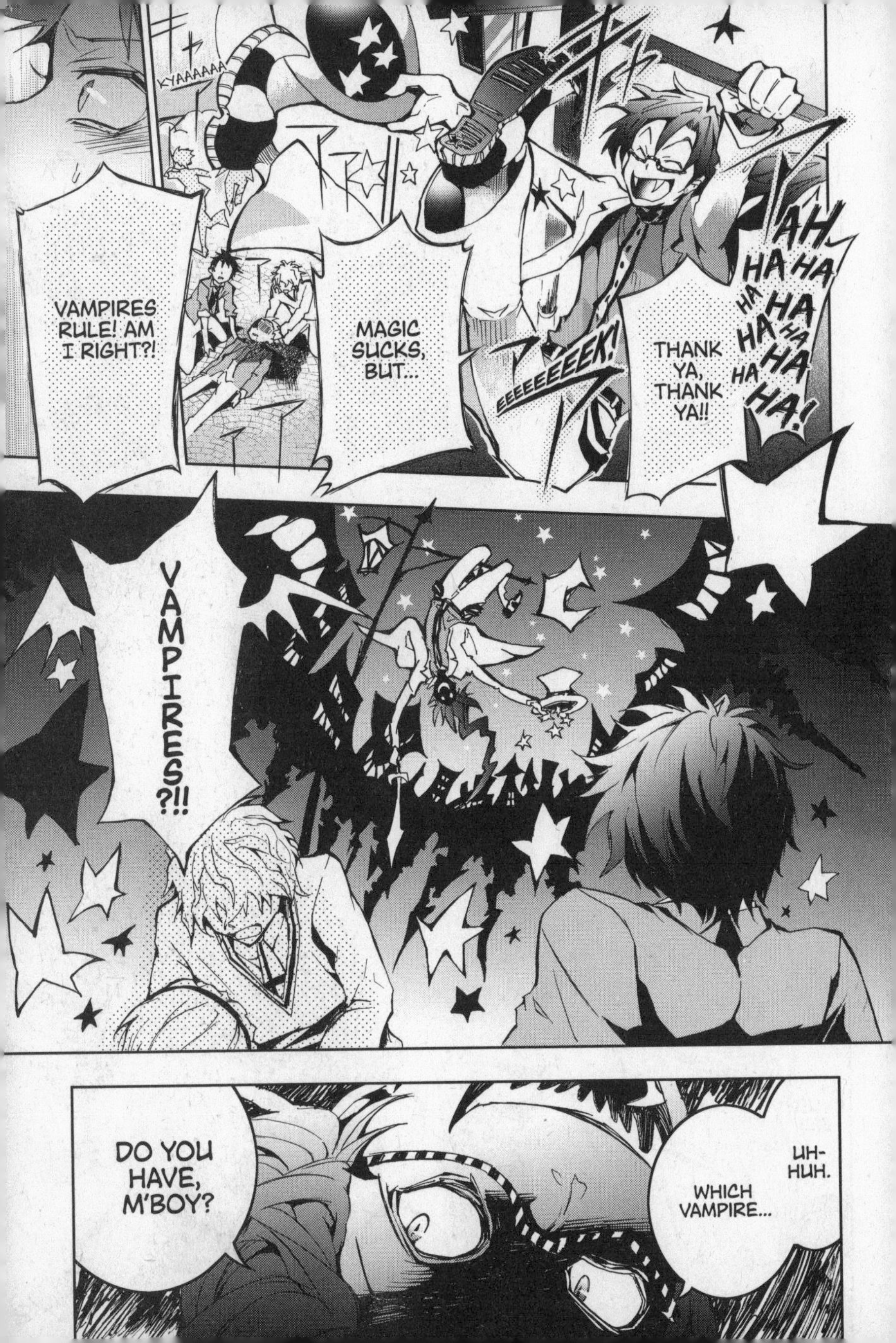
AH HA HA HA HA HA HA HA HA HA!
THANK YA, THANK YA!!
EEEEEEEEEEK!
KYAAAAAAA
MAGIC SUCKS, BUT...
VAMPIRES RULE! AM I RIGHT?!
VAMPIRES?!!
UH-HUH.
WHICH VAMPIRE...
DO YOU HAVE, M'BOY?

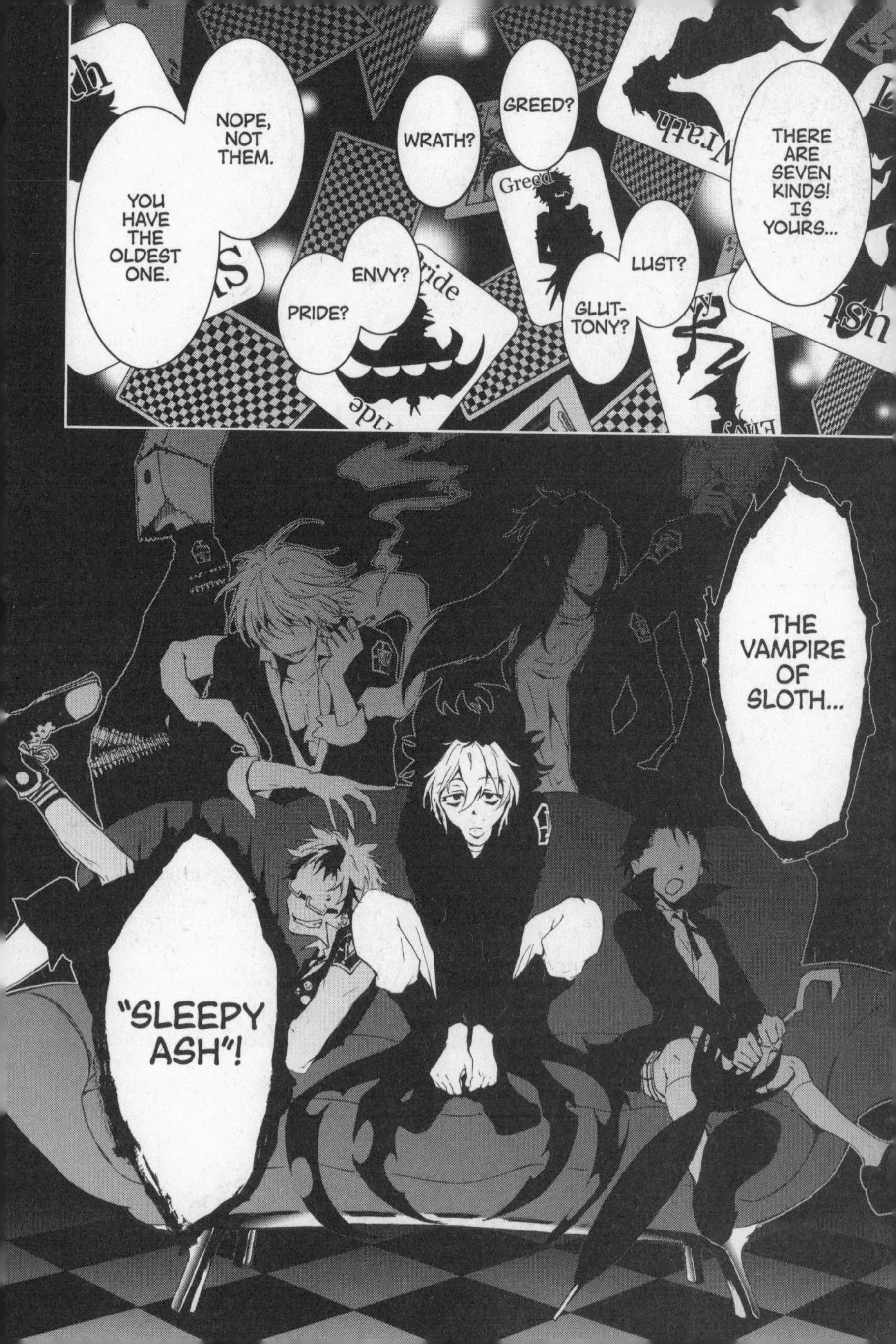
THERE ARE SEVEN KINDS! IS YOURS...
LUST?
GLUT-TONY?
GREED?
WRATH?
ENVY?
PRIDE?
NOPE, NOT THEM.
YOU HAVE THE OLDEST ONE.
Greed
THE VAMPIRE OF SLOTH...
"SLEEPY ASH"!

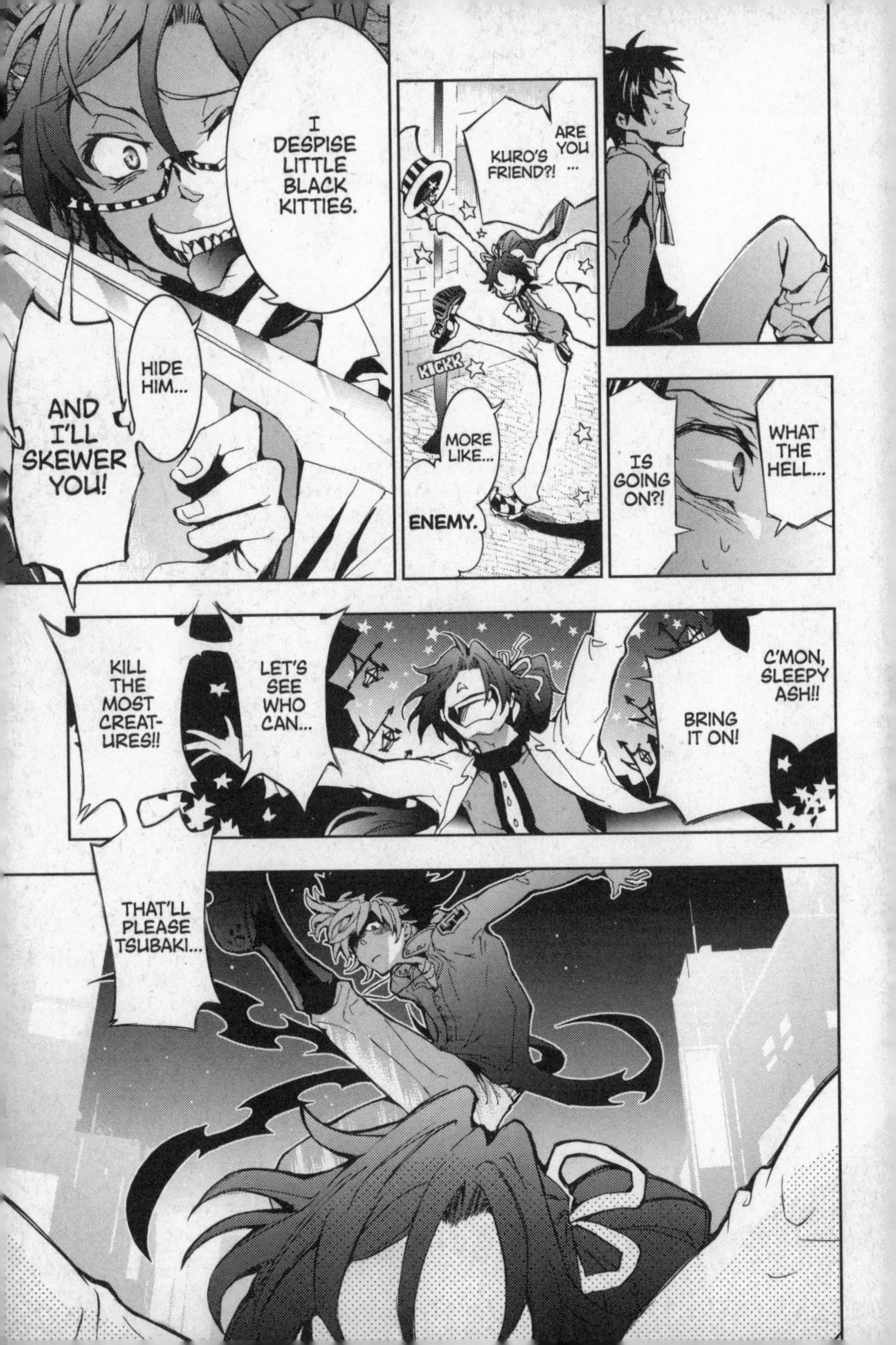
WHAT THE HELL...
IS GOING ON?!
ARE YOU...
KURO'S FRIEND?!
KICKK
MORE LIKE...
ENEMY.
I DESPISE LITTLE BLACK KITTIES.
HIDE HIM...
AND I'LL SKEWER YOU!
C'MON, SLEEPY ASH!!
BRING IT ON!
LET'S SEE WHO CAN...
KILL THE MOST CREATURES!!
THAT'LL PLEASE TSUBAKI...

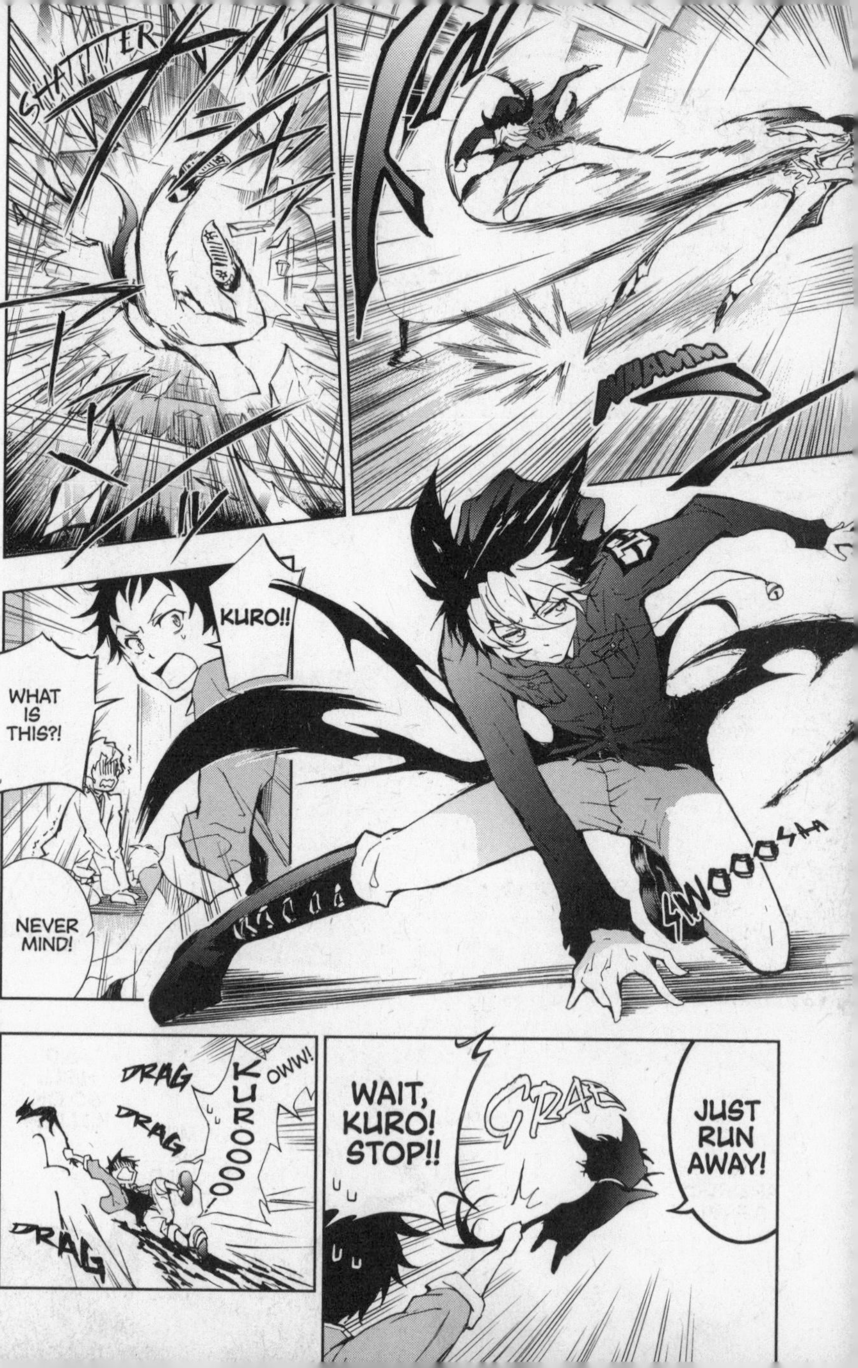
WHAMM
SHATTER
KURO!!
WHAT IS THIS?!
NEVER MIND!
SWOOOSH
JUST RUN AWAY!
GRAB
WAIT, KURO! STOP!!
KUROOOOO!
OWW!
DRAG
DRAG
DRAG

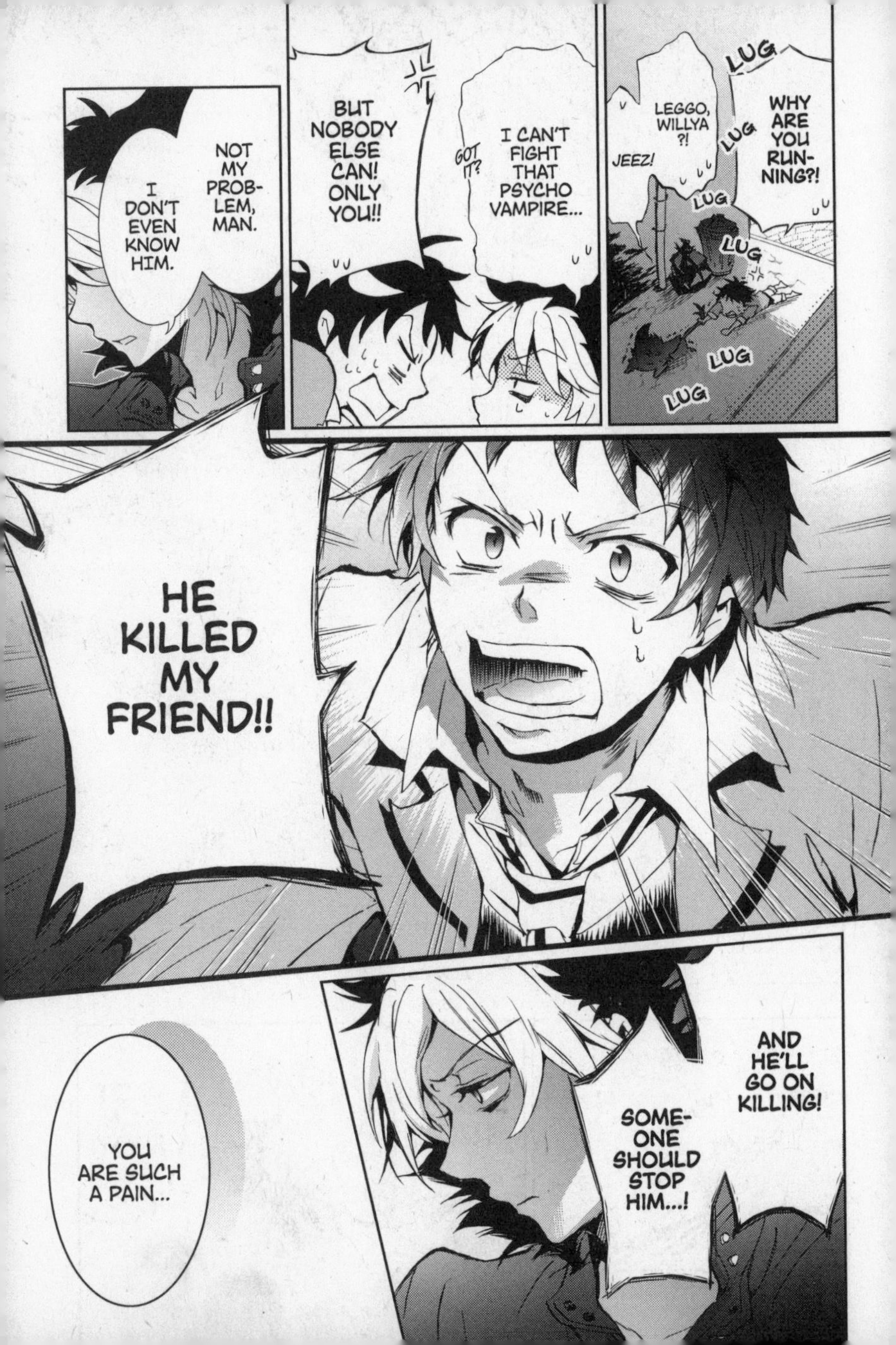
LUG
WHY ARE YOU RUN-NING?!
LEGGO, WILLYA?!
LUG
JEEZ!
LUG
LUG
LUG
LUG
I CAN'T FIGHT THAT PSYCHO VAMPIRE...
GOT IT?
BUT NOBODY ELSE CAN! ONLY YOU!!
NOT MY PROB-LEM, MAN.
I DON'T EVEN KNOW HIM.
HE KILLED MY FRIEND!!
AND HE'LL GO ON KILLING!
SOME-ONE SHOULD STOP HIM...!
YOU ARE SUCH A PAIN...

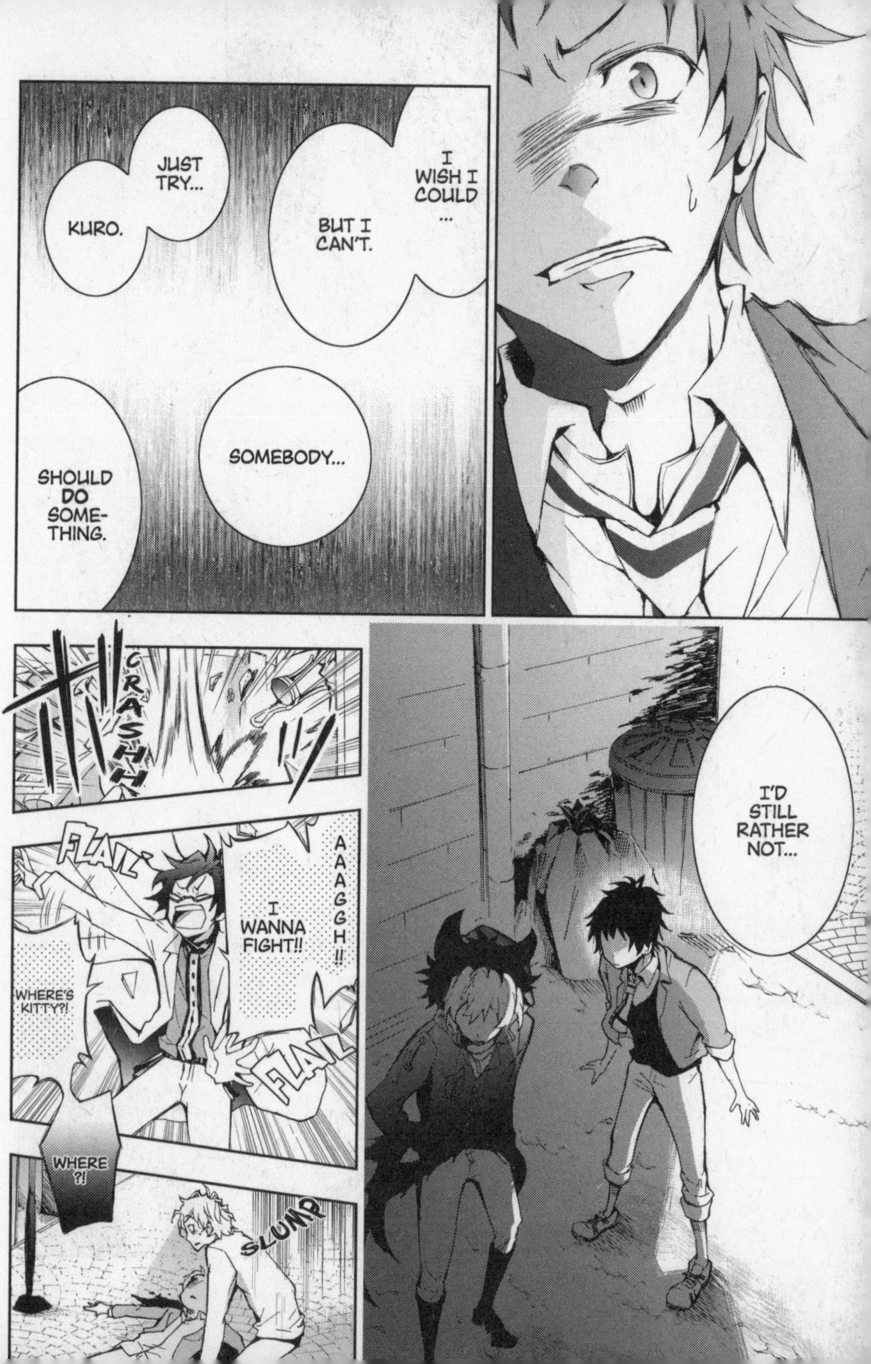
I WISH I COULD ...
BUT I CAN'T.
JUST TRY...
KURO.
SOMEBODY...
SHOULD DO SOME-THING.
I'D STILL RATHER NOT...
CRASHH
AAAAGGH!!
I WANNA FIGHT!!
FLAIL
WHERE'S KITTY?!
FLAIL
WHERE ?!
SLUMP

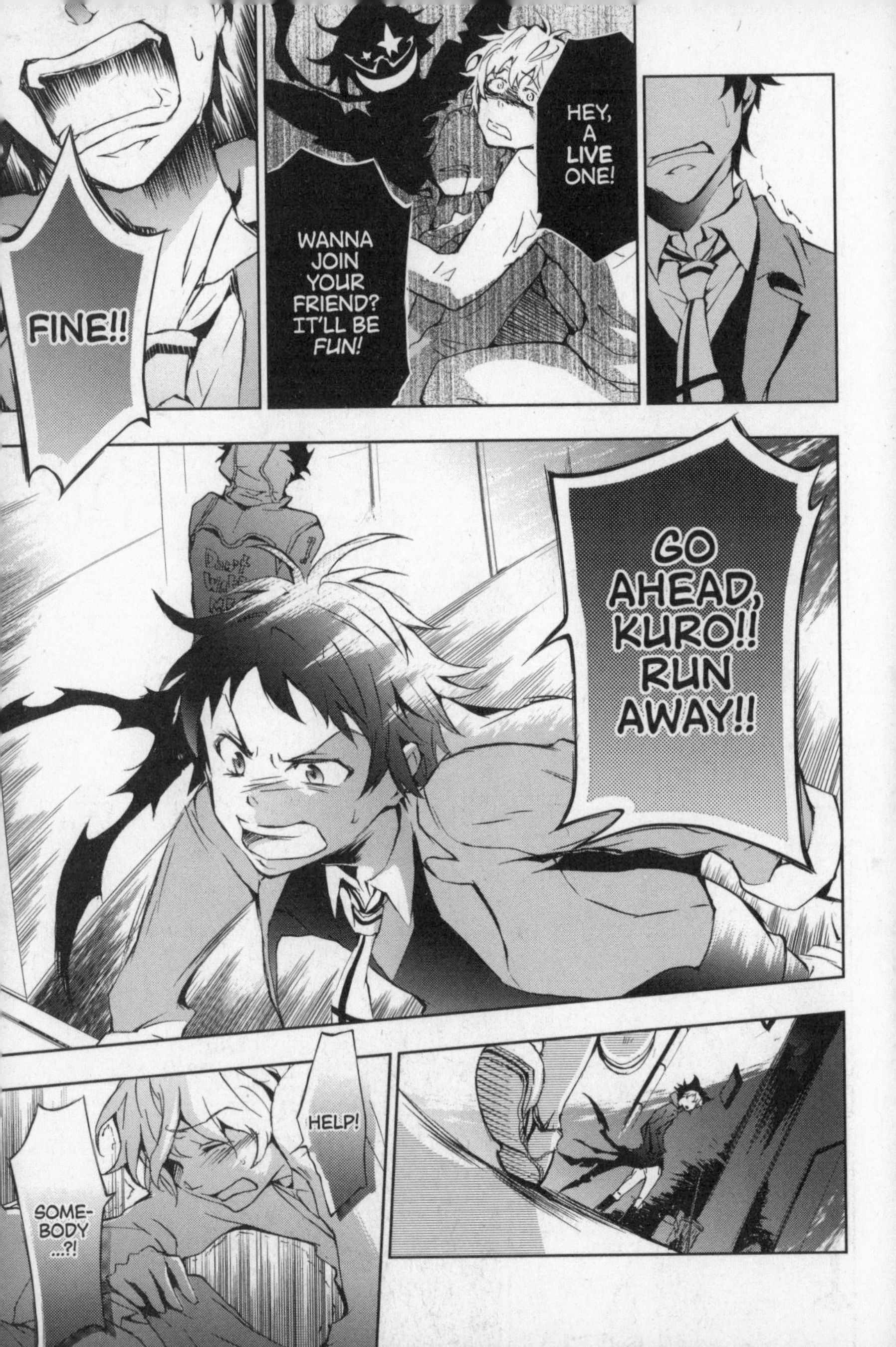
HEY, A LIVE ONE!
WANNA JOIN YOUR FRIEND? IT'LL BE FUN!
FINE!!
GO AHEAD, KURO!! RUN AWAY!!
HELP!
SOMEBODY ...?!

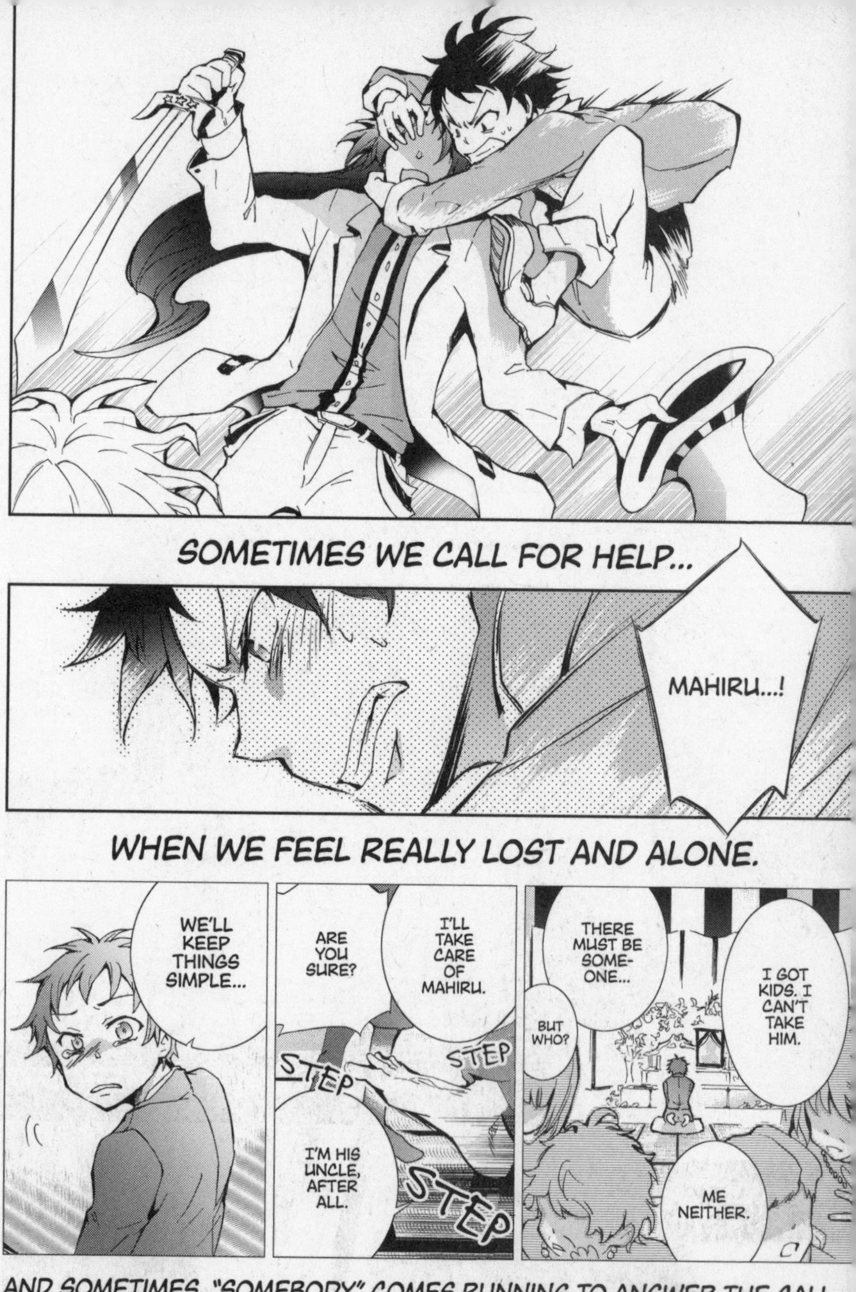
SOMETIMES WE CALL FOR HELP...
MAHIRU...!
WHEN WE FEEL REALLY LOST AND ALONE.
THERE MUST BE SOME-ONE...
I GOT KIDS. I CAN'T TAKE HIM.
BUT WHO?
ME NEITHER.
I'LL TAKE CARE OF MAHIRU.
ARE YOU SURE?
STEP
STEP
I'M HIS UNCLE, AFTER ALL.
STEP
WE'LL KEEP THINGS SIMPLE...
AND SOMETIMES, "SOMEBODY" COMES RUNNING TO ANSWER THE CALL...

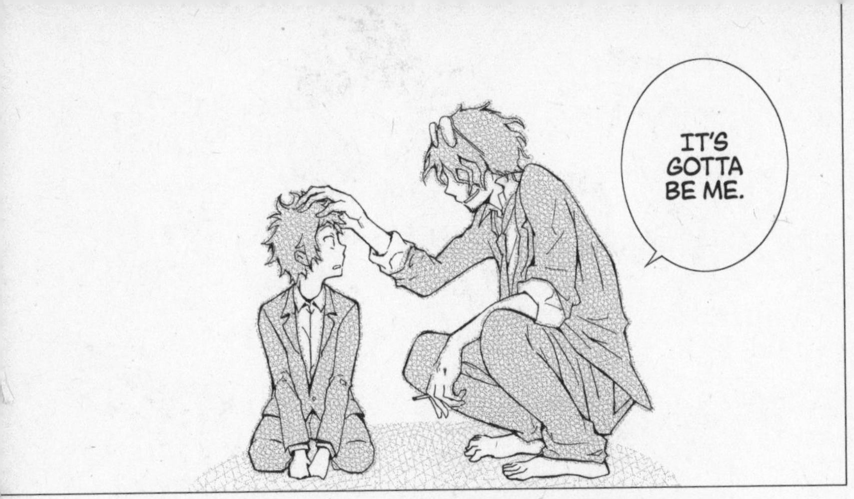
IT'S GOTTA BE ME.

AND THE WORLD KEEPS ON SPINNING.

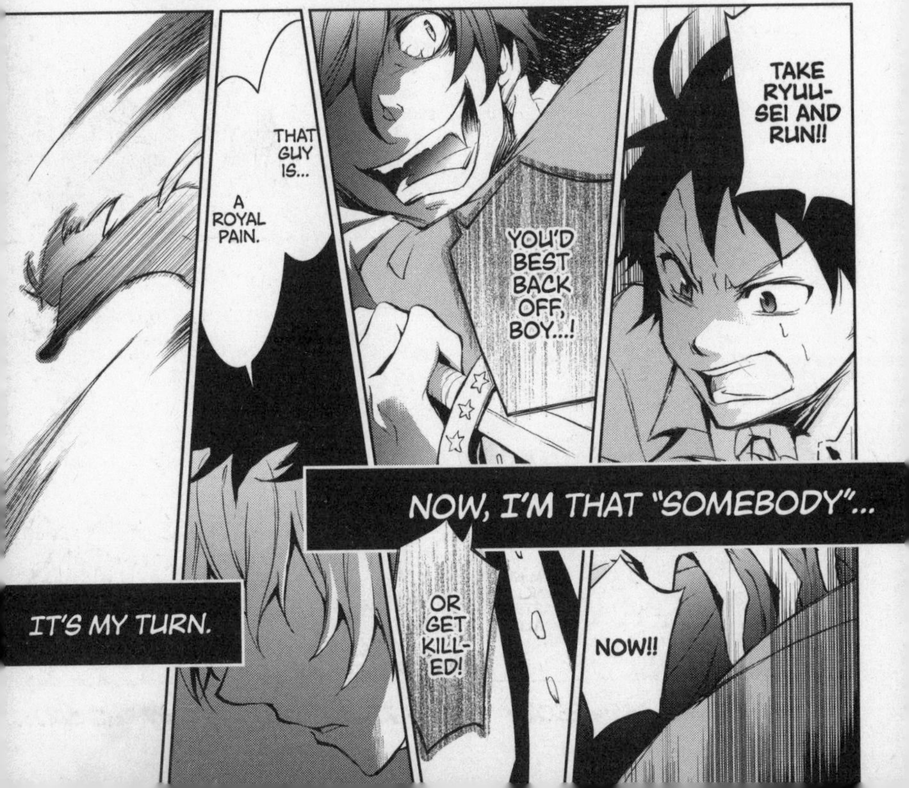
TAKE RYUU-SEI AND RUN!!
YOU'D BEST BACK OFF, BOY...!
THAT GUY IS...
A ROYAL PAIN.
NOW, I'M THAT "SOMEBODY"...
NOW!!
OR GET KILL-ED!
IT'S MY TURN.

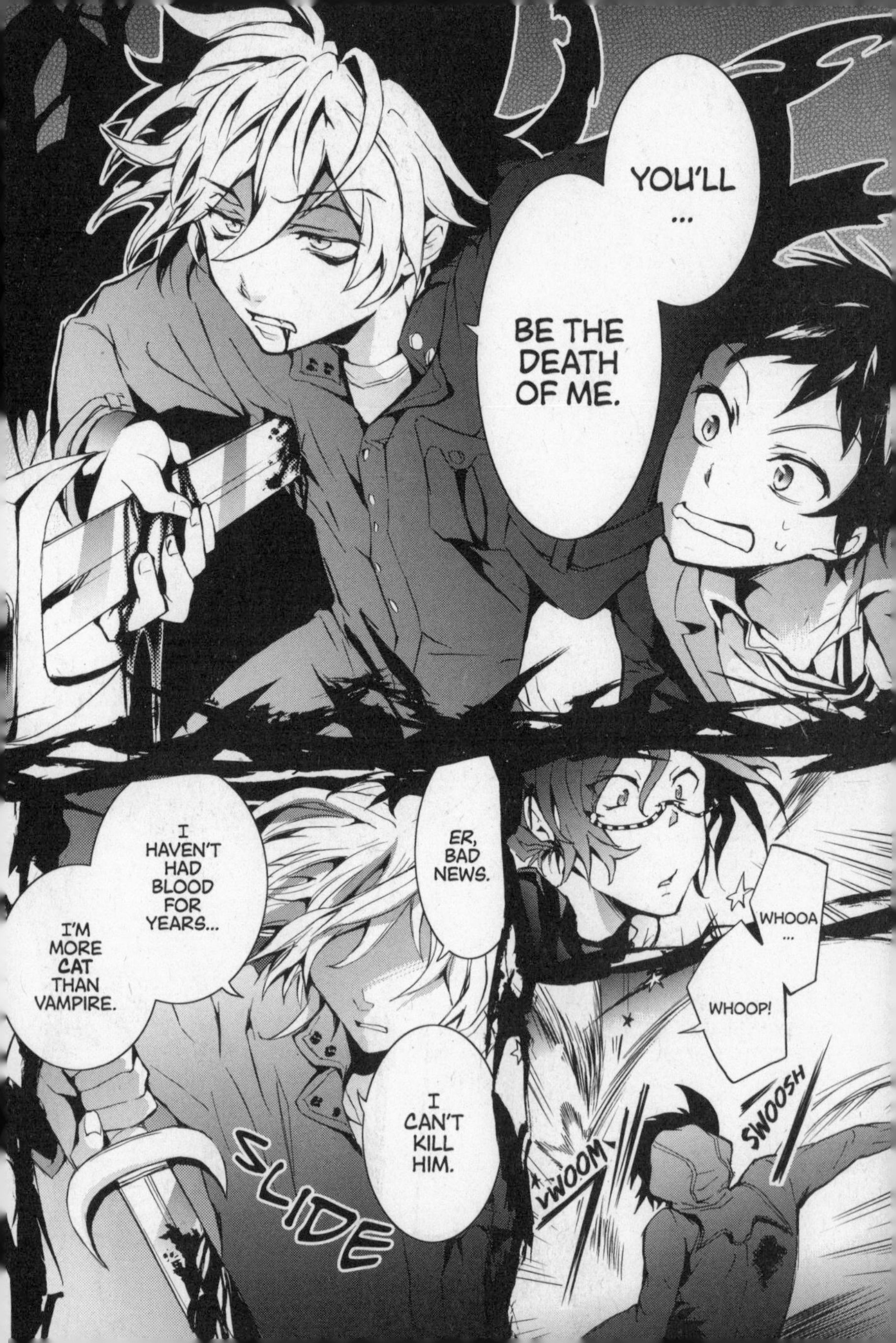
YOU'LL ...
BE THE DEATH OF ME.
WHOOA ...
WHOOP!
SWOOSH
VWOOM
ER, BAD NEWS.
I HAVEN'T HAD BLOOD FOR YEARS...
I'M MORE CAT THAN VAMPIRE.
I CAN'T KILL HIM.
SLIDE

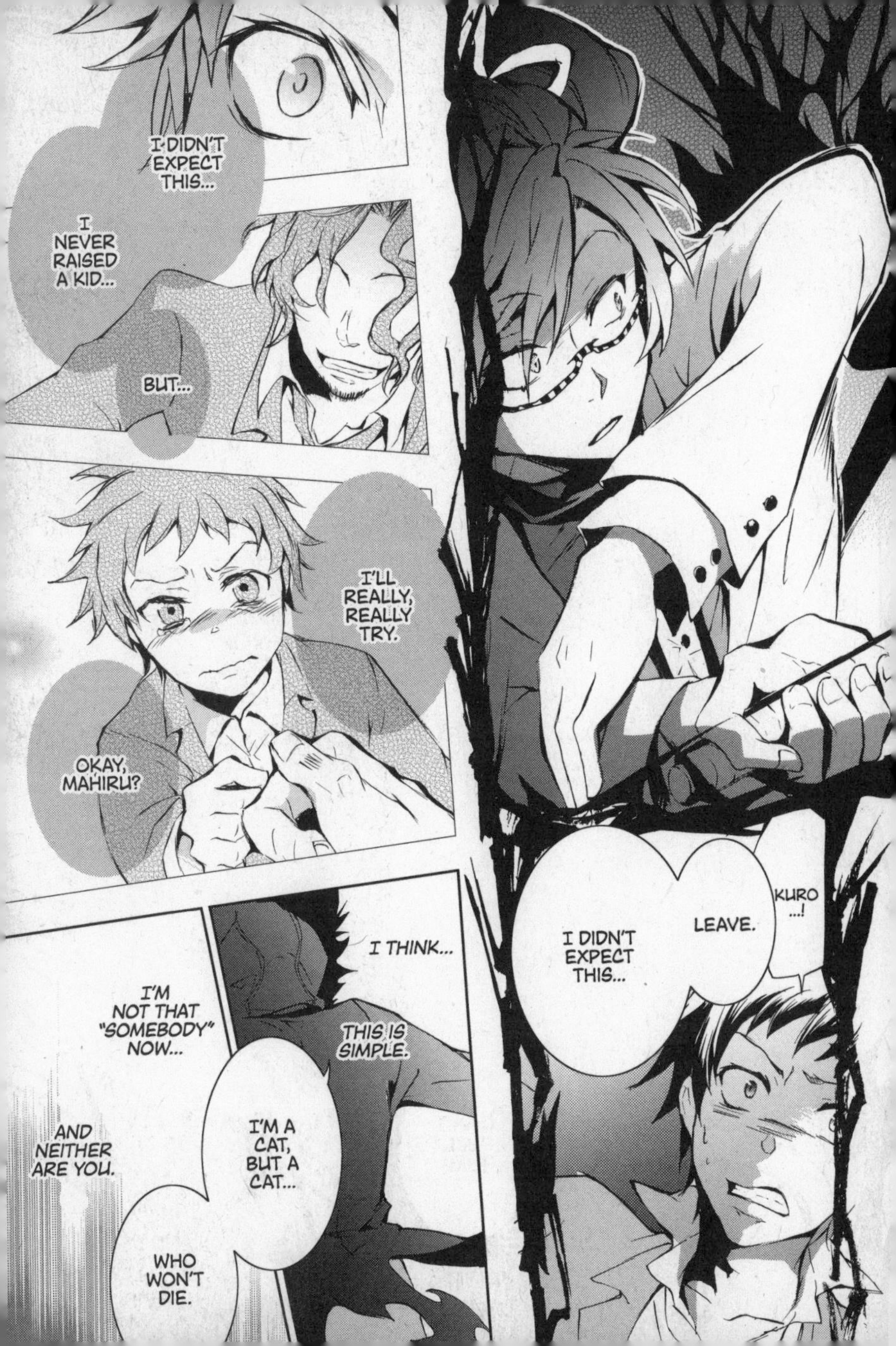
KURO ...!
LEAVE.
I DIDN'T EXPECT THIS...
I DIDN'T EXPECT THIS...
I NEVER RAISED A KID...
BUT...
I'LL REALLY, REALLY TRY.
OKAY, MAHIRU?
I THINK...
THIS IS SIMPLE.
I'M NOT THAT "SOMEBODY" NOW...
I'M A CAT, BUT A CAT...
AND NEITHER ARE YOU.
WHO WON'T DIE.

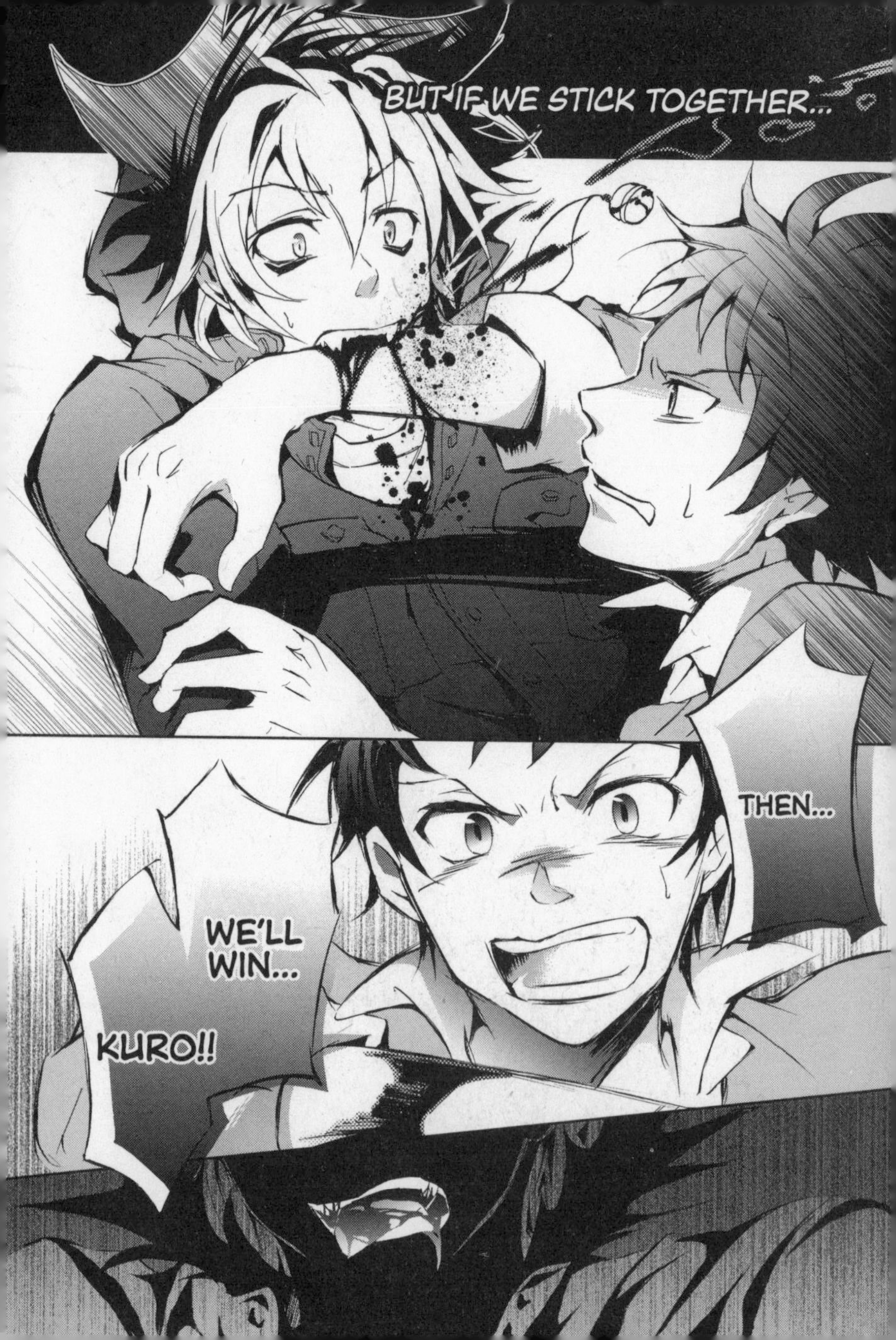
BUT IF WE STICK TOGETHER...
THEN...
WE'LL WIN...
KURO!!

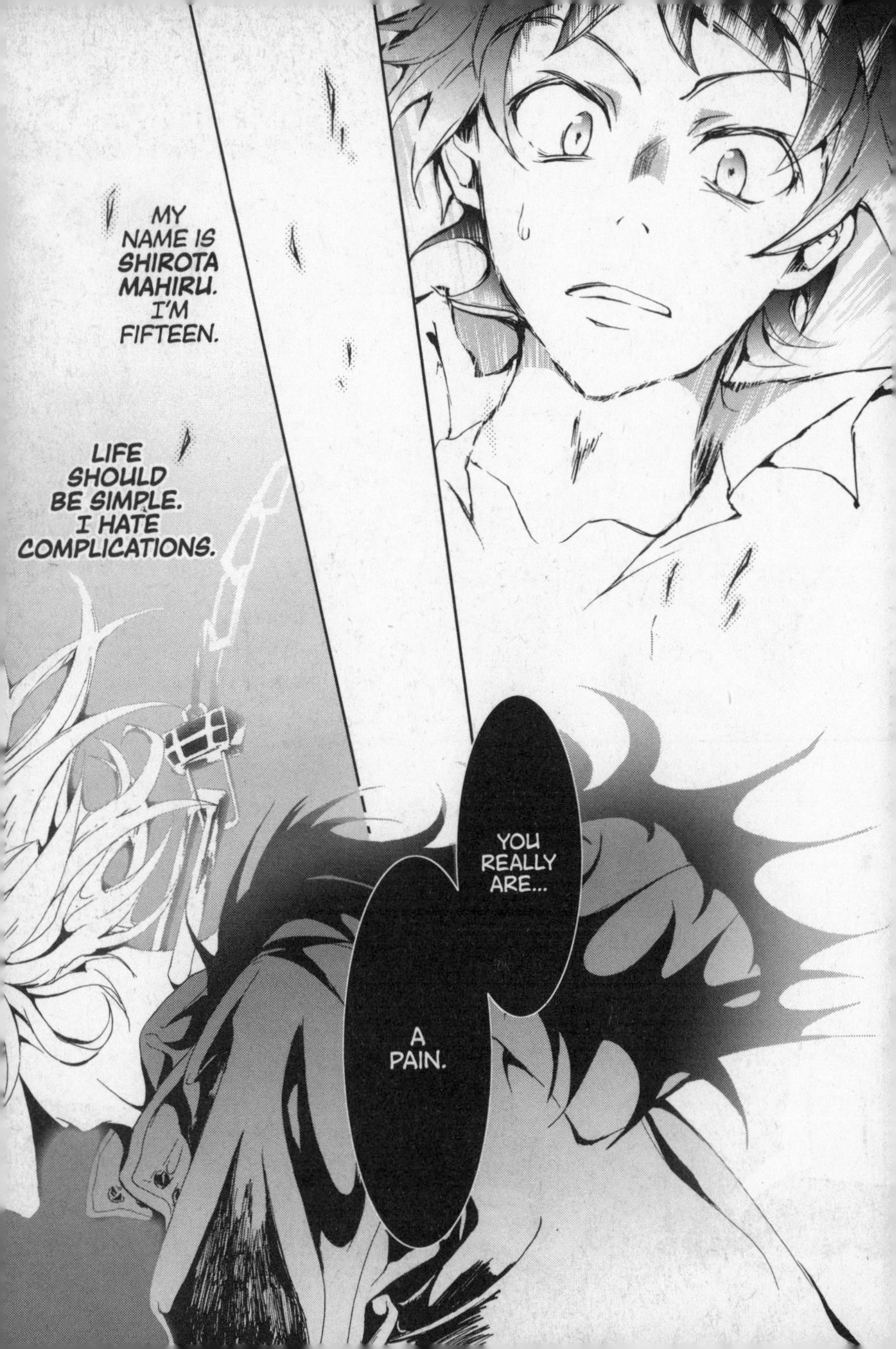
MY NAME IS SHIROTA MAHIRU. I'M FIFTEEN.
LIFE SHOULD BE SIMPLE. I HATE COMPLICATIONS.
YOU REALLY ARE...
A PAIN.

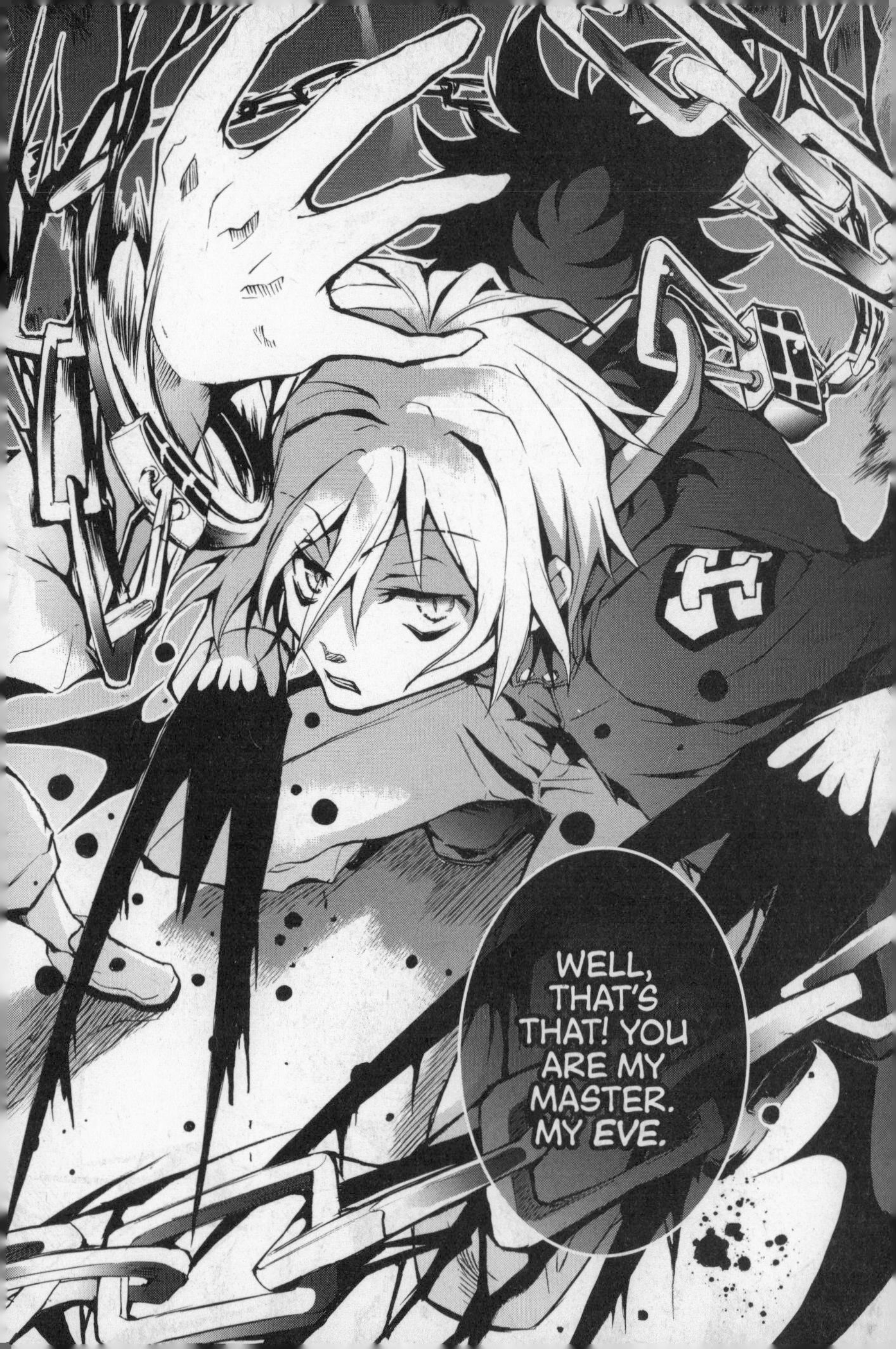
WELL, THAT'S THAT! YOU ARE MY MASTER. MY EVE.

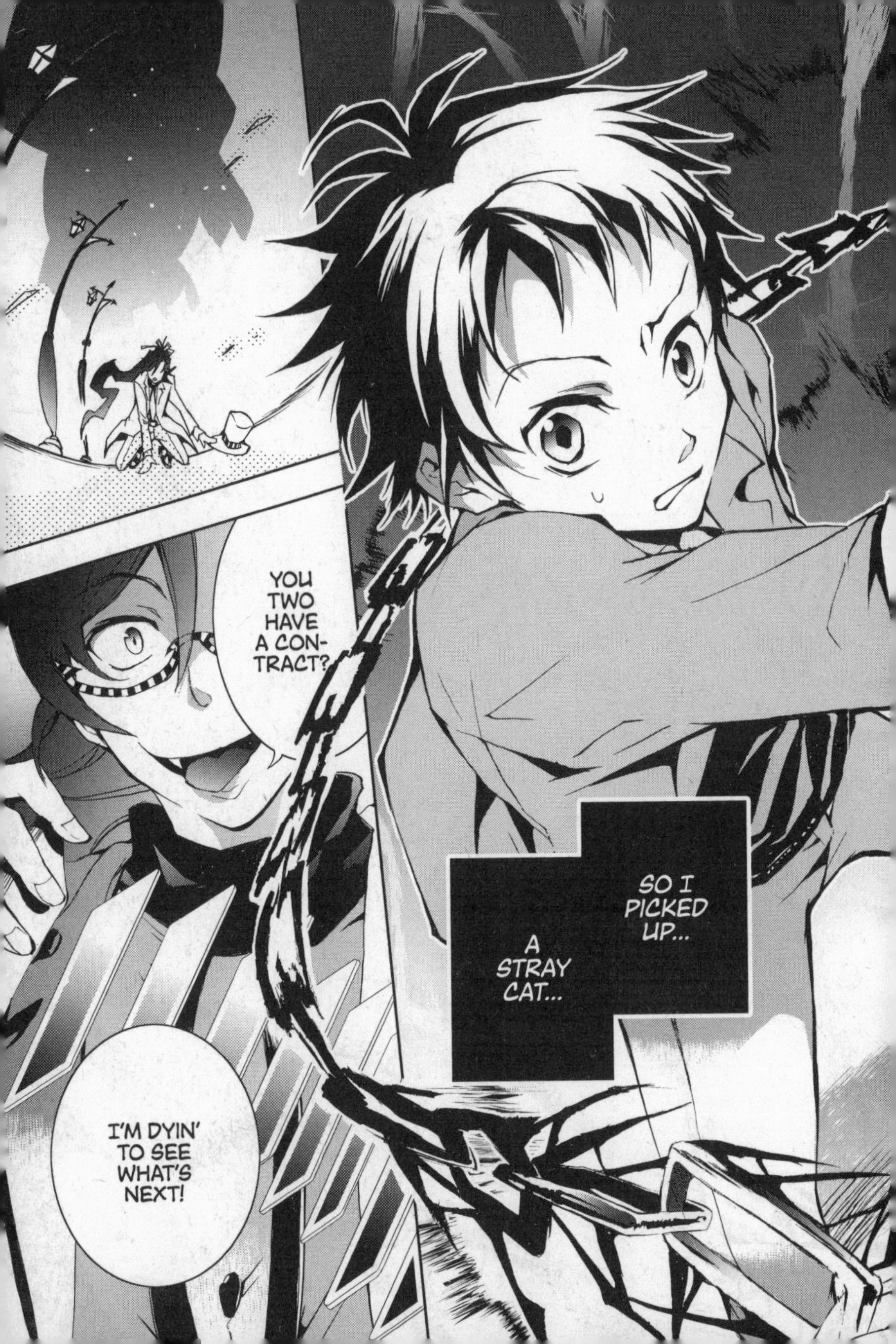
SO I PICKED UP...
A STRAY CAT...
YOU TWO HAVE A CONTRACT?
I'M DYIN' TO SEE WHAT'S NEXT!

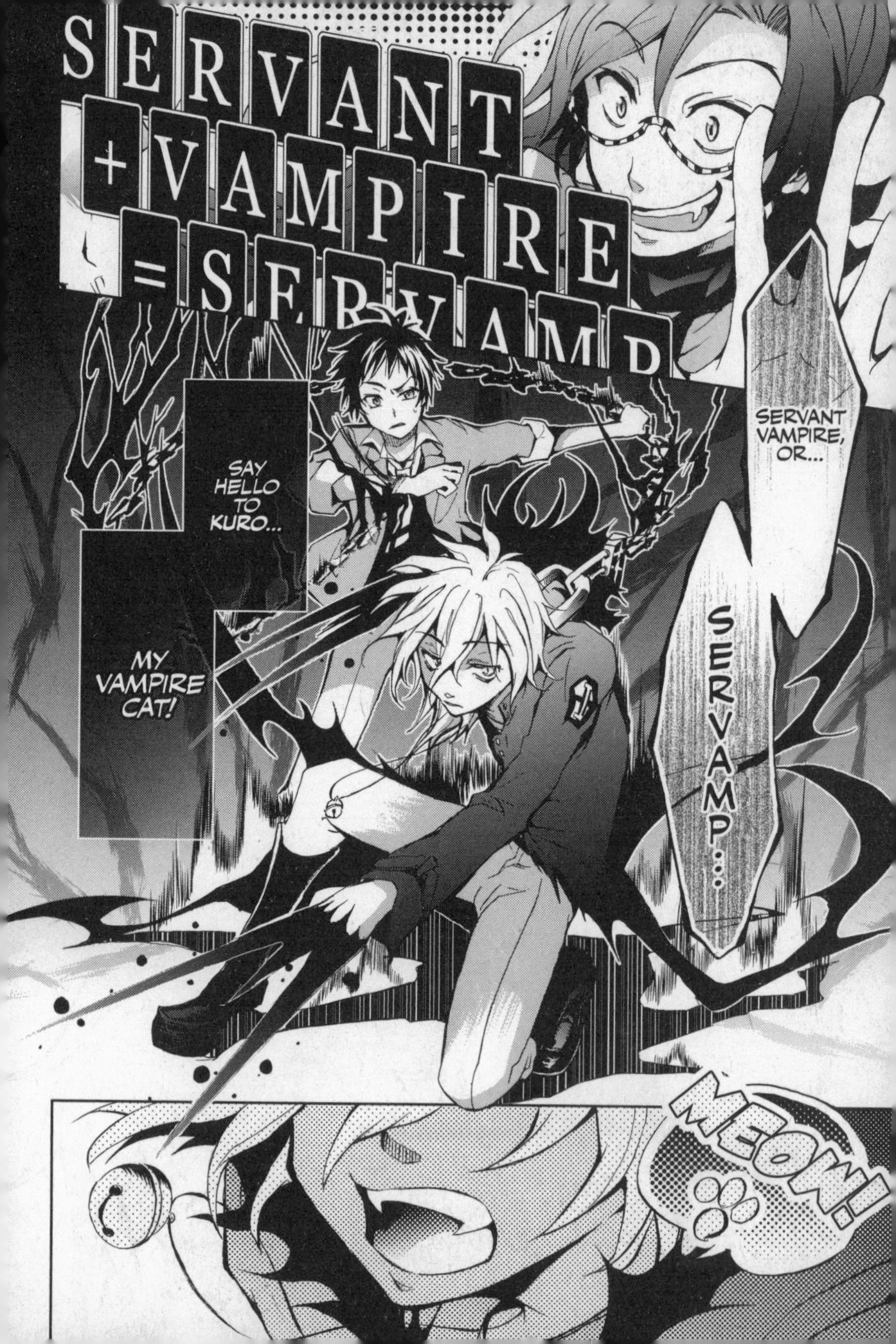
SERVANT + VAMPIRE = SERVAMP
SERVANT VAMPIRE, OR...
SERVAMP...
SAY HELLO TO KURO...
MY VAMPIRE CAT!
MEOW!

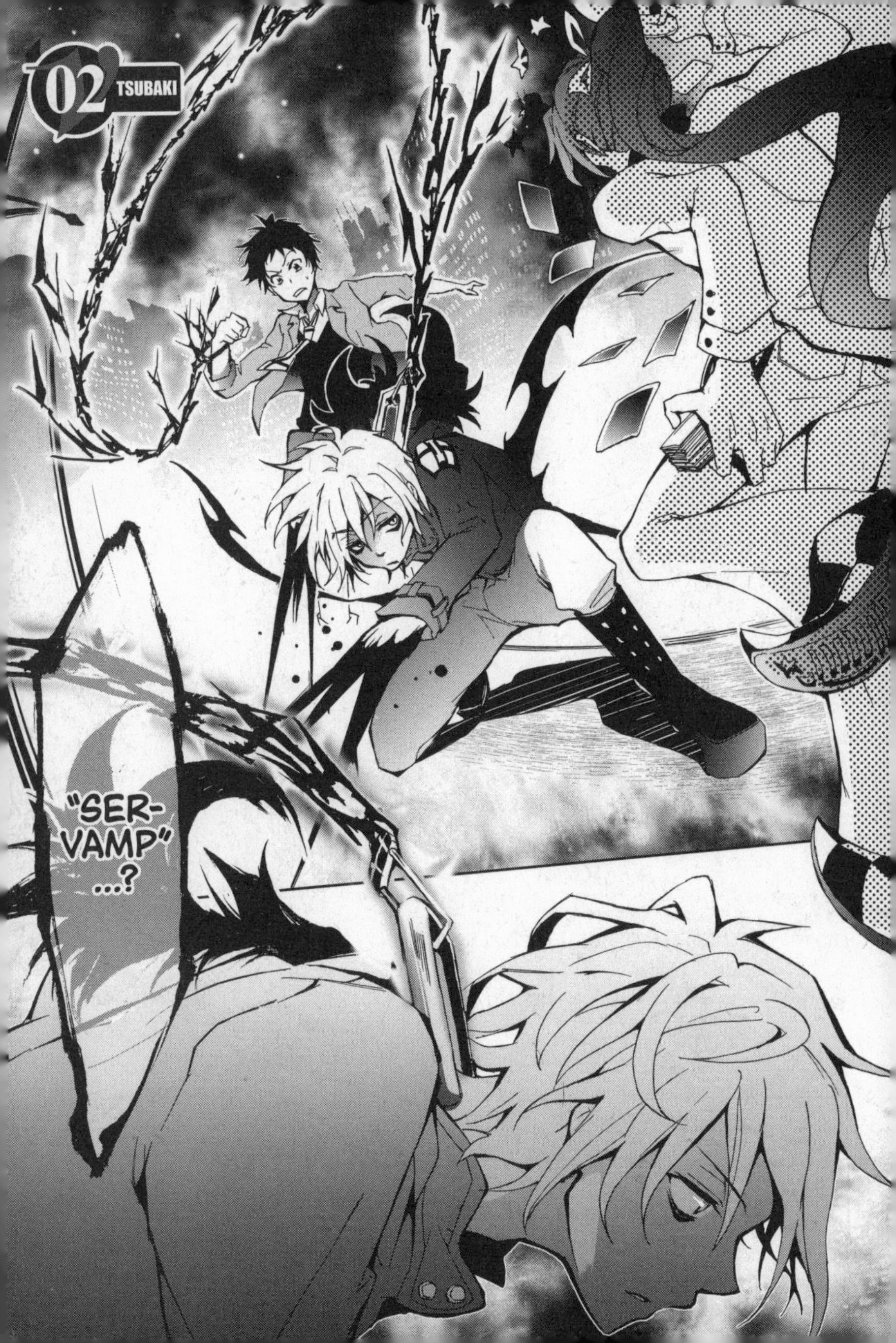
02
TSUBAKI
"SER-
VAMP"
...?

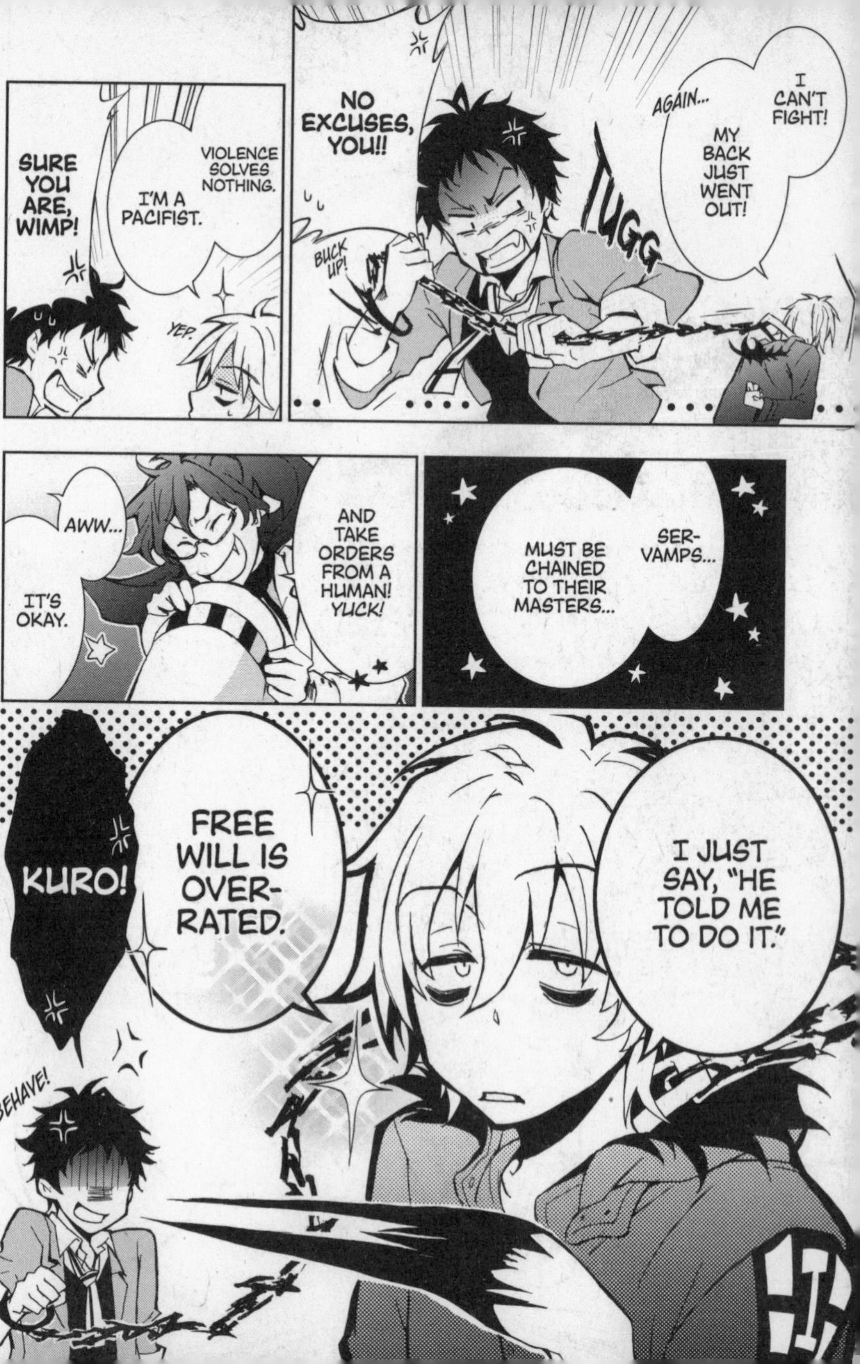

I CAN'T FIGHT!
MY BACK JUST WENT OUT!
AGAIN...
TUGG
NO EXCUSES, YOU!!
BUCK UP!
VIOLENCE SOLVES NOTHING.
I'M A PACIFIST.
YEP.
SURE YOU ARE, WIMP!
SER-VAMPS...
MUST BE CHAINED TO THEIR MASTERS...
AND TAKE ORDERS FROM A HUMAN! YUCK!
AWW...
IT'S OKAY.
I JUST SAY, "HE TOLD ME TO DO IT."
FREE WILL IS OVER-RATED.
KURO!
BEHAVE!

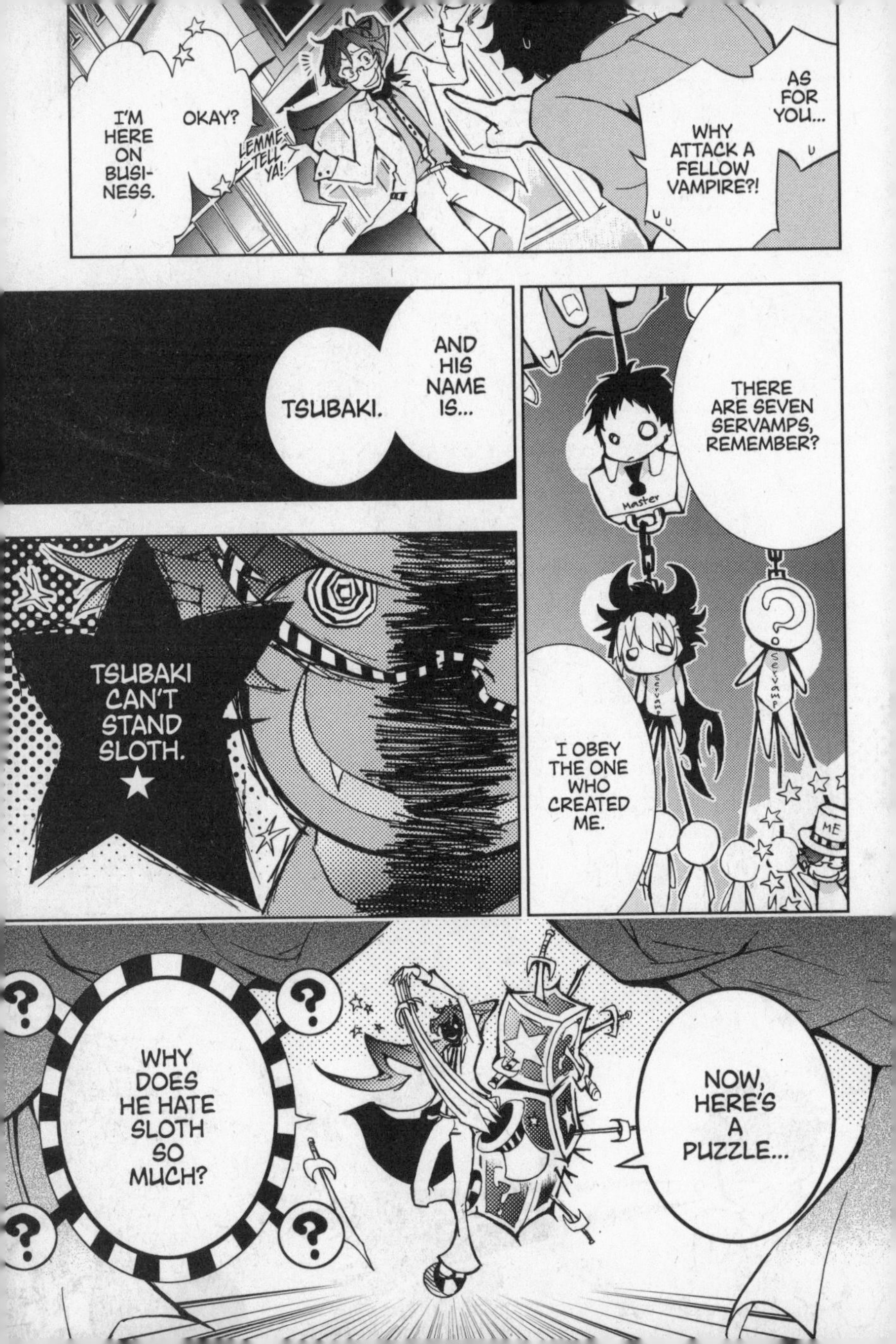
AS FOR YOU...
WHY ATTACK A FELLOW VAMPIRE?!
OKAY?
LEMME TELL YA!
I'M HERE ON BUSINESS.
THERE ARE SEVEN SERVAMPS, REMEMBER?
Master
Servamp
Servamp
I OBEY THE ONE WHO CREATED ME.
ME
AND HIS NAME IS...
TSUBAKI.
TSUBAKI CAN'T STAND SLOTH. ★
NOW, HERE'S A PUZZLE...
WHY DOES HE HATE SLOTH SO MUCH?

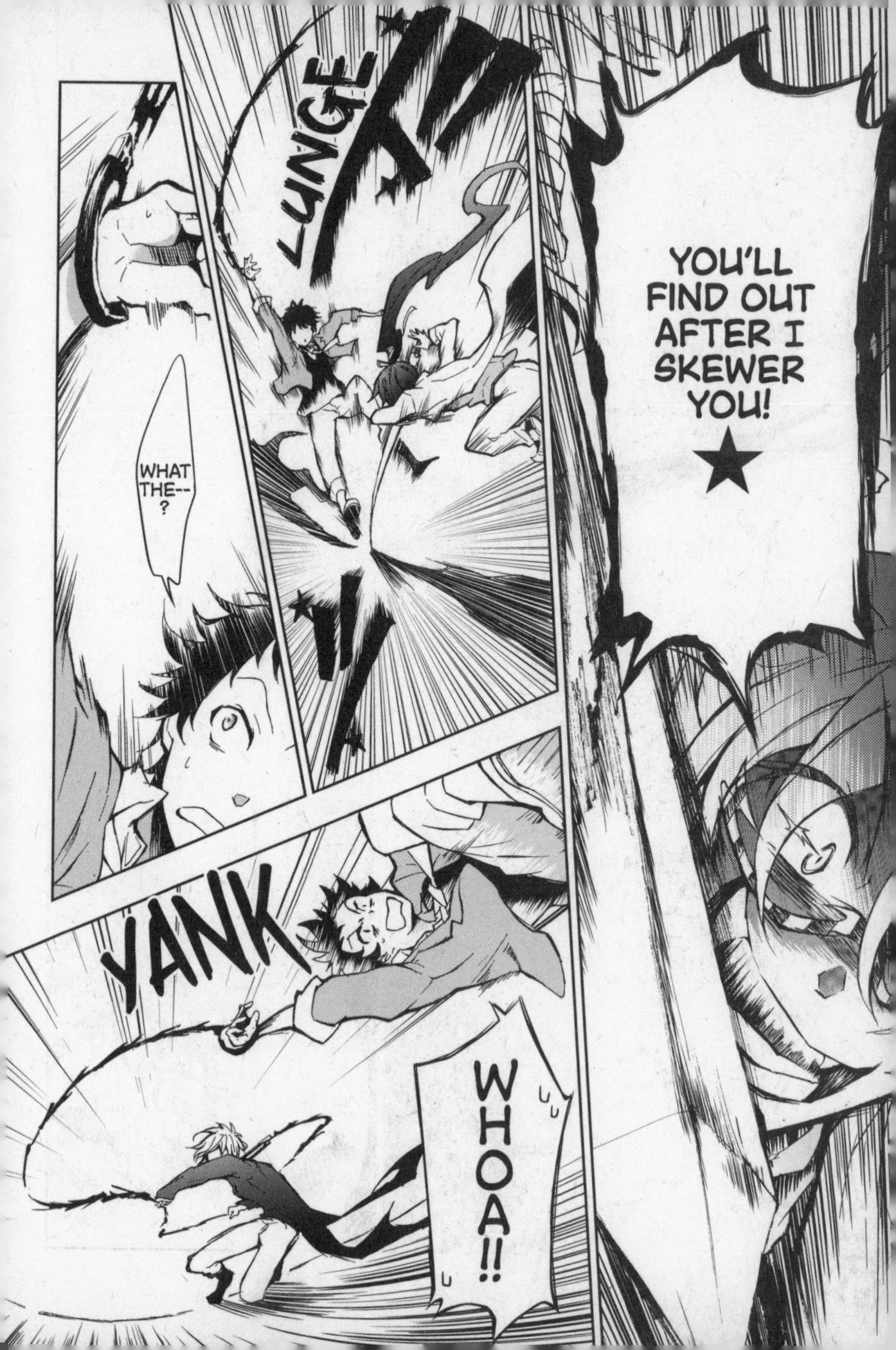
YOU'LL FIND OUT AFTER I SKEWER YOU! ★
LUNGE
WHAT THE-- ?
YANK
WHOA!!

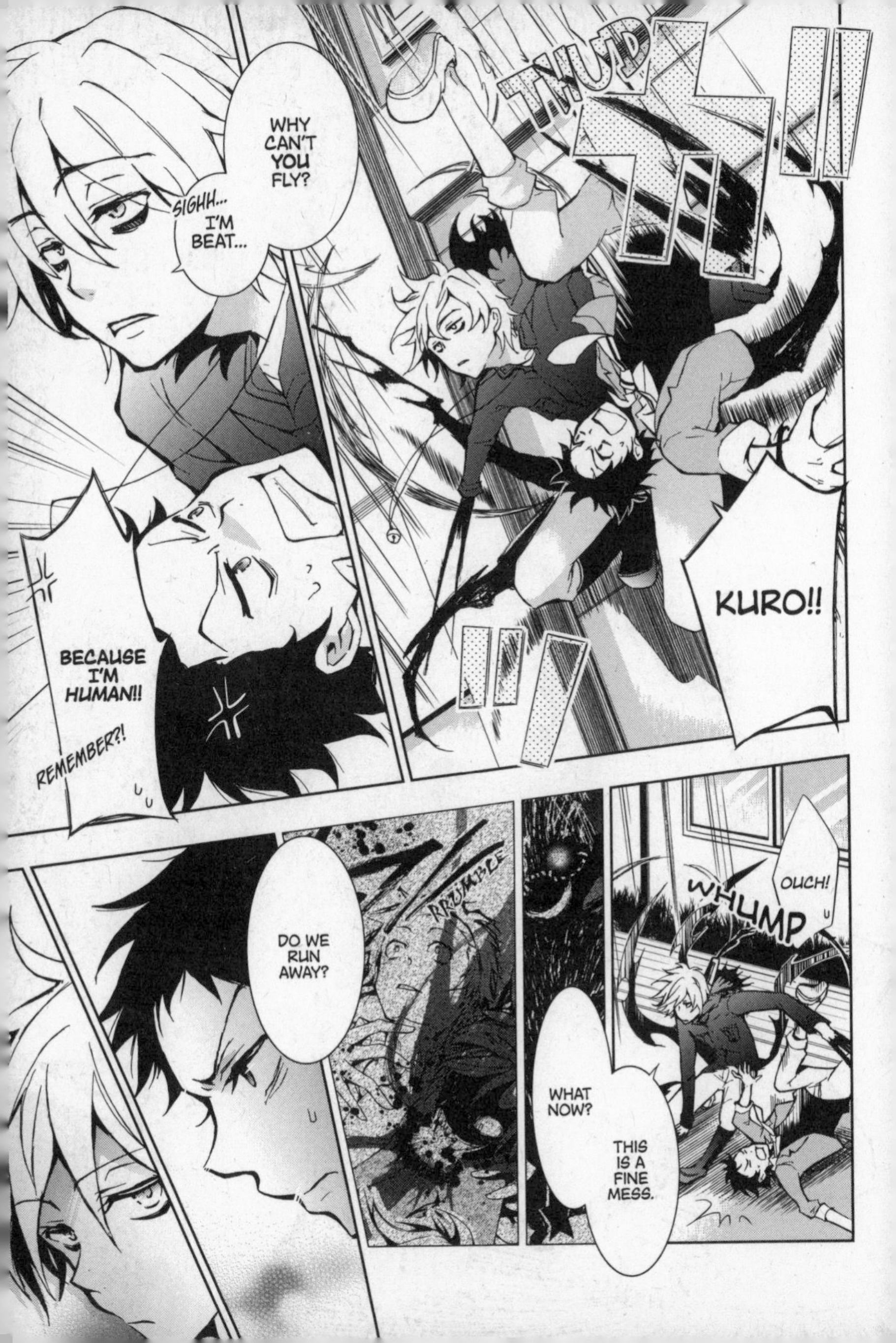
THUD
KURO!!
WHY CAN'T YOU FLY?
SIGHH... I'M BEAT...
BECAUSE I'M HUMAN!!
REMEMBER?!
OUCH!
WHUMP
WHAT NOW?
THIS IS A FINE MESS.
RRUMBLE
DO WE RUN AWAY?

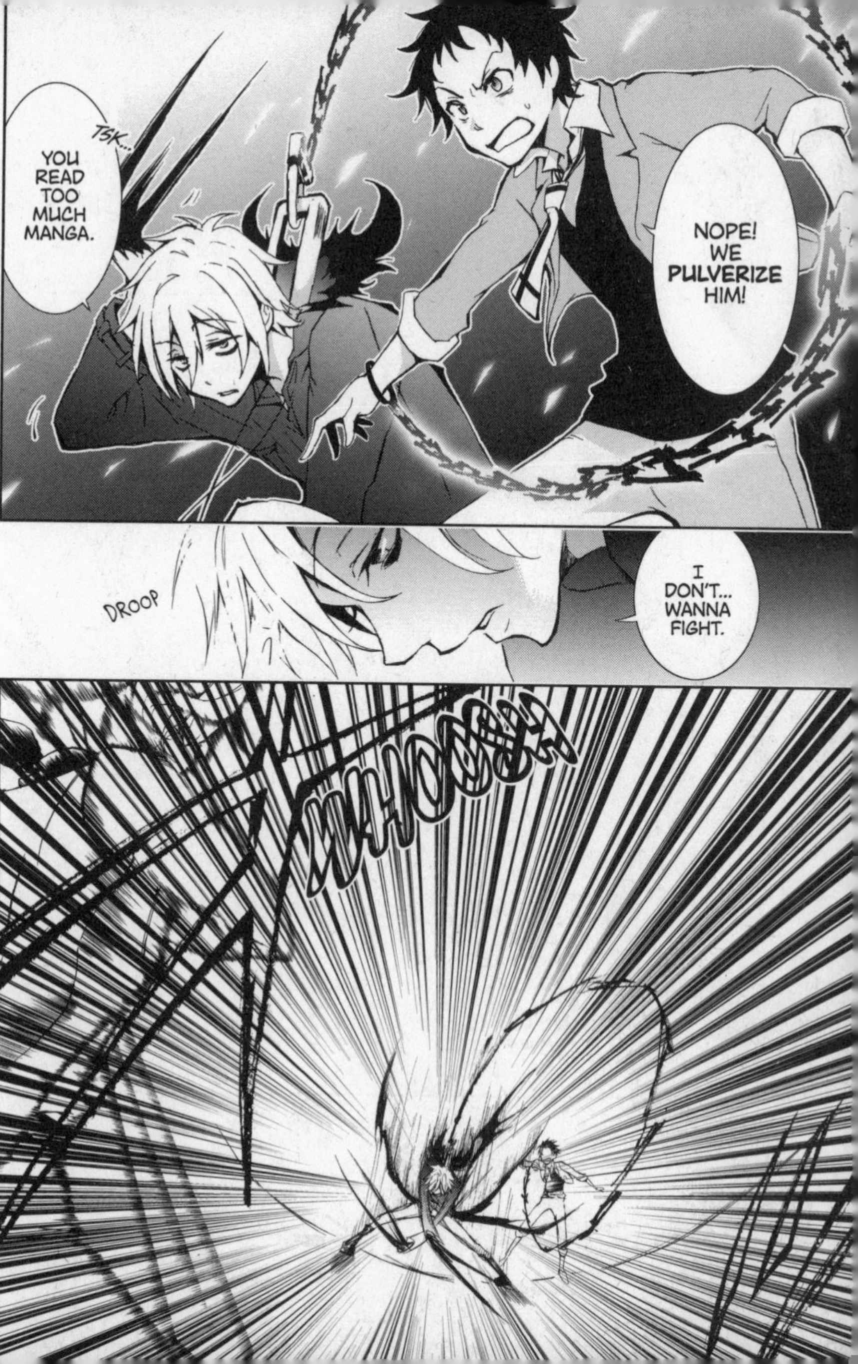
NOPE! WE PULVERIZE HIM!
TSK...
YOU READ TOO MUCH MANGA.
I DON'T... WANNA FIGHT.
DROOP

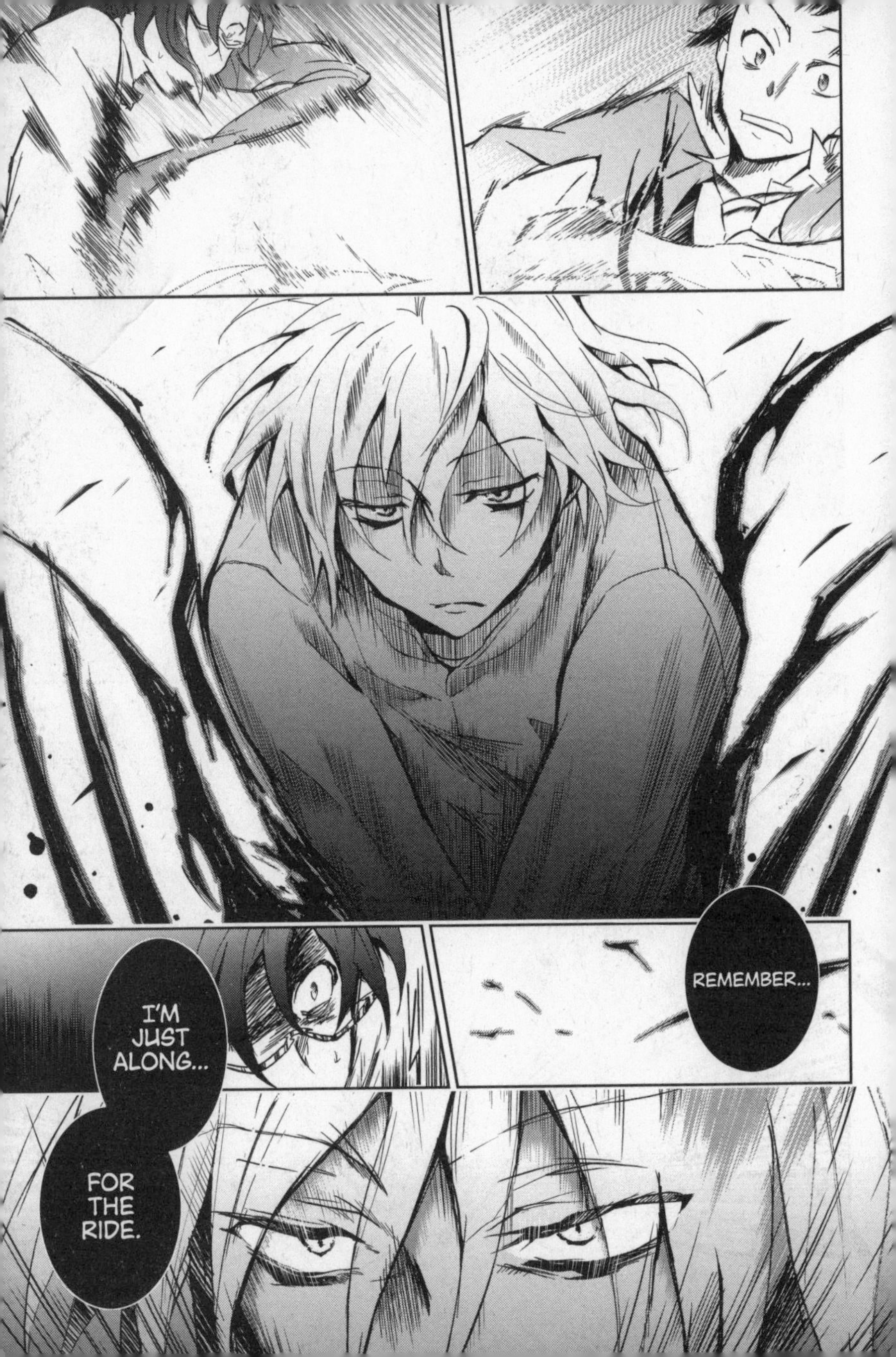
REMEMBER...
I'M JUST ALONG...
FOR THE RIDE.

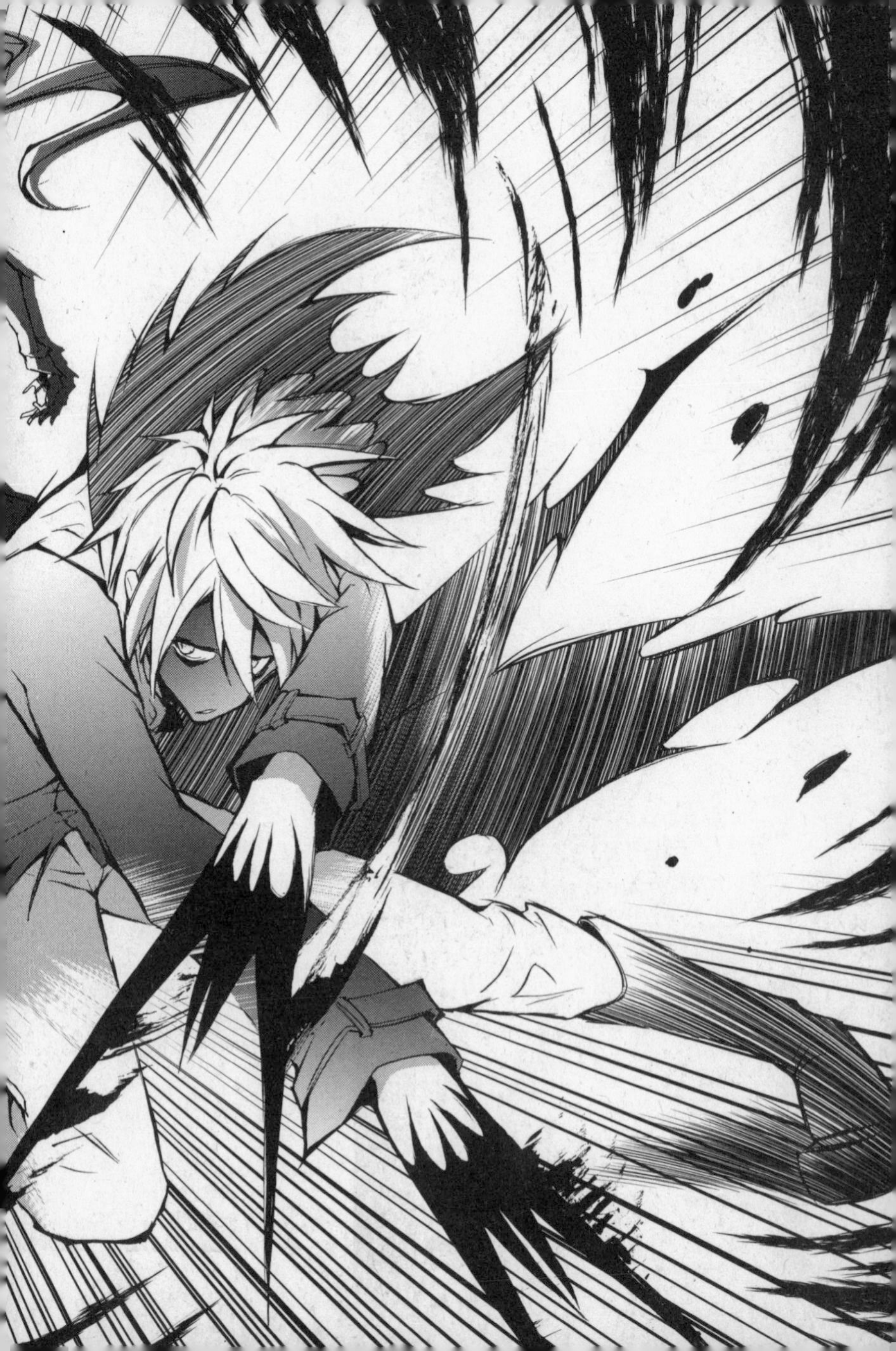

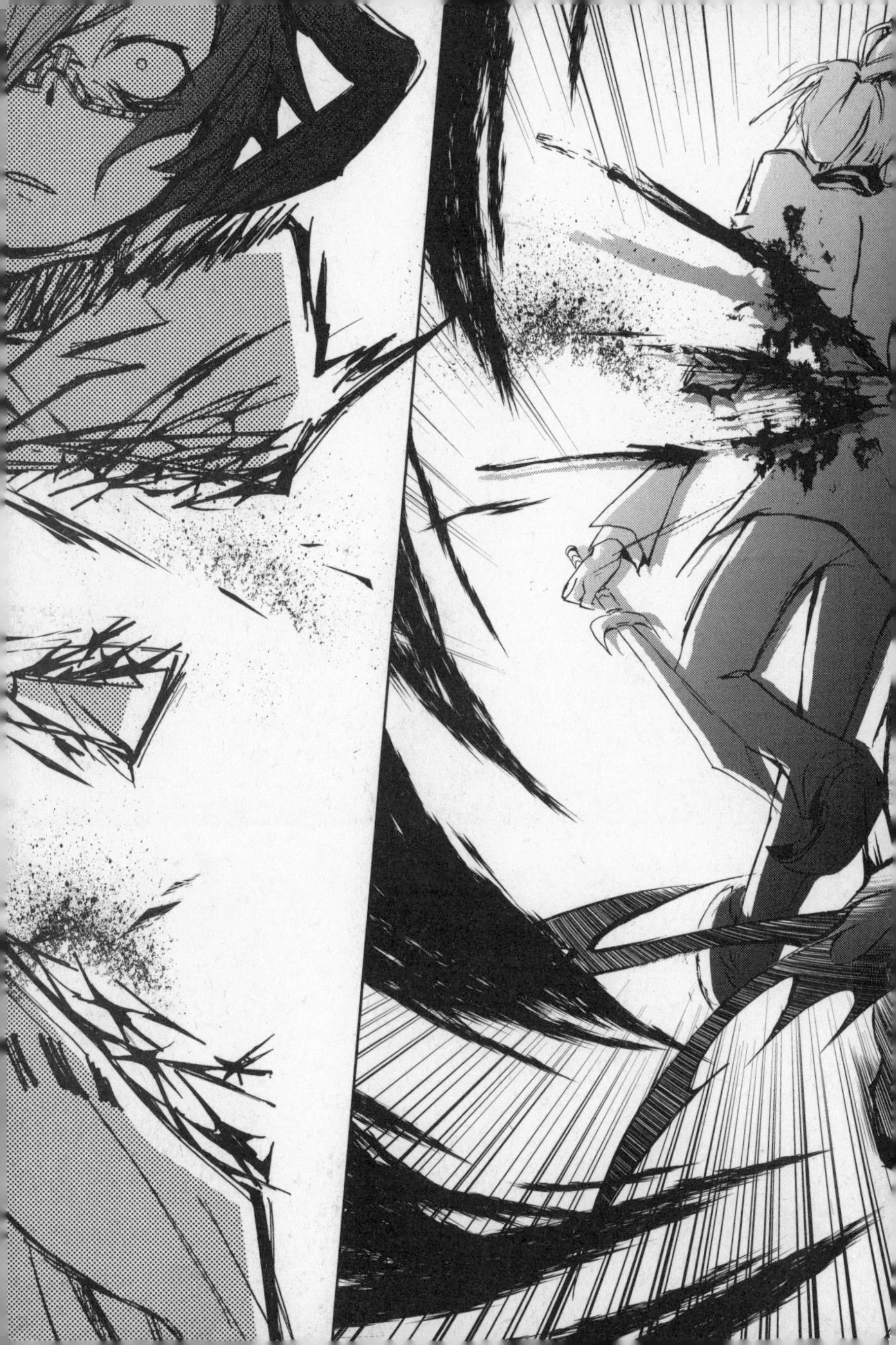

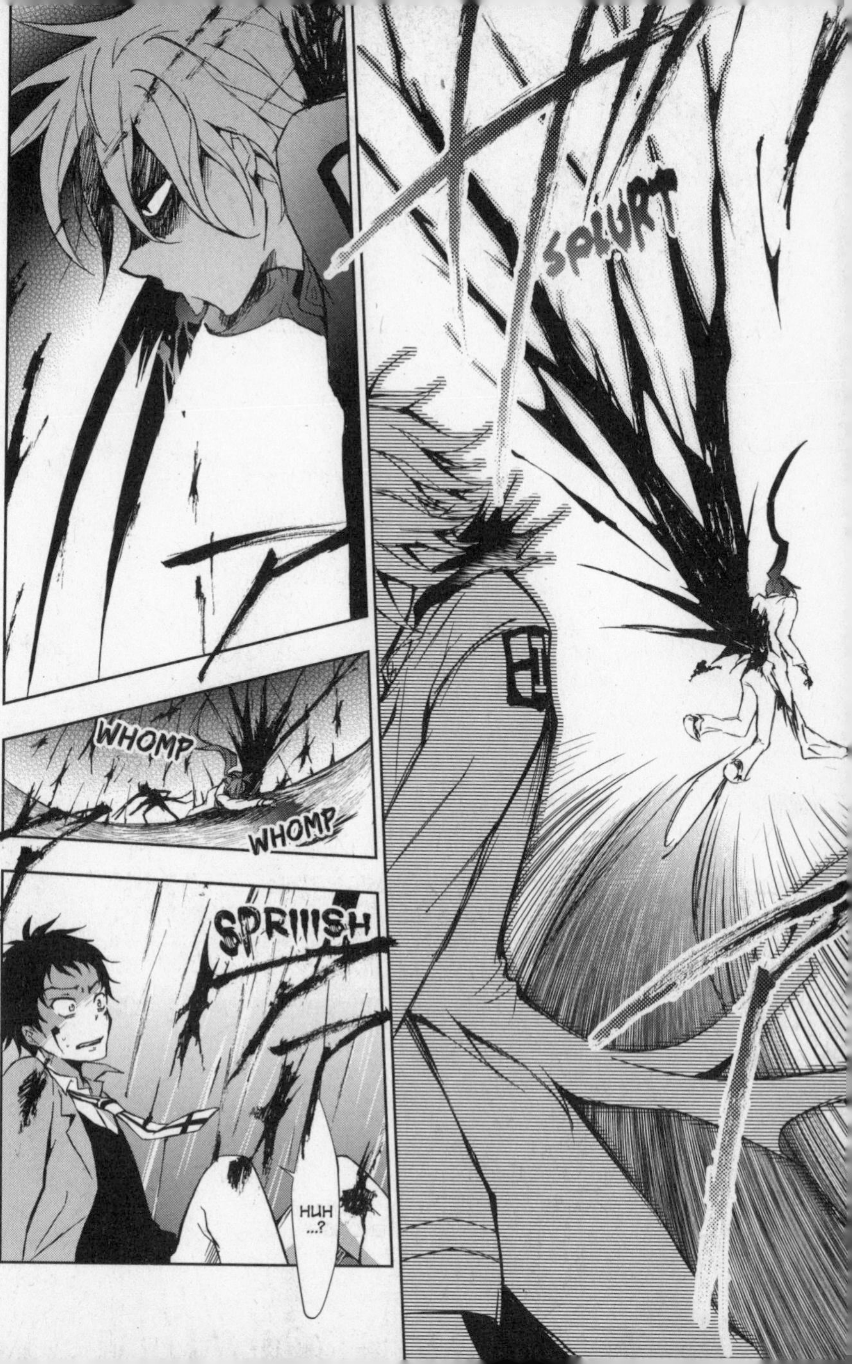
SPLURT
WHOMP
WHOMP
SPRIIISH
HUH ...?

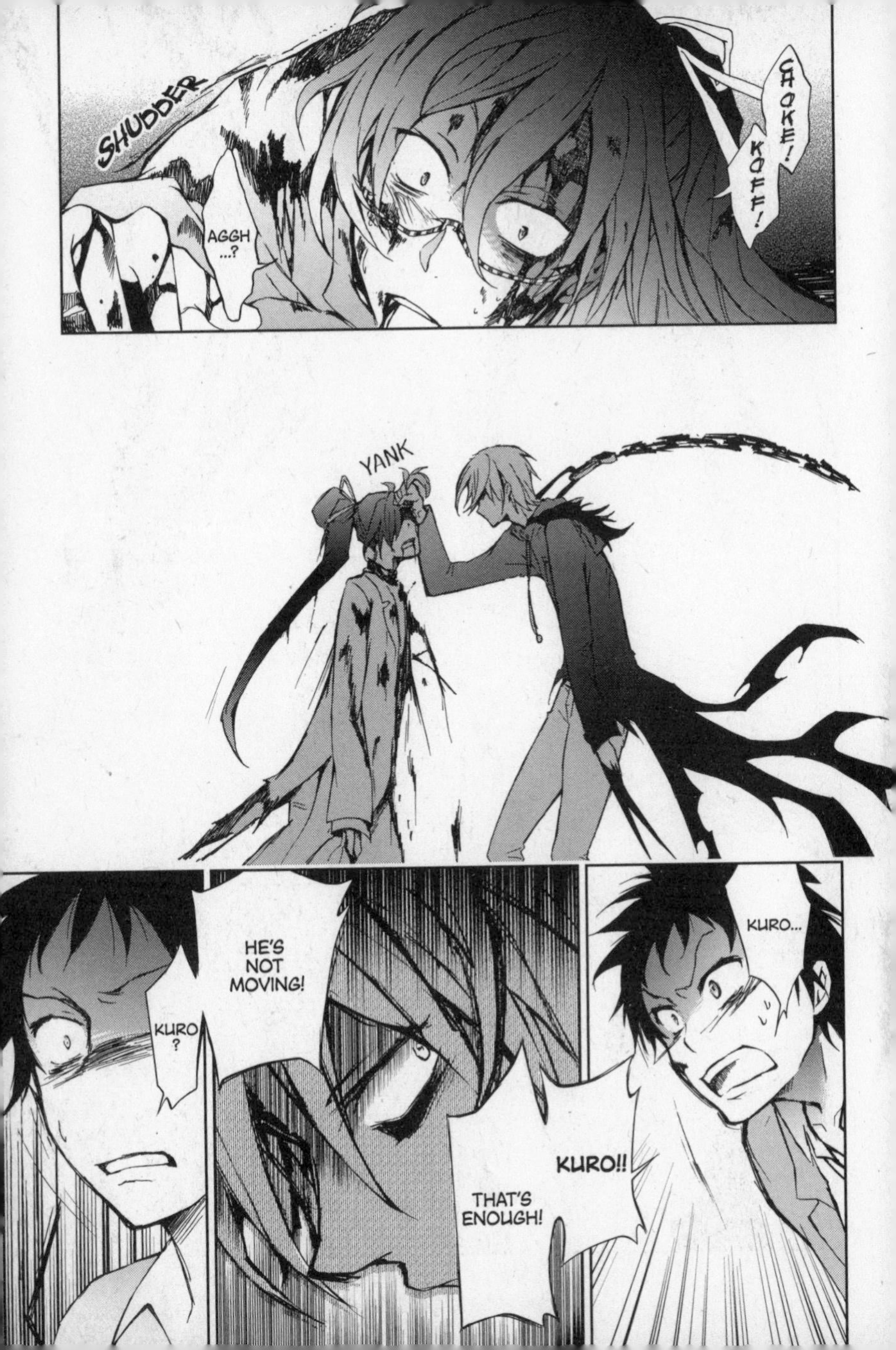
CHOKE! KOFF!
SHUDDER
AGGH ...?
YANK
KURO...
KURO!!
THAT'S ENOUGH!
HE'S NOT MOVING!
KURO ?

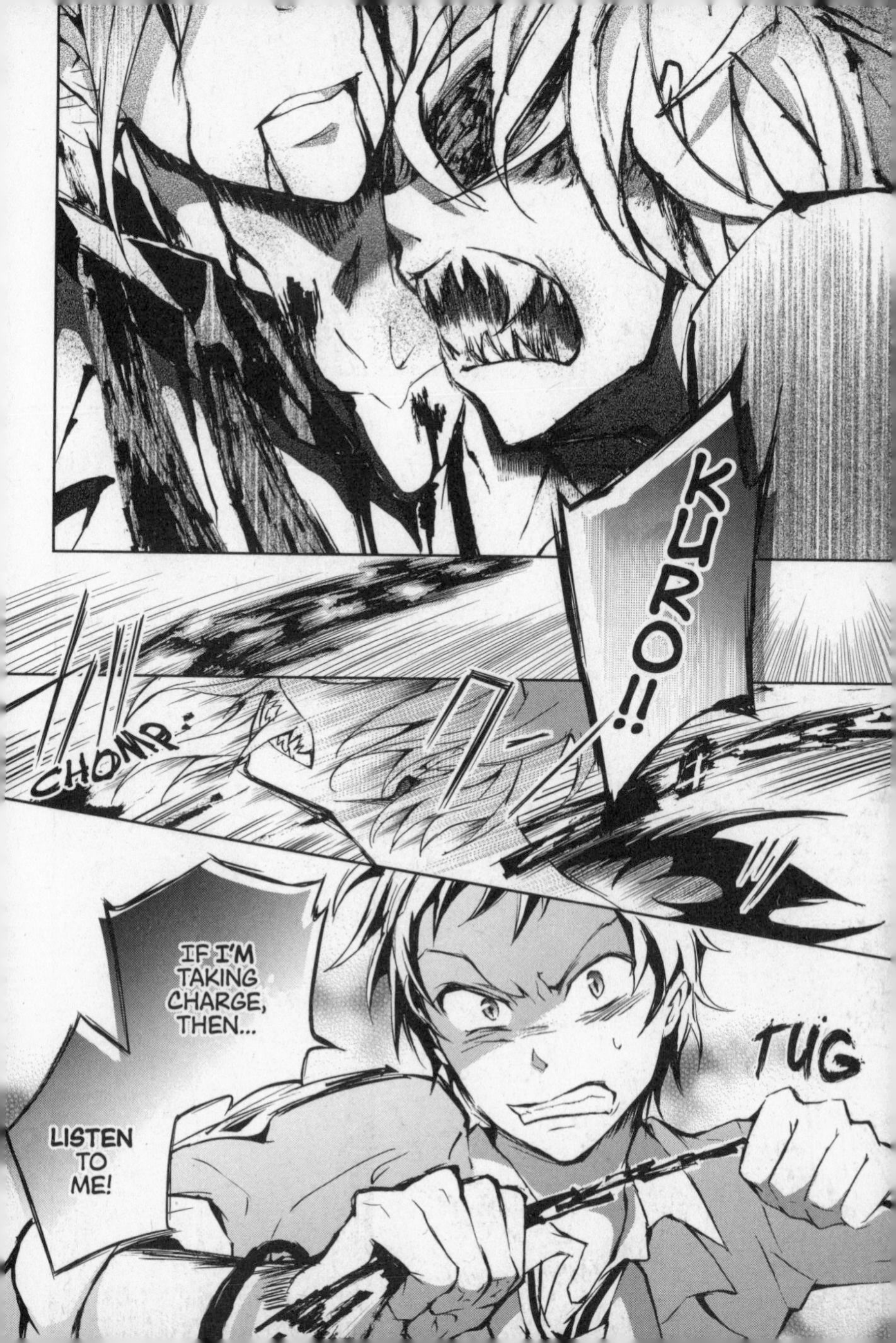
KURO!!
CHOMP
TUG
IF I'M TAKING CHARGE, THEN...
LISTEN TO ME!

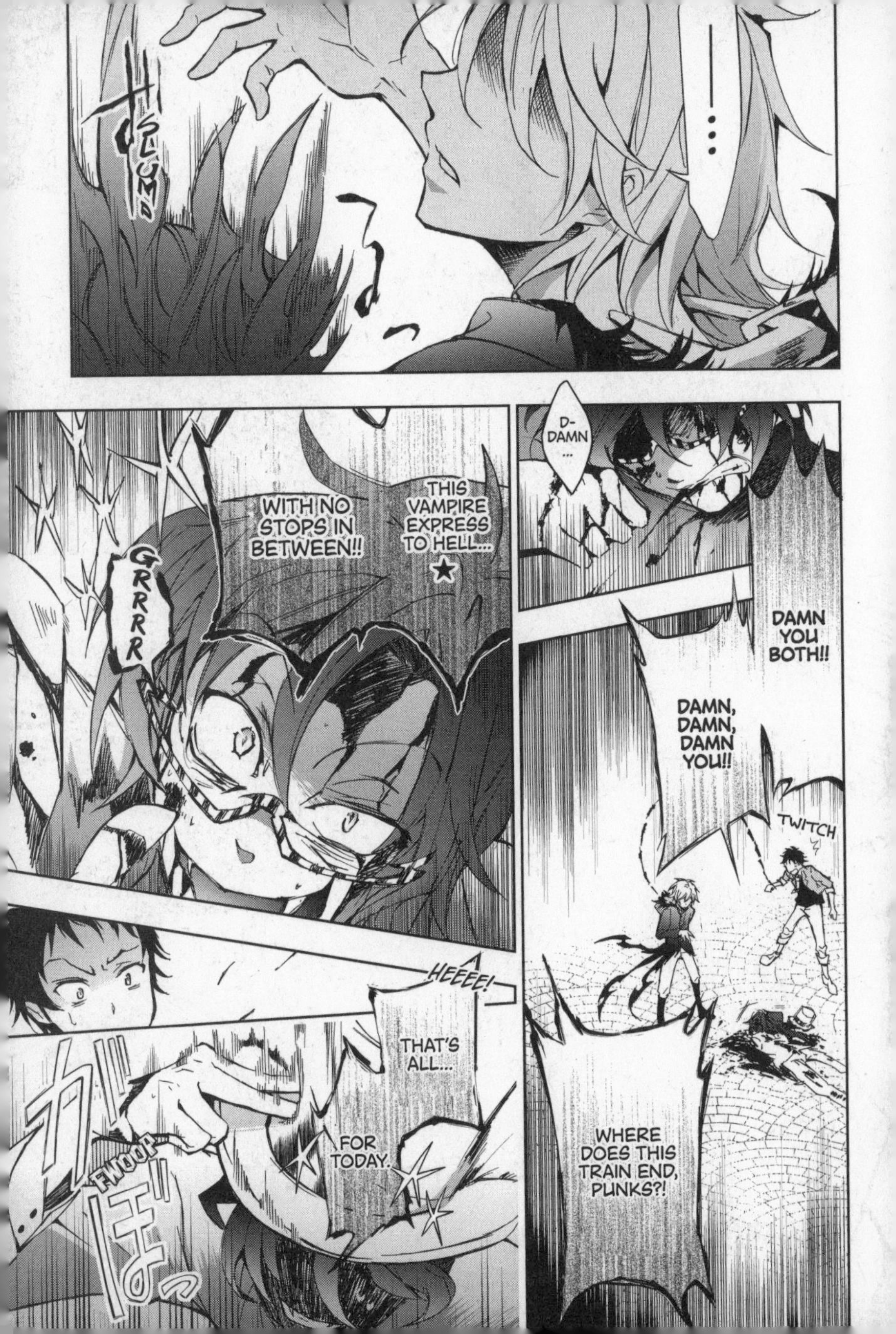

...
SLUMP
D-DAMN...
DAMN YOU BOTH!!
DAMN, DAMN, DAMN YOU!!
TWITCH
WHERE DOES THIS TRAIN END, PUNKS?!
THIS VAMPIRE EXPRESS TO HELL... ★
WITH NO STOPS IN BETWEEN!!
GRRRR
HEEEE!
THAT'S ALL...
FOR TODAY.
FWOOP

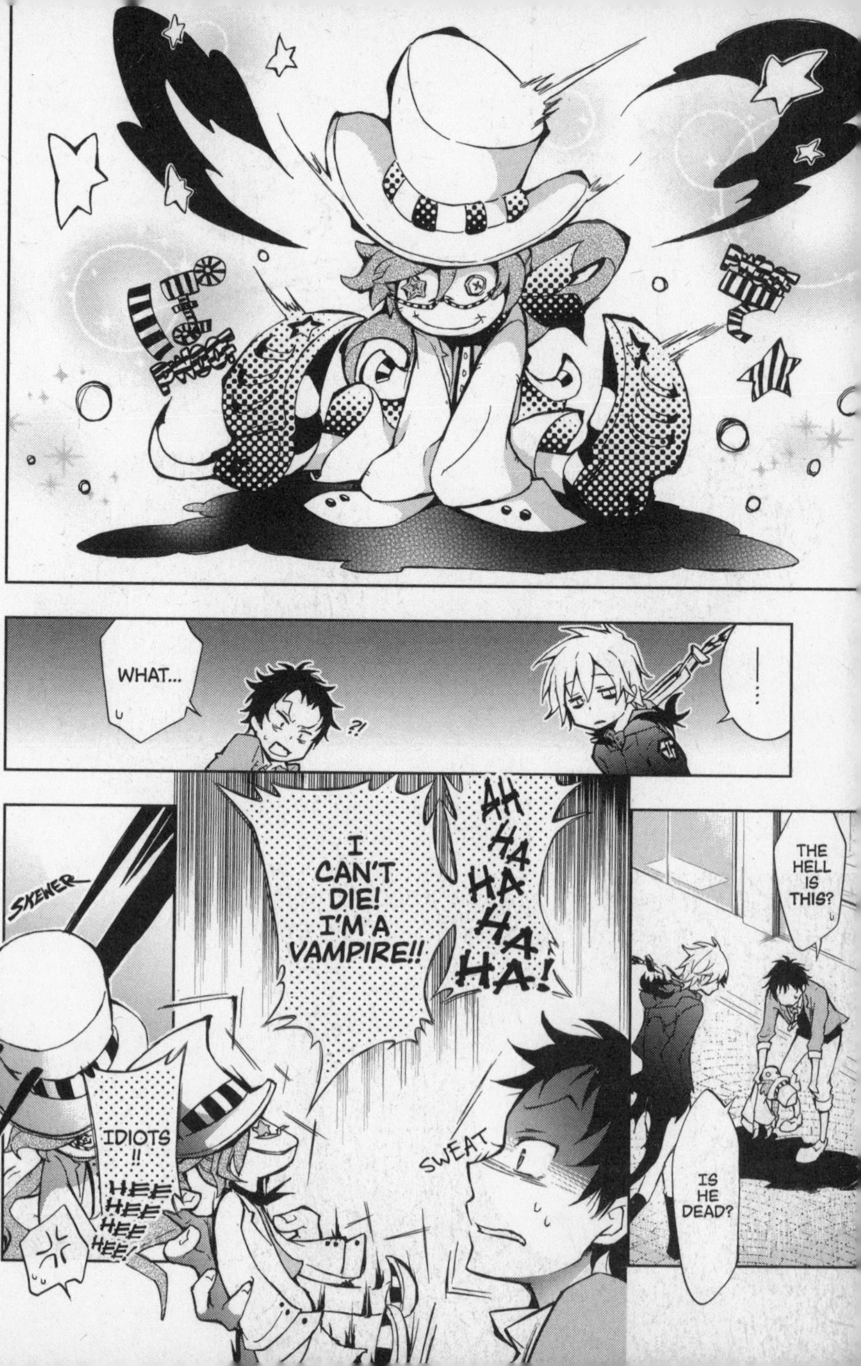

—...
WHAT...
?!
THE HELL IS THIS?
IS HE DEAD?
I CAN'T DIE! I'M A VAMPIRE!!
AH HA HA HA HA HA!
SWEAT
SKEWER
IDIOTS!!
HEE HEE HEE HEE!

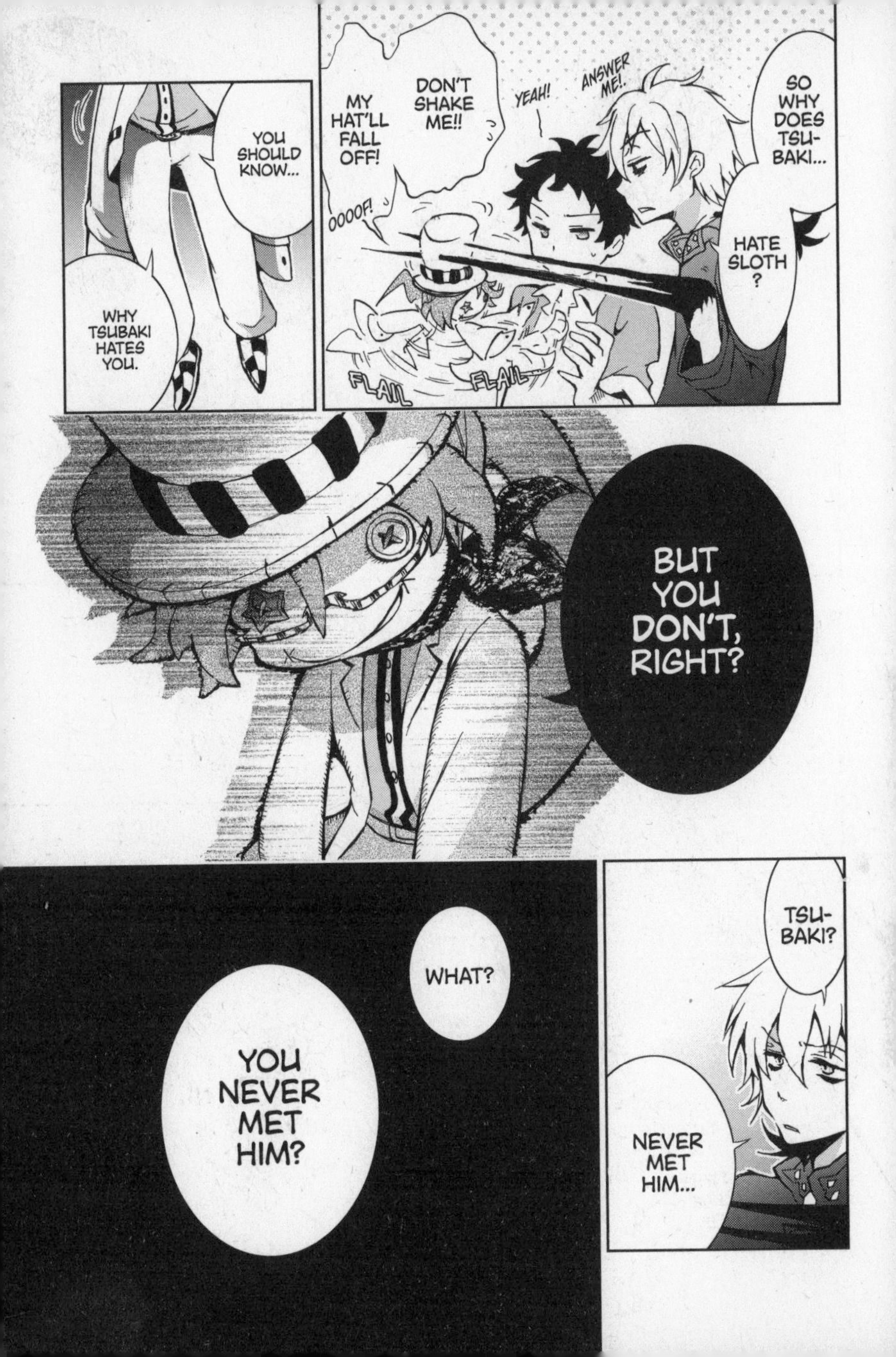
SO WHY DOES TSU-BAKI...
HATE SLOTH?
ANSWER ME!.
YEAH!
DON'T SHAKE ME!!
MY HAT'LL FALL OFF!
OOOOF!
FLAIL
FLAIL
YOU SHOULD KNOW...
WHY TSUBAKI HATES YOU.
BUT YOU DON'T, RIGHT?
TSU-BAKI?
NEVER MET HIM...
WHAT?
YOU NEVER MET HIM?

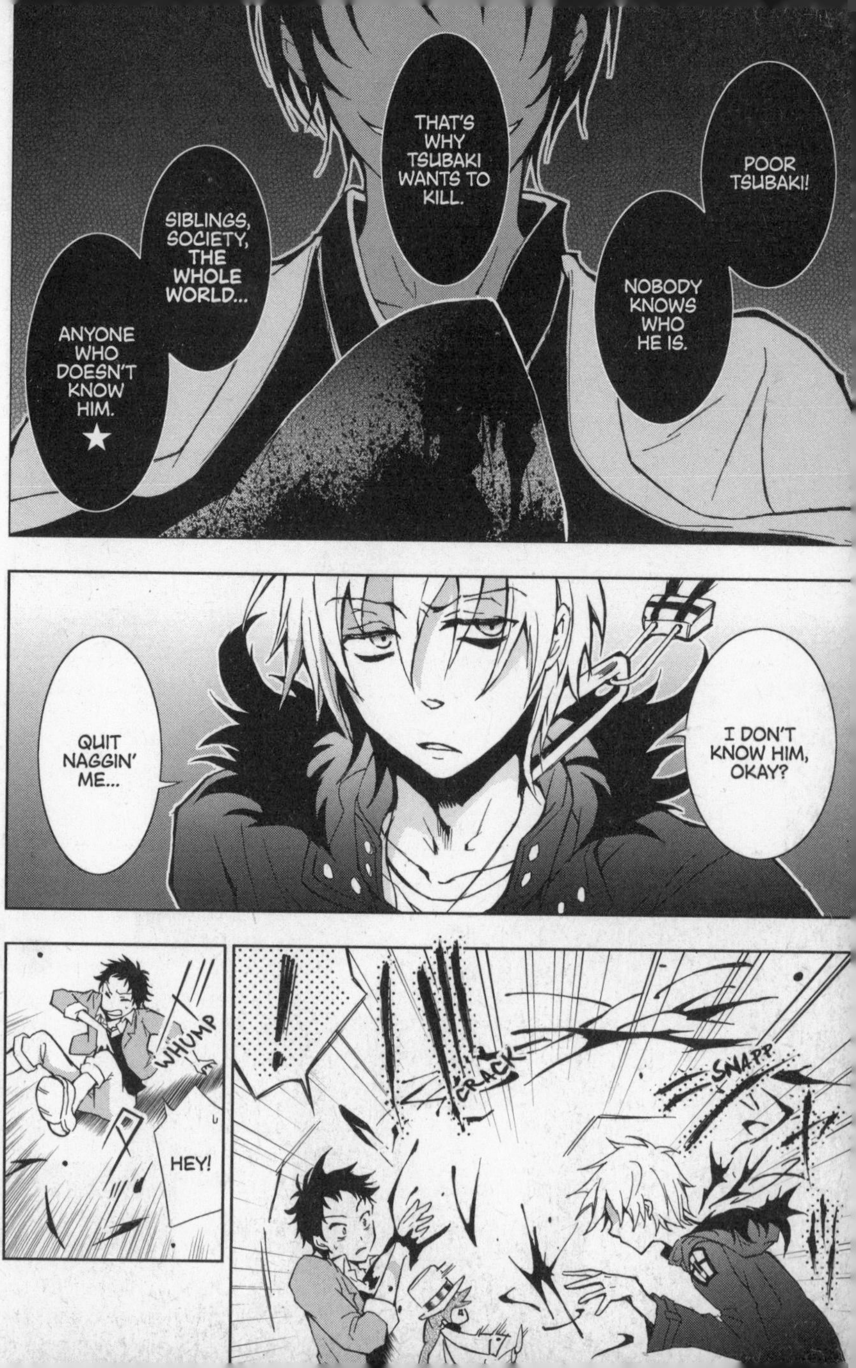
POOR TSUBAKI!
NOBODY KNOWS WHO HE IS.
THAT'S WHY TSUBAKI WANTS TO KILL.
SIBLINGS, SOCIETY, THE WHOLE WORLD...
ANYONE WHO DOESN'T KNOW HIM. ★
I DON'T KNOW HIM, OKAY?
QUIT NAGGIN' ME...
SNAPP
CRACK
WHUMP
HEY!

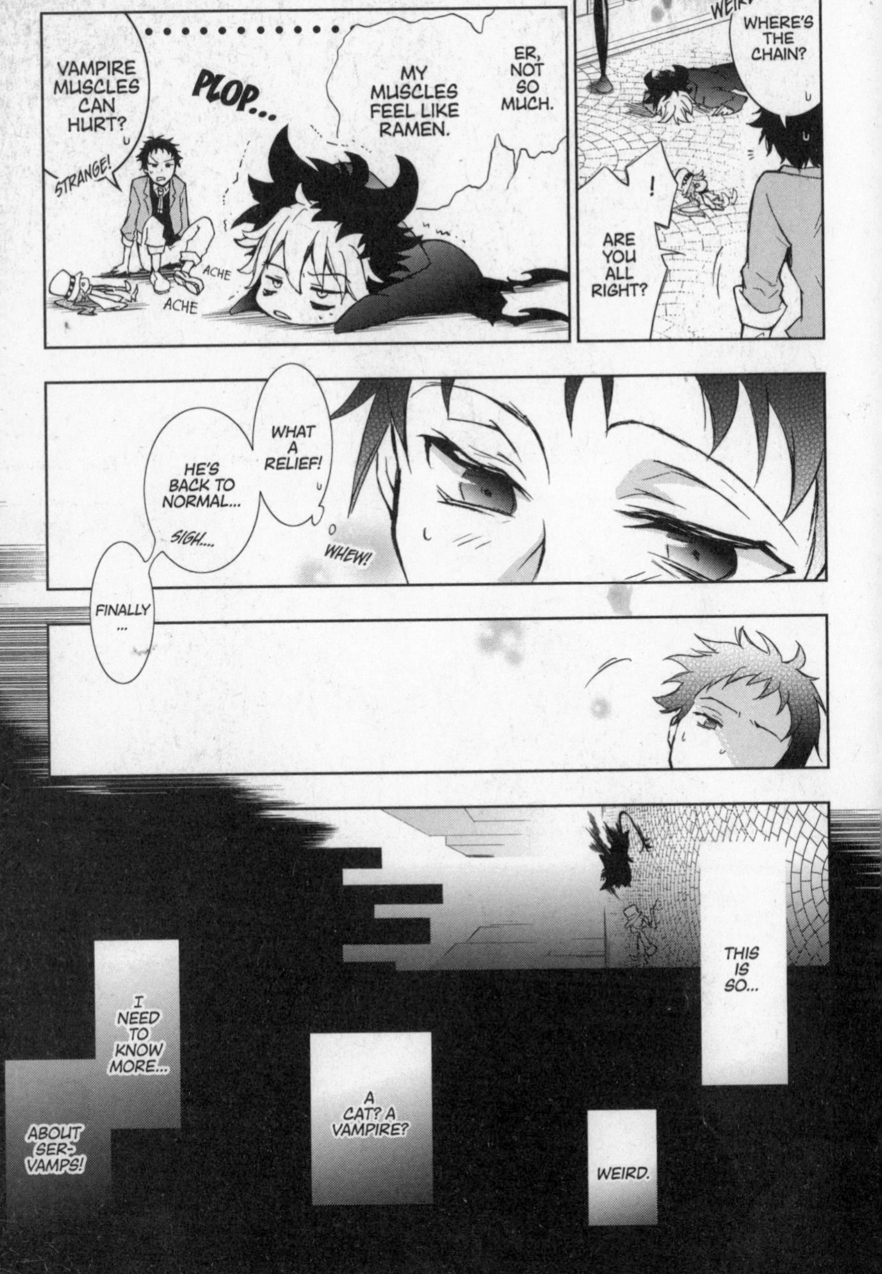
WEIRD!
WHERE'S THE CHAIN?
!
ARE YOU ALL RIGHT?
ER, NOT SO MUCH.
MY MUSCLES FEEL LIKE RAMEN.
....
PLOP...
VAMPIRE MUSCLES CAN HURT?
STRANGE!
ACHE
ACHE
WHAT A RELIEF!
HE'S BACK TO NORMAL...
SIGH....
WHEW!
FINALLY...
THIS IS SO...
WEIRD.
A CAT? A VAMPIRE?
I NEED TO KNOW MORE...
ABOUT SER-VAMPS!

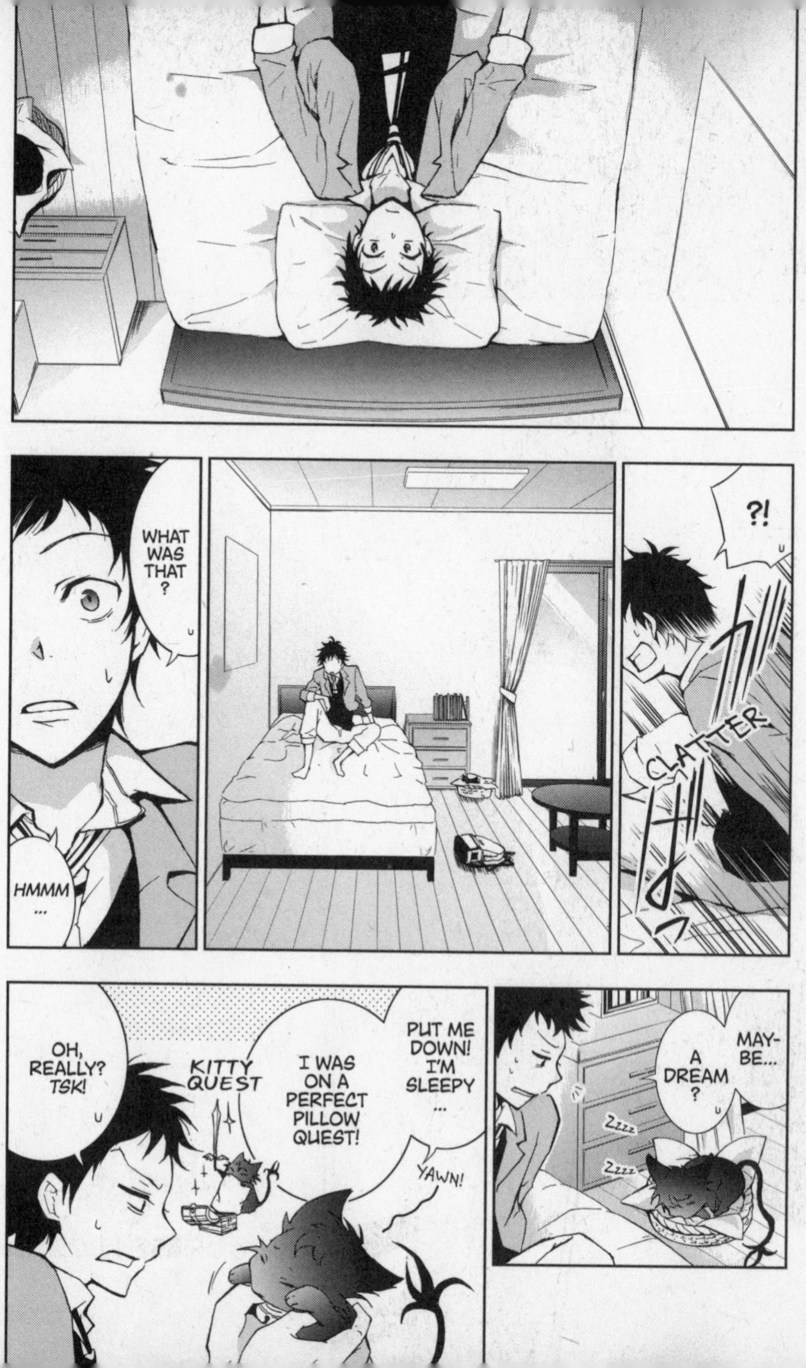
?!
CLATTER
WHAT WAS THAT?
HMMM...
MAY-BE...
A DREAM?
Zzzz
Zzzz
PUT ME DOWN! I'M SLEEPY...
YAWN!
I WAS ON A PERFECT PILLOW QUEST!
KITTY QUEST
OH, REALLY? TSK!

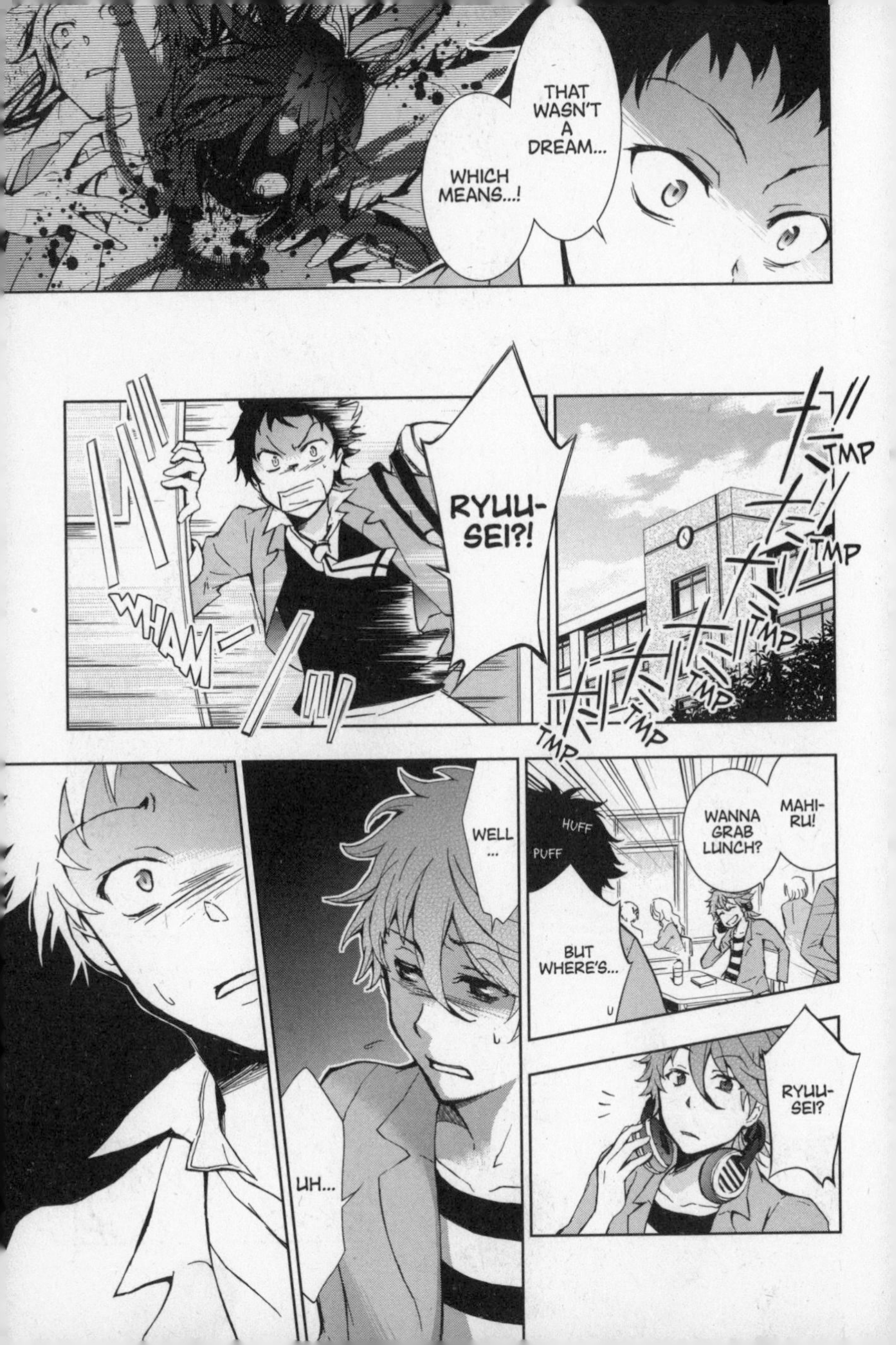
THAT WASN'T A DREAM...
WHICH MEANS...!
TMP
TMP
TMP
TMP
TMP
TMP
RYUU-SEI?!
WHAM
MAHI-RU!
WANNA GRAB LUNCH?
HUFF
PUFF
RYUU-SEI?
WELL ...
BUT WHERE'S...
UH...

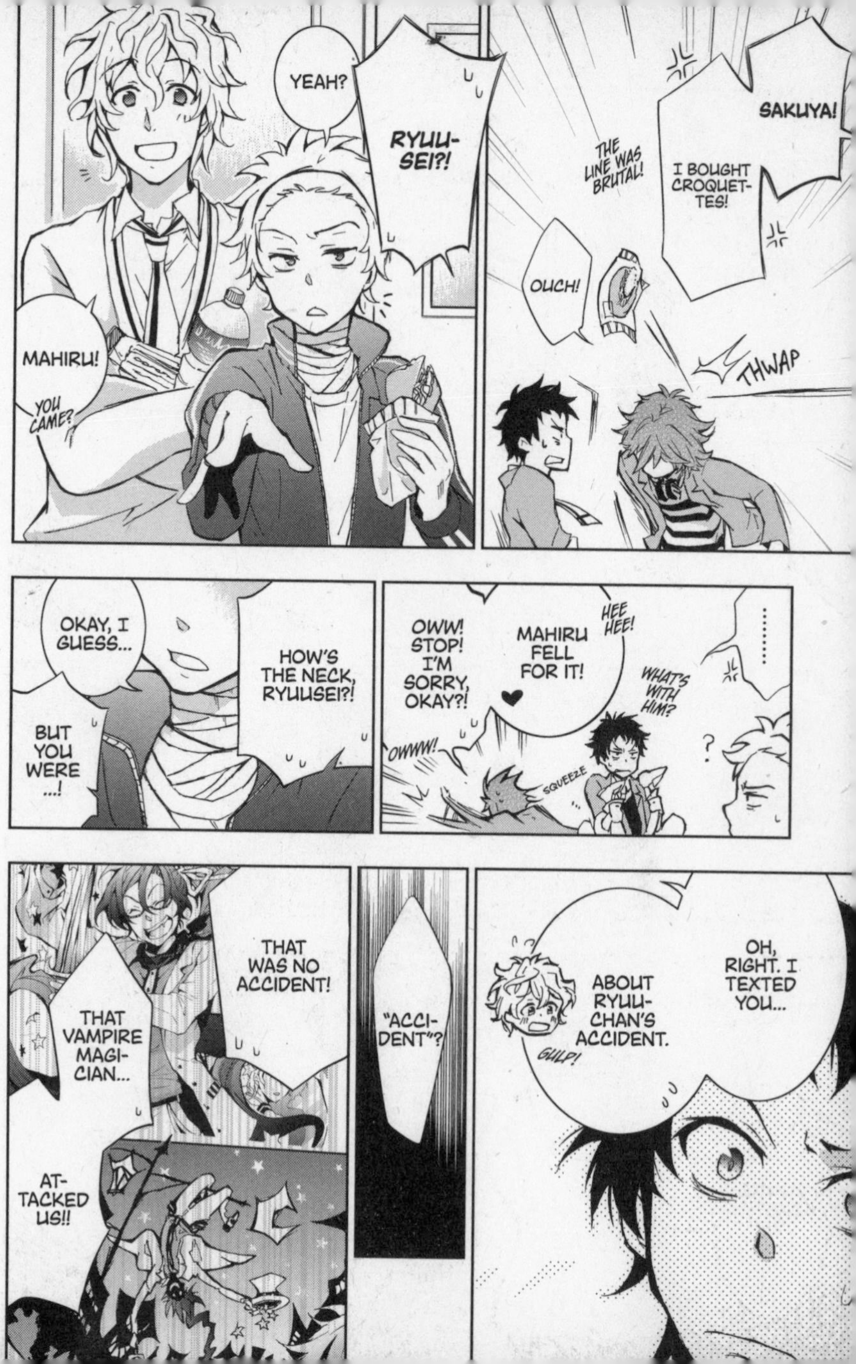
SAKUYA!
I BOUGHT CROQUET-TES!
THE LINE WAS BRUTAL!
OUCH!
THWAP
RYUU-SEI?!
YEAH?
MAHIRU!
YOU CAME?
......
WHAT'S WITH HIM?
?
HEE HEE!
MAHIRU FELL FOR IT!
OWW! STOP! I'M SORRY, OKAY?!
OWWW!
SQUEEZE
HOW'S THE NECK, RYUUSEI?!
OKAY, I GUESS...
BUT YOU WERE ...!
OH, RIGHT. I TEXTED YOU...
ABOUT RYUU-CHAN'S ACCIDENT.
GULP!
"ACCI-DENT"?
THAT WAS NO ACCIDENT!
THAT VAMPIRE MAGI-CIAN...
AT-TACKED US!!

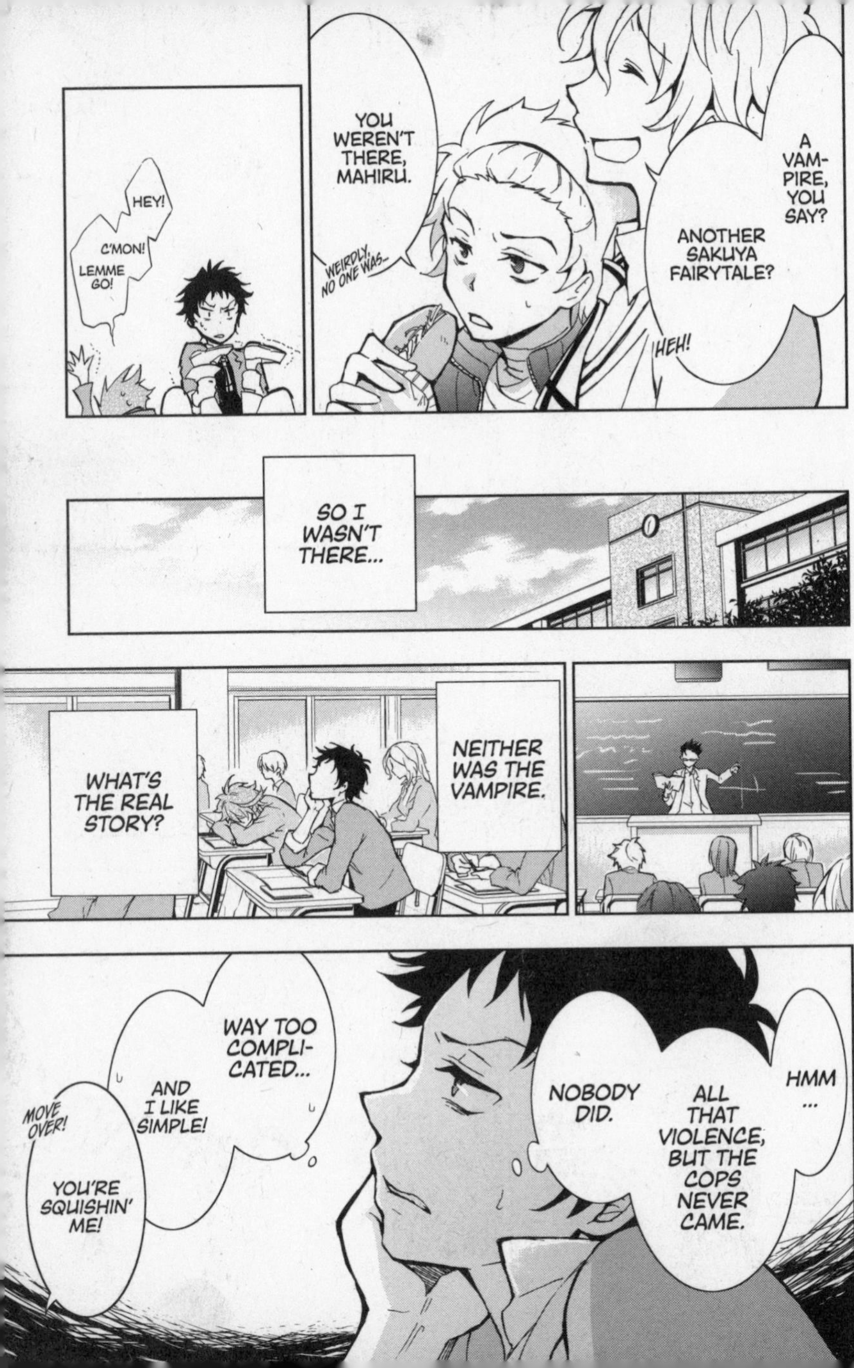
A VAMPIRE, YOU SAY?
ANOTHER SAKUYA FAIRYTALE?
HEH!
YOU WEREN'T THERE, MAHIRU.
WEIRDLY, NO ONE WAS...
HEY!
C'MON!
LEMME GO!
SO I WASN'T THERE...
NEITHER WAS THE VAMPIRE.
WHAT'S THE REAL STORY?
HMM...
ALL THAT VIOLENCE, BUT THE COPS NEVER CAME.
NOBODY DID.
WAY TOO COMPLICATED...
AND I LIKE SIMPLE!
MOVE OVER!
YOU'RE SQUISHIN' ME!

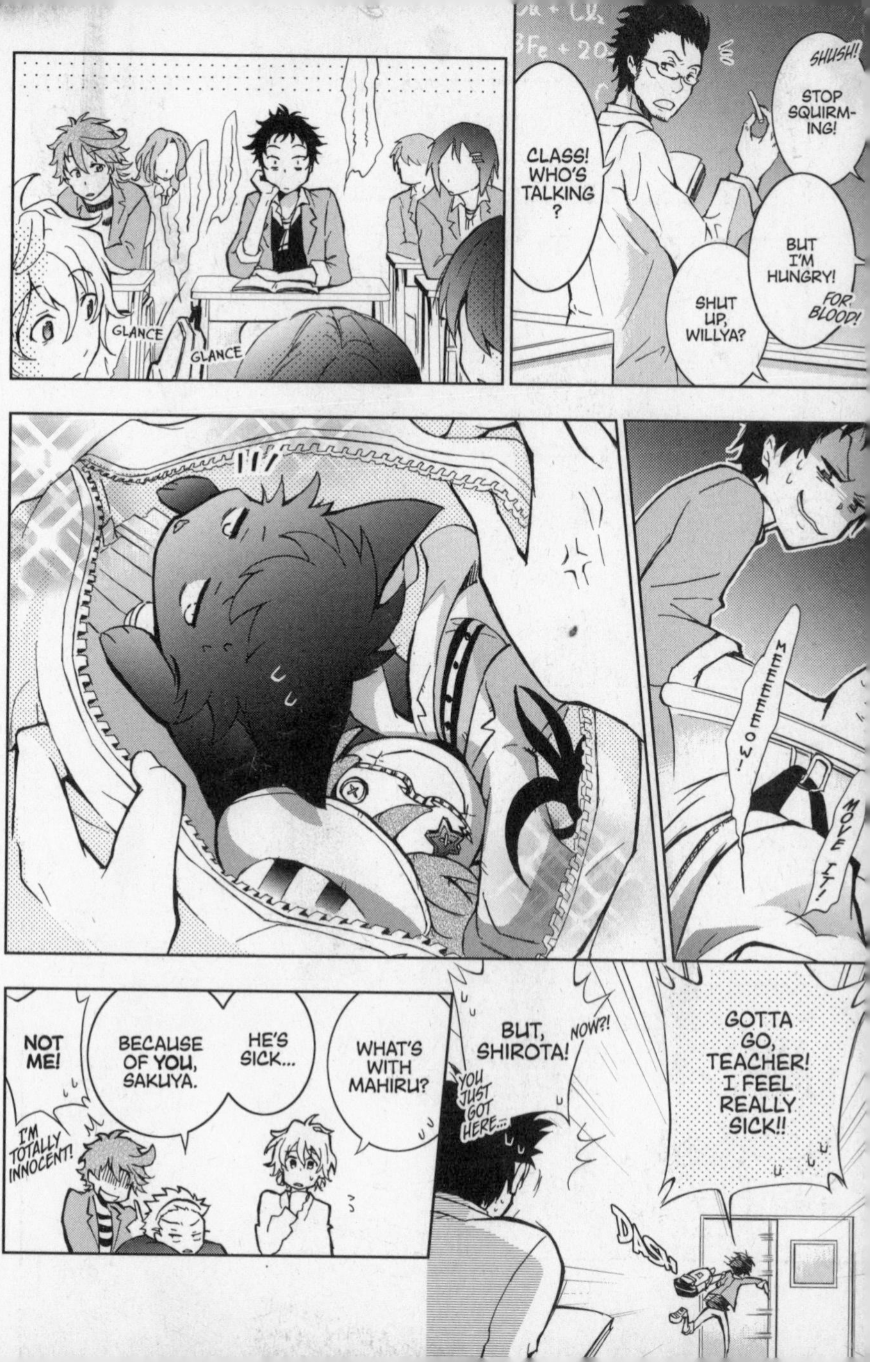
SHUSH!
STOP SQUIRMING!
CLASS! WHO'S TALKING?
BUT I'M HUNGRY!
FOR BLOOD!
SHUT UP, WILLYA?
GLANCE
GLANCE
MEEEEEOW!
MOVE IT!
GOTTA GO, TEACHER! I FEEL REALLY SICK!!
DASH
BUT, SHIROTA!
NOW?!
YOU JUST GOT HERE...
WHAT'S WITH MAHIRU?
HE'S SICK...
BECAUSE OF YOU, SAKUYA.
NOT ME!
I'M TOTALLY INNOCENT!

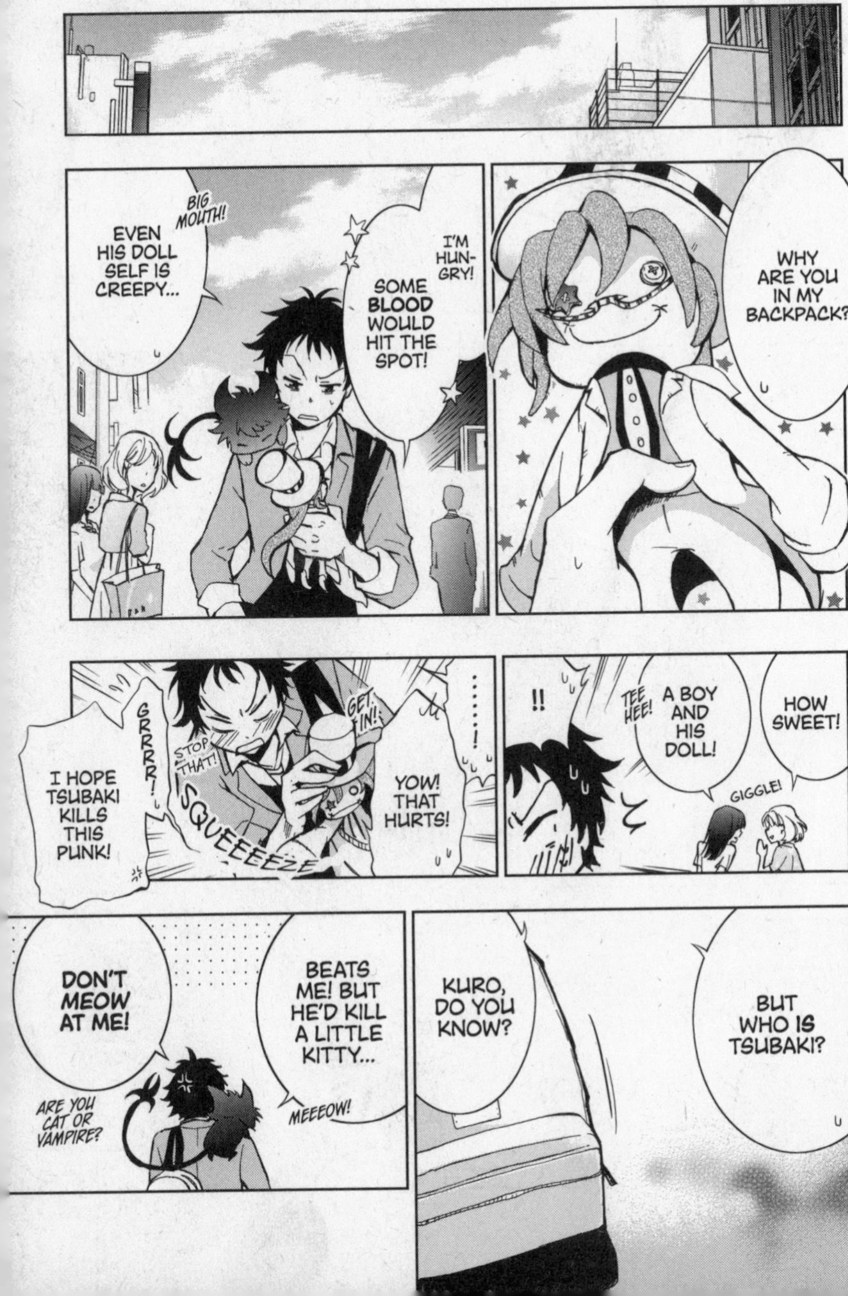
WHY ARE YOU IN MY BACKPACK?
I'M HUNGRY!
SOME BLOOD WOULD HIT THE SPOT!
BIG MOUTH!
EVEN HIS DOLL SELF IS CREEPY...
HOW SWEET!
A BOY AND HIS DOLL!
TEE HEE!
GIGGLE!
!!
......!
YOW! THAT HURTS!
GET IN!
STOP THAT!
SQUEEEEEZE
GRRRR!
I HOPE TSUBAKI KILLS THIS PUNK!
BUT WHO IS TSUBAKI?
KURO, DO YOU KNOW?
BEATS ME! BUT HE'D KILL A LITTLE KITTY...
MEEEOW!
DON'T MEOW AT ME!
ARE YOU CAT OR VAMPIRE?

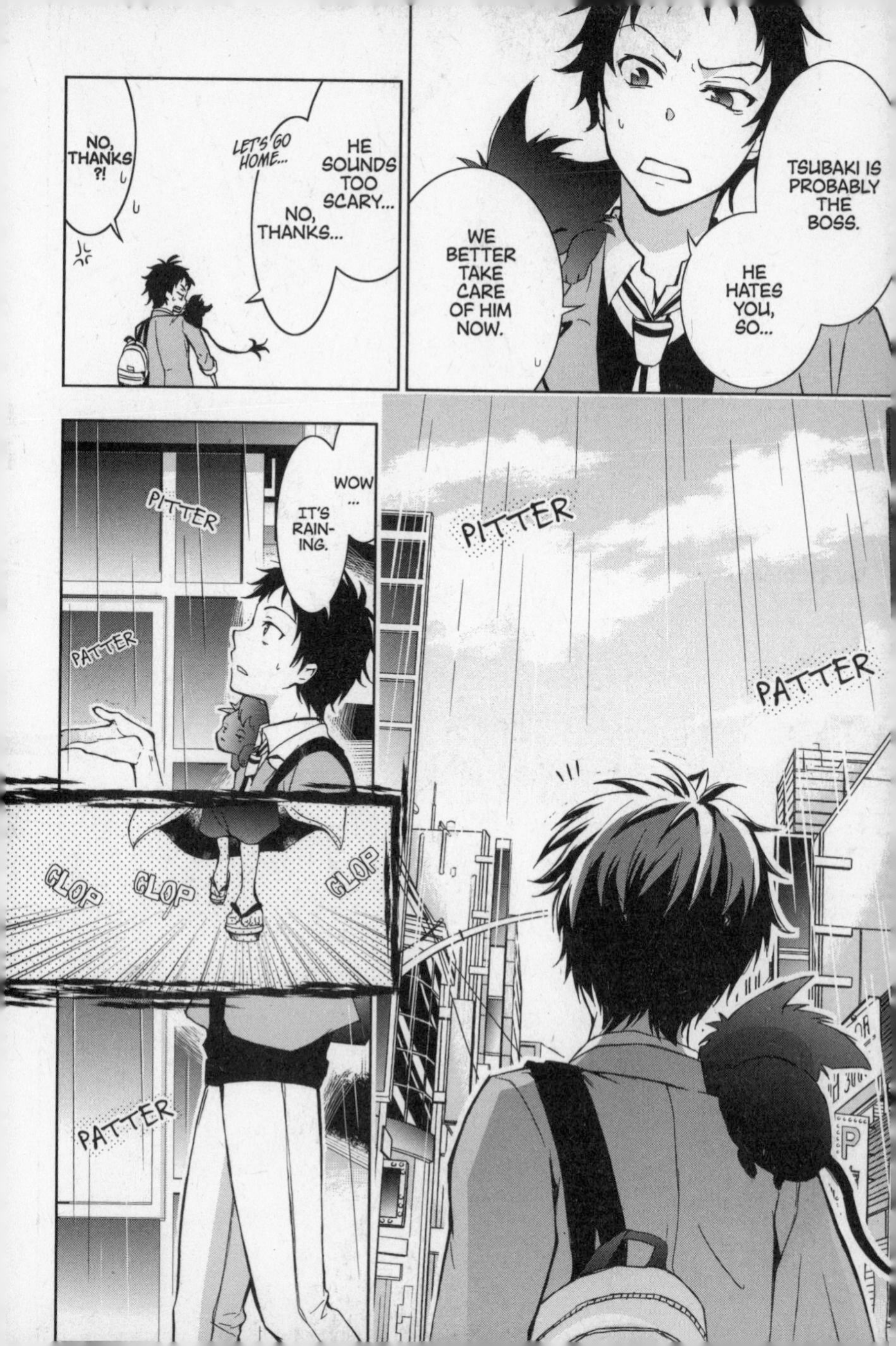
TSUBAKI IS PROBABLY THE BOSS.
HE HATES YOU, SO...
WE BETTER TAKE CARE OF HIM NOW.
HE SOUNDS TOO SCARY...
LET'S GO HOME...
NO, THANKS...
NO, THANKS?!
PITTER
PATTER
WOW... IT'S RAINING.
PITTER
PATTER
GLOP
GLOP
GLOP
PATTER

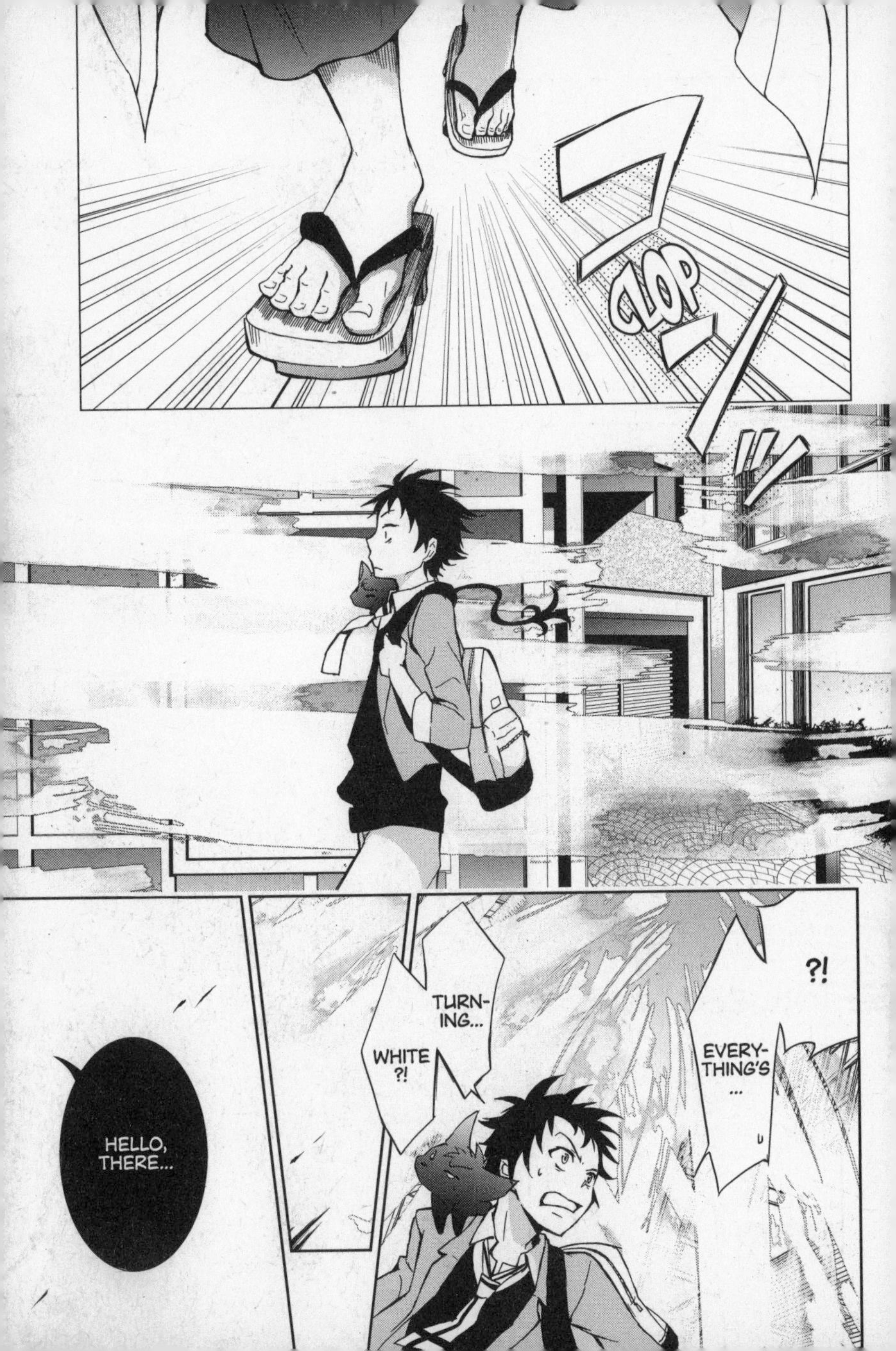
CLOP
?!
EVERY-THING'S...
TURN-ING...
WHITE ?!
HELLO, THERE...

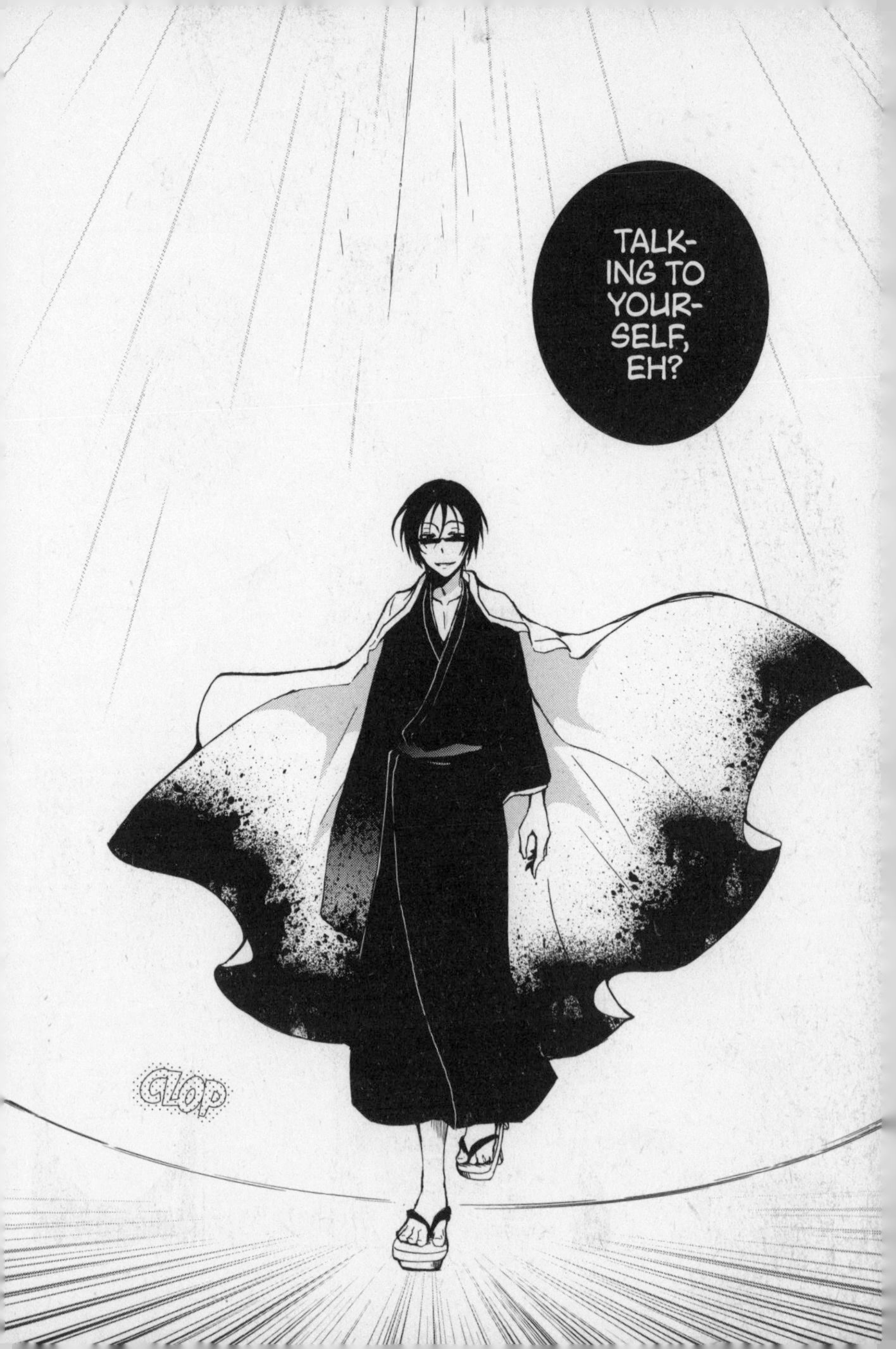
TALK-
ING TO
YOUR-
SELF,
EH?
CLOP

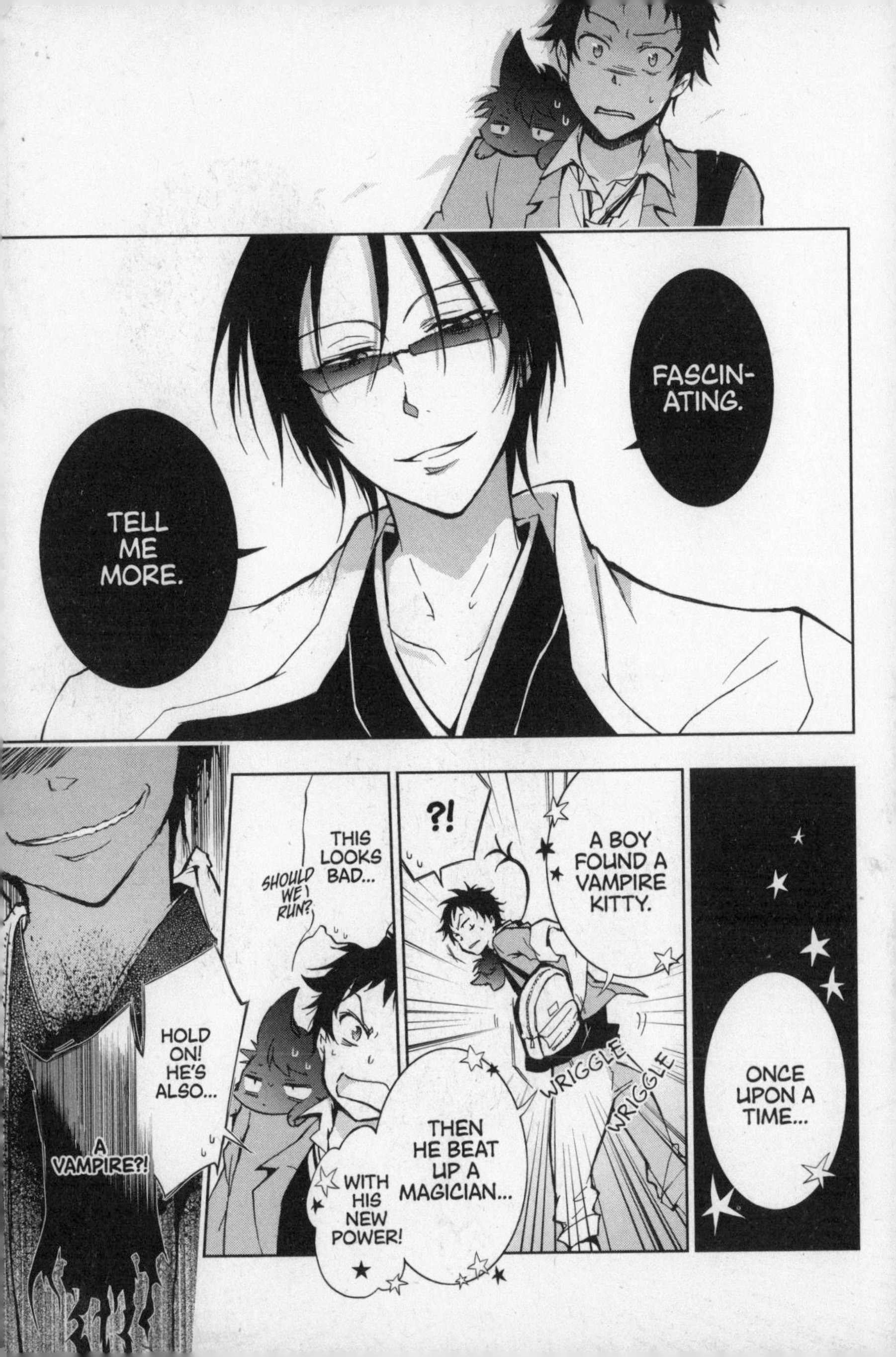
FASCIN-ATING.
TELL ME MORE.
ONCE UPON A TIME...
?!
A BOY FOUND A VAMPIRE KITTY.
WRIGGLE
WRIGGLE
THIS LOOKS BAD...
SHOULD WE RUN?
THEN HE BEAT UP A MAGICIAN...
WITH HIS NEW POWER!
HOLD ON! HE'S ALSO...
A VAMPIRE?!

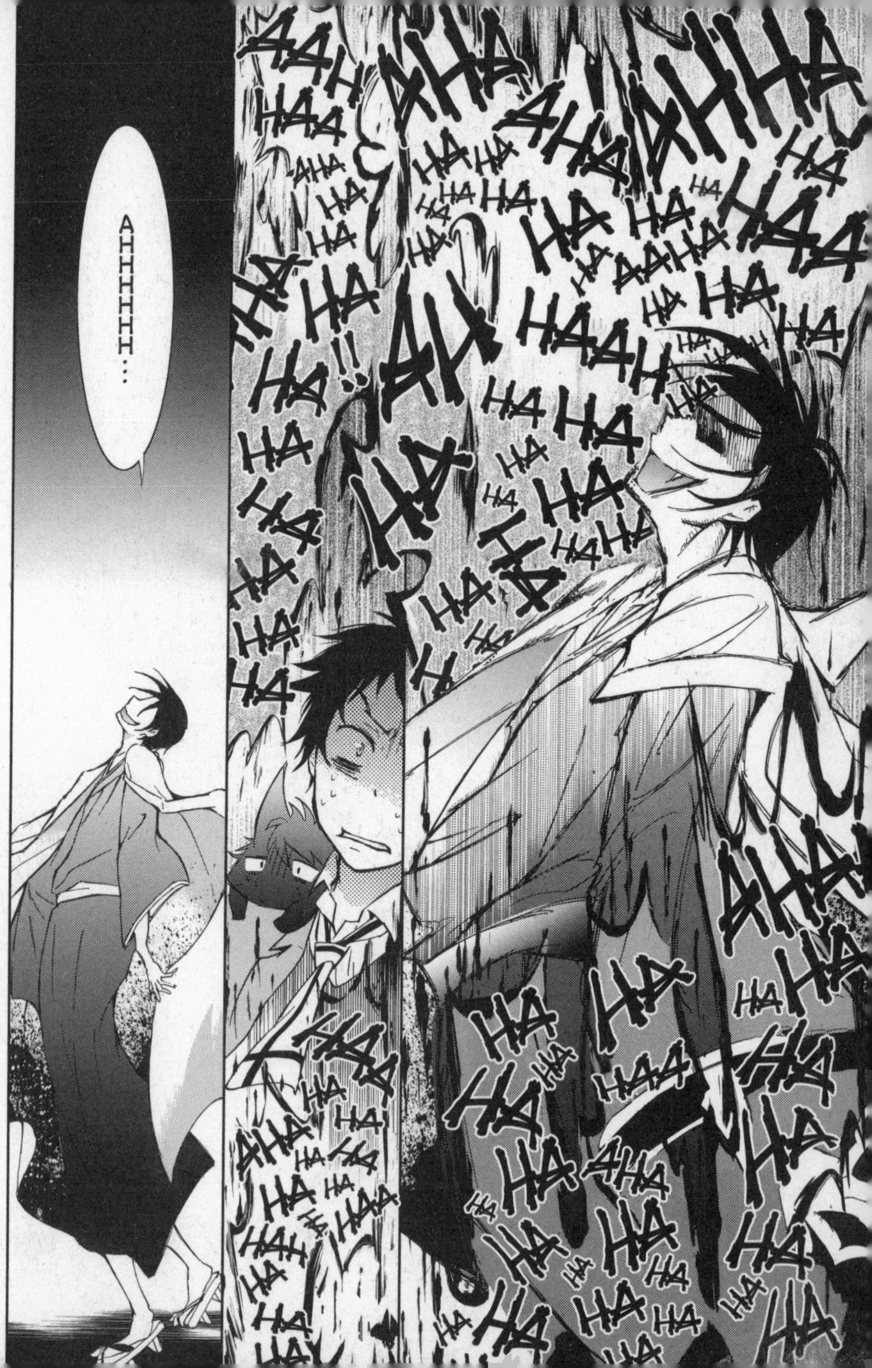
AHAHAHAHA
HA HA HA HA
HAAAH HA HA HA
HA HA HA HAA
AHAHA HA HA HA
HA HA HA HA HA
AHHHHHH...

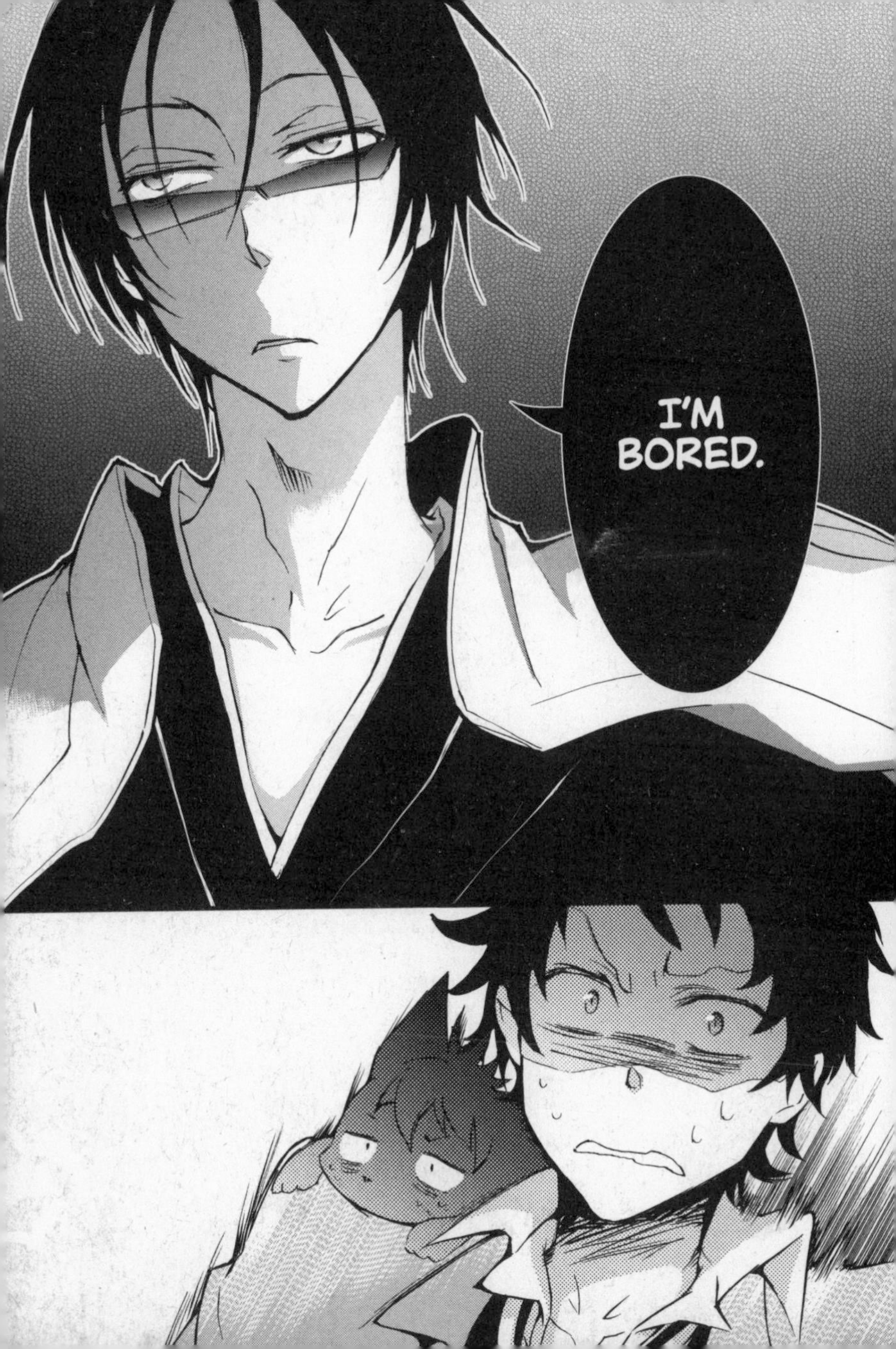
I'M BORED.

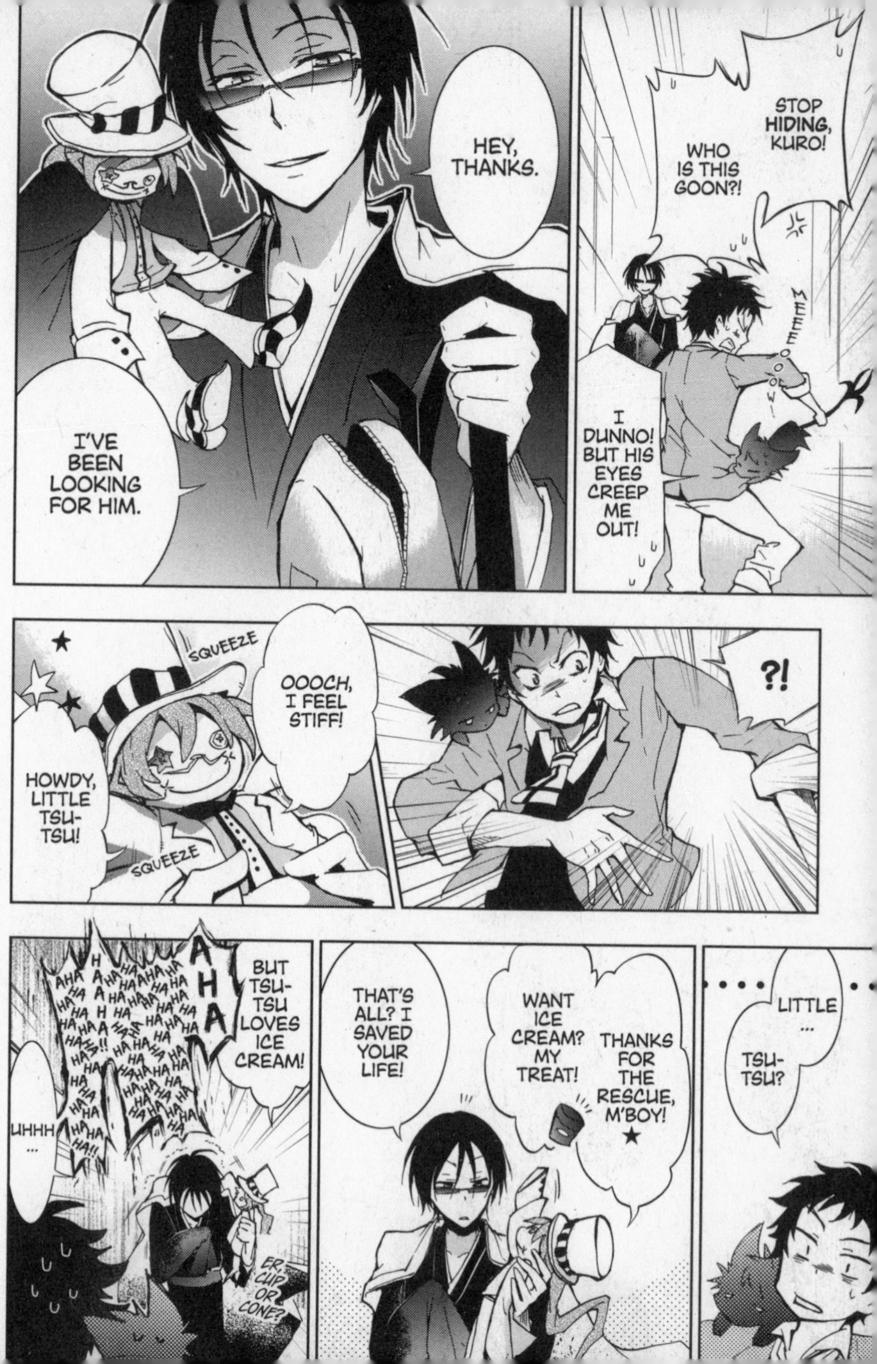
STOP HIDING, KURO!
WHO IS THIS GOON?!
MEEEOOOW!
I DUNNO! BUT HIS EYES CREEP ME OUT!
HEY, THANKS.
I'VE BEEN LOOKING FOR HIM.
?!
SQUEEZE
OOOCH, I FEEL STIFF!
HOWDY, LITTLE TSU-TSU!
SQUEEZE
......
LITTLE ... TSU-TSU?
THANKS FOR THE RESCUE, M'BOY!
WANT ICE CREAM? MY TREAT!
THAT'S ALL? I SAVED YOUR LIFE!
BUT TSU-TSU LOVES ICE CREAM!
AHA
HAHAHA!!
AHA HA HA HA HA HA HA HA HA HA HA!!
ER, CUP OR CONE?
UHHH ...

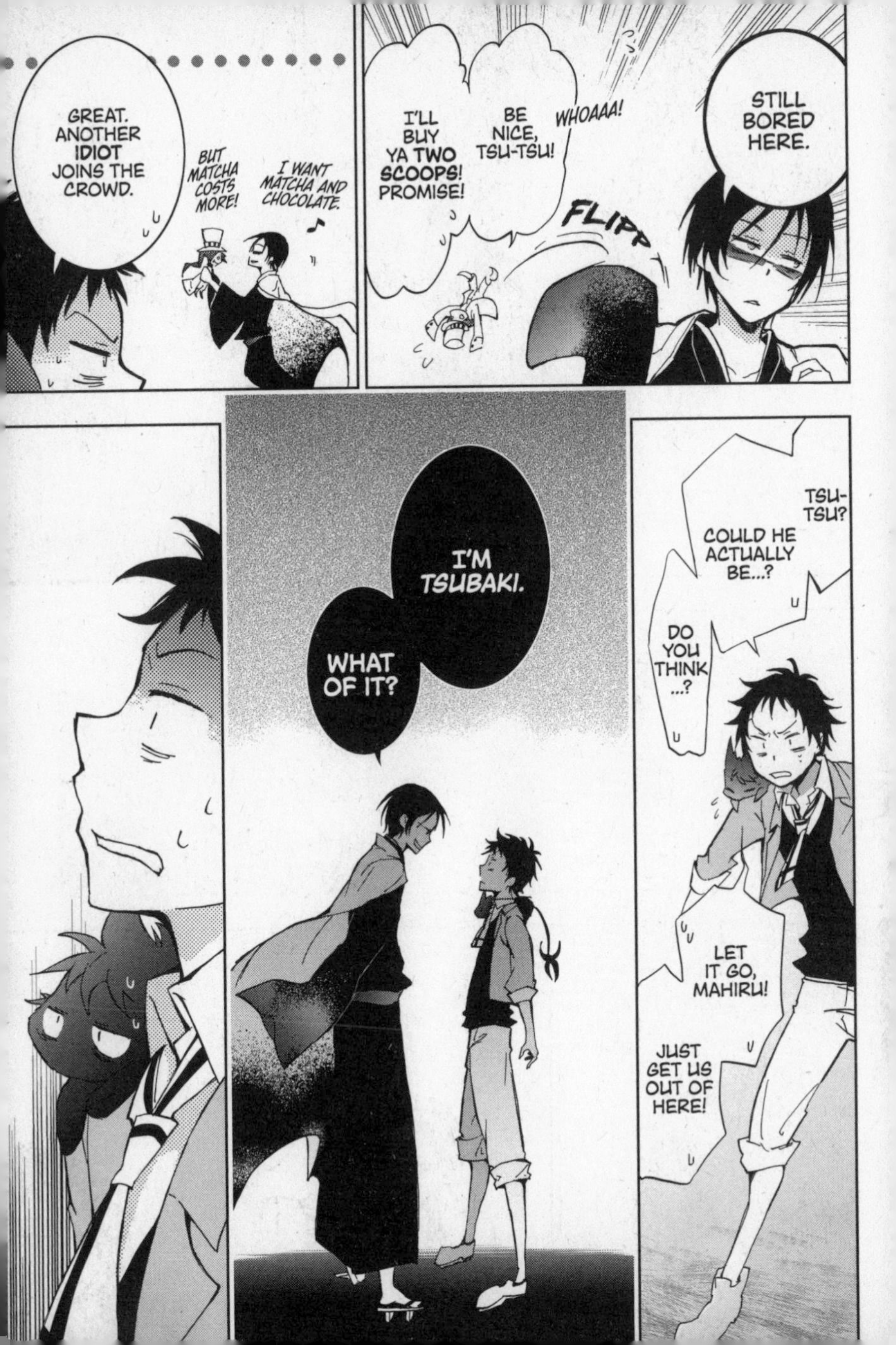
STILL BORED HERE.
WHOAAA!
BE NICE, TSU-TSU!
I'LL BUY YA TWO SCOOPS! PROMISE!
FLIPP
I WANT MATCHA AND CHOCOLATE.
BUT MATCHA COSTS MORE!
GREAT. ANOTHER IDIOT JOINS THE CROWD.
TSU-TSU?
COULD HE ACTUALLY BE...?
DO YOU THINK...?
LET IT GO, MAHIRU!
JUST GET US OUT OF HERE!
I'M TSUBAKI.
WHAT OF IT?

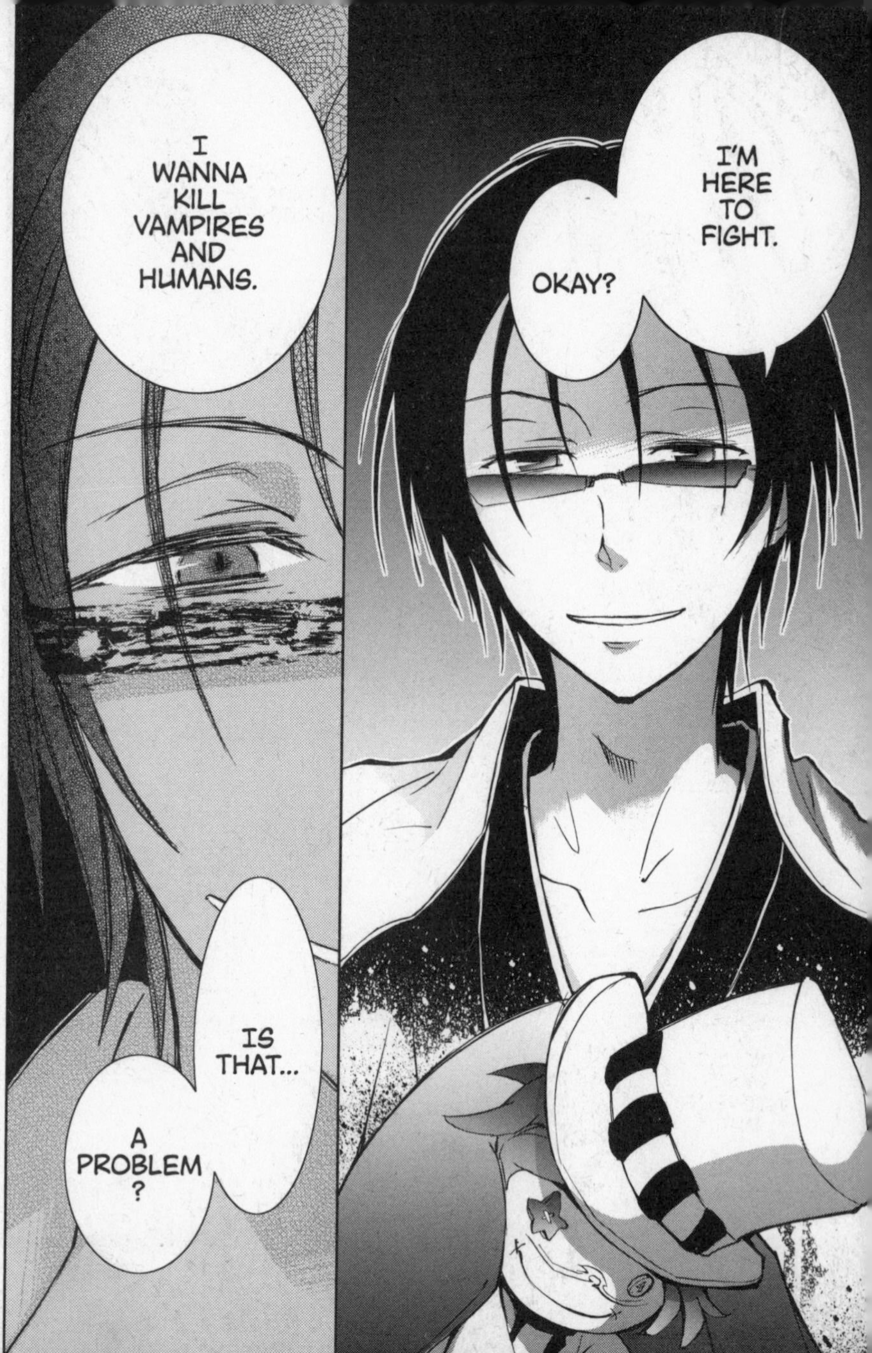
I'M HERE TO FIGHT.
OKAY?
I WANNA KILL VAMPIRES AND HUMANS.
IS THAT...
A PROBLEM?

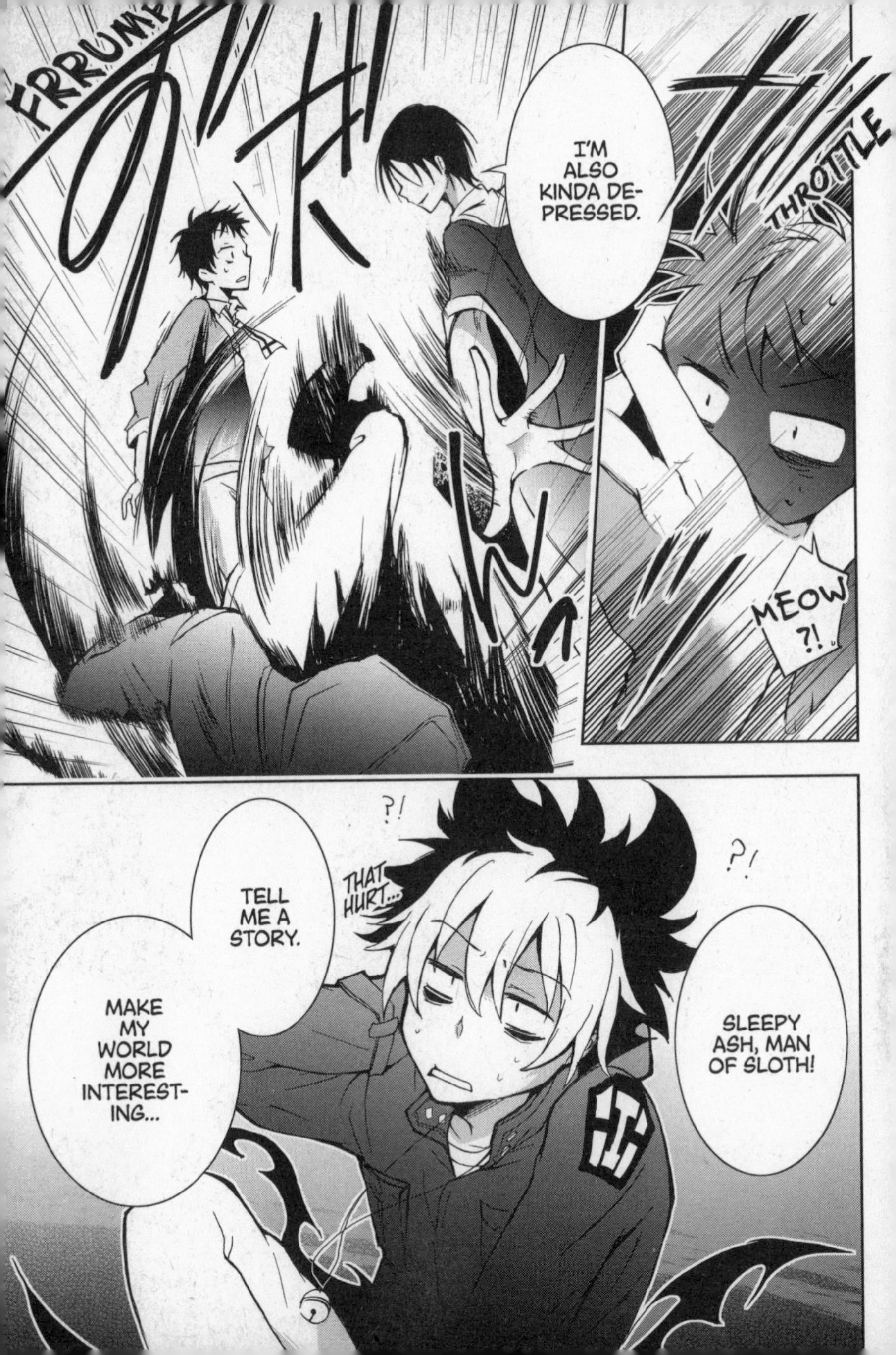
THROTTLE
MEOW ?!
FRRUMP
I'M ALSO KINDA DE-PRESSED.
?!
SLEEPY ASH, MAN OF SLOTH!
?!
THAT HURT...
TELL ME A STORY.
MAKE MY WORLD MORE INTEREST-ING...

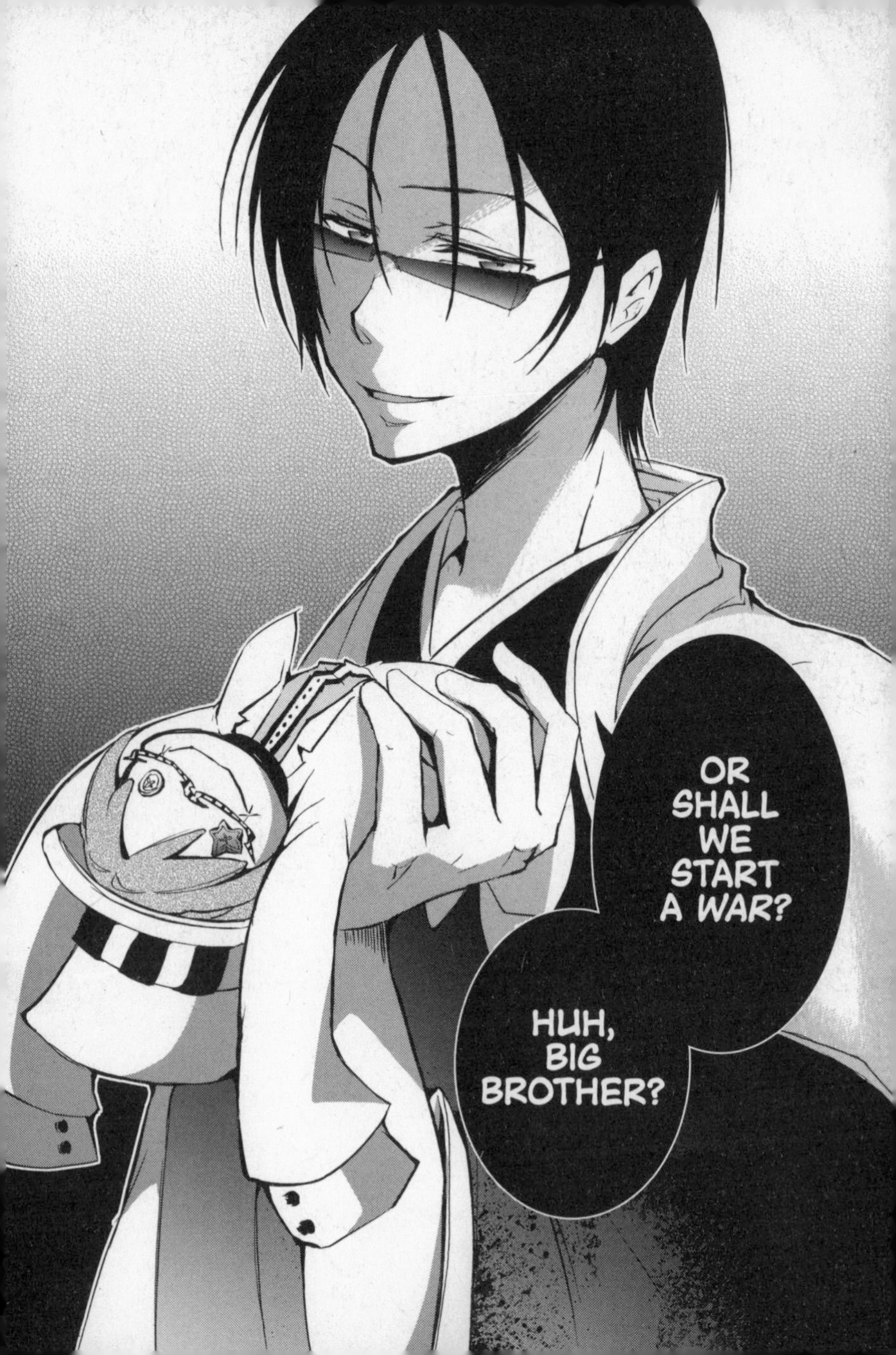
OR SHALL WE START A WAR?
HUH, BIG BROTHER?

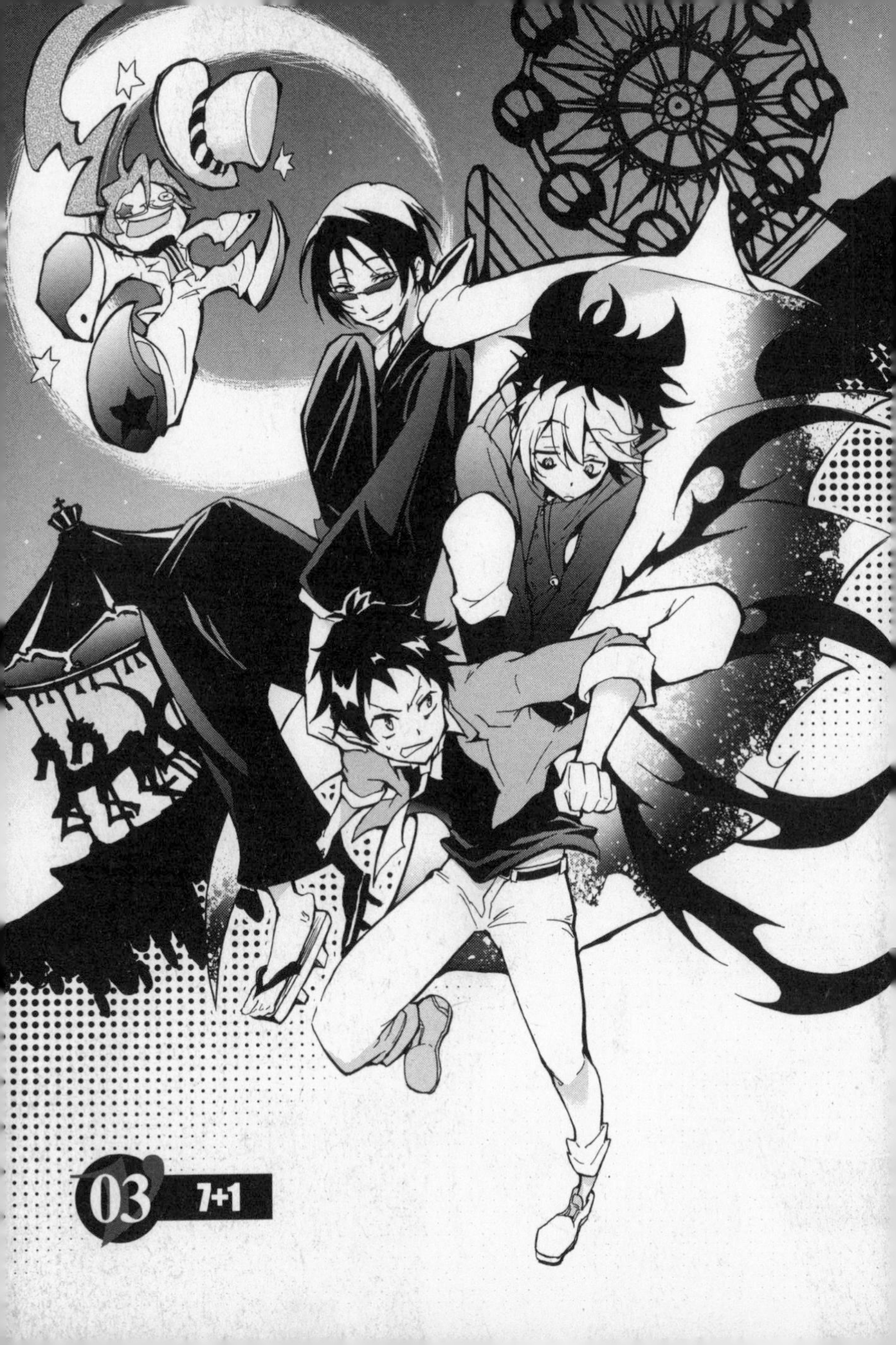

03 7+1

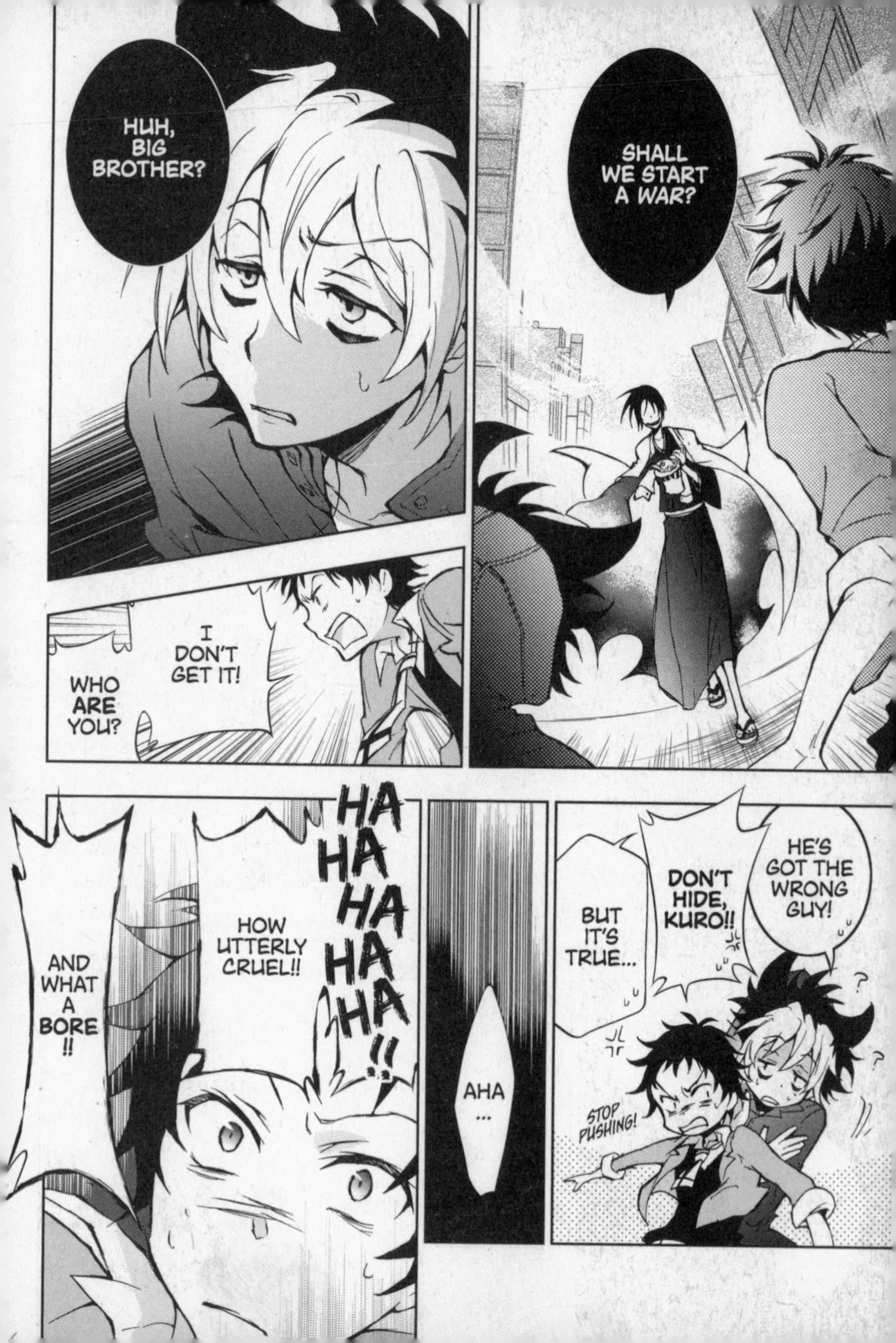
SHALL WE START A WAR?
HUH, BIG BROTHER?
I DON'T GET IT!
WHO ARE YOU?
HE'S GOT THE WRONG GUY!
DON'T HIDE, KURO!!
BUT IT'S TRUE...
STOP PUSHING!
AHA ...
HA HA HA HA HA HA!!
HOW UTTERLY CRUEL!!
AND WHAT A BORE!!

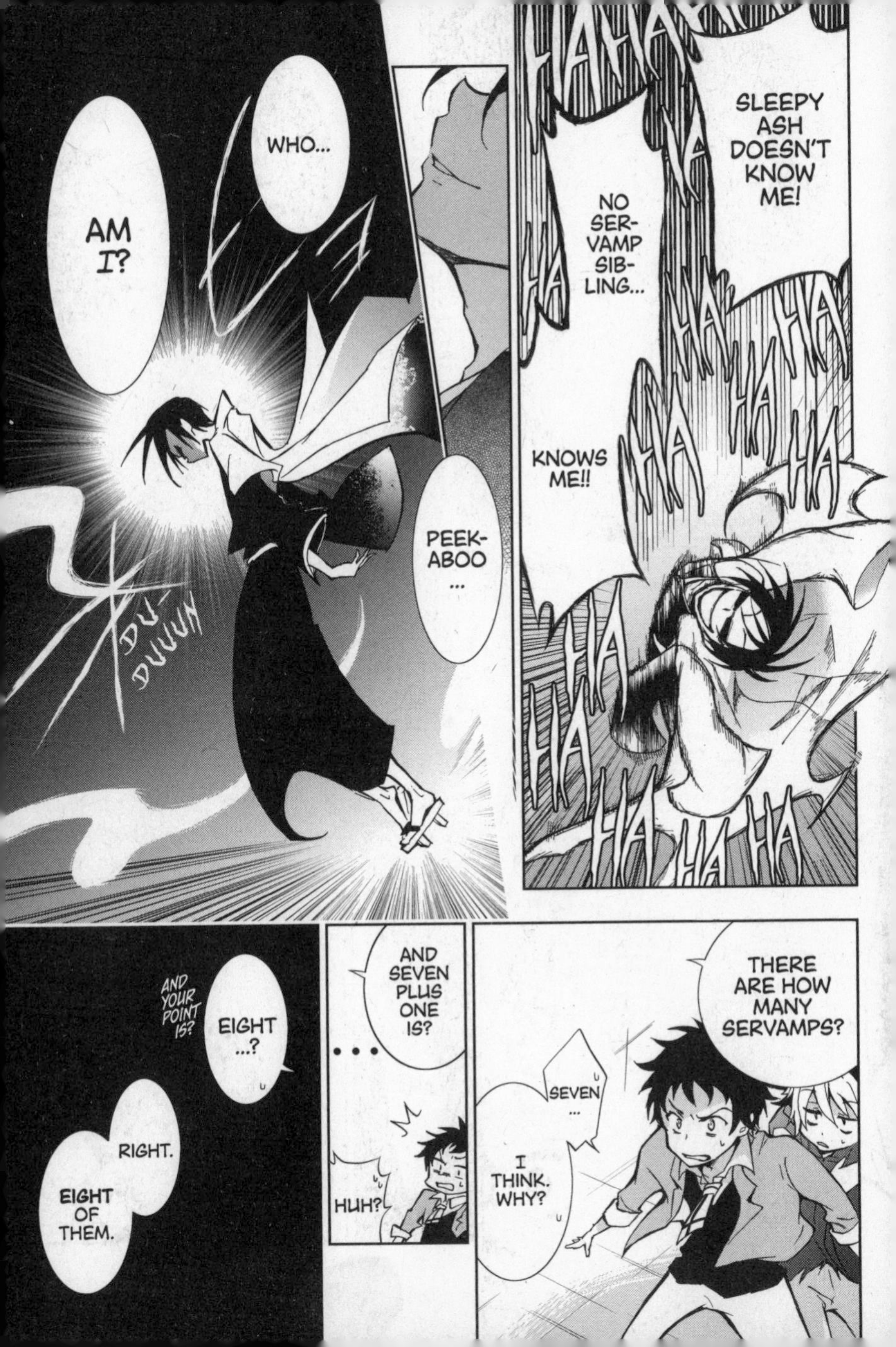
HA HA HA HA HA
SLEEPY ASH DOESN'T KNOW ME!
NO SER-VAMP SIB-LING...
HA HA HA HA HA HA
KNOWS ME!!
HA HA HA HA HA HA HA
PEEK-ABOO ...
WHO...
AM I?
DU-DUUUN
THERE ARE HOW MANY SERVAMPS?
SEVEN ...
I THINK. WHY?
AND SEVEN PLUS ONE IS?
• • •
HUH?
EIGHT ...?
AND YOUR POINT IS?
RIGHT.
EIGHT OF THEM.

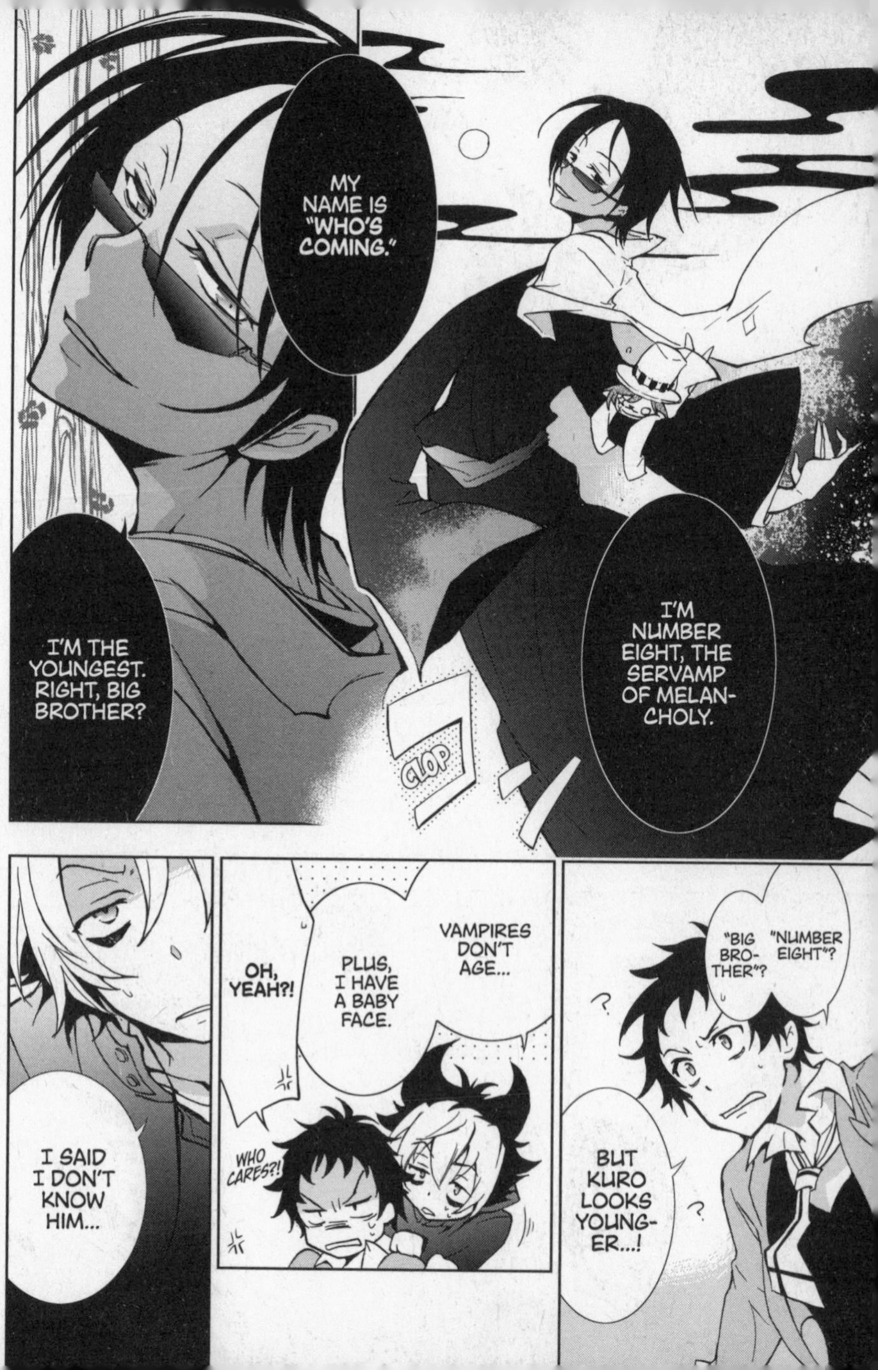
MY NAME IS "WHO'S COMING."
I'M NUMBER EIGHT, THE SERVAMP OF MELAN-CHOLY.
I'M THE YOUNGEST. RIGHT, BIG BROTHER?
CLOP
"NUMBER EIGHT"?
"BIG BRO-THER"?
BUT KURO LOOKS YOUNG-ER...!
VAMPIRES DON'T AGE...
PLUS, I HAVE A BABY FACE.
OH, YEAH?!
WHO CARES?!
I SAID I DON'T KNOW HIM...

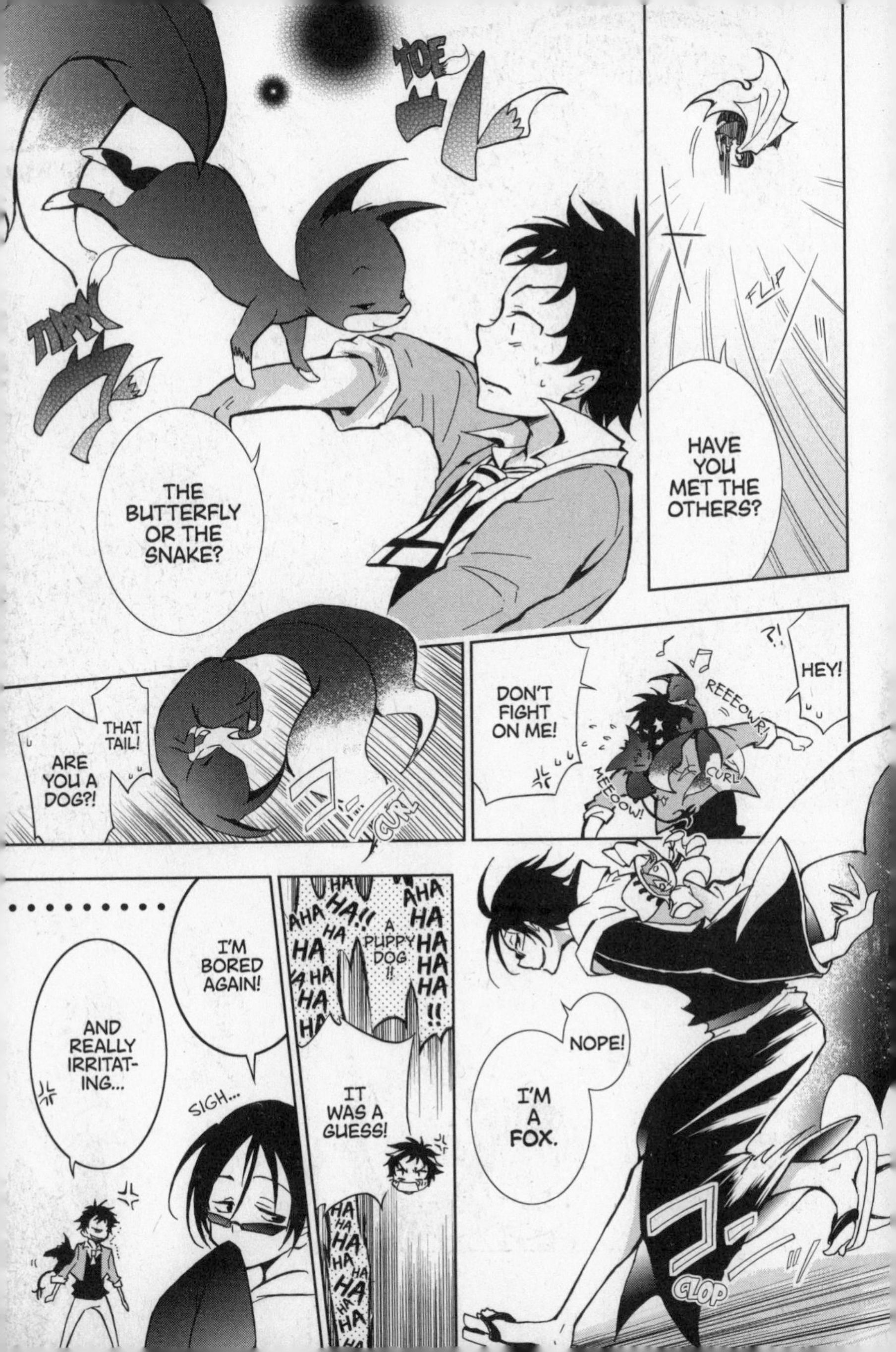
FLIP
HAVE YOU MET THE OTHERS?
TOE
TIPPY
THE BUTTERFLY OR THE SNAKE?
?!
HEY!
REEEOWR!
CURL
MEEOOW!
DON'T FIGHT ON ME!
THAT TAIL!
ARE YOU A DOG?!
CURL
NOPE!
I'M A FOX.
CLOP
HA HA!! AHA HA HA HA HA HA!! AHA HA HA HA HA HA
A PUPPY DOG!!
IT WAS A GUESS!
HA HA HA HA HA HA HA HA HA HA
I'M BORED AGAIN!
AND REALLY IRRITATING...
SIGH...

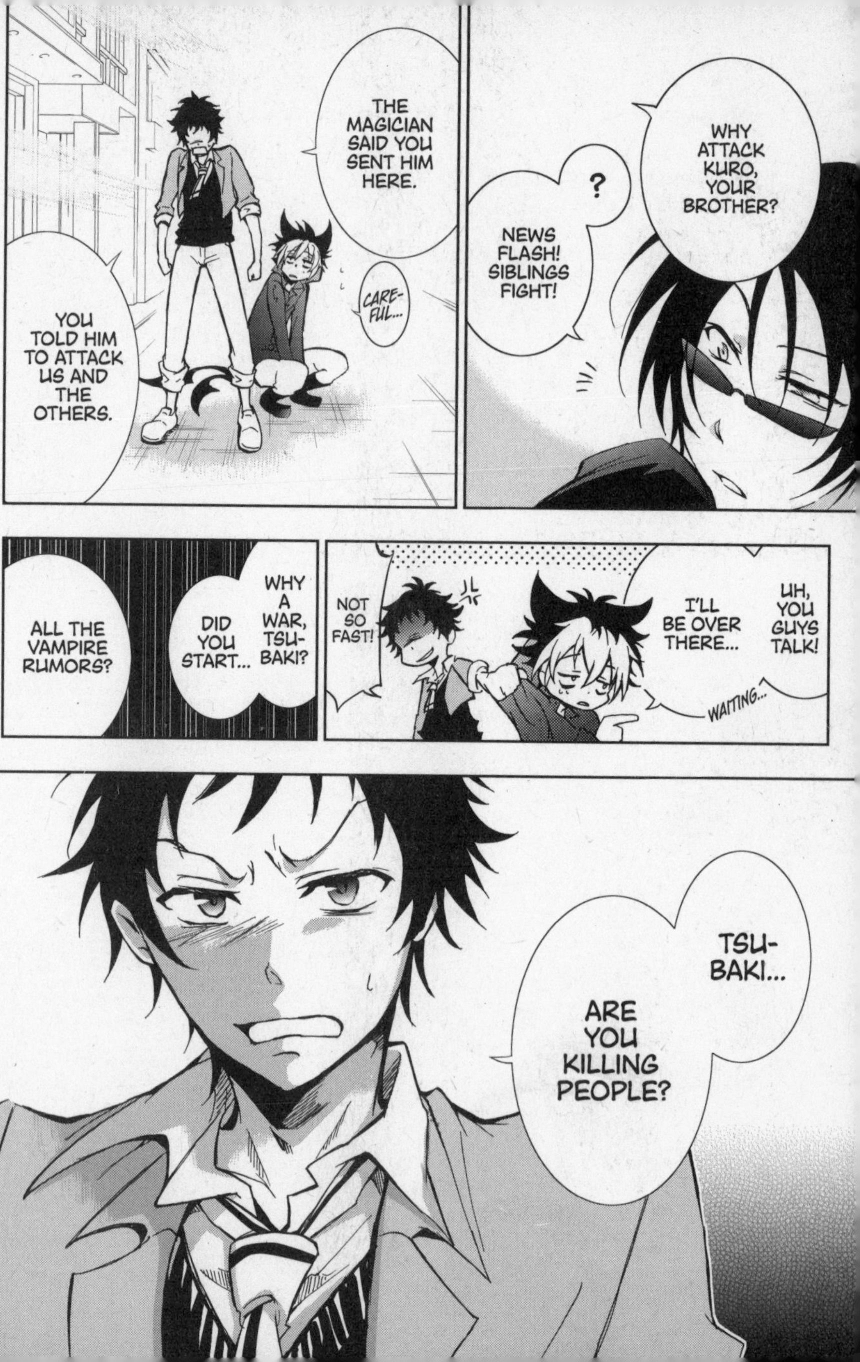
WHY ATTACK KURO, YOUR BROTHER?
?
NEWS FLASH! SIBLINGS FIGHT!
THE MAGICIAN SAID YOU SENT HIM HERE.
CARE-FUL...
YOU TOLD HIM TO ATTACK US AND THE OTHERS.
UH, YOU GUYS TALK!
I'LL BE OVER THERE...
WAITING...
NOT SO FAST!
WHY A WAR, TSU-BAKI?
DID YOU START...
ALL THE VAMPIRE RUMORS?
TSU-BAKI...
ARE YOU KILLING PEOPLE?

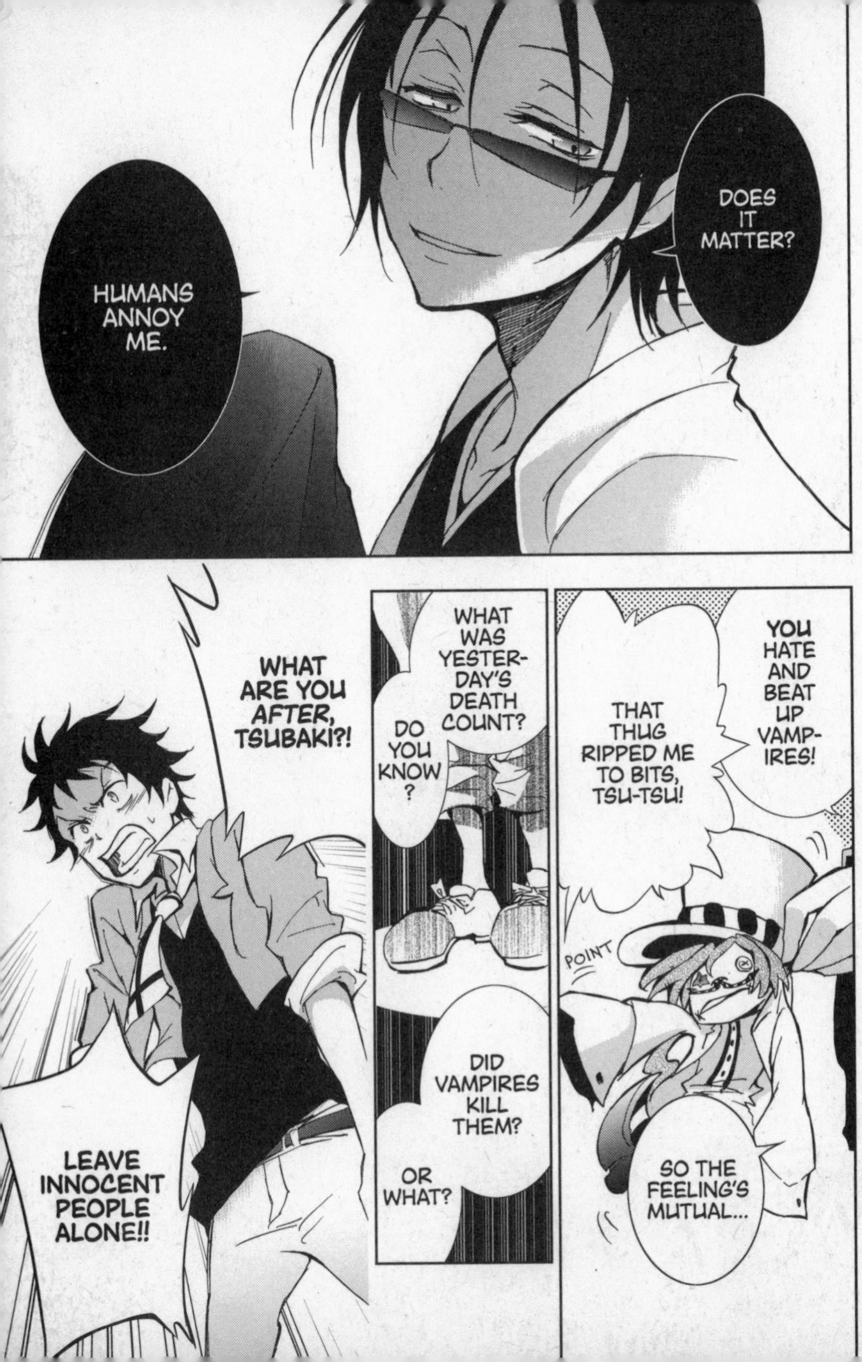
DOES IT MATTER?
HUMANS ANNOY ME.
YOU HATE AND BEAT UP VAMPIRES!
THAT THUG RIPPED ME TO BITS, TSU-TSU!
POINT
SO THE FEELING'S MUTUAL...
WHAT WAS YESTER-DAY'S DEATH COUNT?
DO YOU KNOW?
DID VAMPIRES KILL THEM?
OR WHAT?
WHAT ARE YOU AFTER, TSUBAKI?!
LEAVE INNOCENT PEOPLE ALONE!!

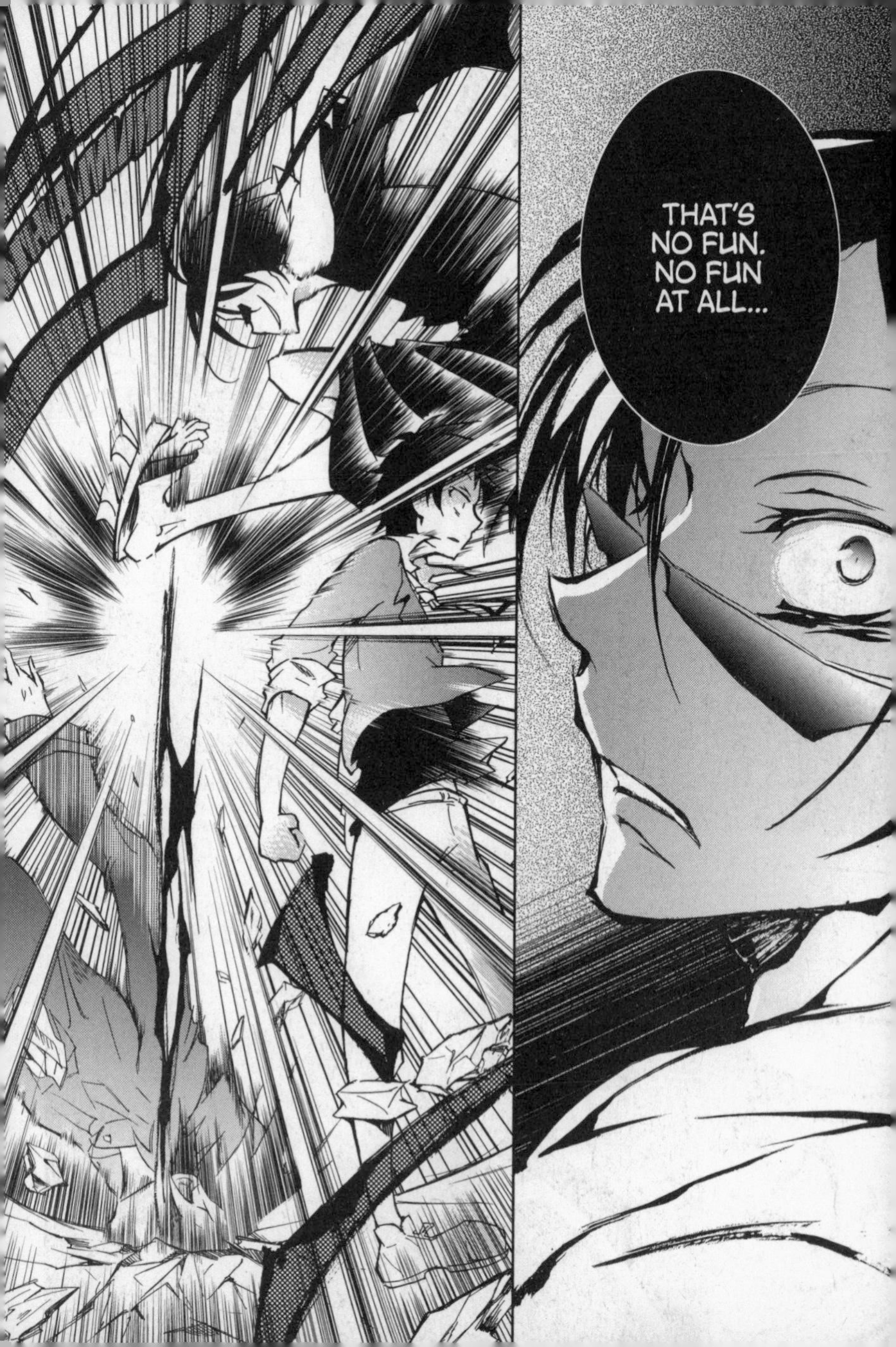
THAT'S NO FUN. NO FUN AT ALL...

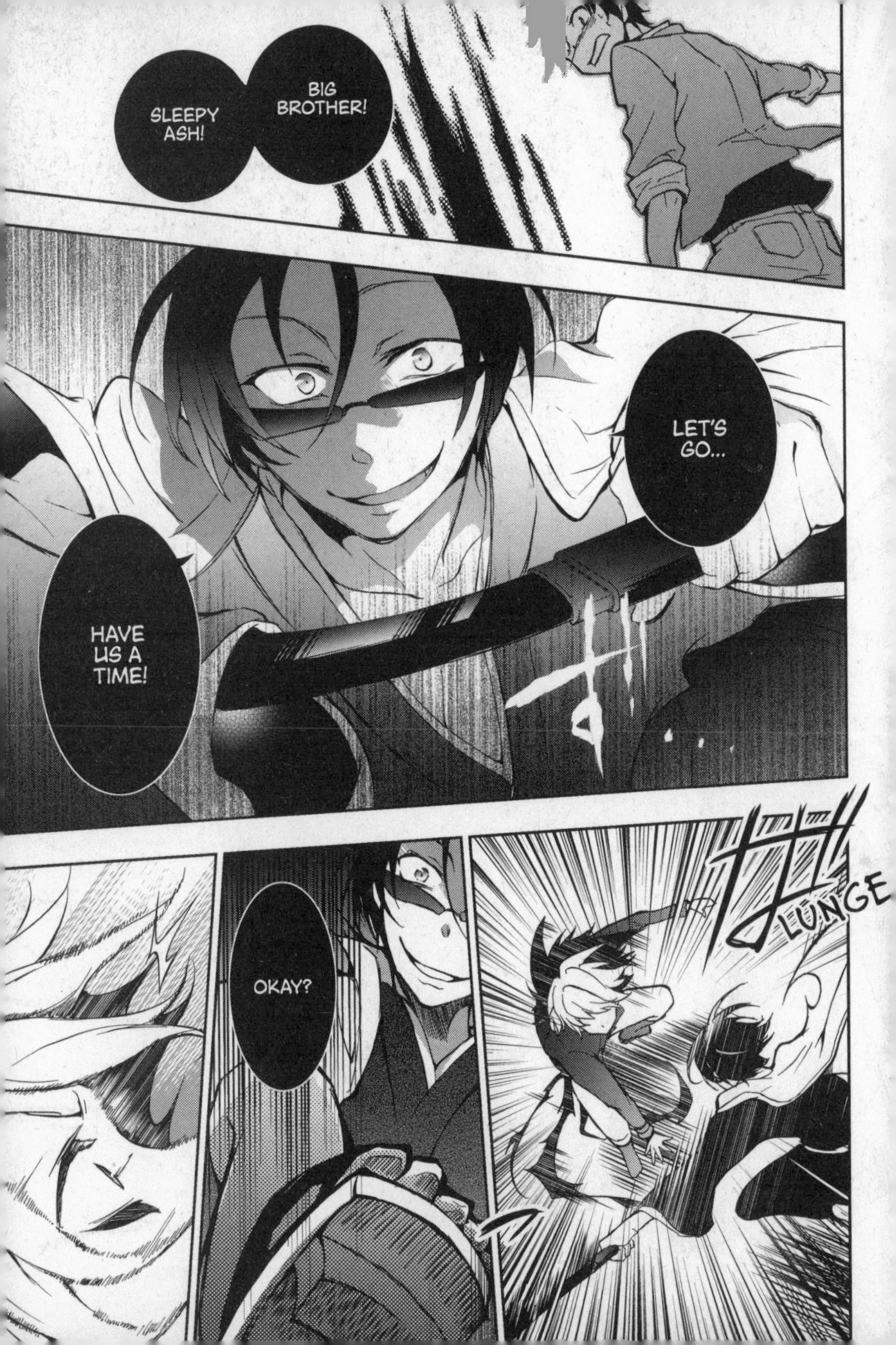
BIG BROTHER!
SLEEPY ASH!
LET'S GO...
HAVE US A TIME!
LUNGE
OKAY?

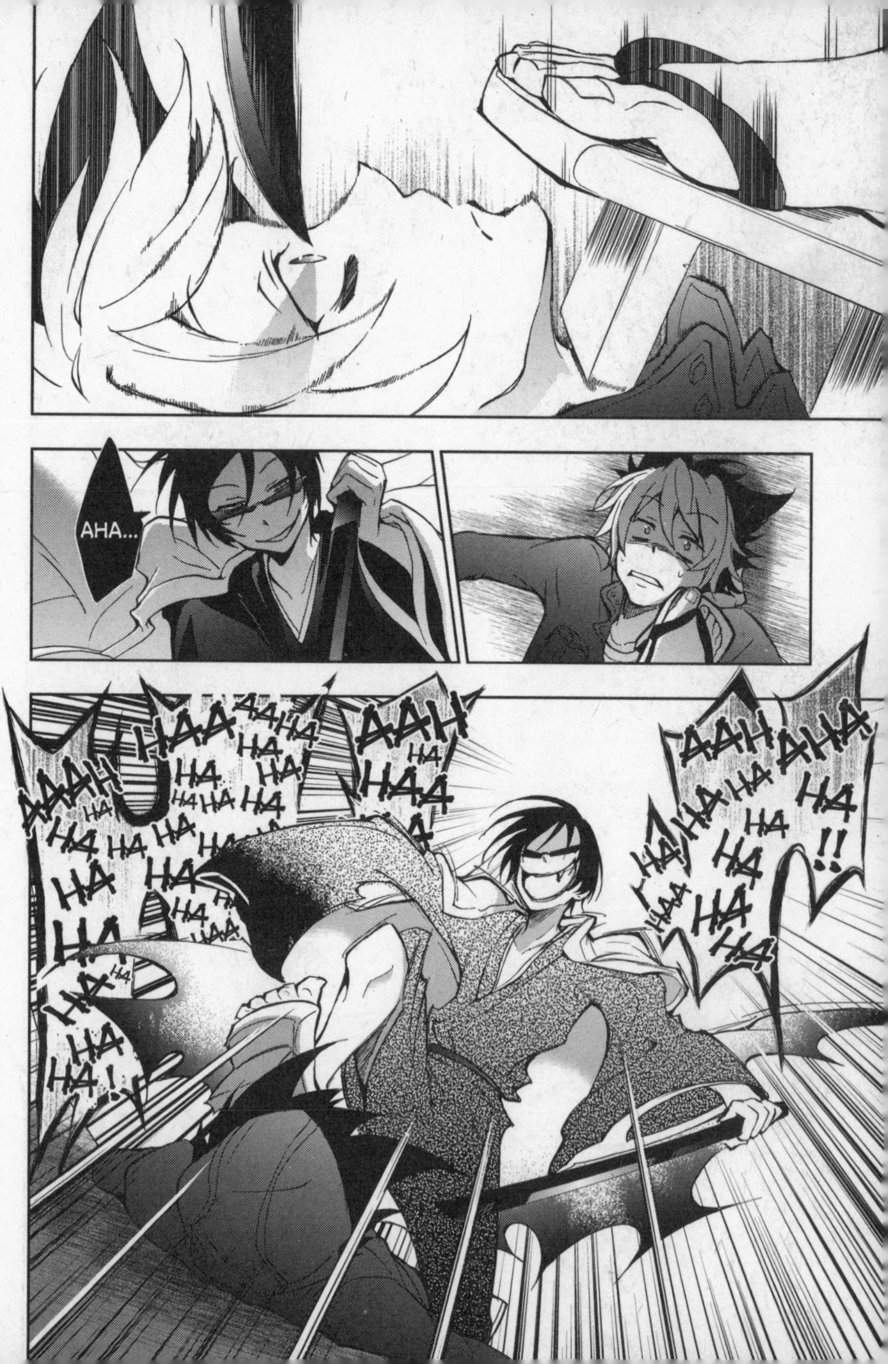
AHA...
AAH AHA HA HA HA HA HA HA HA HA HA!!
AAH HA HAA
HAA HA HA HA HA HA HA
AAAH HA HA HA HA HA HA HA HA HA HA HA!

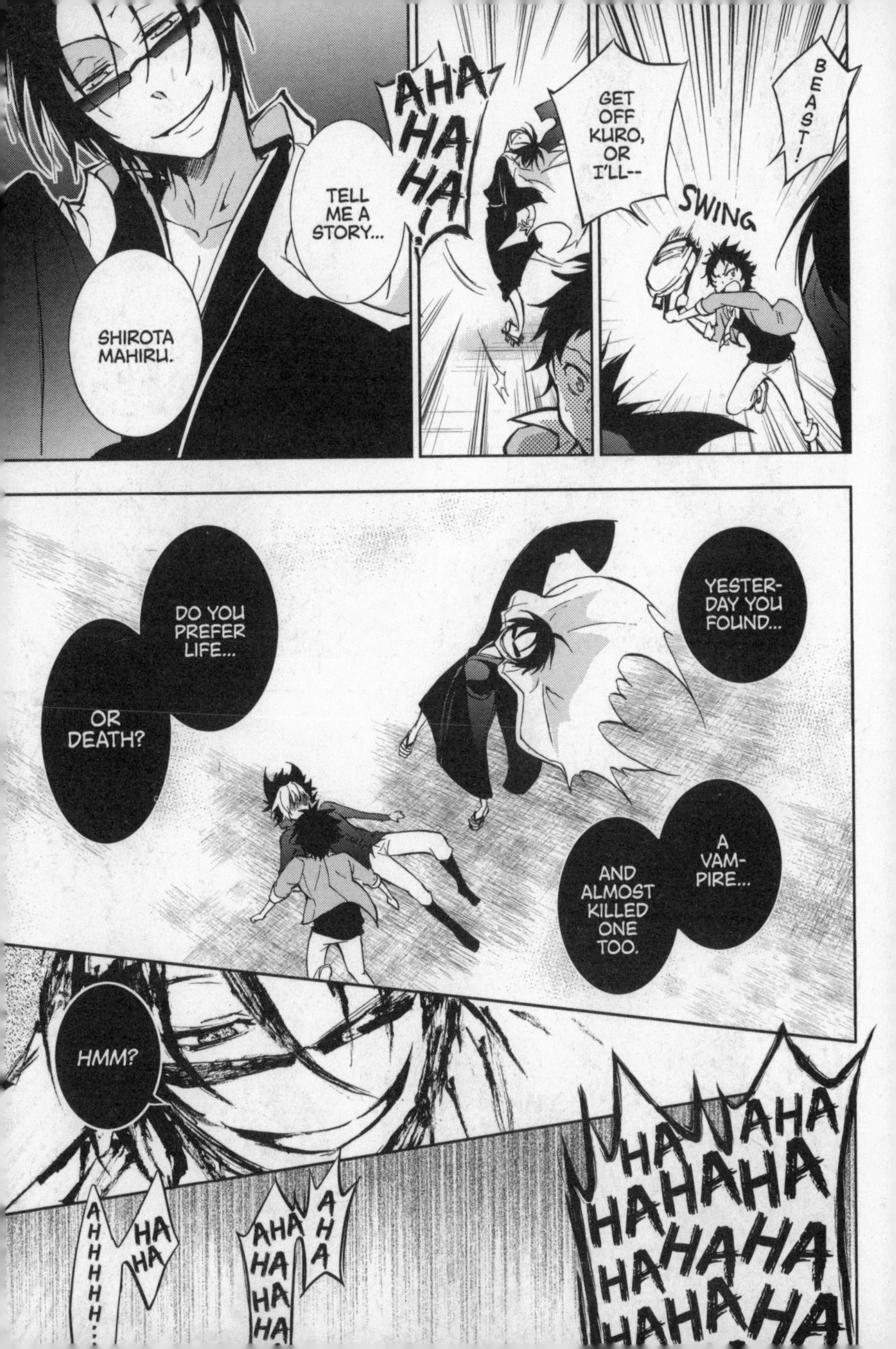
BEAST!
SWING
GET OFF KURO, OR I'LL--
AHAHAHA!
TELL ME A STORY...
SHIROTA MAHIRU.
YESTERDAY YOU FOUND...
A VAMPIRE...
AND ALMOST KILLED ONE TOO.
DO YOU PREFER LIFE...
OR DEATH?
HMM?
HAHAHAHAHAHAHAHAHAHAHAHAHAHAHAHA
AHA
AHAHAHAHAHA
HAHA
AHHHHHH...

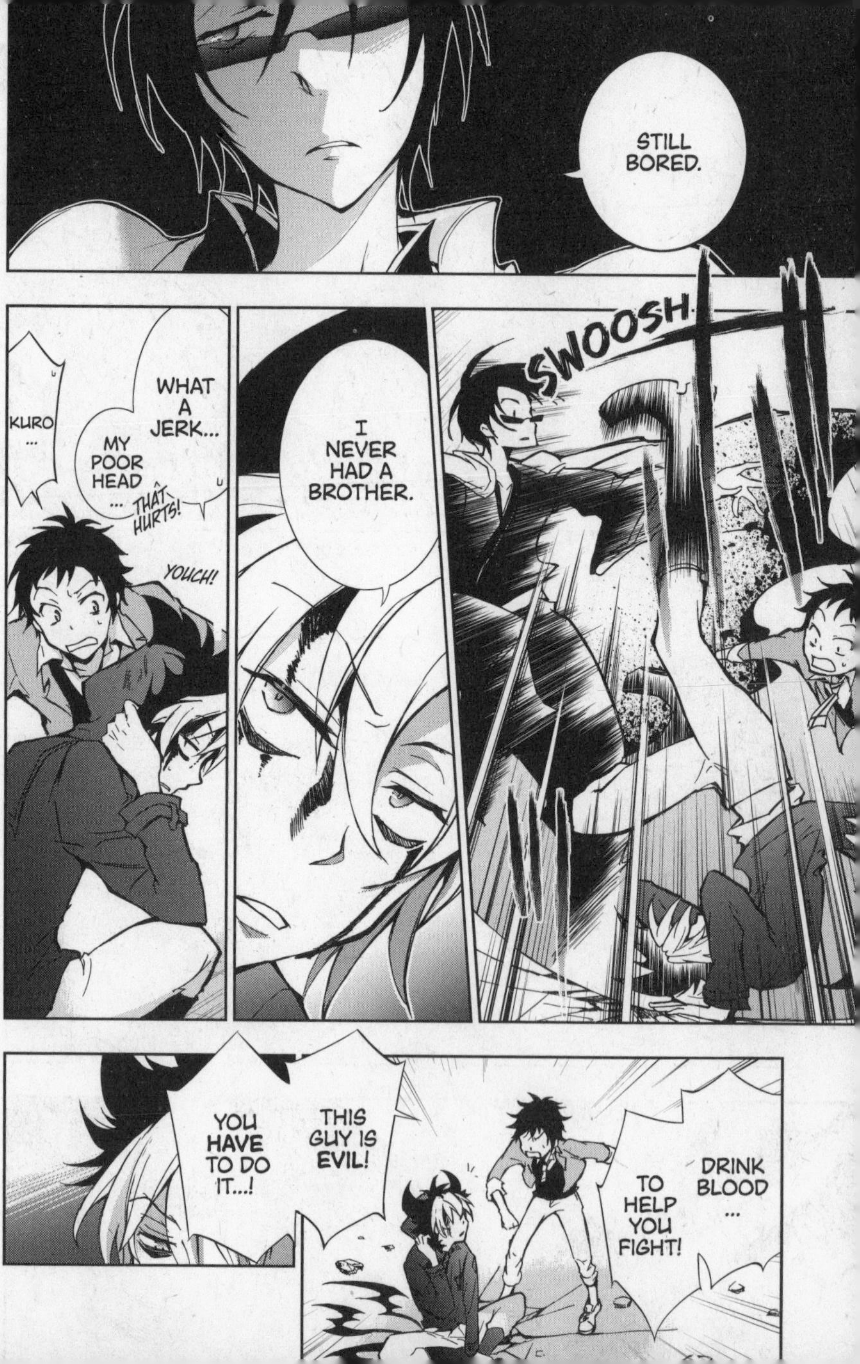

STILL BORED.
SWOOSH
I NEVER HAD A BROTHER.
WHAT A JERK...
MY POOR HEAD ...
THAT HURTS!
YOUCH!
KURO ...
DRINK BLOOD ...
TO HELP YOU FIGHT!
THIS GUY IS EVIL!
YOU HAVE TO DO IT...!

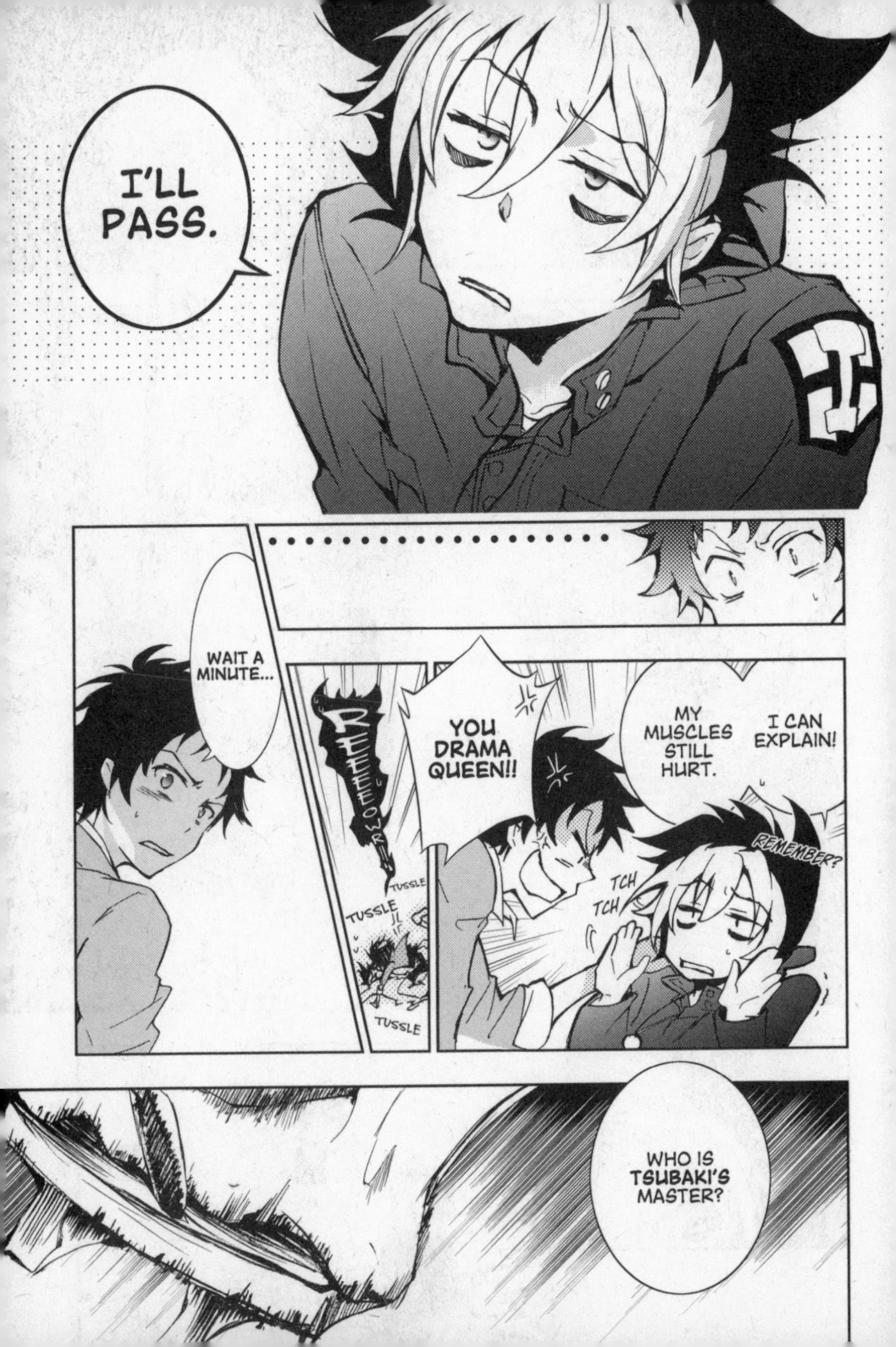

I'LL PASS.
....
I CAN EXPLAIN!
MY MUSCLES STILL HURT.
YOU DRAMA QUEEN!!
REMEMBER?
TCH TCH
REEEOWR
TUSSLE
TUSSLE
TUSSLE
WAIT A MINUTE...
WHO IS TSUBAKI'S MASTER?

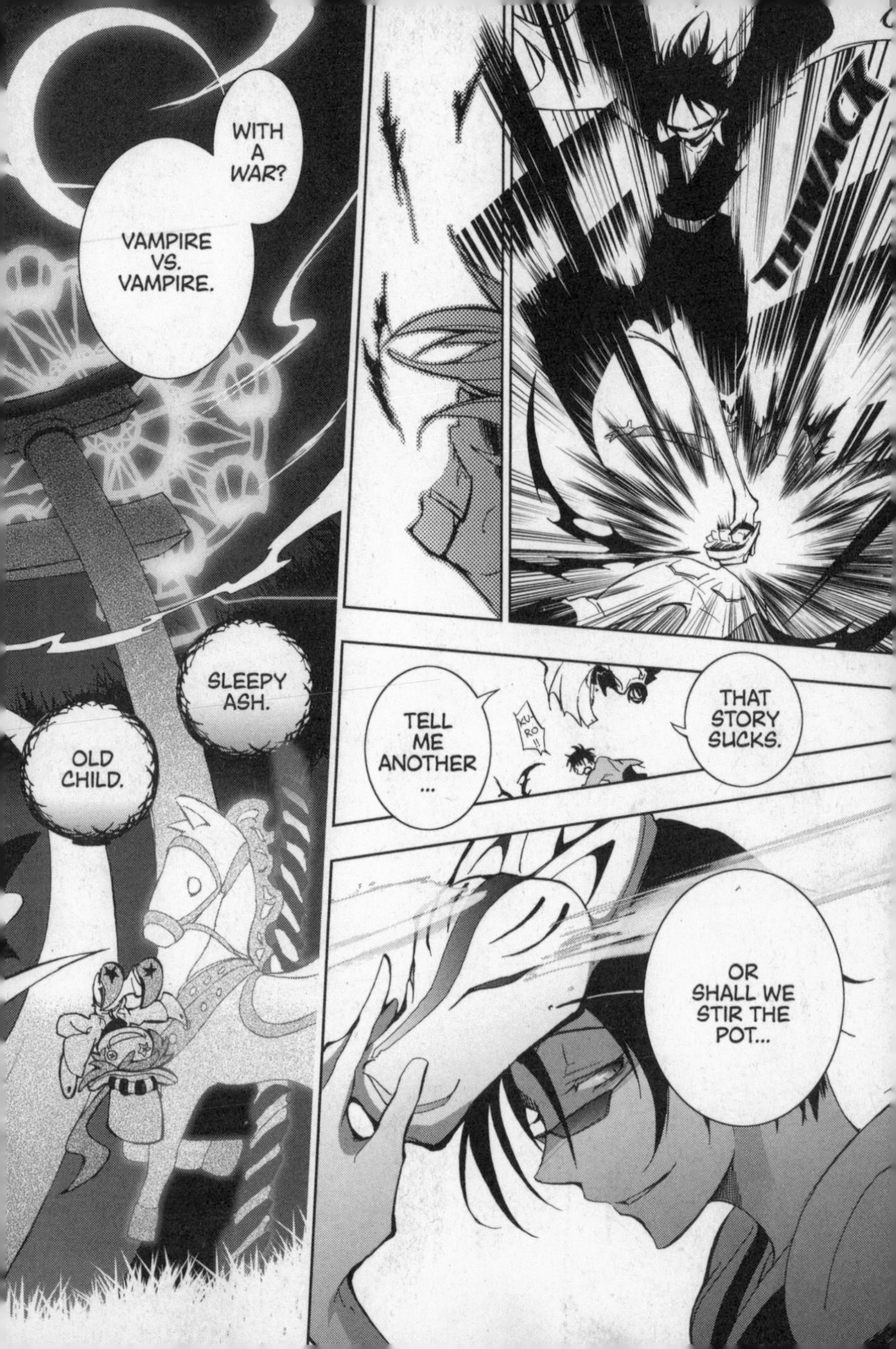
THWACK
THAT STORY SUCKS.
KU-RO!!
TELL ME ANOTHER ...
OR SHALL WE STIR THE POT...
WITH A WAR?
VAMPIRE VS. VAMPIRE.
SLEEPY ASH.
OLD CHILD.

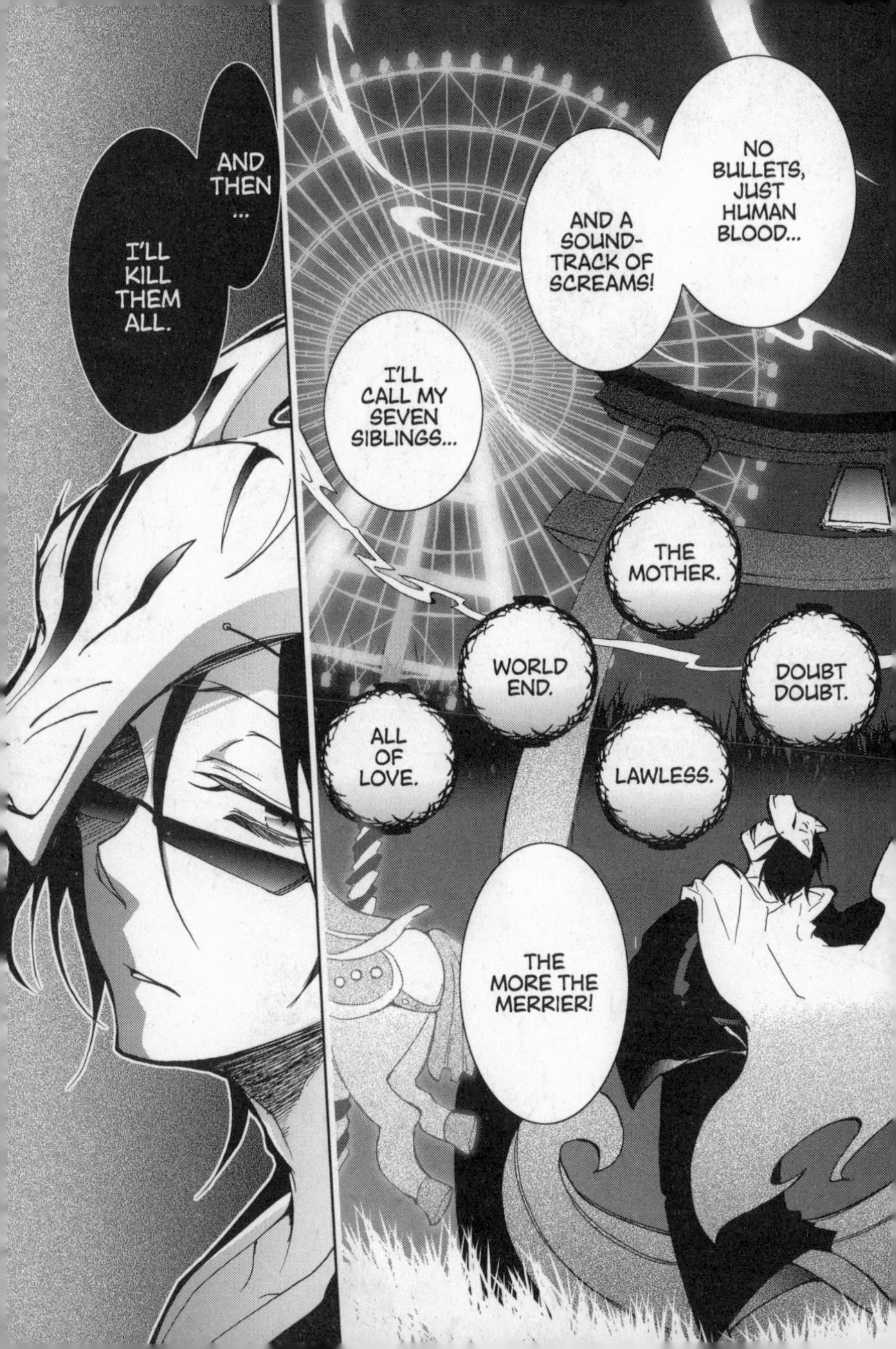
NO BULLETS, JUST HUMAN BLOOD...
AND A SOUND-TRACK OF SCREAMS!
I'LL CALL MY SEVEN SIBLINGS...
THE MOTHER.
DOUBT DOUBT.
WORLD END.
LAWLESS.
ALL OF LOVE.
THE MORE THE MERRIER!
AND THEN ...
I'LL KILL THEM ALL.

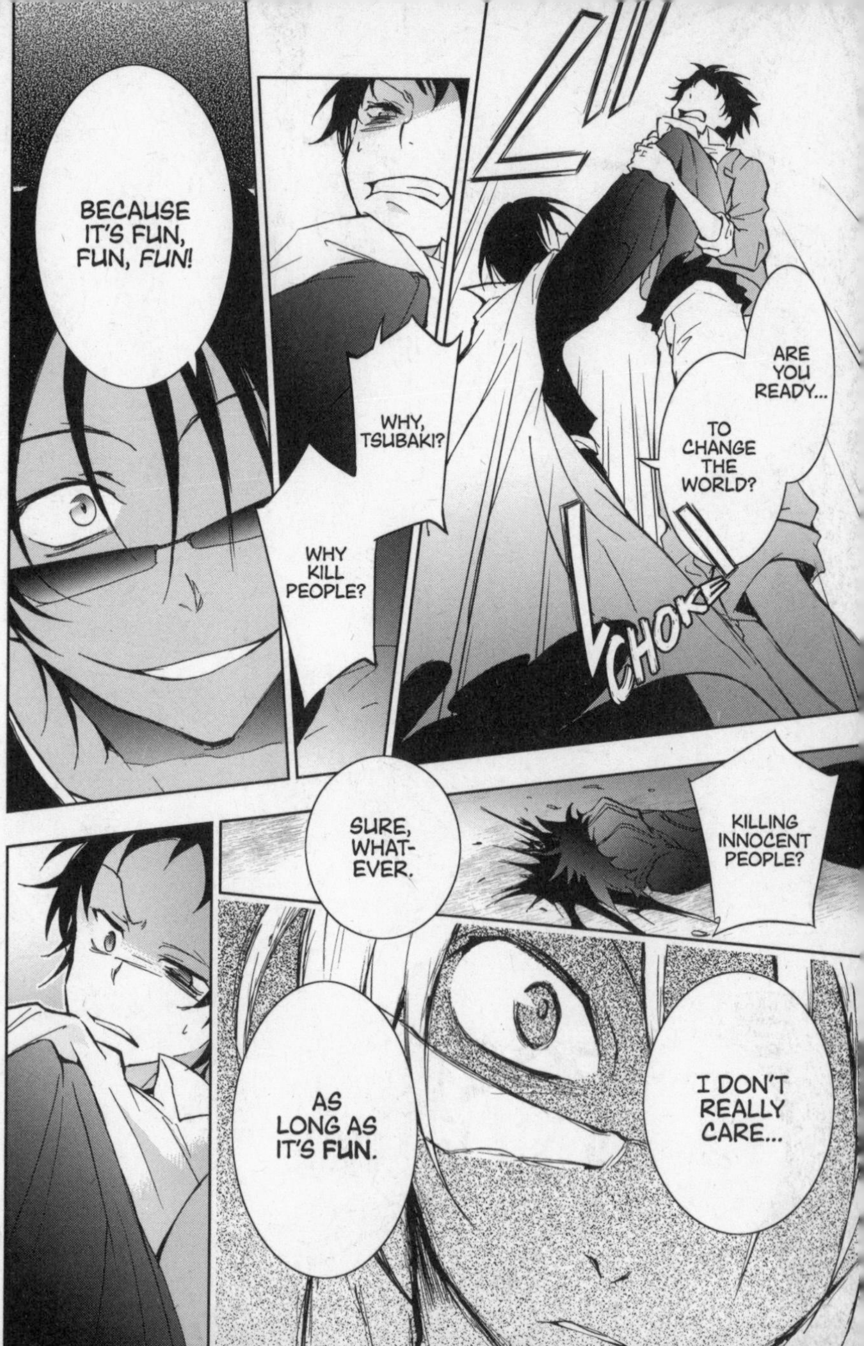
ARE YOU READY...
TO CHANGE THE WORLD?
CHOKE
WHY, TSUBAKI?
WHY KILL PEOPLE?
BECAUSE IT'S FUN, FUN, FUN!
KILLING INNOCENT PEOPLE?
SURE, WHAT-EVER.
I DON'T REALLY CARE...
AS LONG AS IT'S FUN.

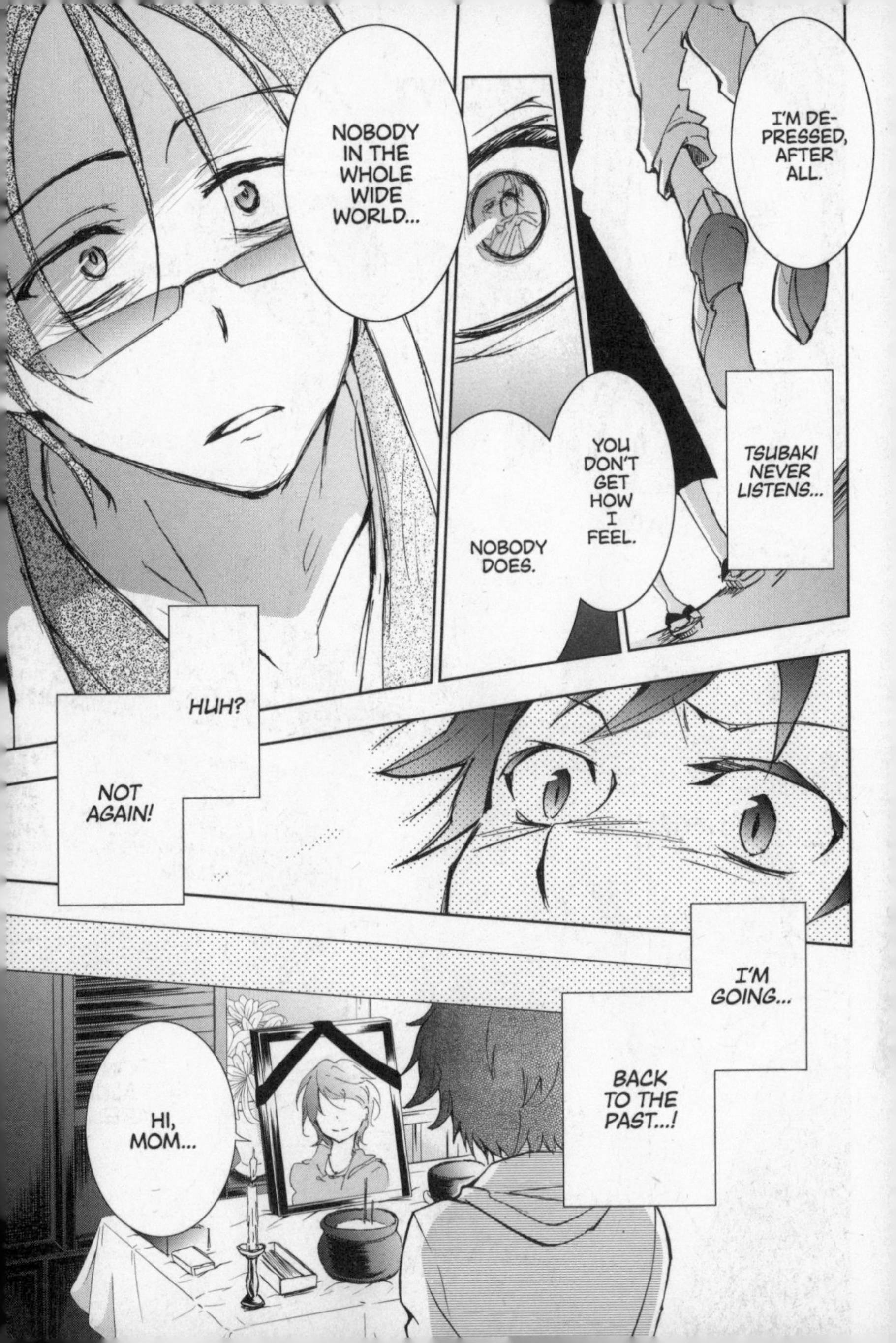
I'M DE-PRESSED, AFTER ALL.
TSUBAKI NEVER LISTENS...
YOU DON'T GET HOW I FEEL.
NOBODY DOES.
NOBODY IN THE WHOLE WIDE WORLD...
HUH?
NOT AGAIN!
I'M GOING...
BACK TO THE PAST...!
HI, MOM...

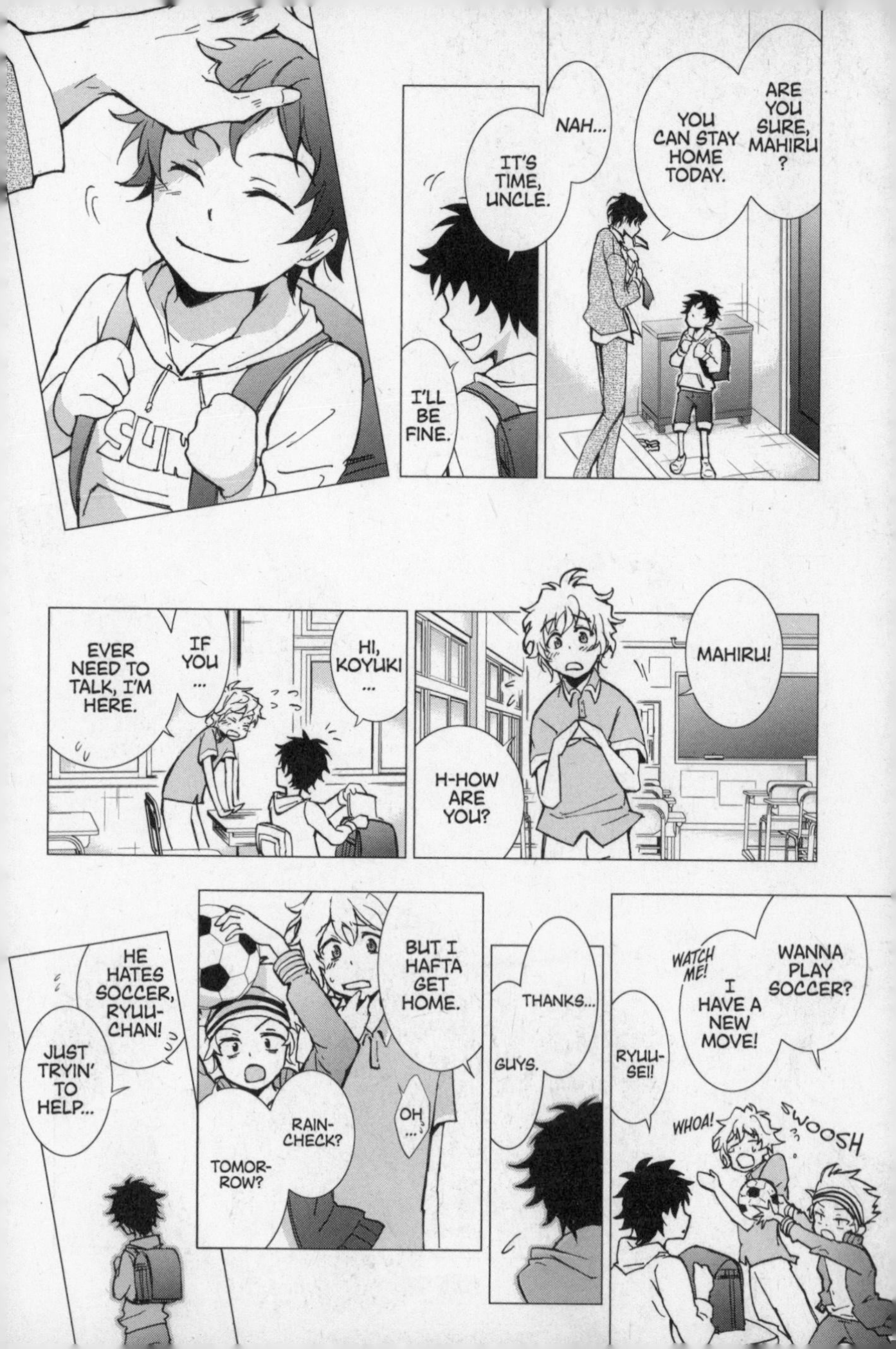
ARE YOU SURE, MAHIRU?
YOU CAN STAY HOME TODAY.
NAH...
IT'S TIME, UNCLE.
I'LL BE FINE.
MAHIRU!
H-HOW ARE YOU?
HI, KOYUKI...
IF YOU...
EVER NEED TO TALK, I'M HERE.
WANNA PLAY SOCCER?
I HAVE A NEW MOVE!
WATCH ME!
RYUU-SEI!
WHOA!
SWOOSH
THANKS...
GUYS.
BUT I HAFTA GET HOME.
OH...
RAIN-CHECK?
TOMOR-ROW?
HE HATES SOCCER, RYUU-CHAN!
JUST TRYIN' TO HELP...

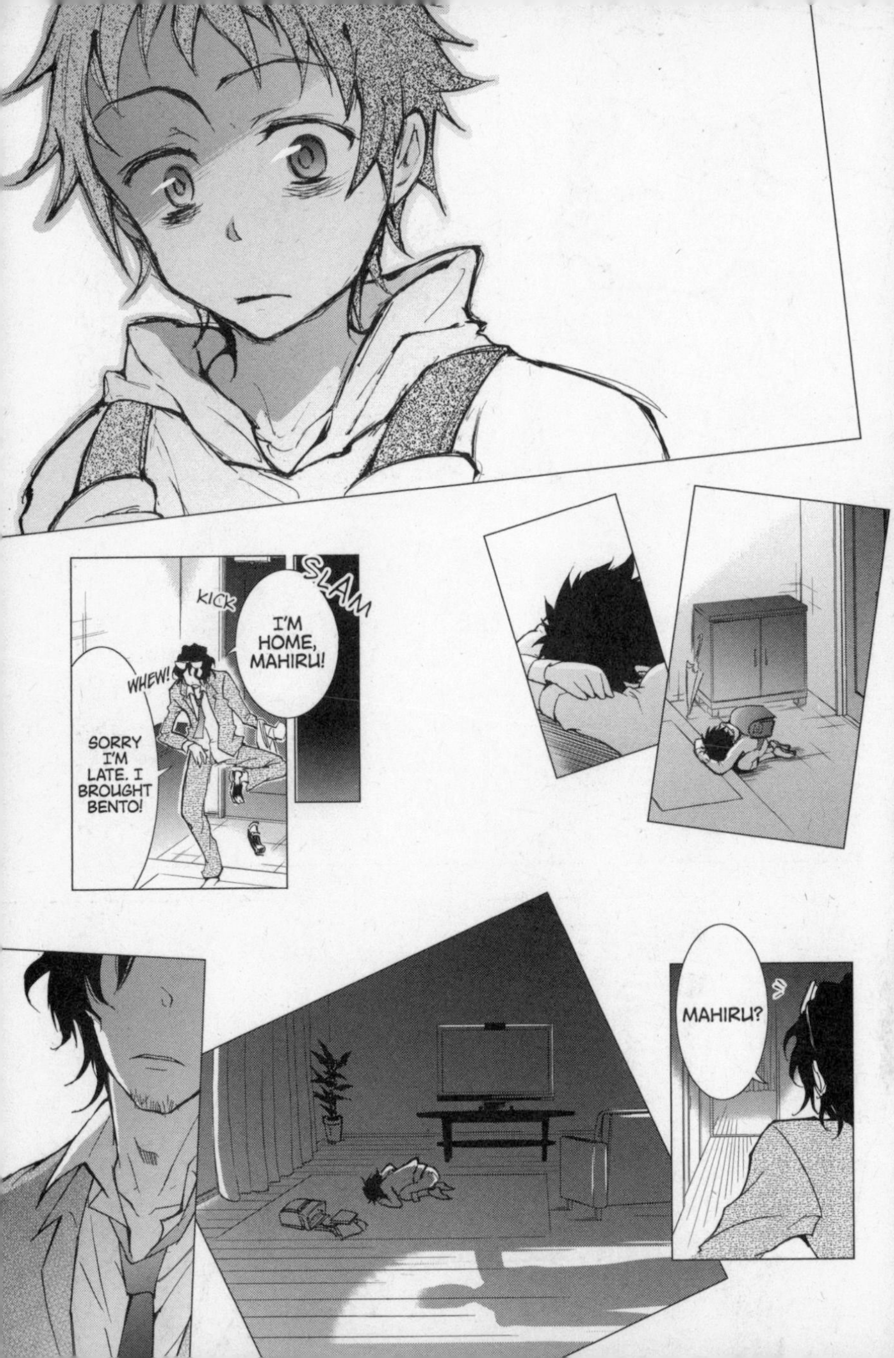
SLAM
KICK
I'M HOME, MAHIRU!
WHEW!
SORRY I'M LATE. I BROUGHT BENTO!
MAHIRU?

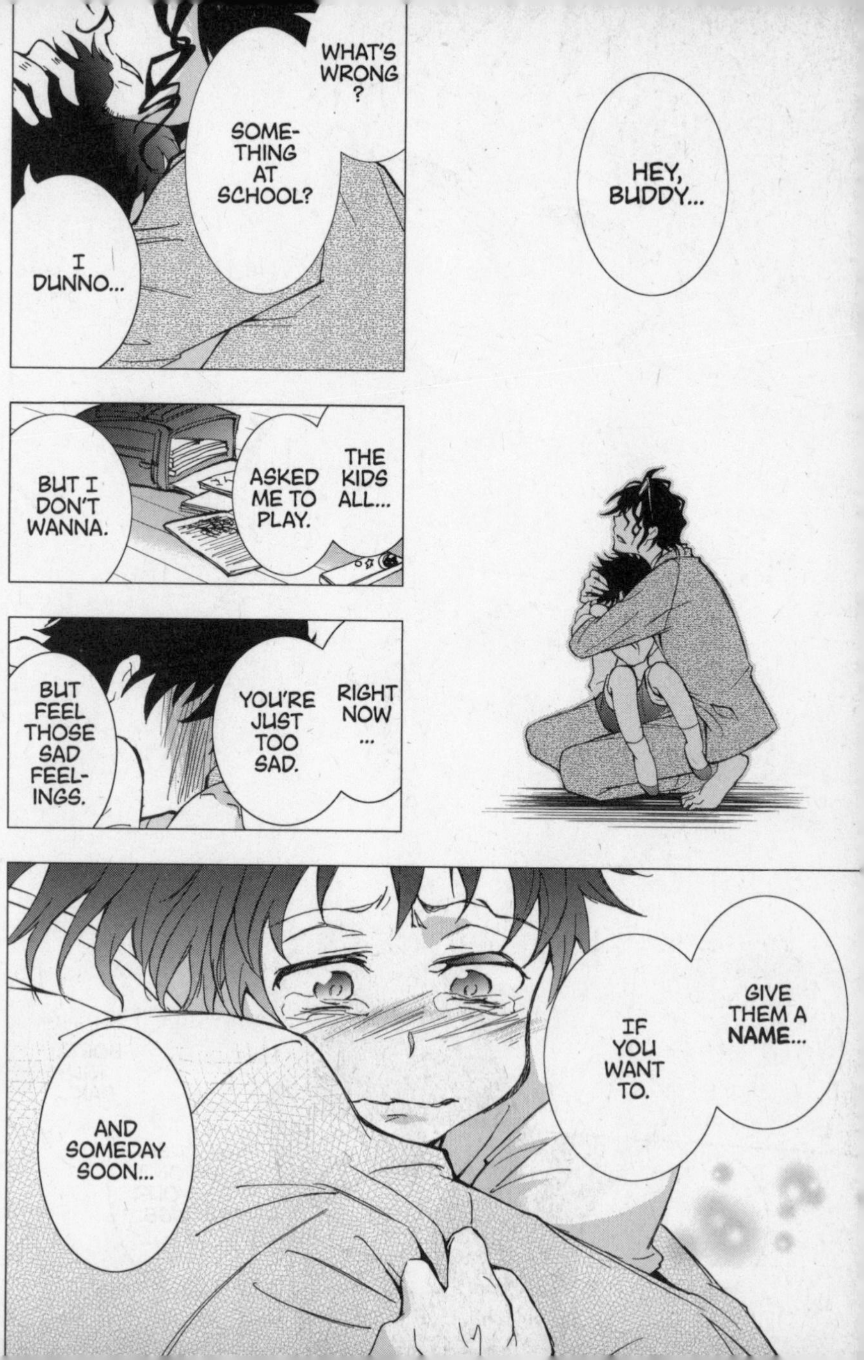
HEY, BUDDY...
WHAT'S WRONG?
SOMETHING AT SCHOOL?
I DUNNO...
THE KIDS ALL...
ASKED ME TO PLAY.
BUT I DON'T WANNA.
RIGHT NOW...
YOU'RE JUST TOO SAD.
BUT FEEL THOSE SAD FEELINGS.
GIVE THEM A NAME...
IF YOU WANT TO.
AND SOMEDAY SOON...

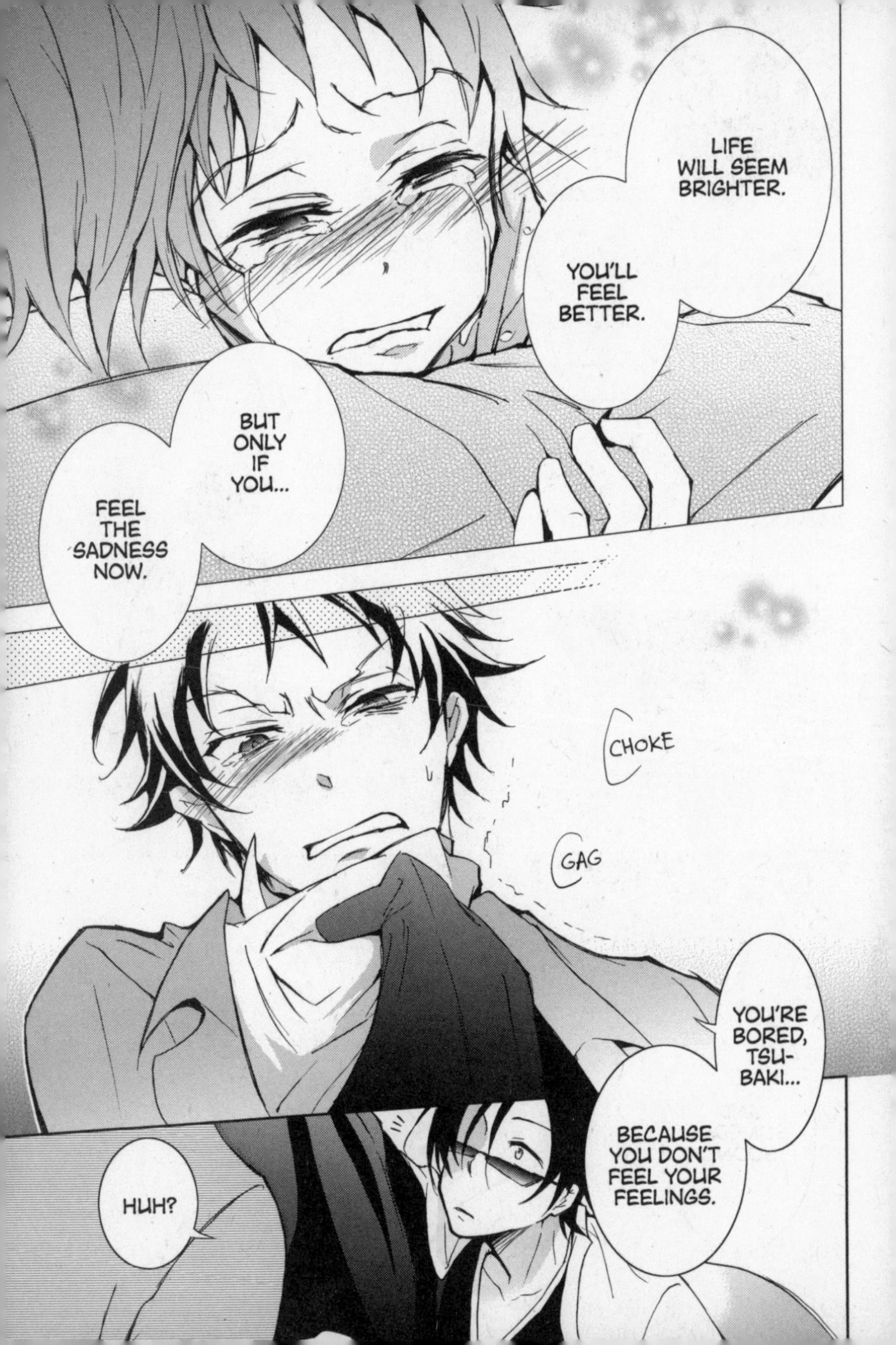
LIFE WILL SEEM BRIGHTER.
YOU'LL FEEL BETTER.
BUT ONLY IF YOU...
FEEL THE SADNESS NOW.
CHOKE
GAG
YOU'RE BORED, TSU-BAKI...
BECAUSE YOU DON'T FEEL YOUR FEELINGS.
HUH?

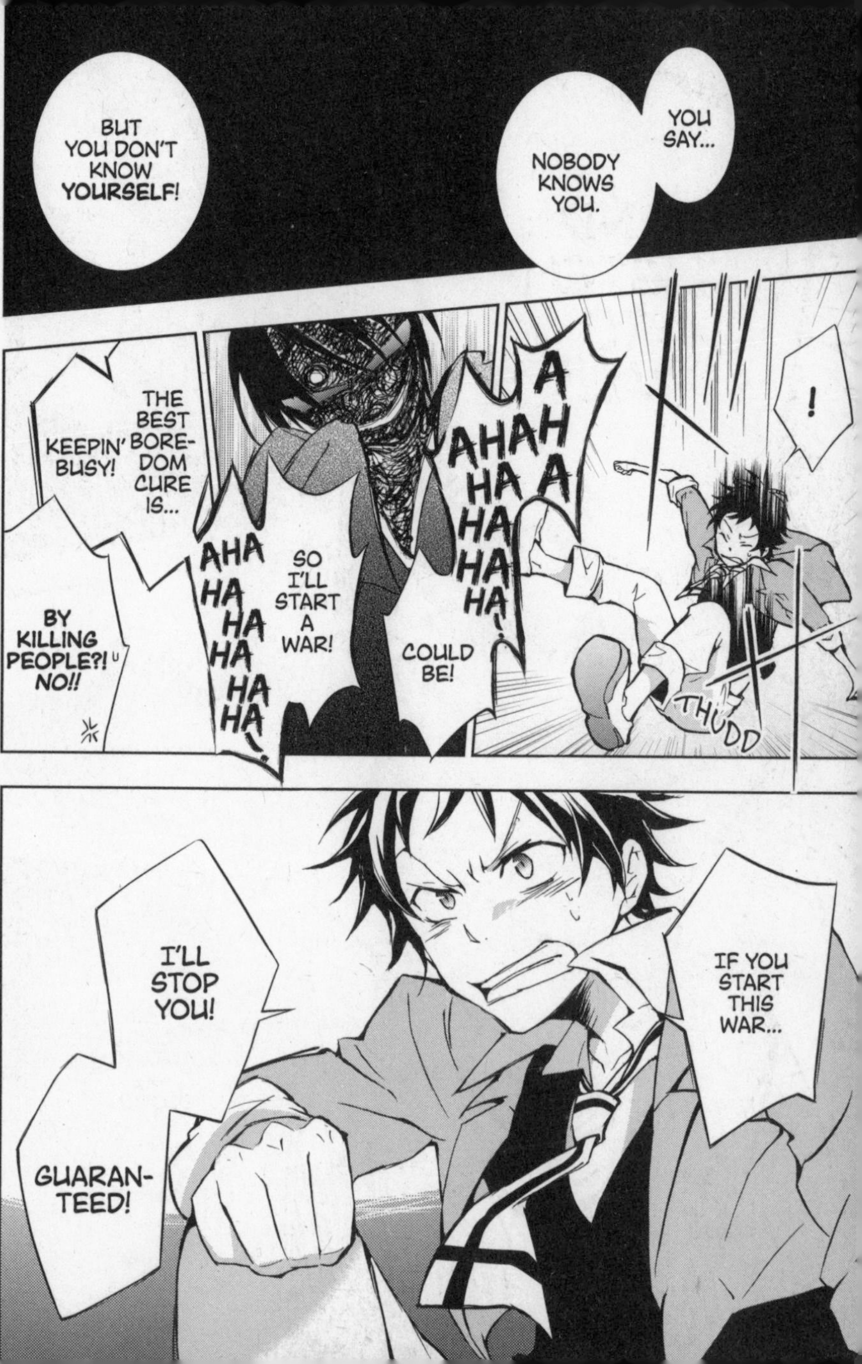
YOU SAY...
NOBODY KNOWS YOU.
BUT YOU DON'T KNOW YOURSELF!
!
THUDD
AHAHAHA HA HA HA HA
COULD BE!
SO I'LL START A WAR!
AHA HA HA HA HA HA
THE BEST BORE-DOM CURE IS...
KEEPIN' BUSY!
BY KILLING PEOPLE?! NO!!
IF YOU START THIS WAR...
I'LL STOP YOU!
GUARAN-TEED!

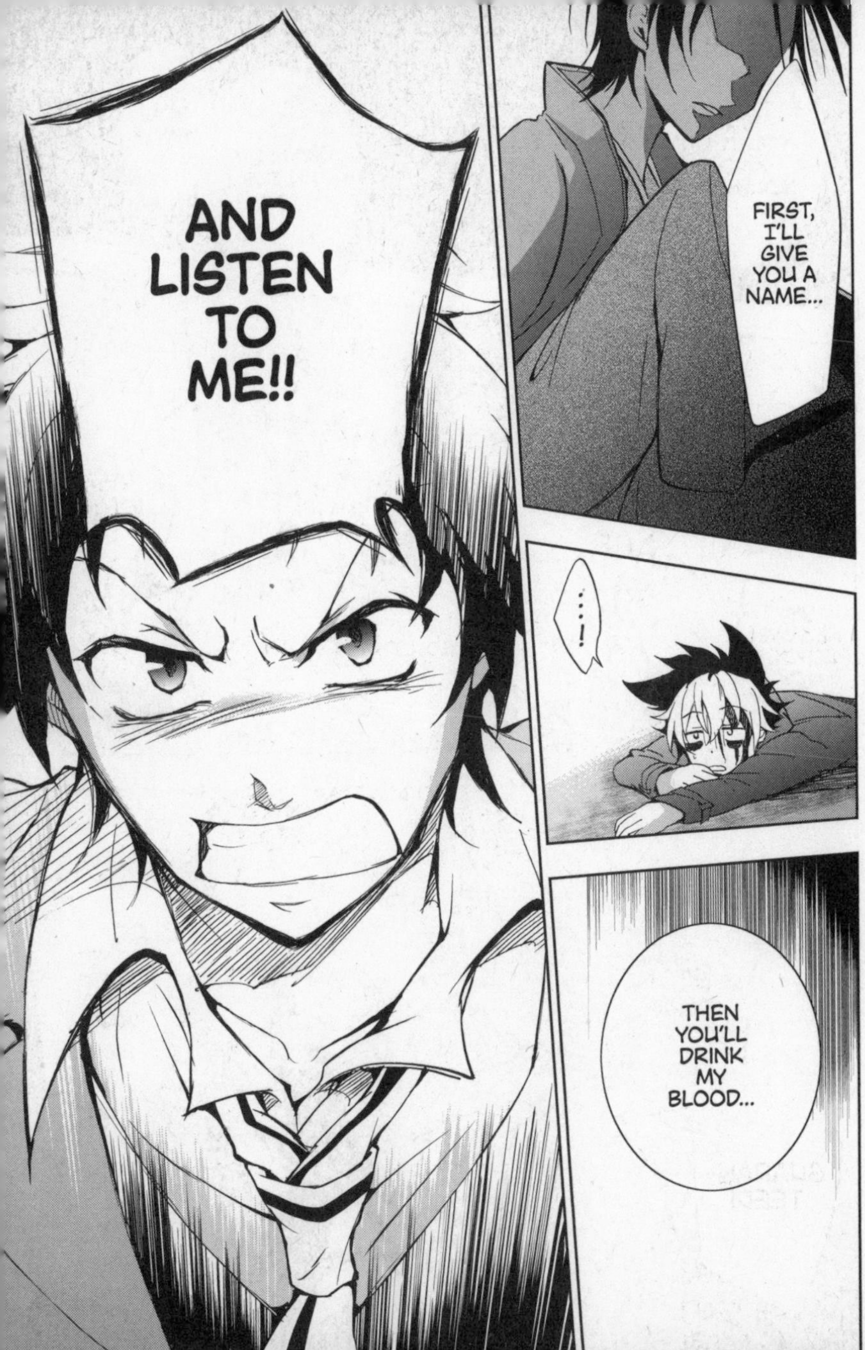
FIRST, I'LL GIVE YOU A NAME...
...!
THEN YOU'LL DRINK MY BLOOD...
AND LISTEN TO ME!!

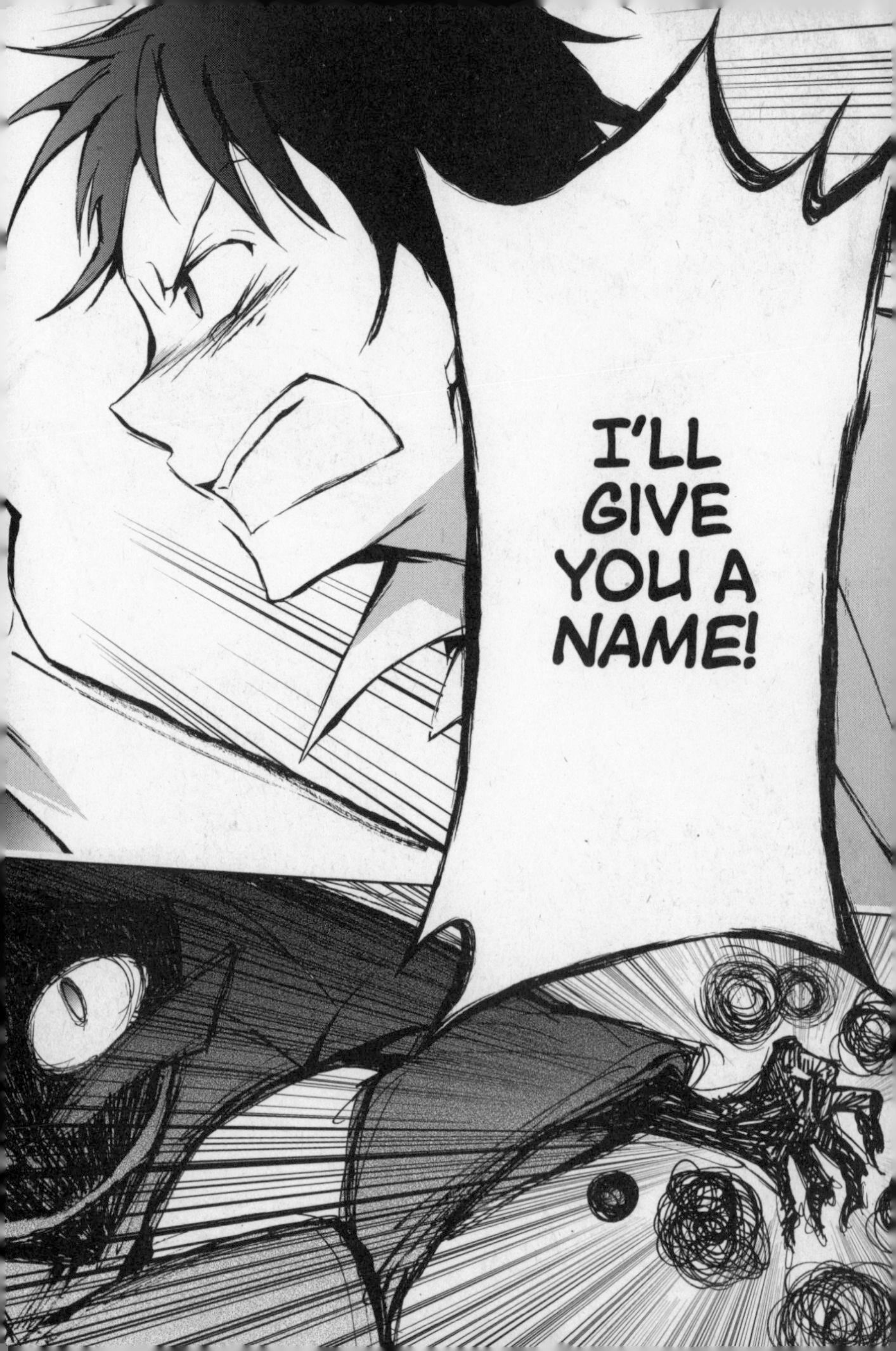
I'LL GIVE YOU A NAME!

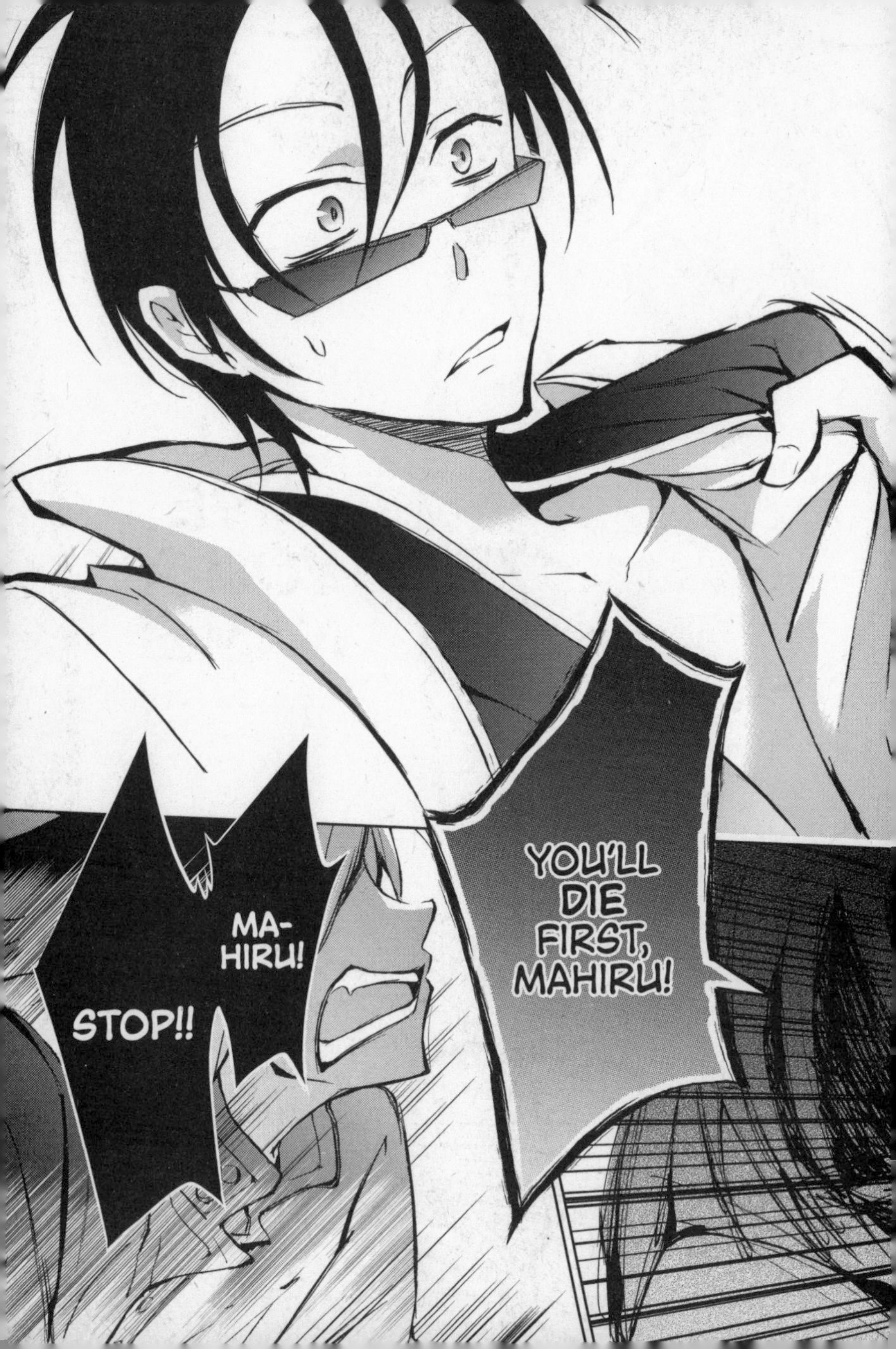
YOU'LL DIE FIRST, MAHIRU!
MA-HIRU!
STOP!!

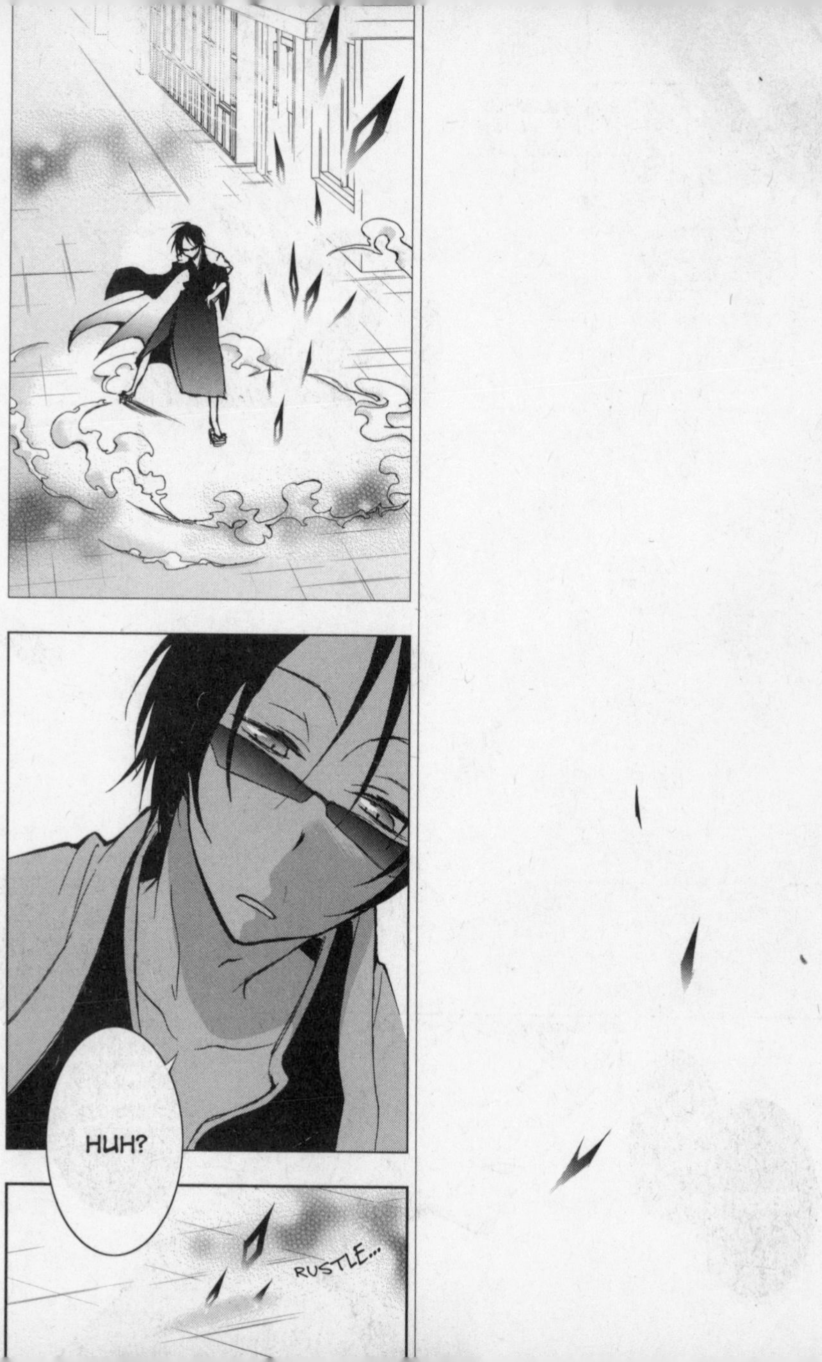
HUH?
RUSTLE...

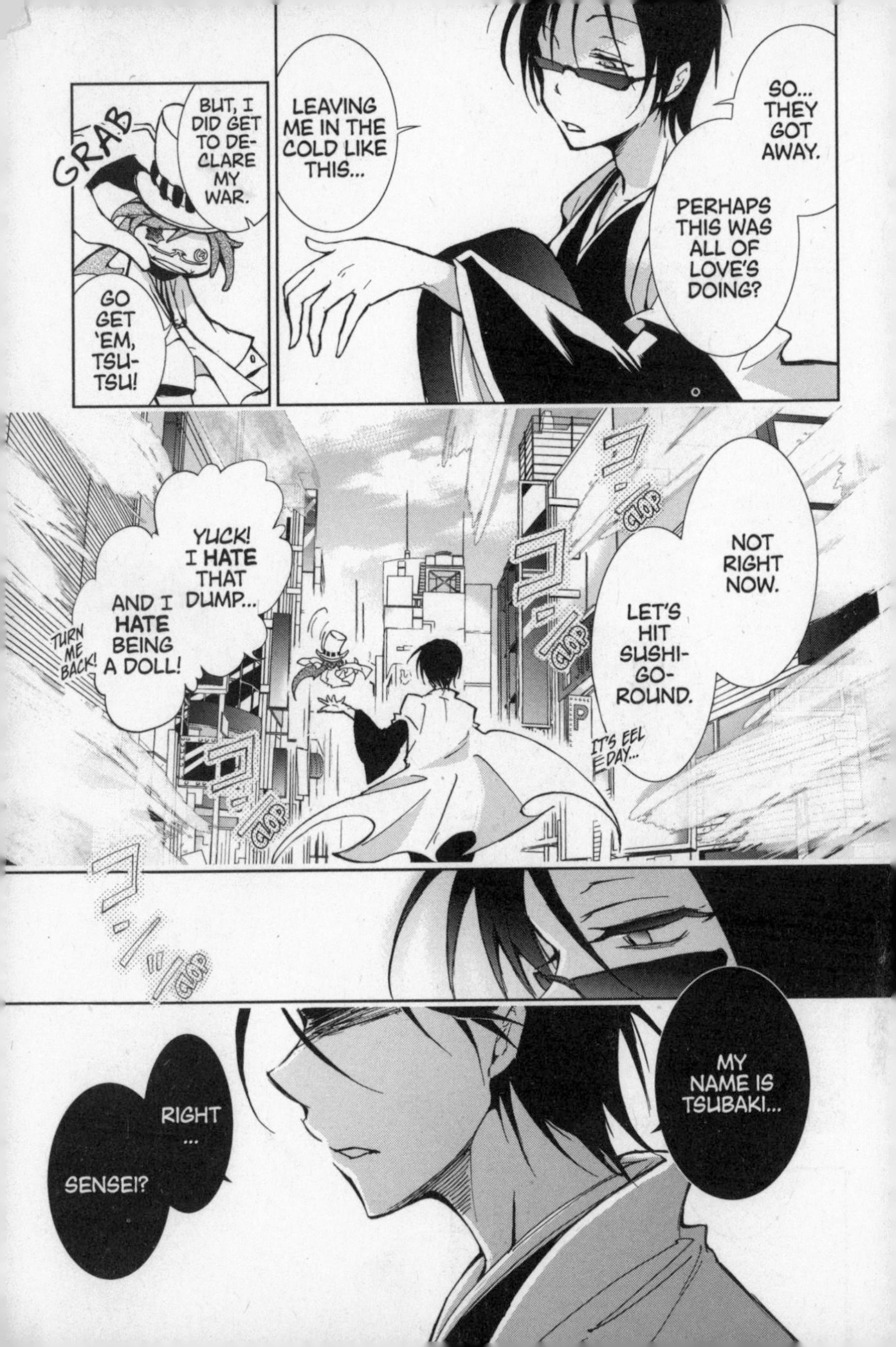
SO... THEY GOT AWAY.
PERHAPS THIS WAS ALL OF LOVE'S DOING?
LEAVING ME IN THE COLD LIKE THIS...
GRAB
BUT, I DID GET TO DE-CLARE MY WAR.
GO GET 'EM, TSU-TSU!
CLOP
NOT RIGHT NOW.
LET'S HIT SUSHI-GO-ROUND.
CLOP
IT'S EEL DAY...
YUCK! I HATE THAT DUMP...
AND I HATE BEING A DOLL!
TURN ME BACK!
CLOP
CLOP
MY NAME IS TSUBAKI...
RIGHT ... SENSEI?

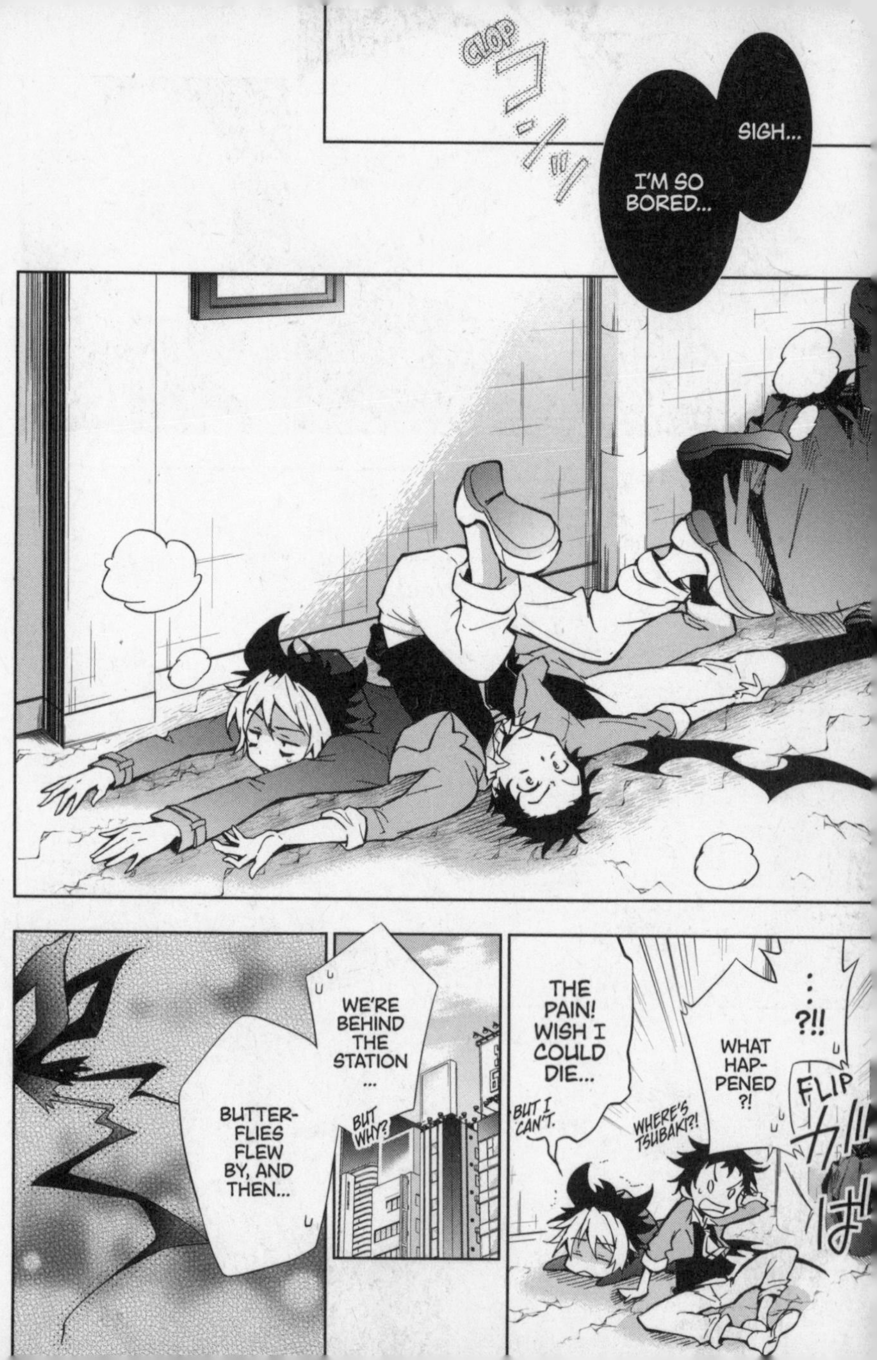
SIGH...
I'M SO BORED...
CLOP
...
?!!
WHAT HAP-PENED?!
FLIP
WHERE'S TSUBAKI?!
THE PAIN! WISH I COULD DIE...
BUT I CAN'T.
WE'RE BEHIND THE STATION ...
BUT WHY?
BUTTER-FLIES FLEW BY, AND THEN...

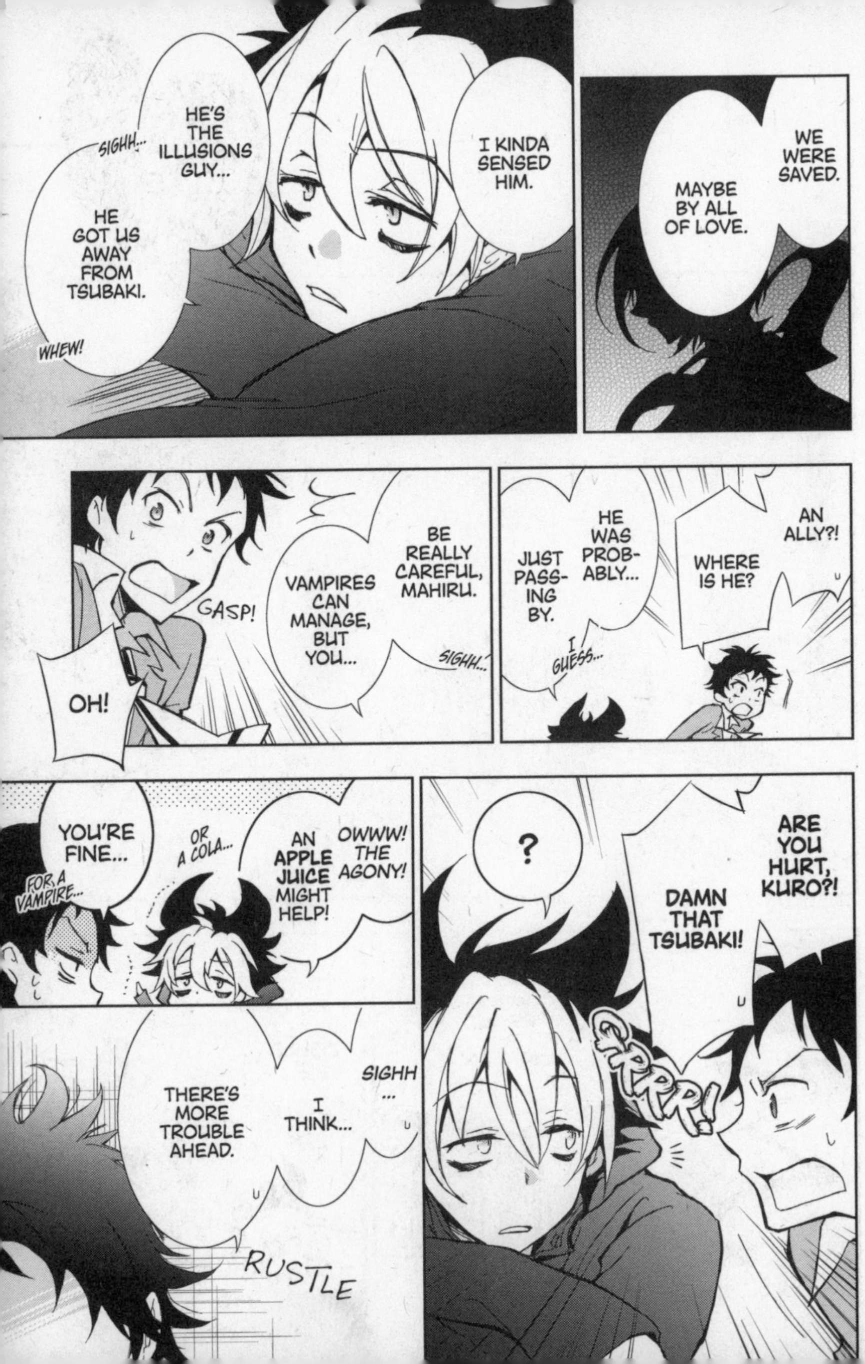
WE WERE SAVED.
MAYBE BY ALL OF LOVE.
I KINDA SENSED HIM.
HE'S THE ILLUSIONS GUY...
SIGHH...
HE GOT US AWAY FROM TSUBAKI.
WHEW!
AN ALLY?!
WHERE IS HE?
HE WAS PROBABLY...
JUST PASSING BY.
I GUESS...
BE REALLY CAREFUL, MAHIRU.
VAMPIRES CAN MANAGE, BUT YOU...
SIGHH...
GASP!
OH!
ARE YOU HURT, KURO?!
DAMN THAT TSUBAKI!
?
GRRR!
OWWW! THE AGONY!
AN APPLE JUICE MIGHT HELP!
OR A COLA...
YOU'RE FINE...
FOR A VAMPIRE...
SIGHH...
I THINK...
THERE'S MORE TROUBLE AHEAD.
RUSTLE

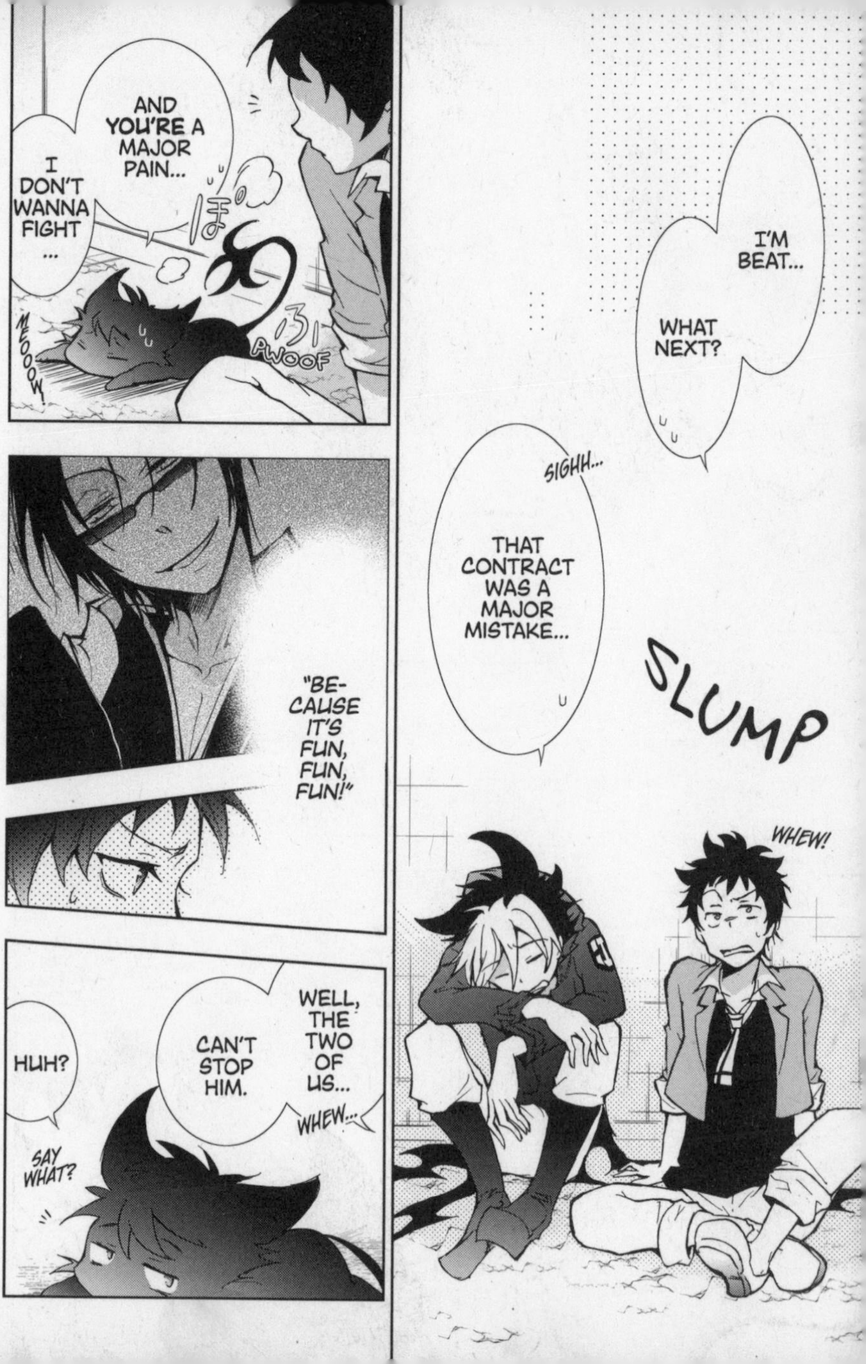
I'M BEAT...
WHAT NEXT?
SIGHH...
THAT CONTRACT WAS A MAJOR MISTAKE...
SLUMP
WHEW!
AND YOU'RE A MAJOR PAIN...
I DON'T WANNA FIGHT ...
ぼ
PWOOF
MEOOOW!
"BE-CAUSE IT'S FUN, FUN, FUN!"
WELL, THE TWO OF US...
CAN'T STOP HIM.
WHEW...
HUH?
SAY WHAT?

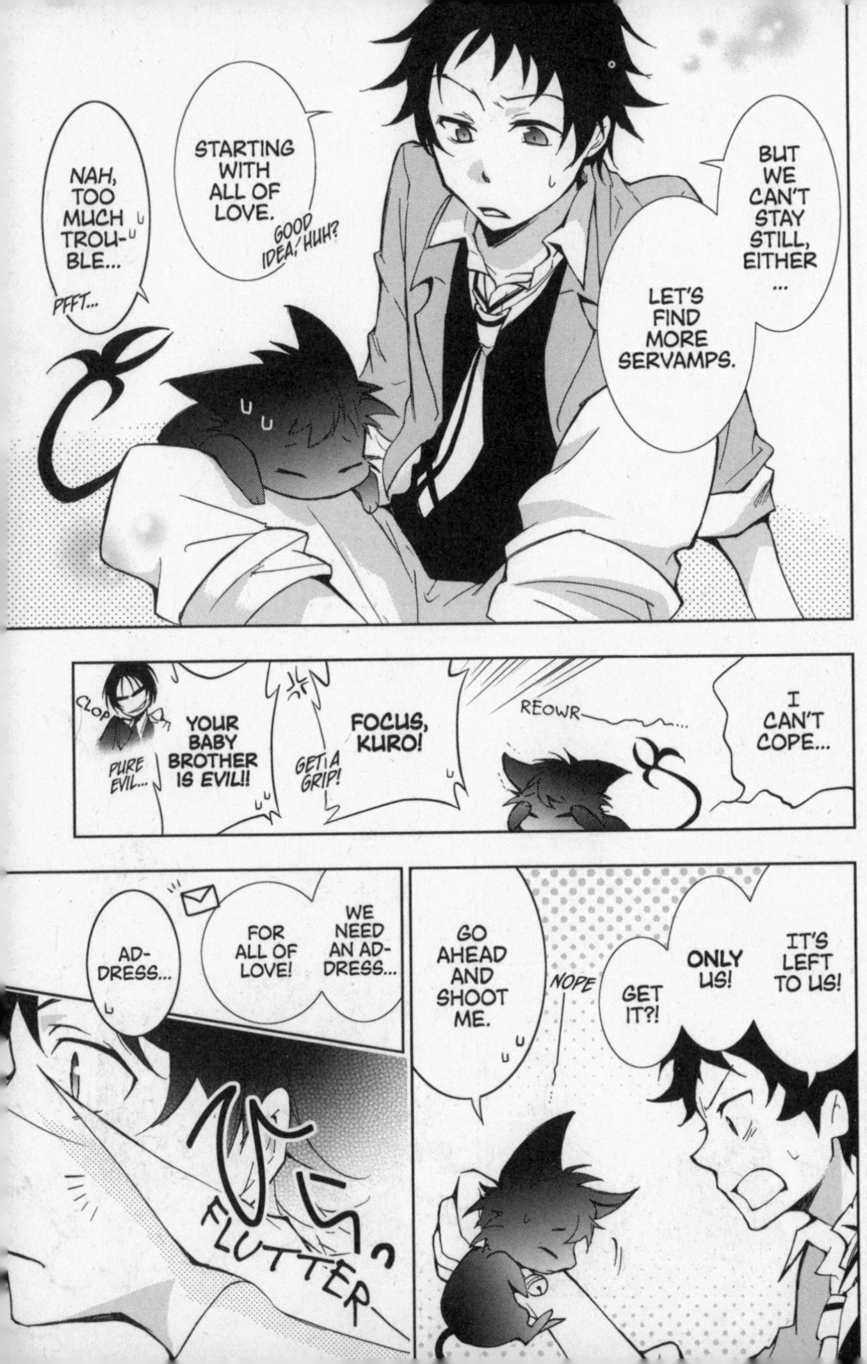
BUT WE CAN'T STAY STILL, EITHER ...
LET'S FIND MORE SERVAMPS.
STARTING WITH ALL OF LOVE.
GOOD IDEA, HUH?
NAH, TOO MUCH TROUBLE...
PFFT...
I CAN'T COPE...
REOWR...
FOCUS, KURO!
GET A GRIP!
YOUR BABY BROTHER IS EVIL!!
PURE EVIL...
CLOP
IT'S LEFT TO US!
ONLY US!
GET IT?!
NOPE
GO AHEAD AND SHOOT ME.
WE NEED AN ADDRESS...
FOR ALL OF LOVE!
AD-DRESS...
FLUTTER

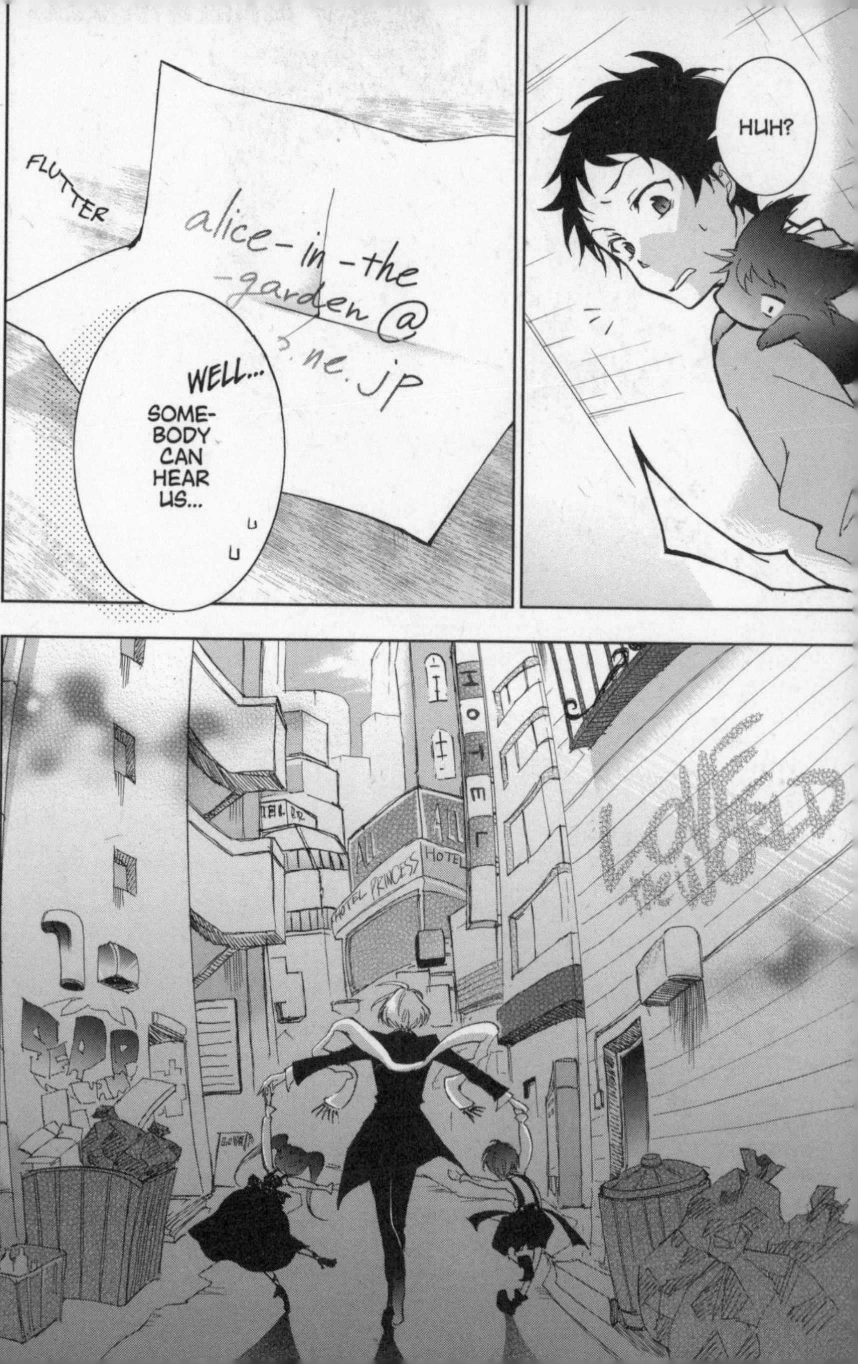
HUH?
FLUTTER
alice-in-the
-garden@
ne.jp
WELL...
SOMEBODY CAN HEAR US...
HOTEL
HOTEL
HOTEL PRINCESS

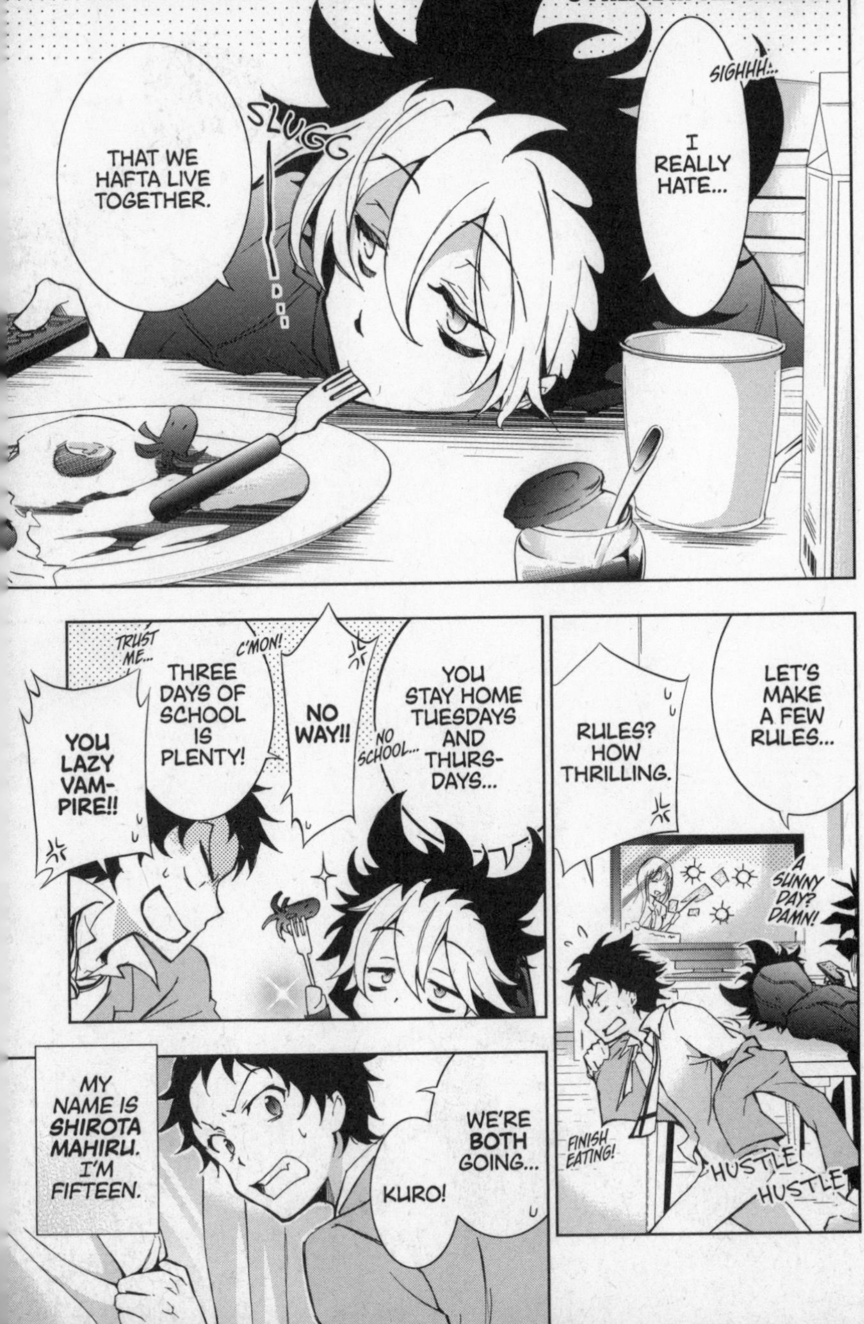
SIGHHH...
I REALLY HATE...
SLUGG
THAT WE HAFTA LIVE TOGETHER.
LET'S MAKE A FEW RULES...
RULES? HOW THRILLING.
A SUNNY DAY? DAMN!
FINISH EATING!
HUSTLE
HUSTLE
YOU STAY HOME TUESDAYS AND THURS-DAYS...
NO SCHOOL...
NO WAY!!
C'MON!
THREE DAYS OF SCHOOL IS PLENTY!
TRUST ME...
YOU LAZY VAM-PIRE!!
WE'RE BOTH GOING...
KURO!
MY NAME IS SHIROTA MAHIRU. I'M FIFTEEN.

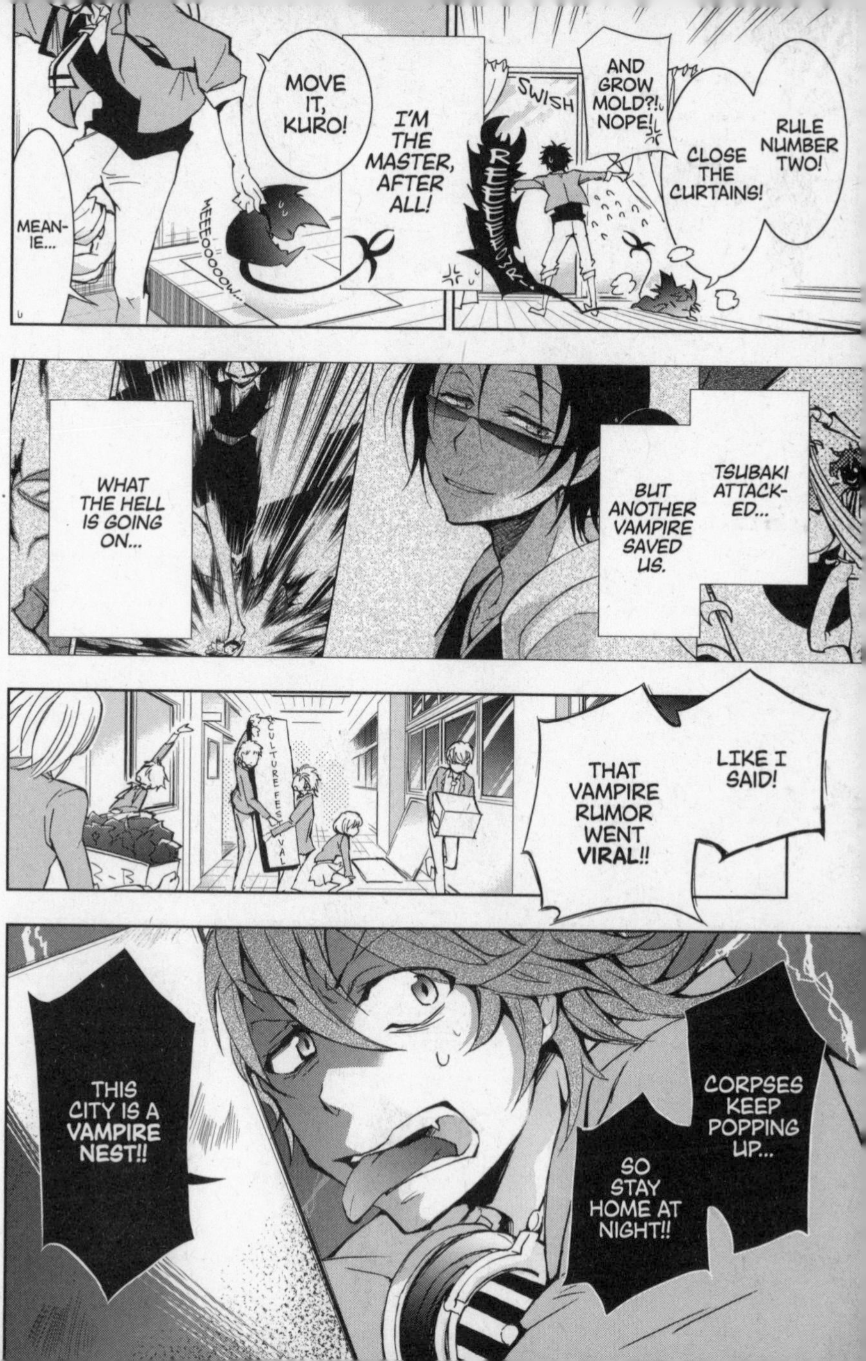
RULE NUMBER TWO!
CLOSE THE CURTAINS!
AND GROW MOLD?! NOPE!
SWISH
REEEEOWR!
I'M THE MASTER, AFTER ALL!
MOVE IT, KURO!
MEEEOOOOOW...
MEAN-IE...
TSUBAKI ATTACK-ED...
BUT ANOTHER VAMPIRE SAVED US.
WHAT THE HELL IS GOING ON...
LIKE I SAID!
THAT VAMPIRE RUMOR WENT VIRAL!!
CULTURE FESTIVAL
CORPSES KEEP POPPING UP...
SO STAY HOME AT NIGHT!!
THIS CITY IS A VAMPIRE NEST!!

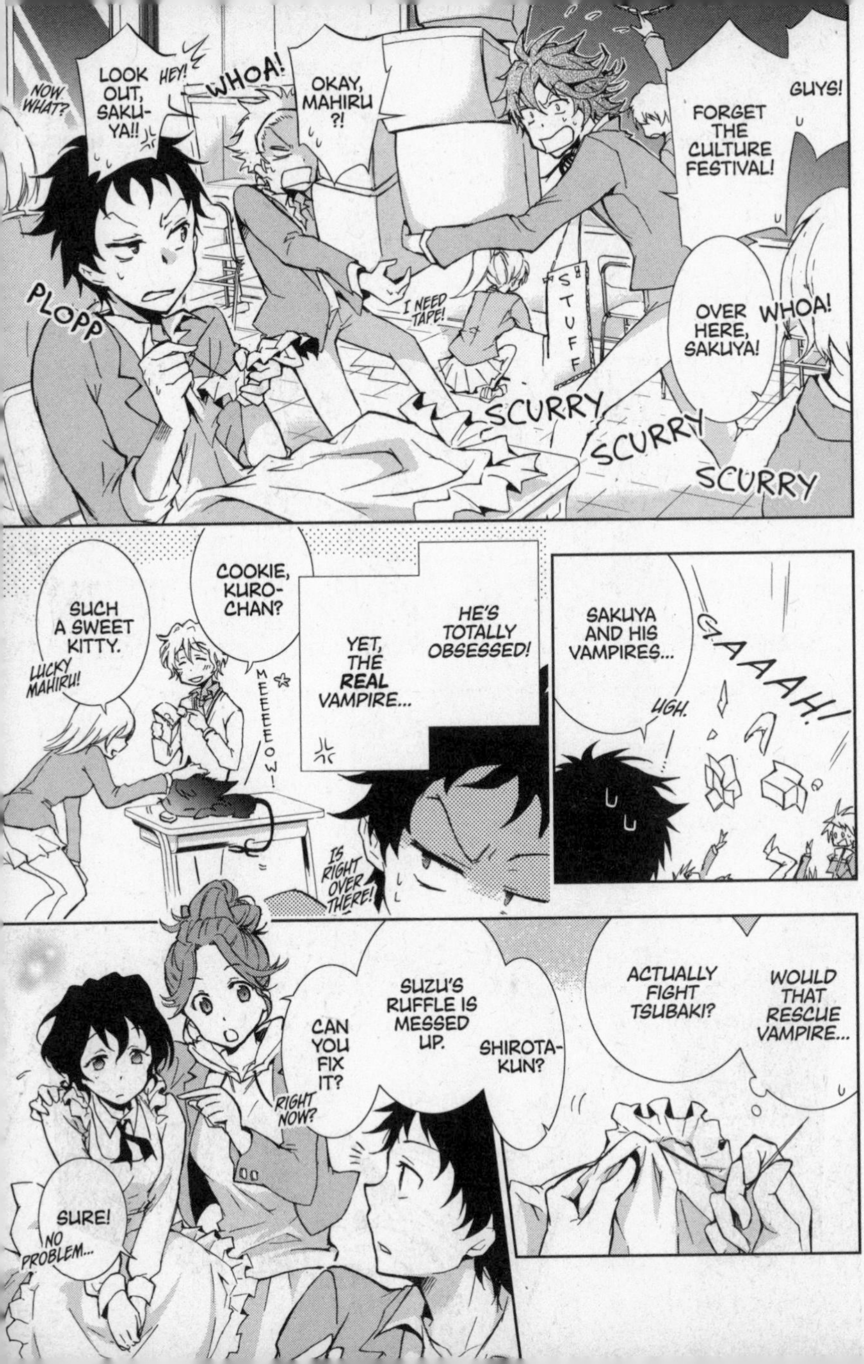
GUYS!
FORGET THE CULTURE FESTIVAL!
WHOA!
OVER HERE, SAKUYA!
OKAY, MAHIRU?!
WHOA!
HEY!
LOOK OUT, SAKU-YA!!
NOW WHAT?
STUFF
I NEED TAPE!
PLOPP
SCURRY
SCURRY
SCURRY
GAAAAH!
SAKUYA AND HIS VAMPIRES...
UGH.
HE'S TOTALLY OBSESSED!
YET, THE **REAL** VAMPIRE...
IS RIGHT OVER THERE!
COOKIE, KURO-CHAN?
MEEEEEOW!
SUCH A SWEET KITTY.
LUCKY MAHIRU!
WOULD THAT RESCUE VAMPIRE...
ACTUALLY FIGHT TSUBAKI?
SHIROTA-KUN?
SUZU'S RUFFLE IS MESSED UP.
CAN YOU FIX IT?
RIGHT NOW?
SURE!
NO PROBLEM...

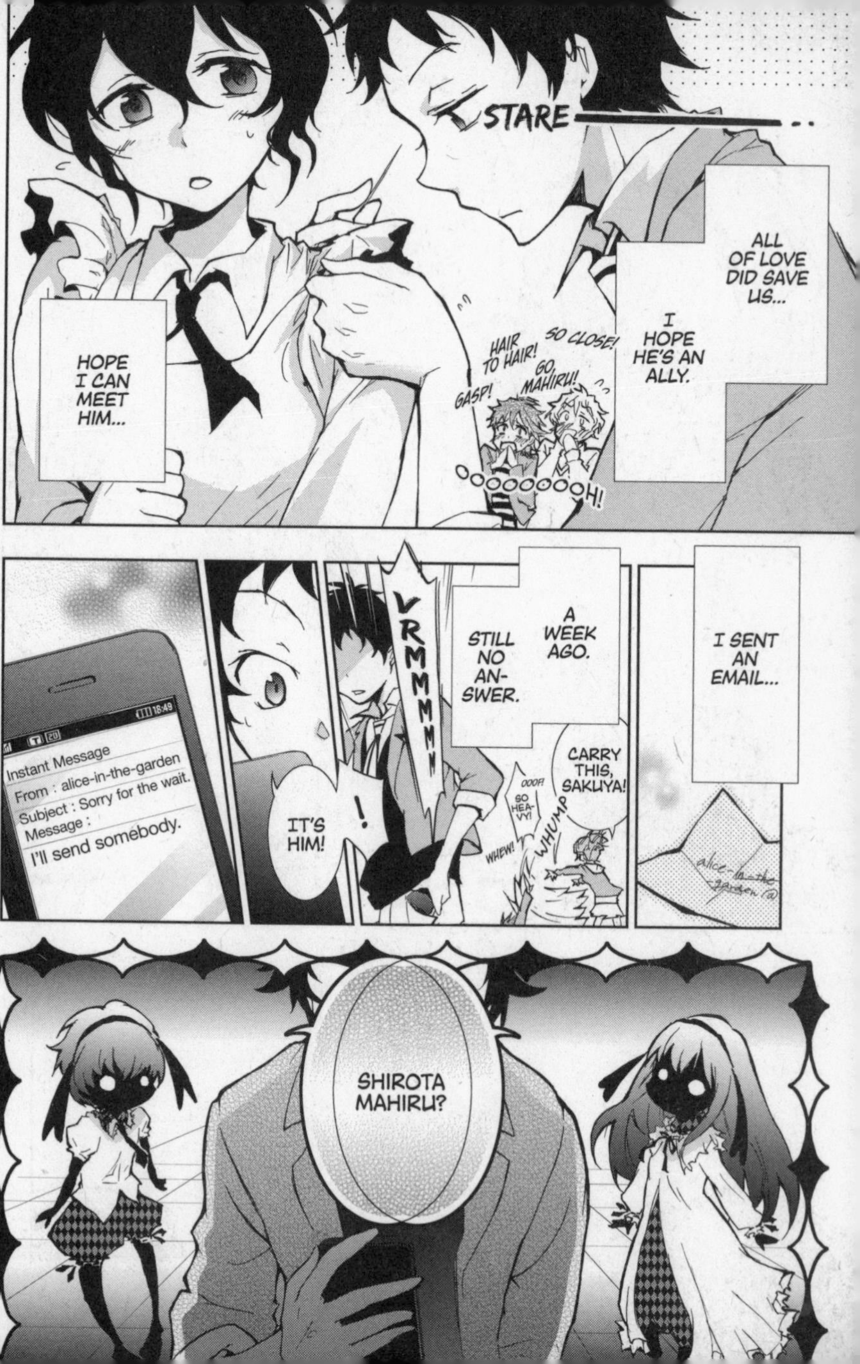
STARE
ALL OF LOVE DID SAVE US...
I HOPE HE'S AN ALLY.
SO CLOSE!
GO MAHIRU!
HAIR TO HAIR!
GASP!
OOOOOOOOOH!
HOPE I CAN MEET HIM...
I SENT AN EMAIL...
alice-in-the-garden@
A WEEK AGO.
STILL NO ANSWER.
CARRY THIS, SAKUYA!
OOOF! SO HEAVY!
WHUMP
WHEW!
VRMMMMM
!
IT'S HIM!
18:49
Instant Message
From : alice-in-the-garden
Subject : Sorry for the wait.
Message :
I'll send somebody.
SHIROTA MAHIRU?

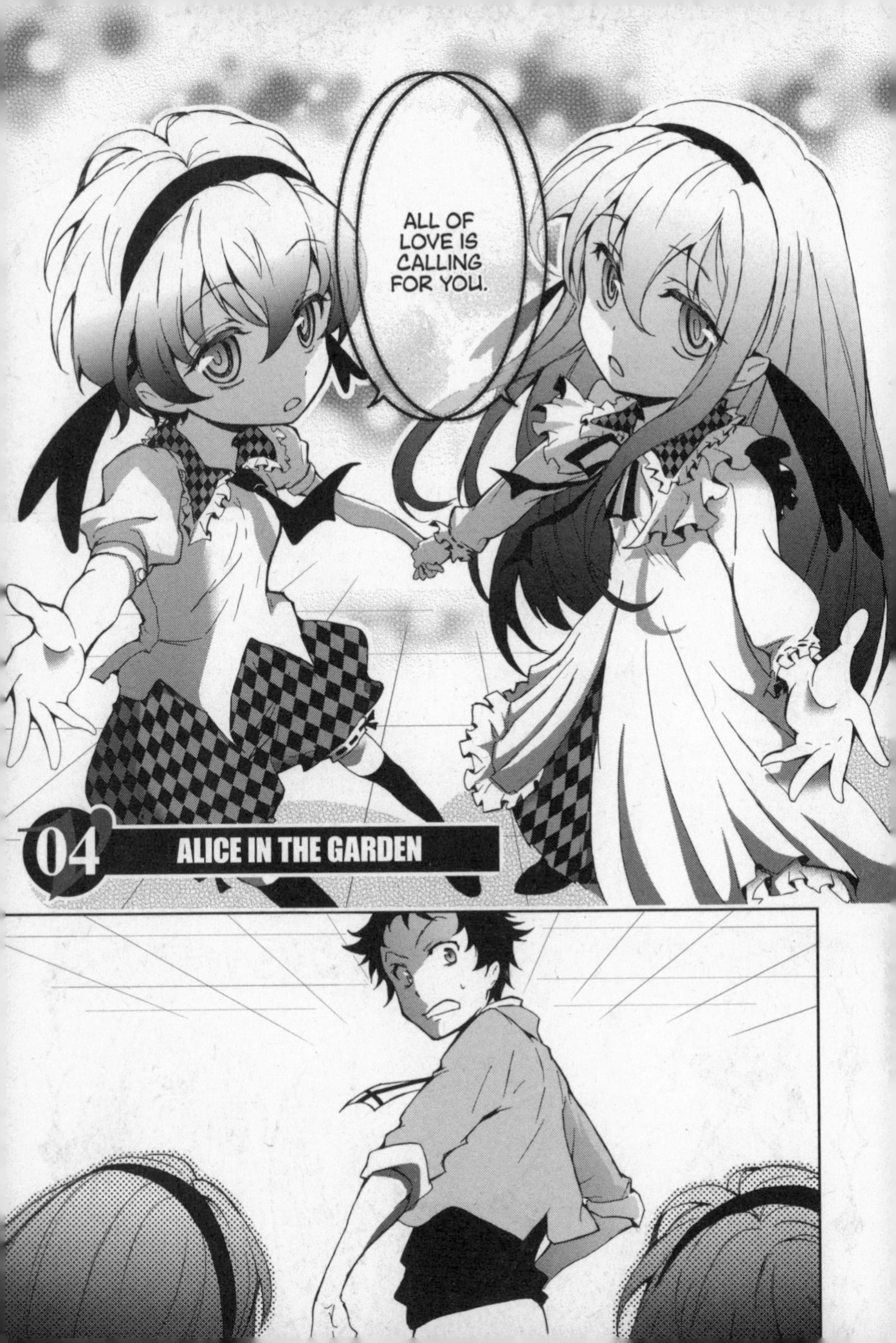
ALL OF LOVE IS CALLING FOR YOU.
04
ALICE IN THE GARDEN

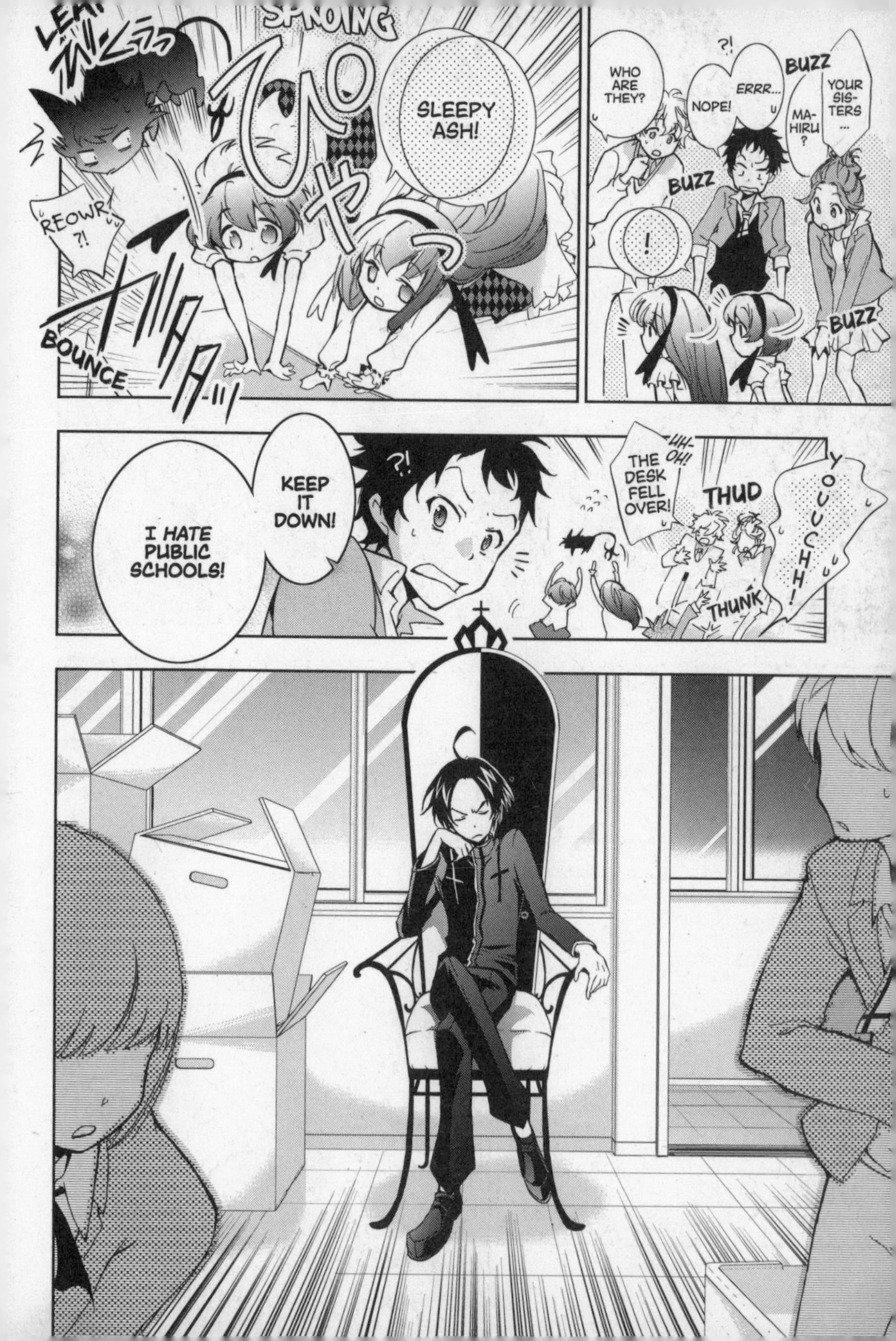
YOUR SISTERS...
BUZZ
MAHIRU?
ERRR...
?!
NOPE!
WHO ARE THEY?
BUZZ
!
BUZZ
SPROING
SLEEPY ASH!
LEA
REOWR ?!
BOUNCE
YOUUUCH!
THUD
UH-OH!
THE DESK FELL OVER!
THUNK
?!
KEEP IT DOWN!
I HATE PUBLIC SCHOOLS!

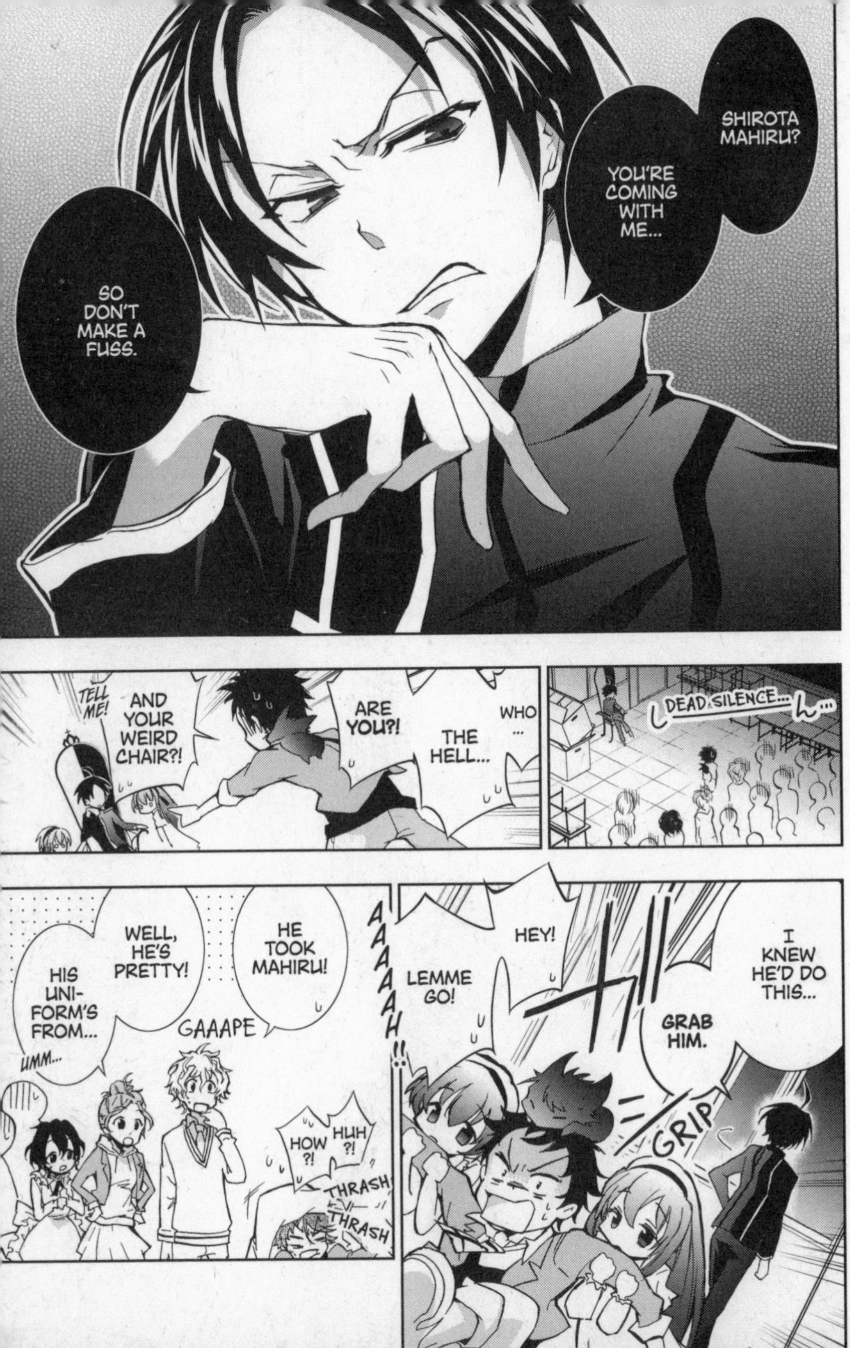
SHIROTA MAHIRU?
YOU'RE COMING WITH ME...
SO DON'T MAKE A FUSS.
DEAD SILENCE...
WHO ... THE HELL...
ARE YOU?!
AND YOUR WEIRD CHAIR?!
TELL ME!
I KNEW HE'D DO THIS...
GRAB HIM.
HEY!
LEMME GO!
GRIP
AAAAAH!!
HE TOOK MAHIRU!
WELL, HE'S PRETTY!
HIS UNI-FORM'S FROM...
GAAAPE
UMM...
HUH?!
HOW?!
THRASH
THRASH

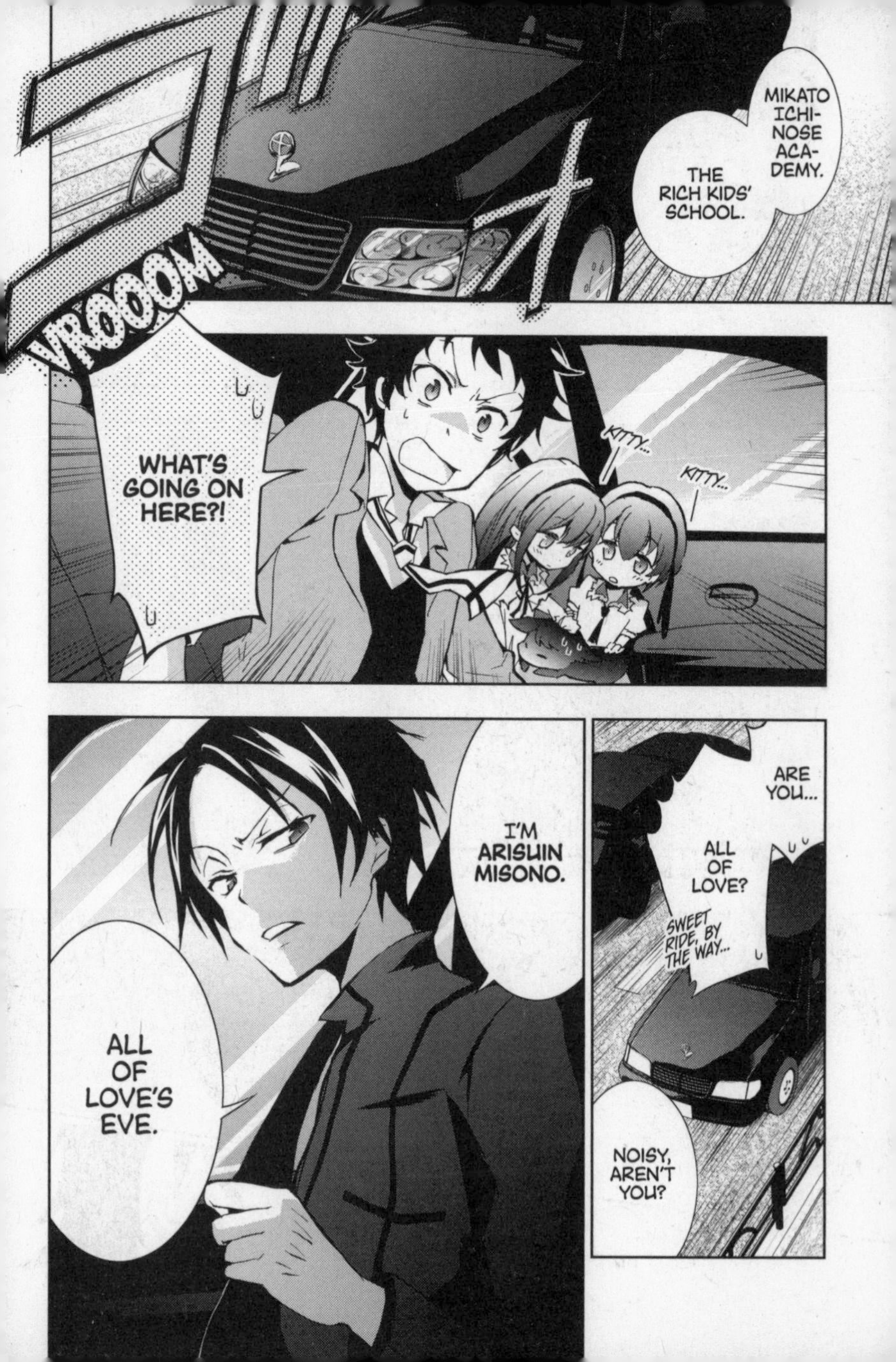
MIKATO ICHINOSE ACADEMY.
THE RICH KIDS' SCHOOL.
VROOOM
KITTY...
KITTY...
WHAT'S GOING ON HERE?!
ARE YOU...
ALL OF LOVE?
SWEET RIDE, BY THE WAY...
NOISY, AREN'T YOU?
I'M ARISUIN MISONO.
ALL OF LOVE'S EVE.

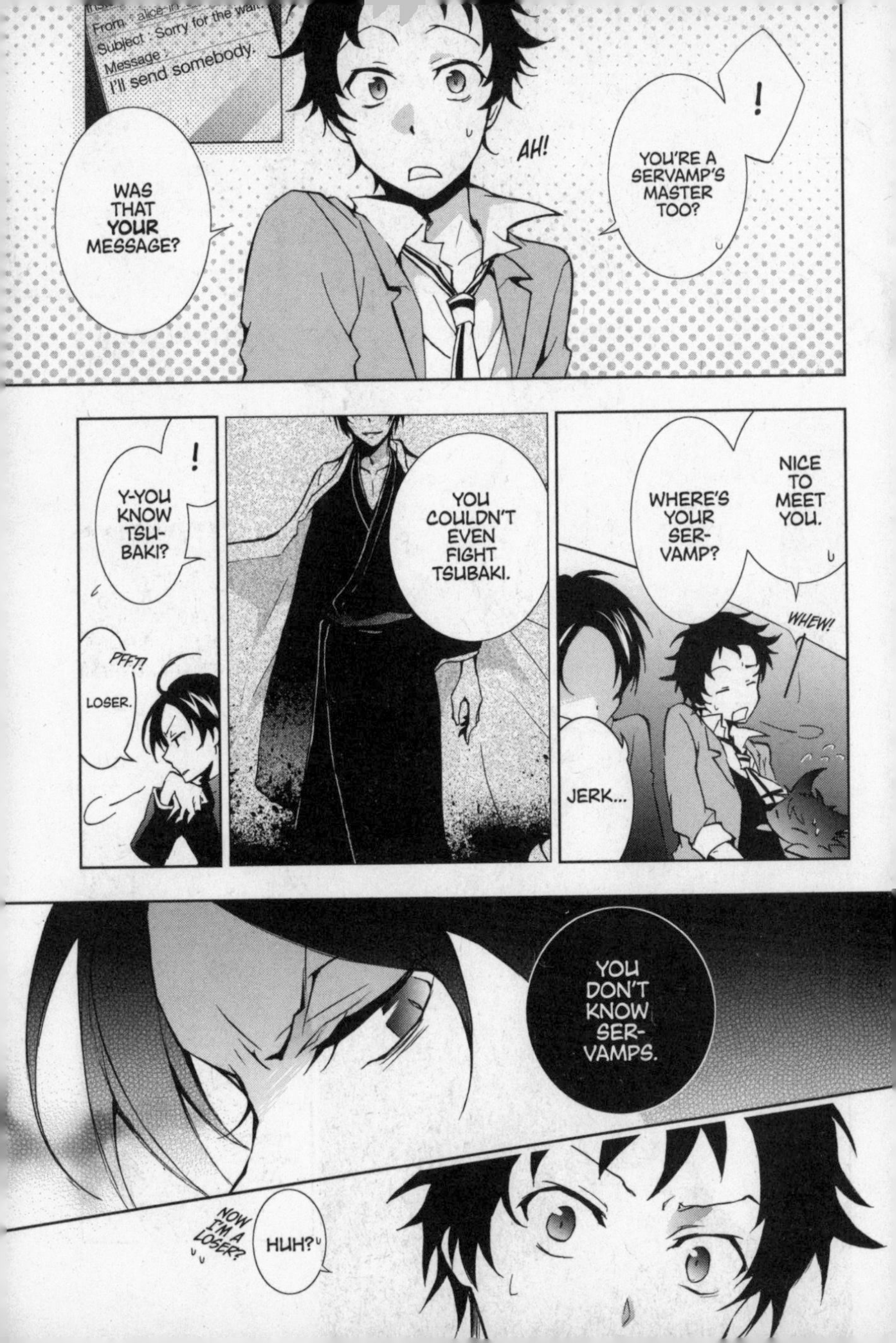
!
YOU'RE A SERVAMP'S MASTER TOO?
AH!
From : alice-in
Subject : Sorry for the wait.
Message :
I'll send somebody.
WAS THAT **YOUR** MESSAGE?
NICE TO MEET YOU.
WHERE'S YOUR SER-VAMP?
WHEW!
JERK...
YOU COULDN'T EVEN FIGHT TSUBAKI.
!
Y-YOU KNOW TSU-BAKI?
PFFT!
LOSER.
YOU DON'T KNOW SER-VAMPS.
HUH?
NOW I'M A LOSER?

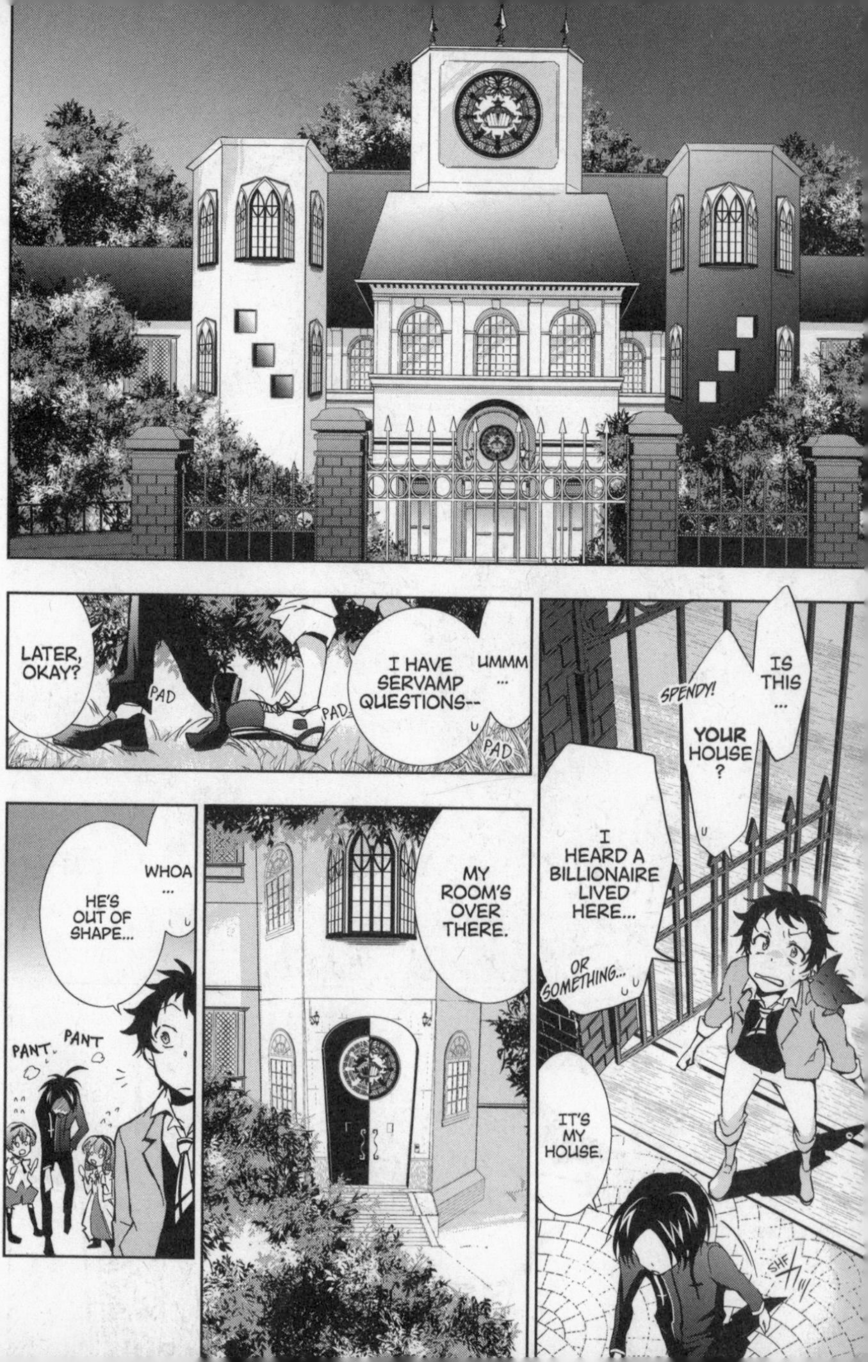
IS THIS ...
YOUR HOUSE ?
SPENDY!
I HEARD A BILLIONAIRE LIVED HERE...
OR SOMETHING...
IT'S MY HOUSE.
SHF
UMMM ...
I HAVE SERVAMP QUESTIONS--
PAD
PAD
LATER, OKAY?
PAD
MY ROOM'S OVER THERE.
WHOA ...
HE'S OUT OF SHAPE...
PANT
PANT

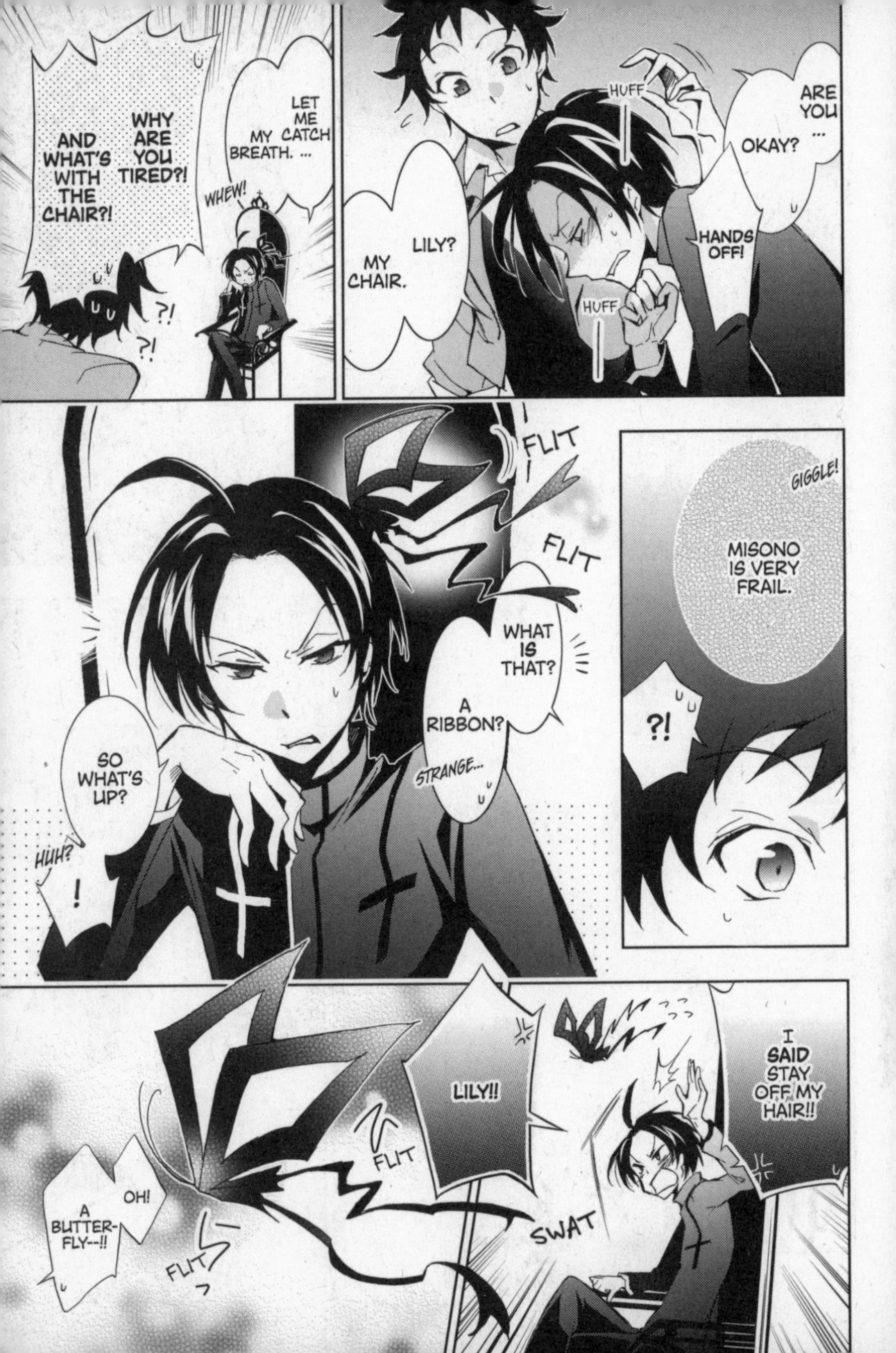
ARE YOU ... OKAY?
HUFF
HANDS OFF!
LILY? MY CHAIR.
HUFF
LET ME CATCH MY BREATH. ...
WHEW!
WHY ARE YOU TIRED?!
AND WHAT'S WITH THE CHAIR?!
?!
?!
GIGGLE!
MISONO IS VERY FRAIL.
?!
FLIT
FLIT
WHAT IS THAT?
A RIBBON?
STRANGE...
SO WHAT'S UP?
HUH?
!
I SAID STAY OFF MY HAIR!!
LILY!!
SWAT
FLIT
OH!
A BUTTER-FLY--!!
FLIT

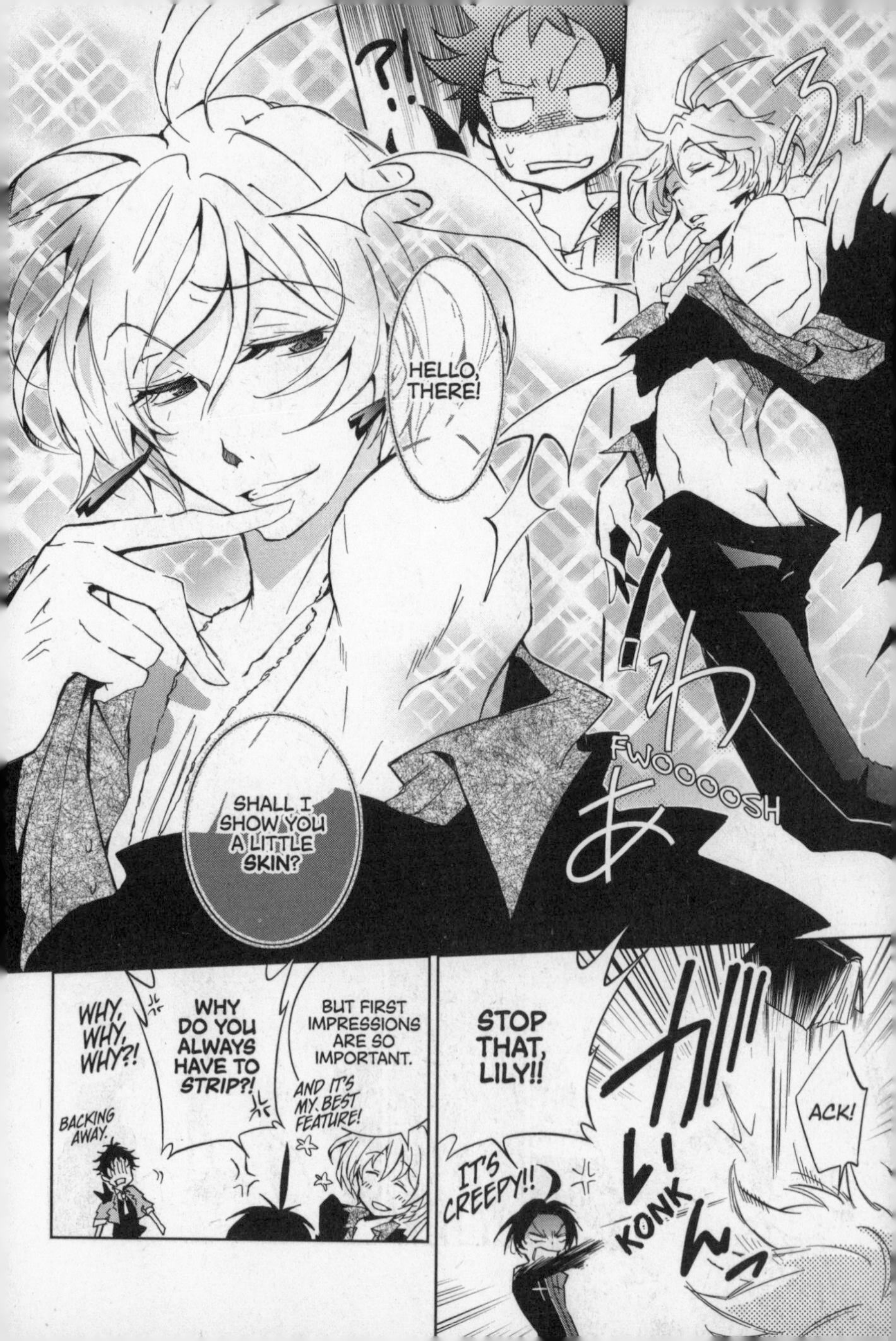
?!
HELLO, THERE!
FWOOOOOSH
SHALL I SHOW YOU A LITTLE SKIN?
ACK!
STOP THAT, LILY!!
KONK
IT'S CREEPY!!
BUT FIRST IMPRESSIONS ARE SO IMPORTANT.
AND IT'S MY BEST FEATURE!
WHY DO YOU ALWAYS HAVE TO STRIP?!
WHY, WHY, WHY?!
BACKING AWAY.

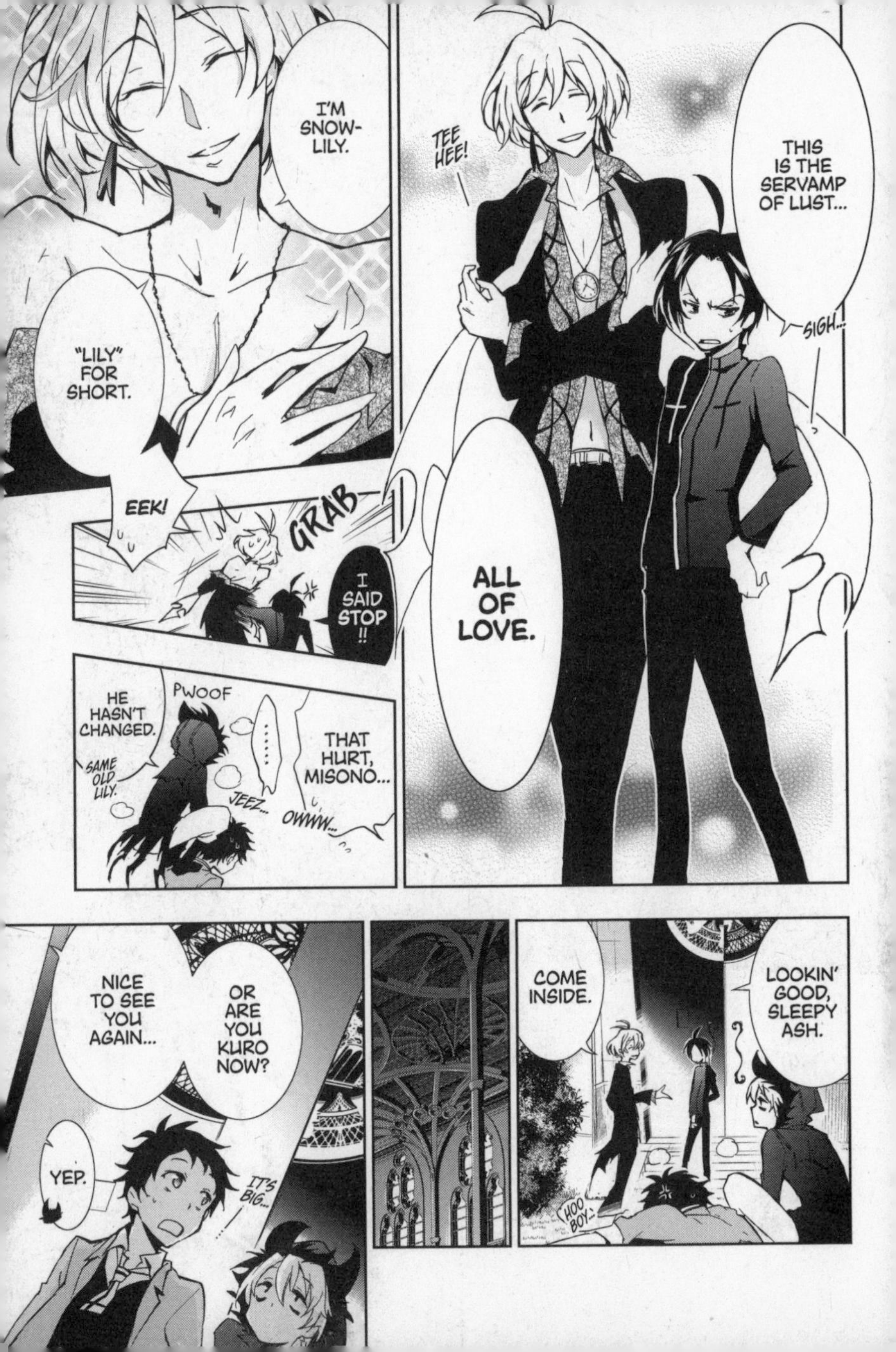
THIS IS THE SERVAMP OF LUST...
TEE HEE!
SIGH...
ALL OF LOVE.
I'M SNOW-LILY.
"LILY" FOR SHORT.
I SAID STOP!!
GRAB
EEK!
THAT HURT, MISONO...
OWWW...
......
PWOOF
HE HASN'T CHANGED.
SAME OLD LILY.
JEEZ...
LOOKIN' GOOD, SLEEPY ASH.
COME INSIDE.
HOO BOY.
NICE TO SEE YOU AGAIN...
OR ARE YOU KURO NOW?
IT'S BIG...
YEP.

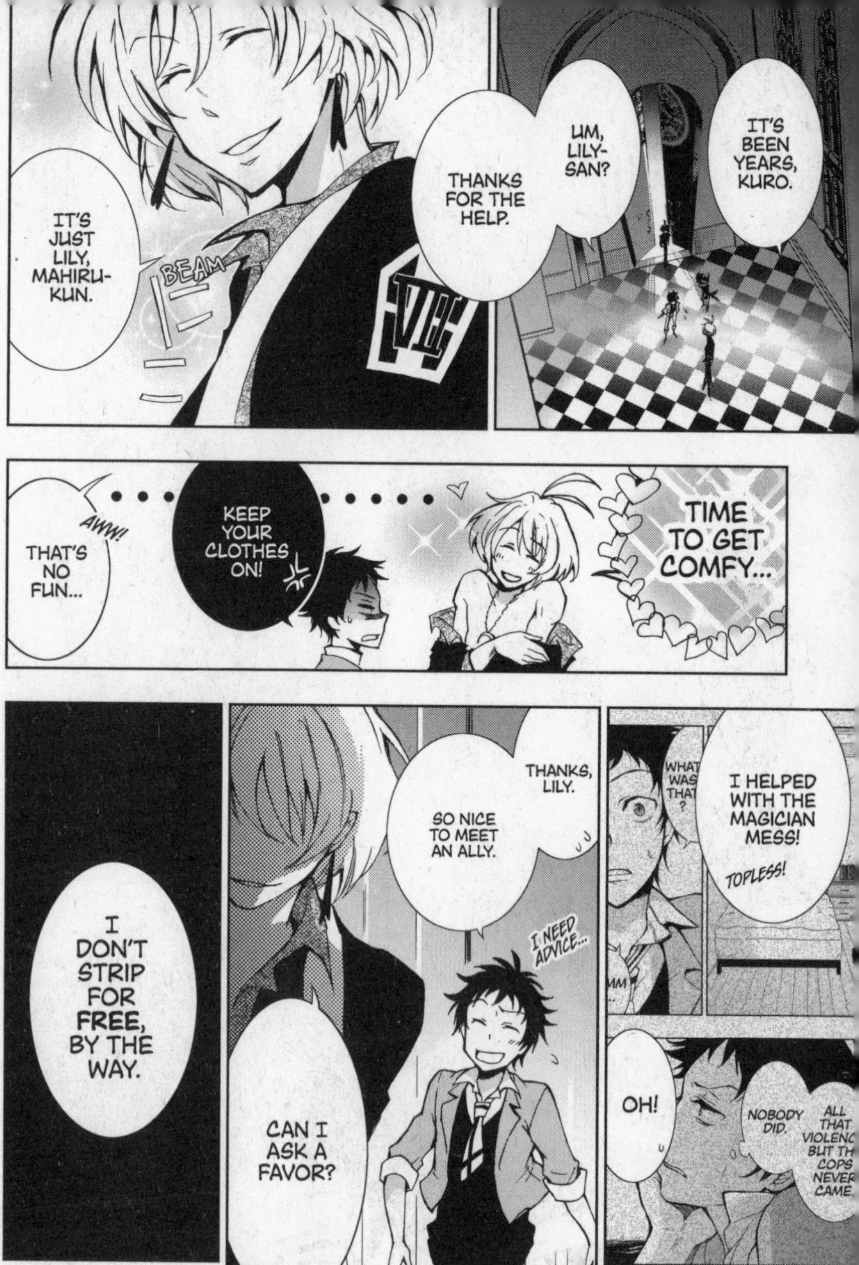
IT'S BEEN YEARS, KURO.
UM, LILY-SAN?
THANKS FOR THE HELP.
BEAM
IT'S JUST LILY, MAHIRU-KUN.
TIME TO GET COMFY...
KEEP YOUR CLOTHES ON!
AWW!
THAT'S NO FUN...
I HELPED WITH THE MAGICIAN MESS!
TOPLESS!
WHAT WAS THAT?
ALL THAT VIOLENC BUT TH COPS NEVER CAME.
NOBODY DID.
OH!
THANKS, LILY.
SO NICE TO MEET AN ALLY.
I NEED ADVICE...
CAN I ASK A FAVOR?
I DON'T STRIP FOR FREE, BY THE WAY.

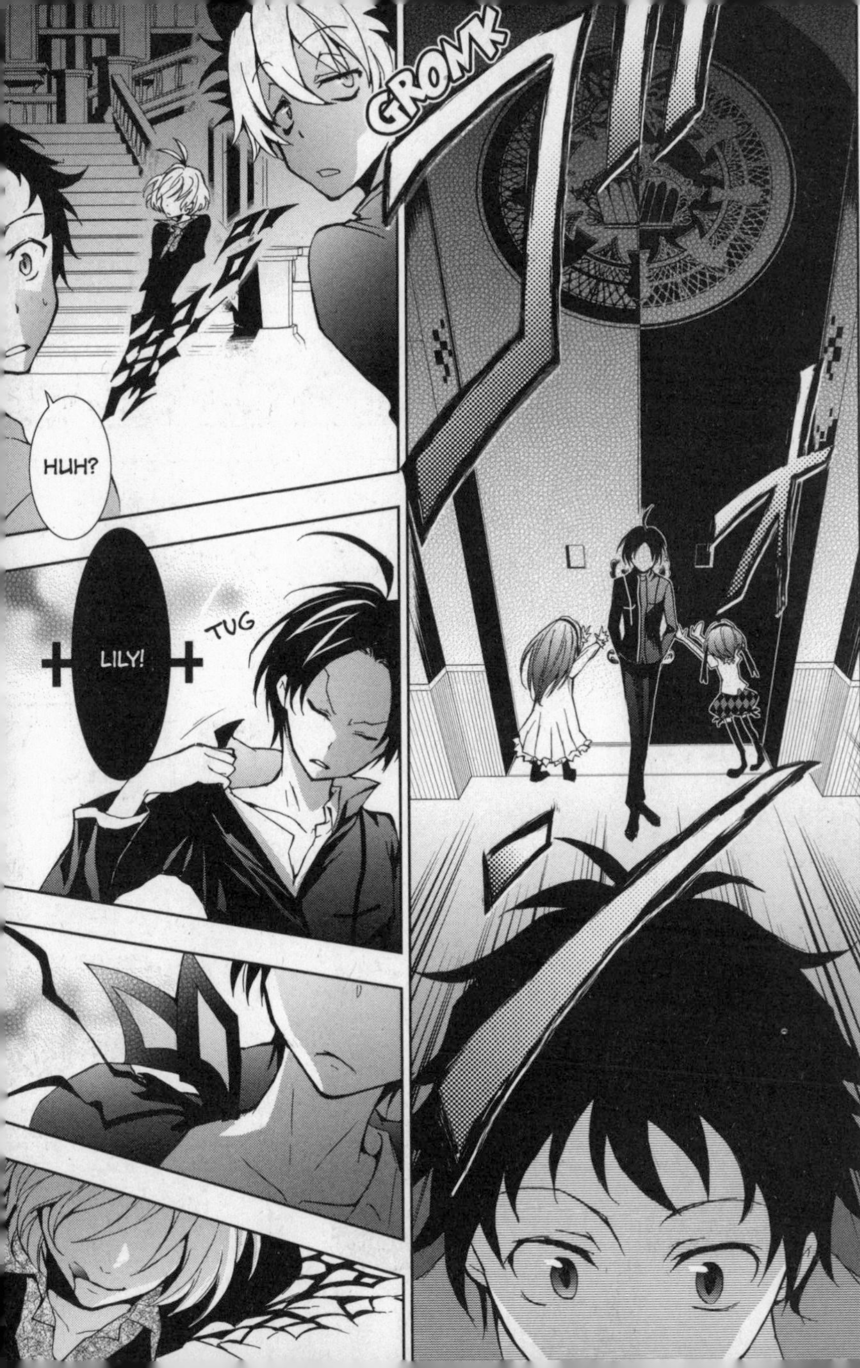
GRONK
HUH?
TUG
LILY!

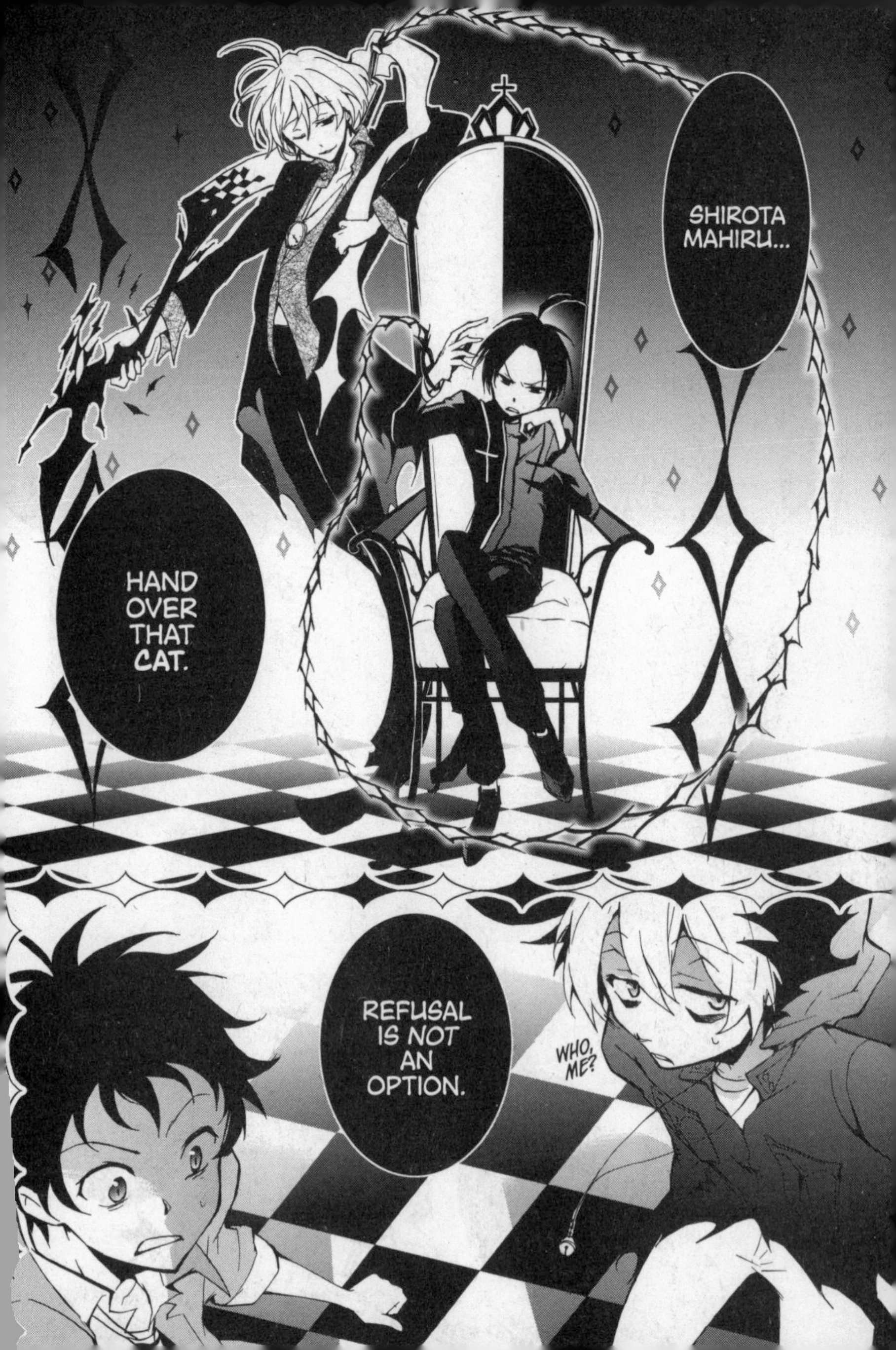
SHIROTA MAHIRU...
HAND OVER THAT CAT.
REFUSAL IS NOT AN OPTION.
WHO, ME?

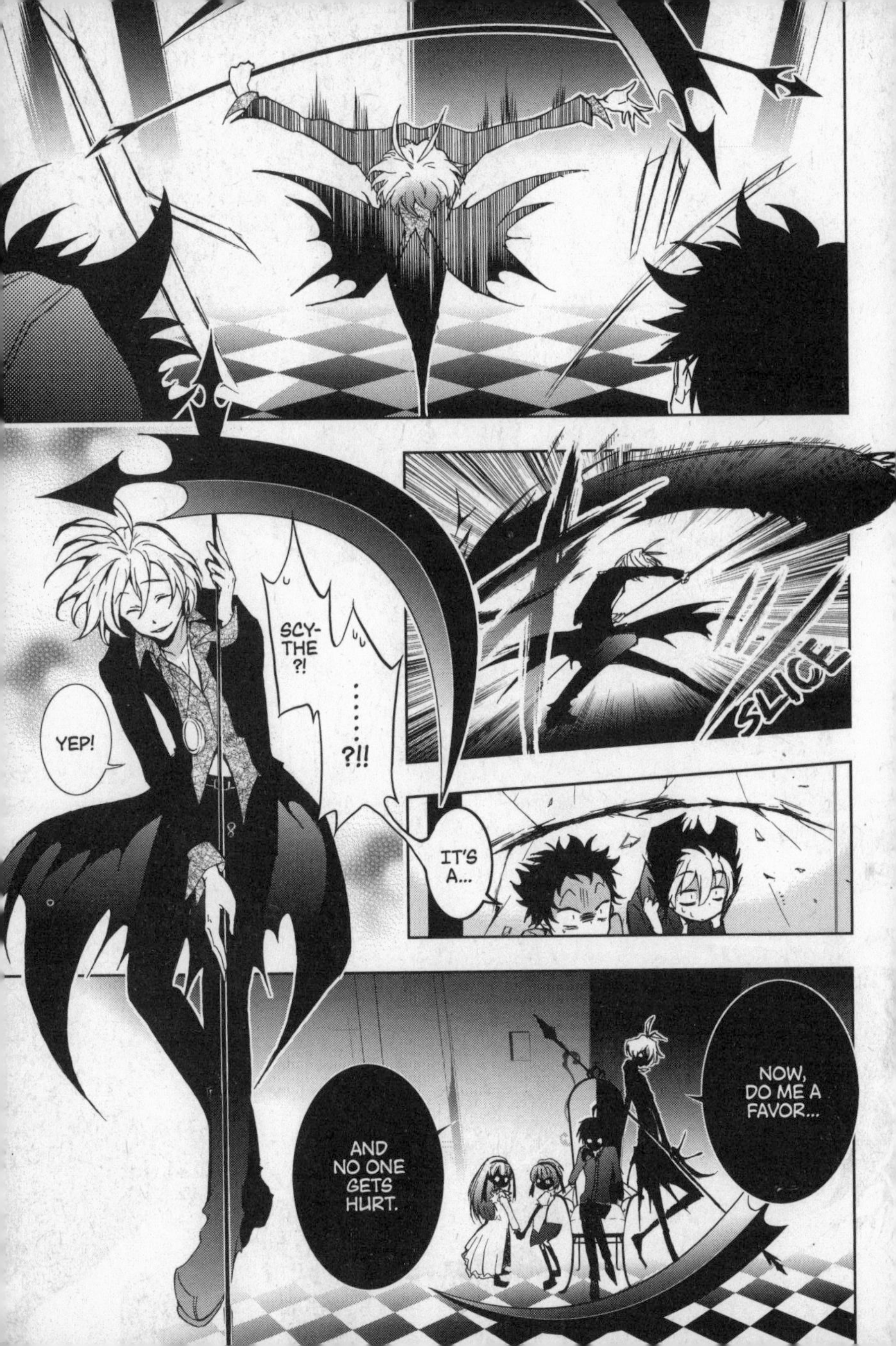
SLICE
IT'S A...
SCY-THE ?!
......?!!
YEP!
NOW, DO ME A FAVOR...
AND NO ONE GETS HURT.

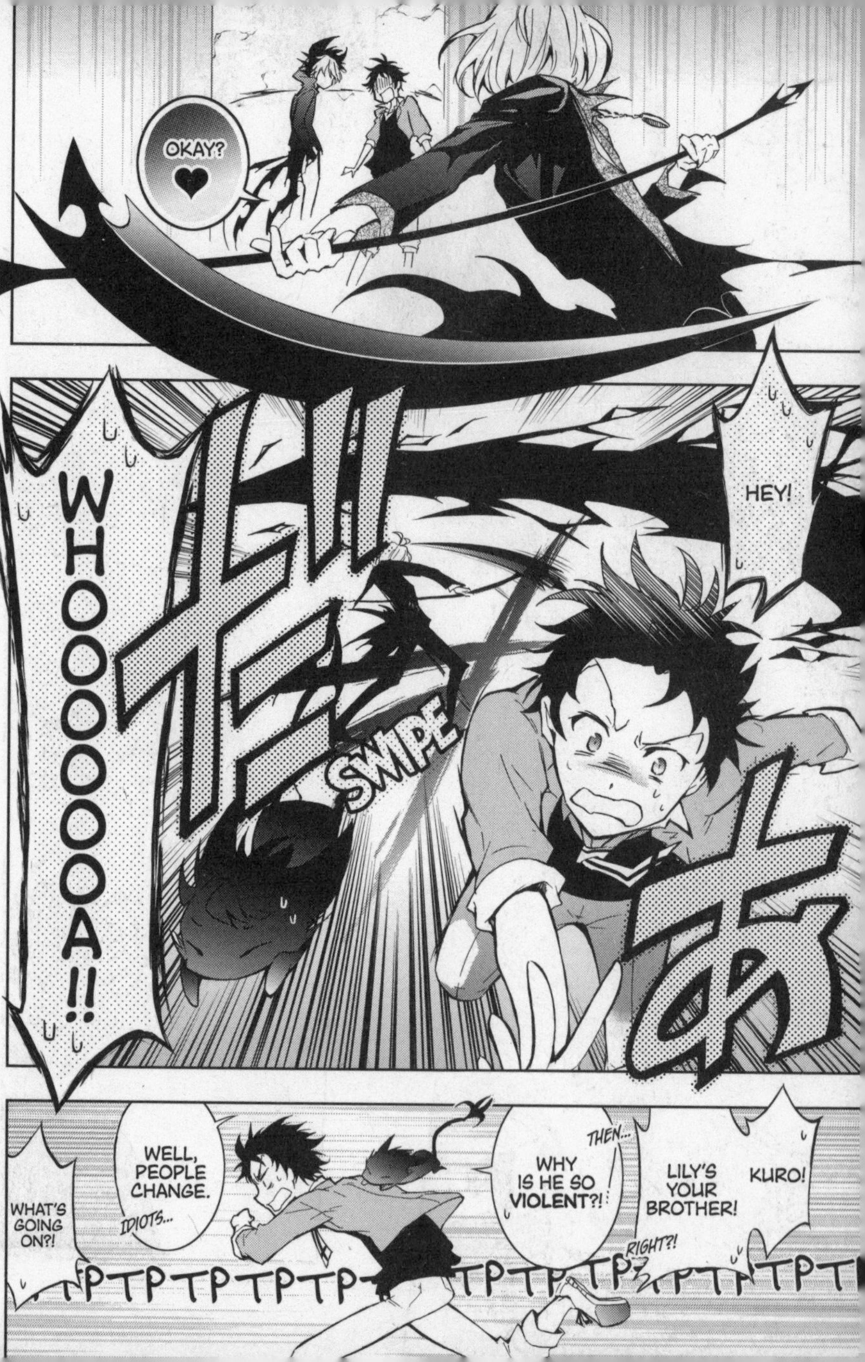

OKAY? ♥
HEY!
SWIPE
WHOOOOOOA!!
KURO!
LILY'S YOUR BROTHER!
RIGHT?!
THEN...
WHY IS HE SO VIOLENT?!
WELL, PEOPLE CHANGE.
IDIOTS...
WHAT'S GOING ON?!
TPTPTPTPTPTP

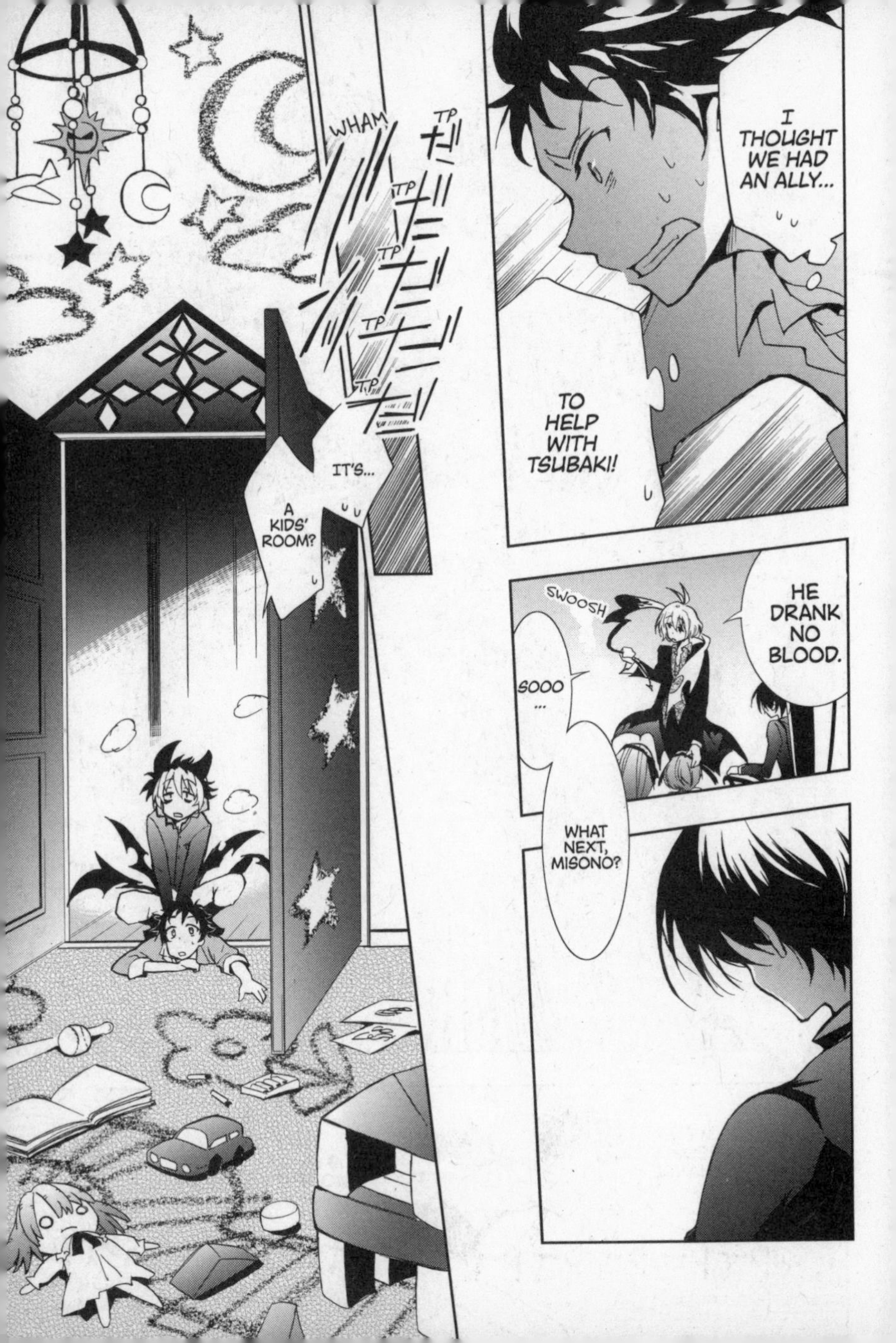
I THOUGHT WE HAD AN ALLY...
TO HELP WITH TSUBAKI!
HE DRANK NO BLOOD.
SWOOSH
SOOO ...
WHAT NEXT, MISONO?
WHAM
TP
TP
TP
TP
TP
IT'S...
A KIDS' ROOM?

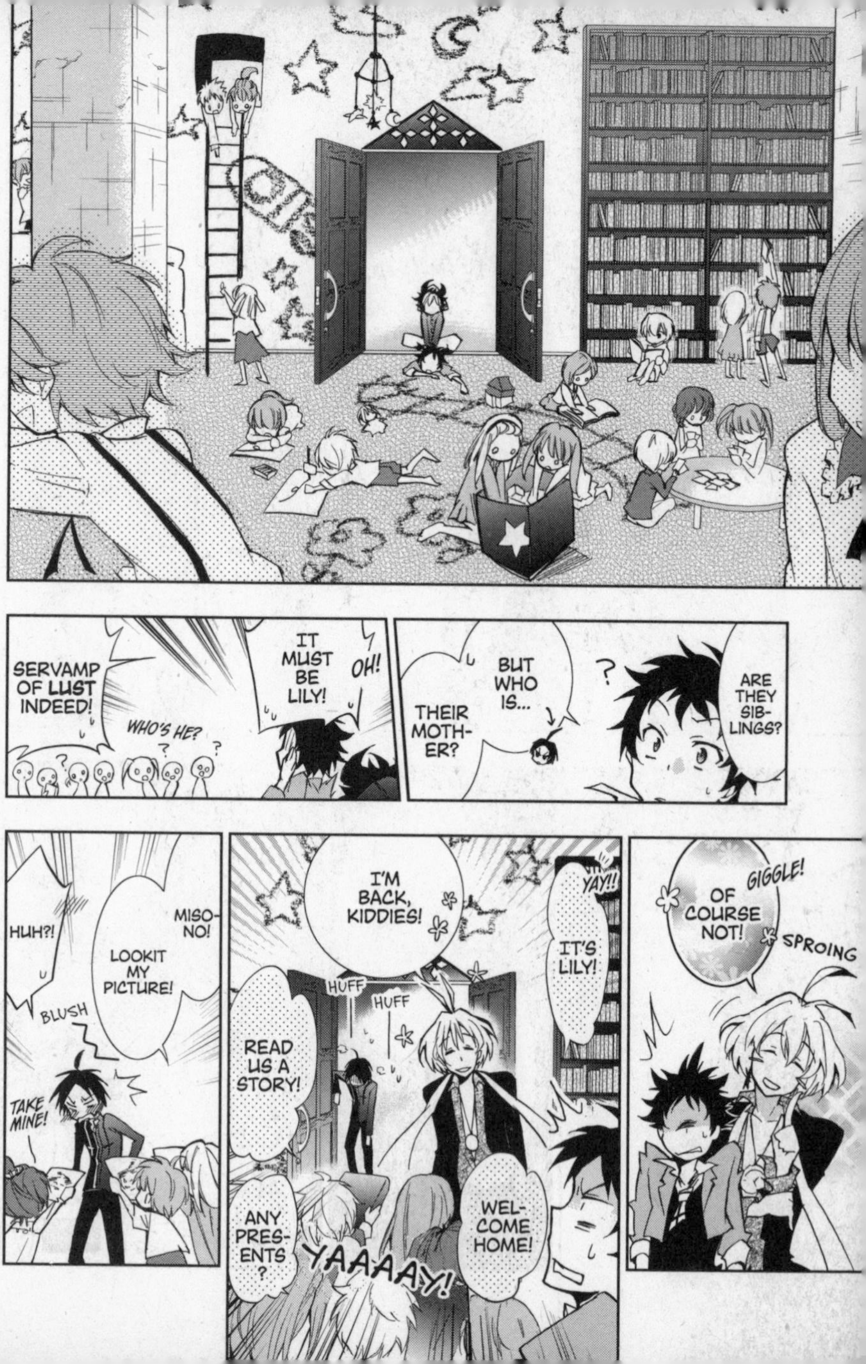
ARE THEY SIB-LINGS?
BUT WHO IS...
THEIR MOTHER?
OH!
IT MUST BE LILY!
SERVAMP OF LUST INDEED!
WHO'S HE?
GIGGLE!
OF COURSE NOT!
SPROING
I'M BACK, KIDDIES!
YAY!!
IT'S LILY!
HUFF
HUFF
READ US A STORY!
WEL-COME HOME!
ANY PRES-ENTS?
YAAAAAY!
MISO-NO!
LOOKIT MY PICTURE!
HUH?!
BLUSH
TAKE MINE!

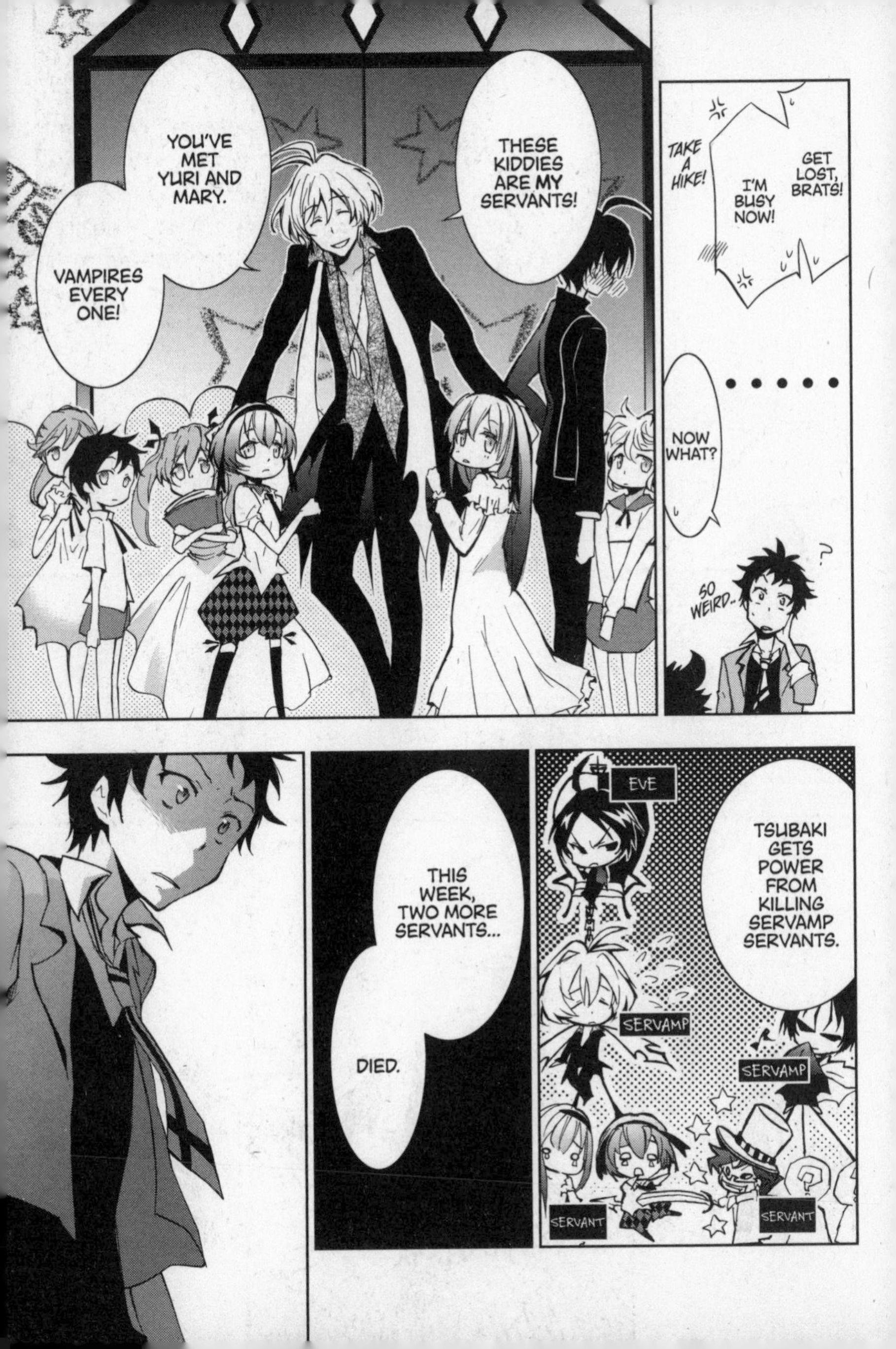

GET LOST, BRATS!
I'M BUSY NOW!
TAKE A HIKE!
.....
NOW WHAT?
SO WEIRD...
THESE KIDDIES ARE MY SERVANTS!
YOU'VE MET YURI AND MARY.
VAMPIRES EVERY ONE!
EVE
TSUBAKI GETS POWER FROM KILLING SERVAMP SERVANTS.
SERVAMP
SERVAMP
SERVANT
SERVANT
THIS WEEK, TWO MORE SERVANTS...
DIED.

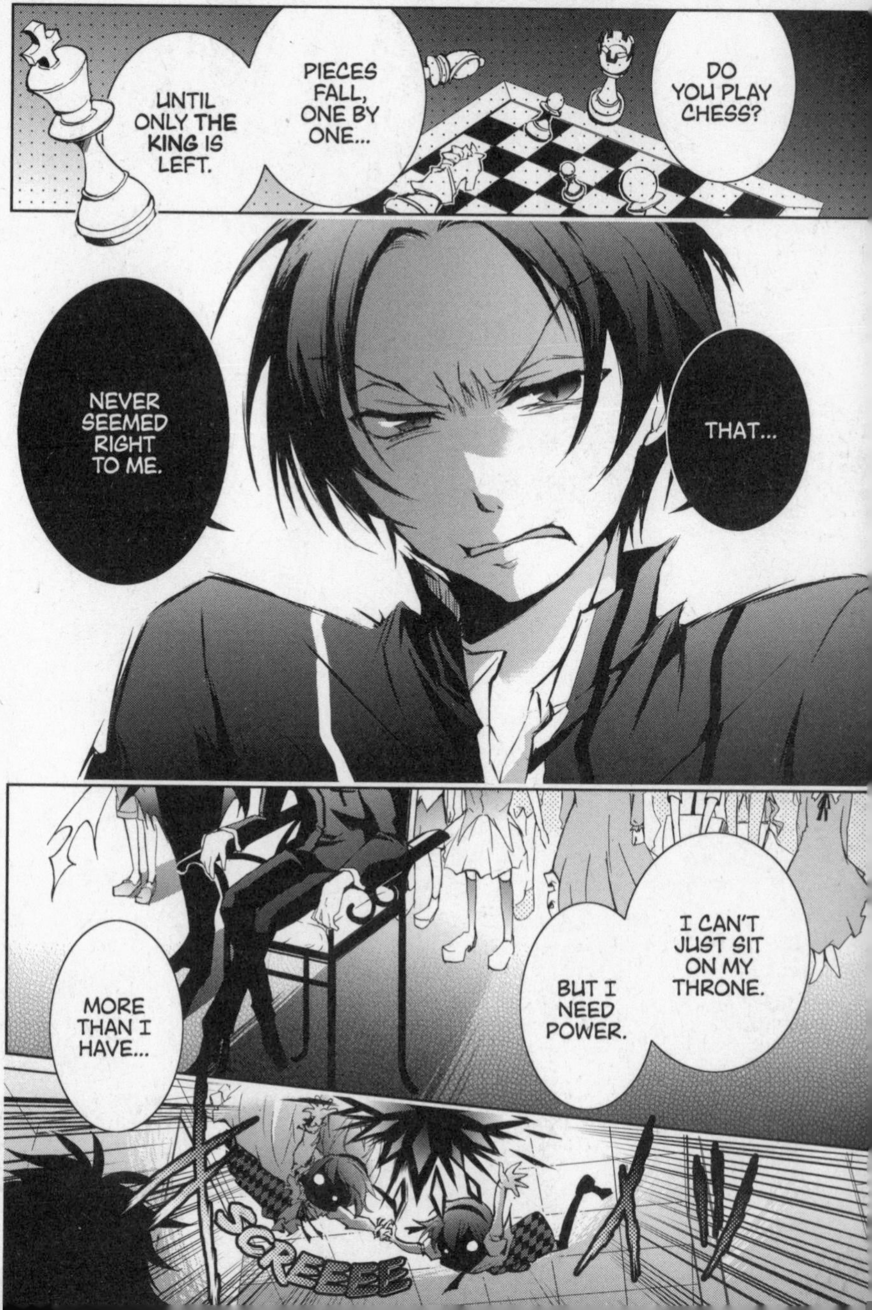
DO YOU PLAY CHESS?
PIECES FALL, ONE BY ONE...
UNTIL ONLY THE KING IS LEFT.
THAT...
NEVER SEEMED RIGHT TO ME.
I CAN'T JUST SIT ON MY THRONE.
BUT I NEED POWER.
MORE THAN I HAVE...
SCREEEEE

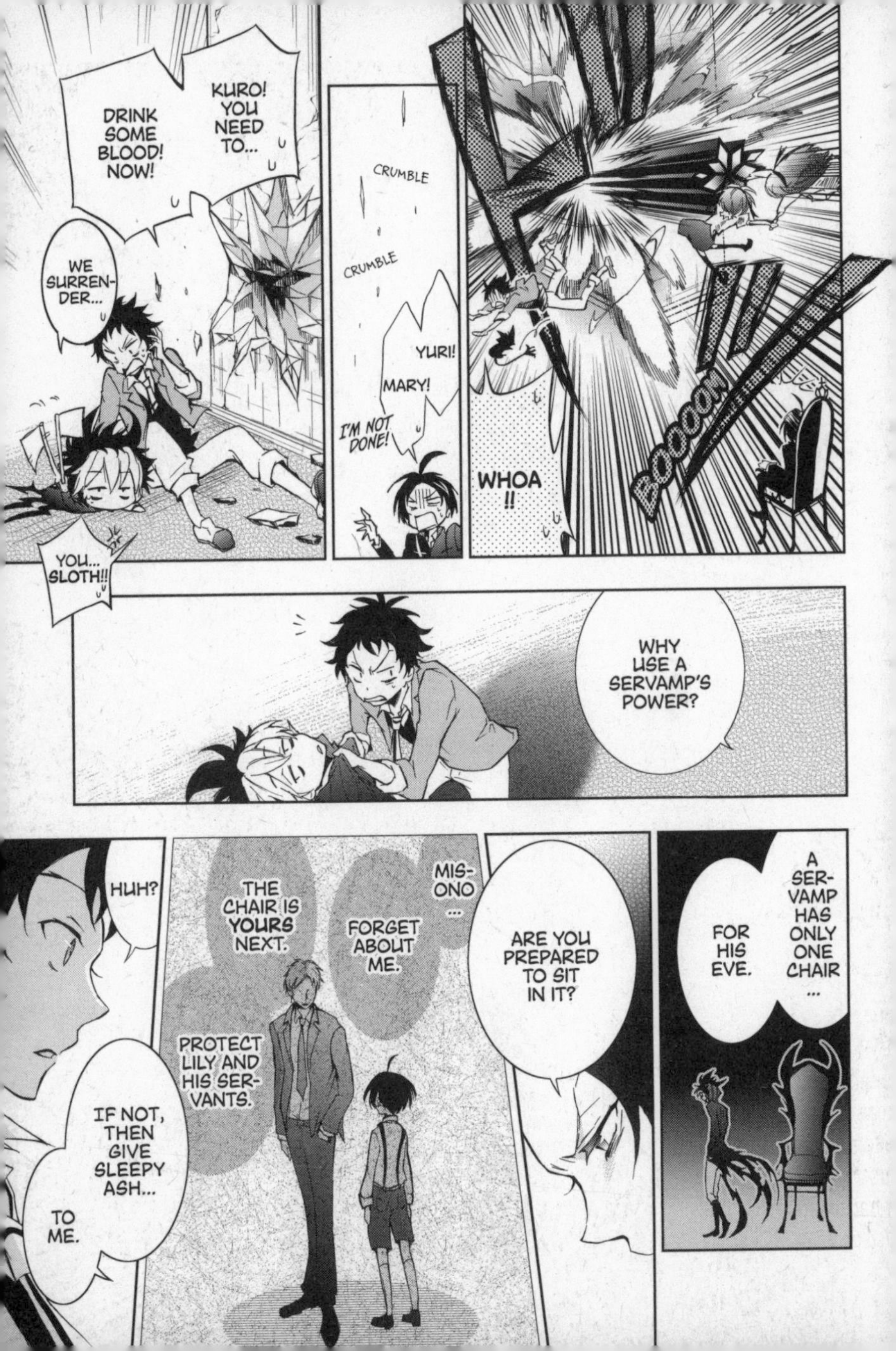
BOOOOM
WHOA!!
CRUMBLE
CRUMBLE
YURI!
MARY!
I'M NOT DONE!
KURO! YOU NEED TO...
DRINK SOME BLOOD! NOW!
WE SURRENDER...
YOU... SLOTH!!
WHY USE A SERVAMP'S POWER?
A SERVAMP HAS ONLY ONE CHAIR...
FOR HIS EVE.
ARE YOU PREPARED TO SIT IN IT?
MISONO...
FORGET ABOUT ME.
THE CHAIR IS YOURS NEXT.
PROTECT LILY AND HIS SERVANTS.
HUH?
IF NOT, THEN GIVE SLEEPY ASH...
TO ME.

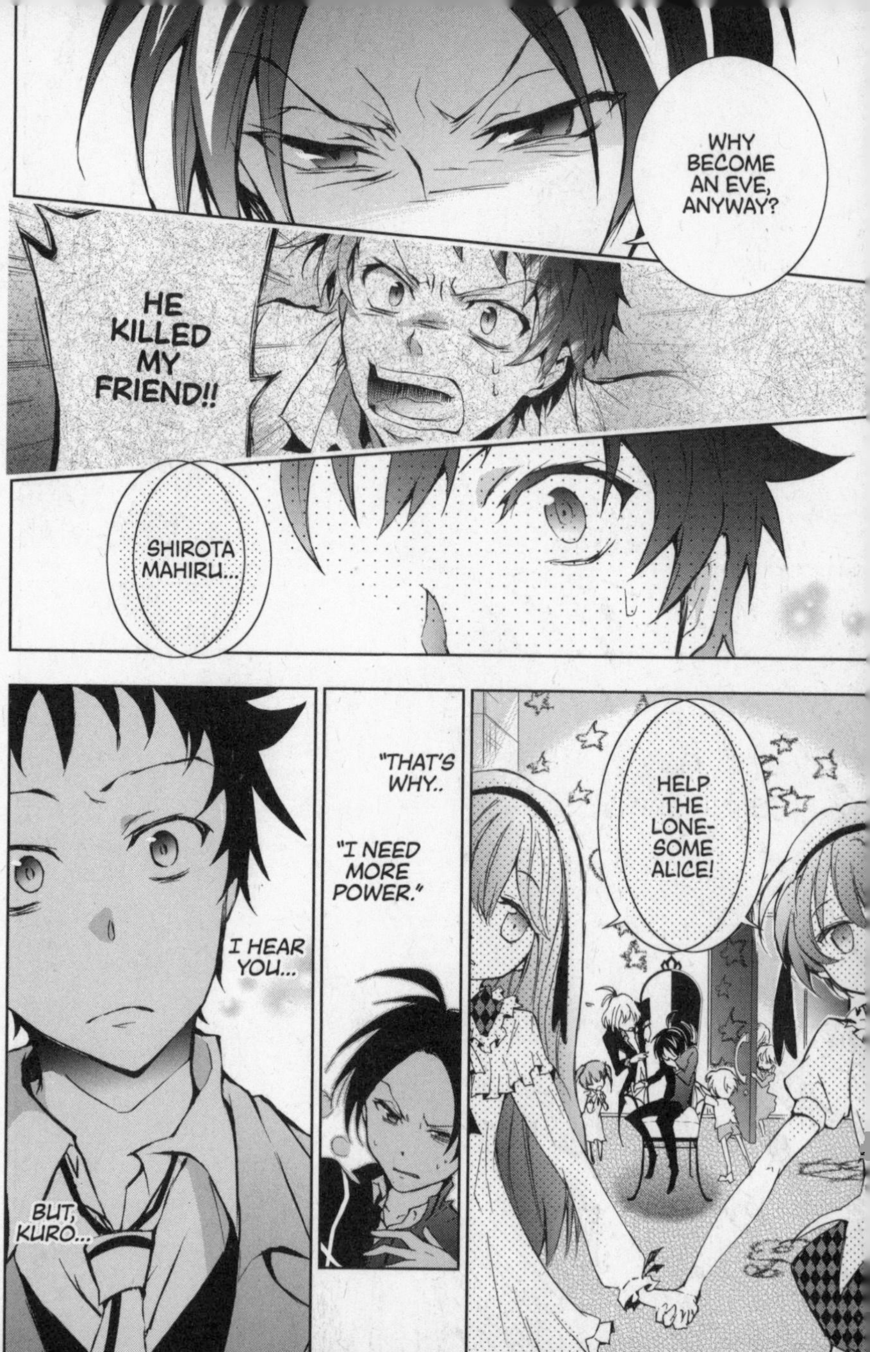
WHY BECOME AN EVE, ANYWAY?
HE KILLED MY FRIEND!!
SHIROTA MAHIRU...
HELP THE LONE-SOME ALICE!
"THAT'S WHY..
"I NEED MORE POWER."
I HEAR YOU...
BUT, KURO...

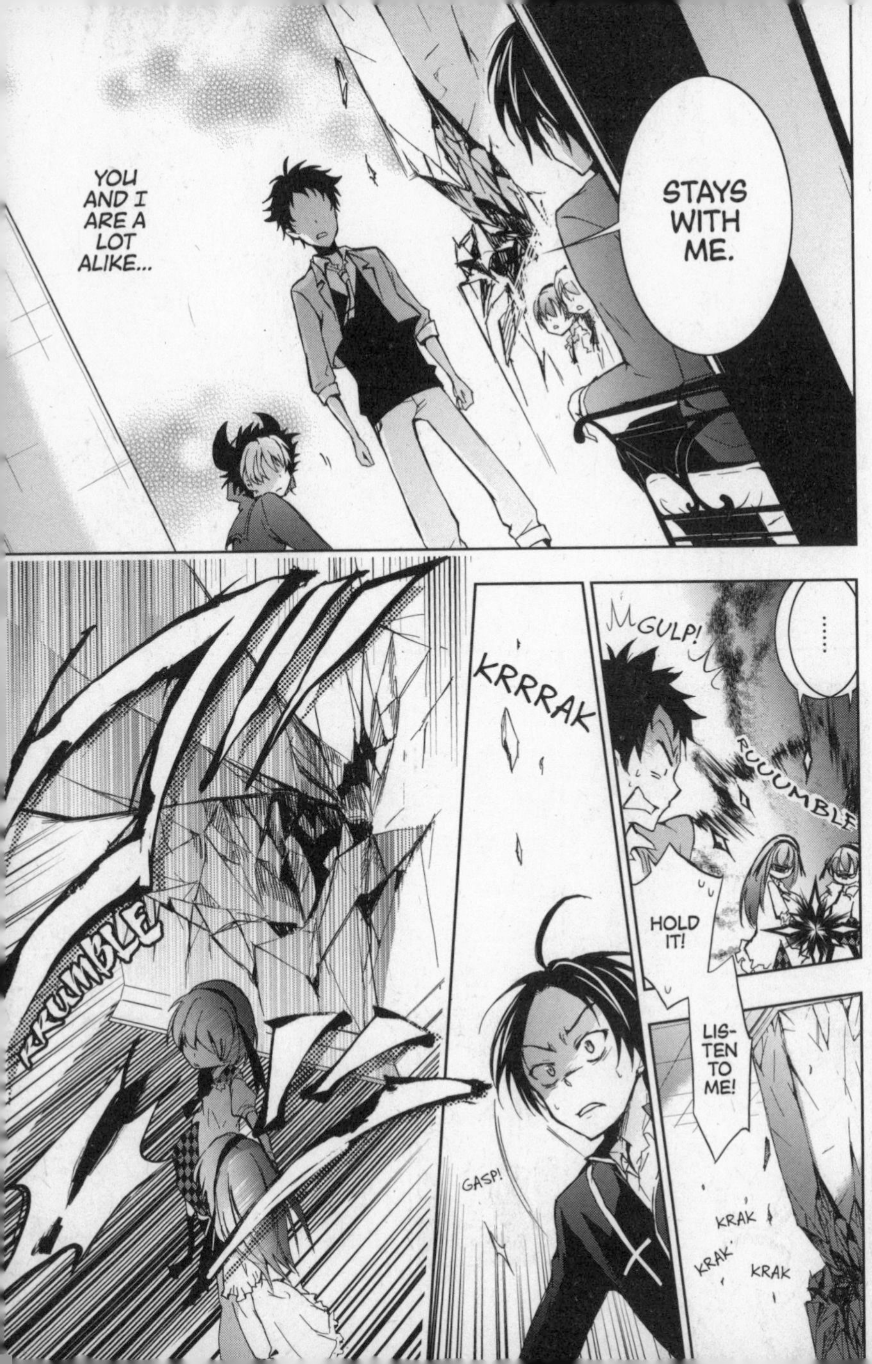
STAYS WITH ME.
YOU AND I ARE A LOT ALIKE...
......
GULP!
RUUUMBLE
HOLD IT!
LIS-TEN TO ME!
KRAK
KRAK
KRAK
KRRRAK
GASP!
KRUMBLE

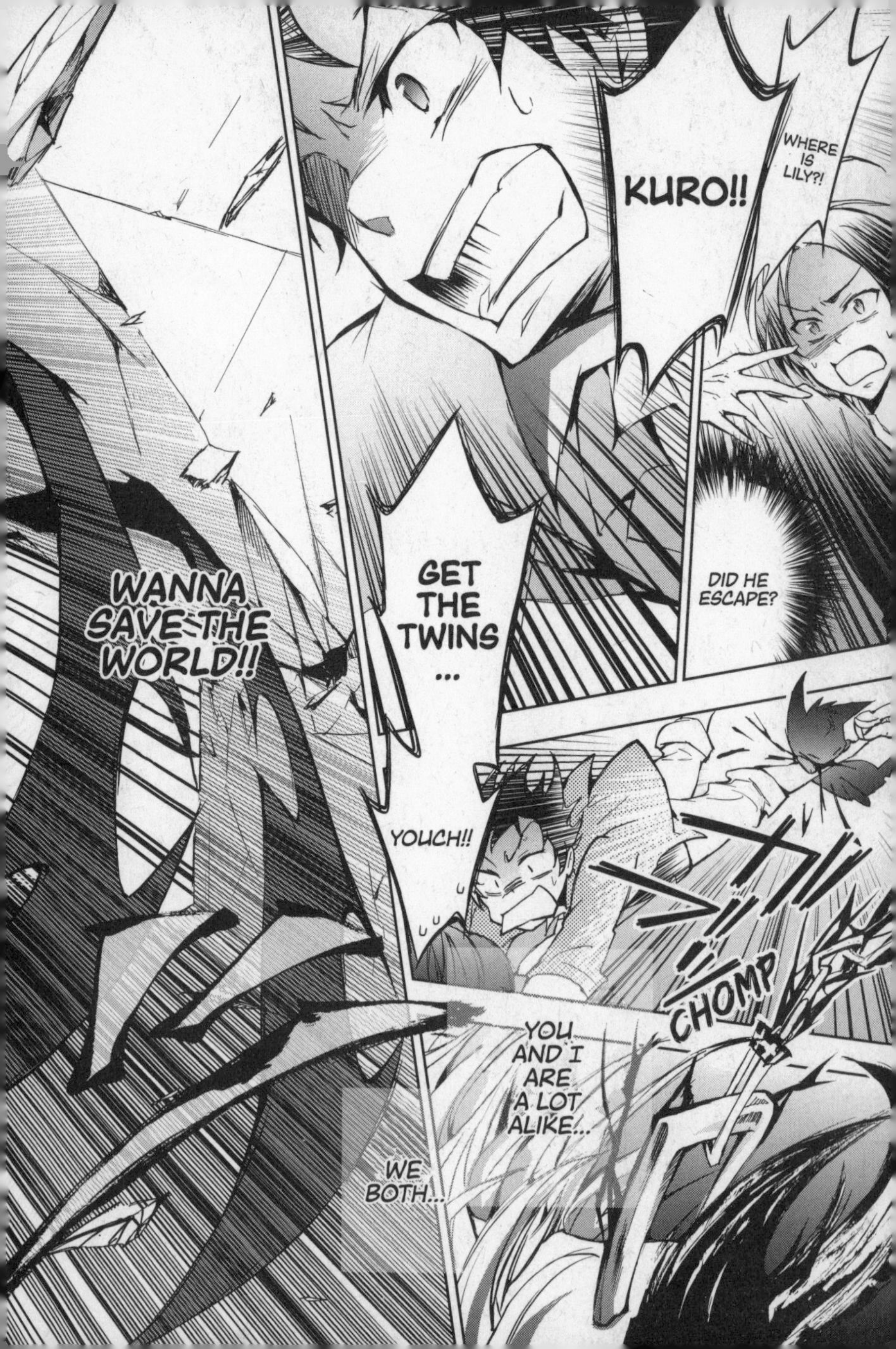
WHERE IS LILY?!
KURO!!
DID HE ESCAPE?
YOUCH!!
CHOMP
GET THE TWINS...
YOU AND I ARE A LOT ALIKE...
WE BOTH...
WANNA SAVE THE WORLD!!

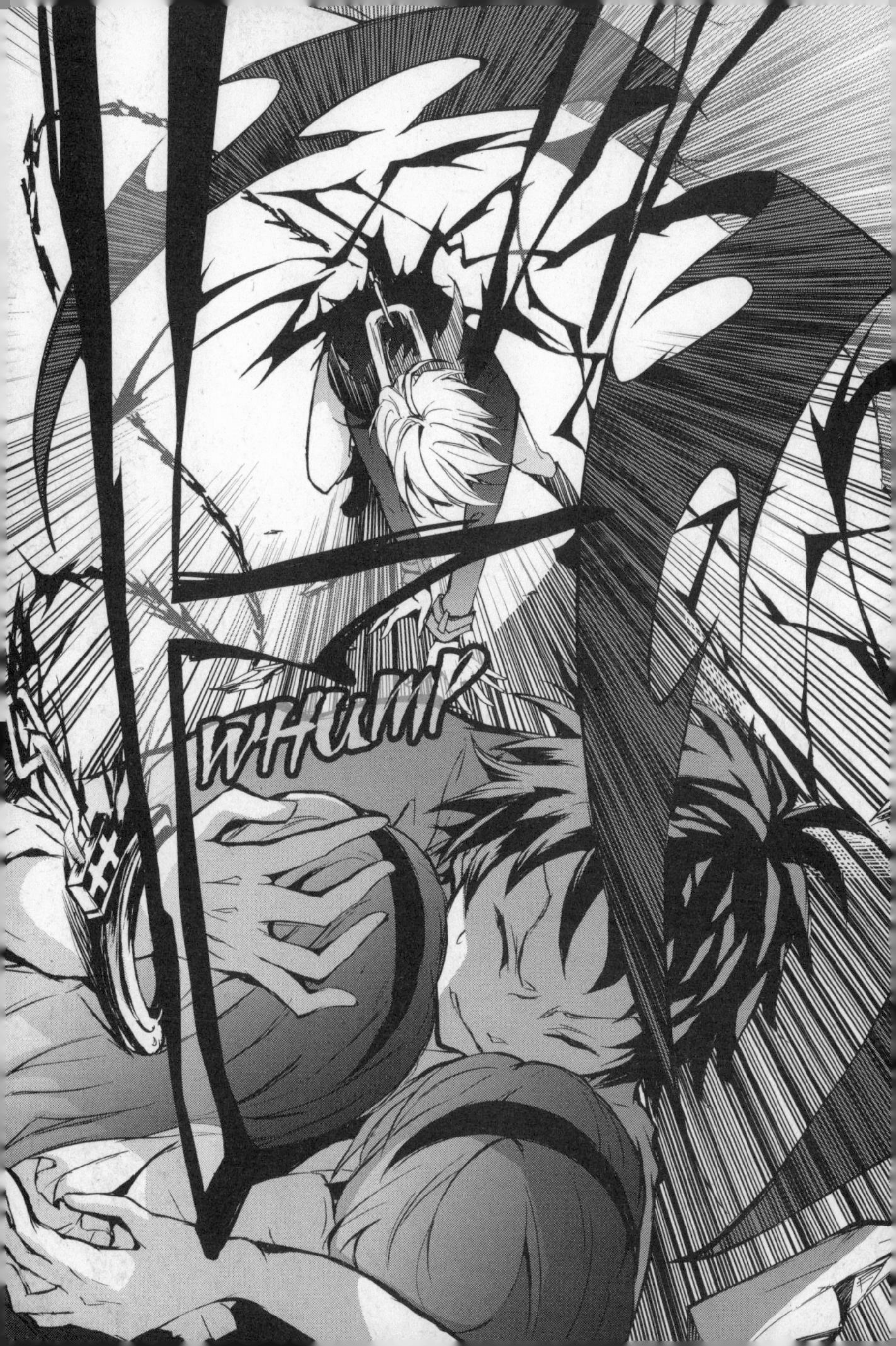
WHUMP

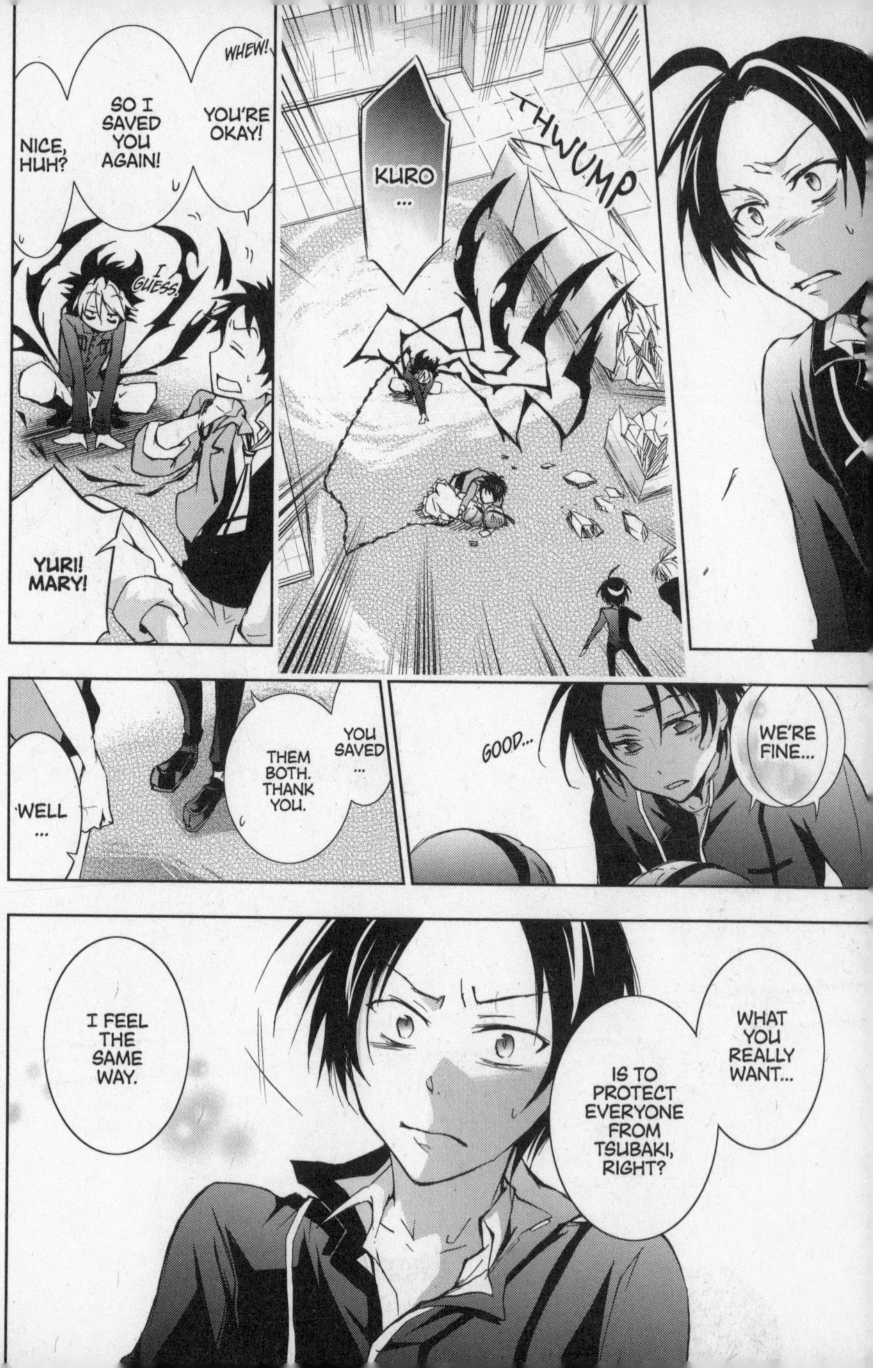
THWUMP
KURO...
WHEW!
YOU'RE OKAY!
SO I SAVED YOU AGAIN!
NICE, HUH?
I GUESS.
YURI! MARY!
WE'RE FINE...
GOOD...
YOU SAVED...
THEM BOTH. THANK YOU.
WELL...
WHAT YOU REALLY WANT...
IS TO PROTECT EVERYONE FROM TSUBAKI, RIGHT?
I FEEL THE SAME WAY.

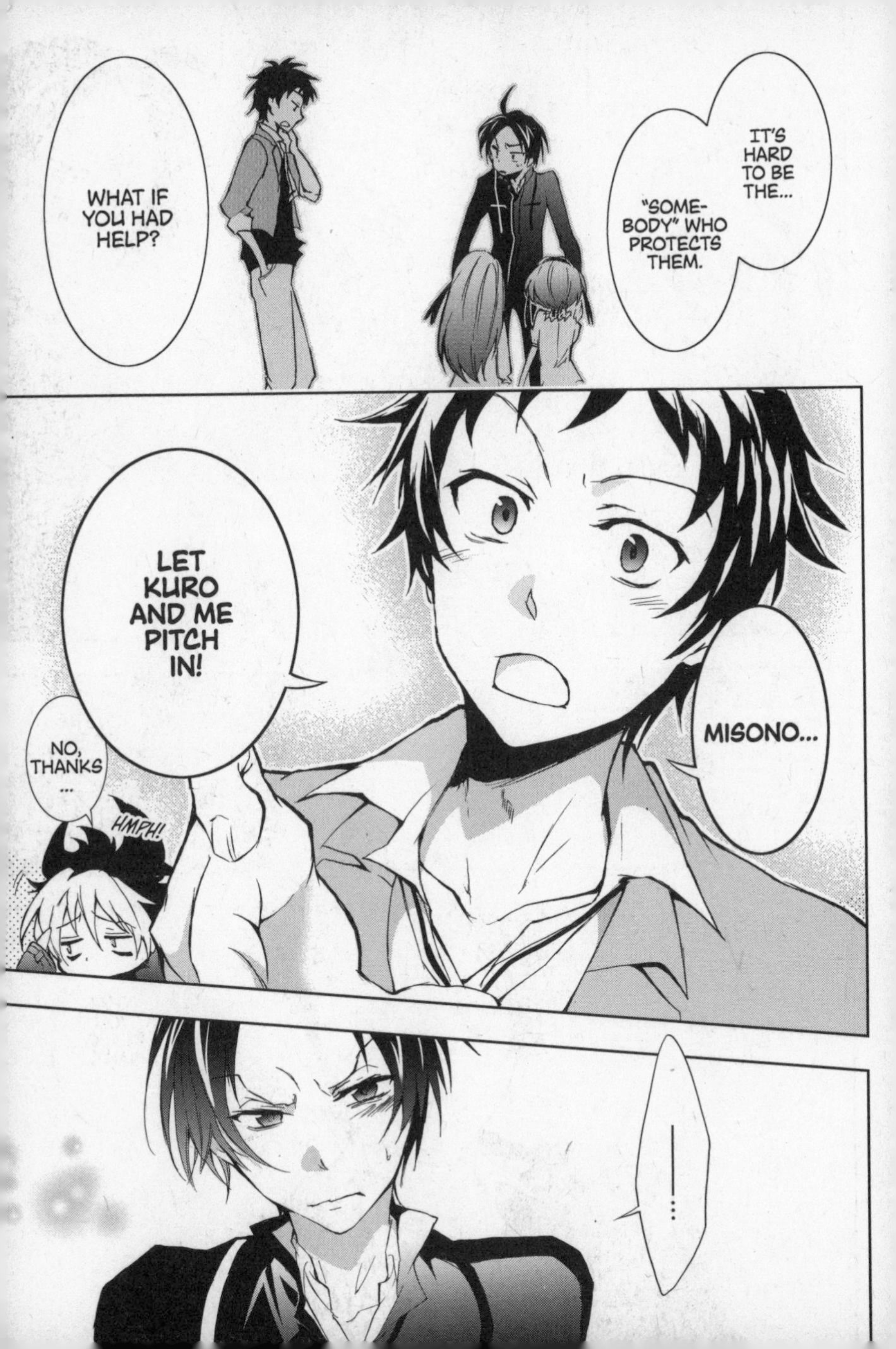
IT'S HARD TO BE THE... "SOME-BODY" WHO PROTECTS THEM.
WHAT IF YOU HAD HELP?
MISONO...
LET KURO AND ME PITCH IN!
NO, THANKS...
HMPH!
......

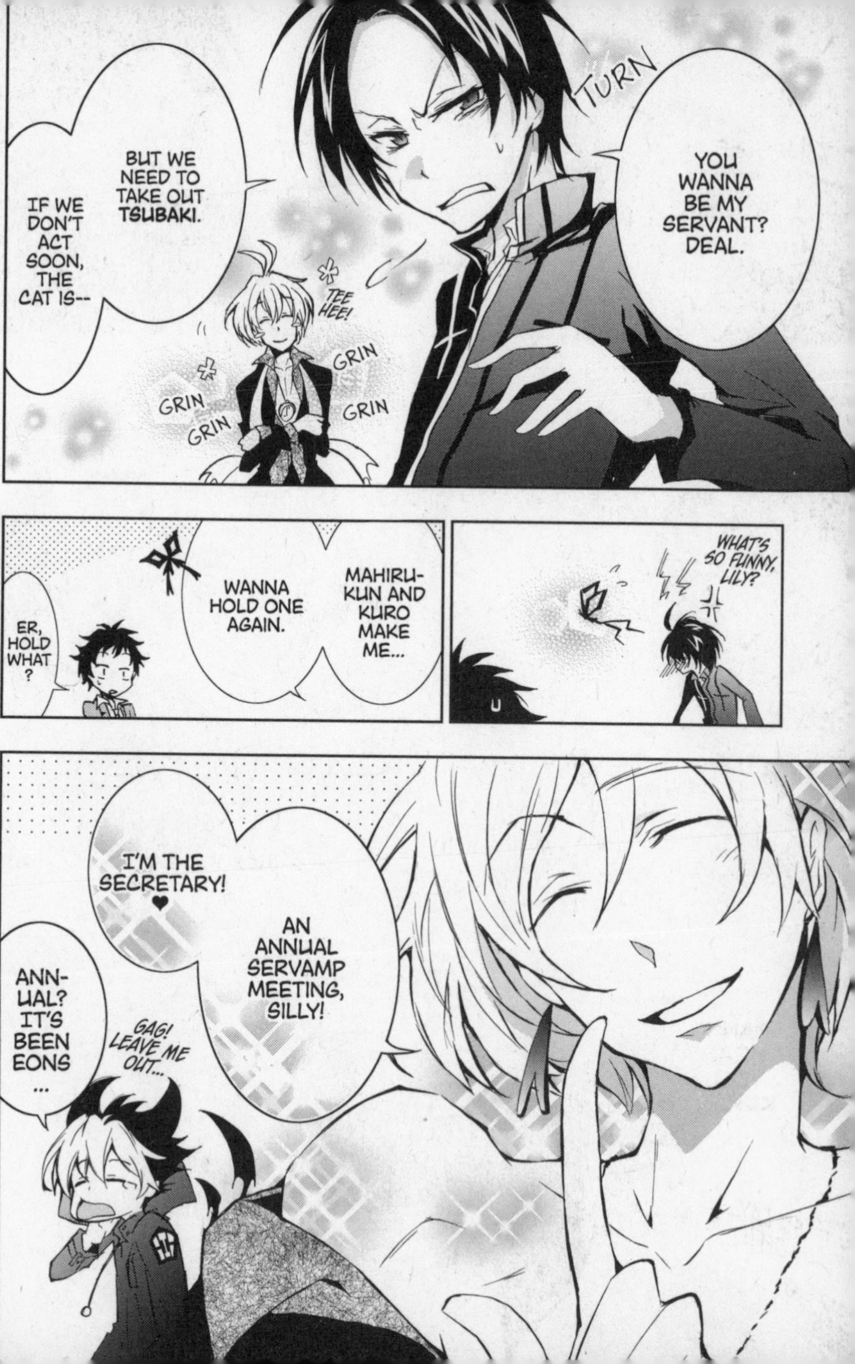

TURN
YOU WANNA BE MY SERVANT? DEAL.
TEE HEE!
GRIN
GRIN
GRIN
GRIN
BUT WE NEED TO TAKE OUT TSUBAKI.
IF WE DON'T ACT SOON, THE CAT IS--
WHAT'S SO FUNNY, LILY?
MAHIRU-KUN AND KURO MAKE ME...
WANNA HOLD ONE AGAIN.
ER, HOLD WHAT?
I'M THE SECRETARY! ♥
AN ANNUAL SERVAMP MEETING, SILLY!
ANN-UAL? IT'S BEEN EONS...
GAG! LEAVE ME OUT...

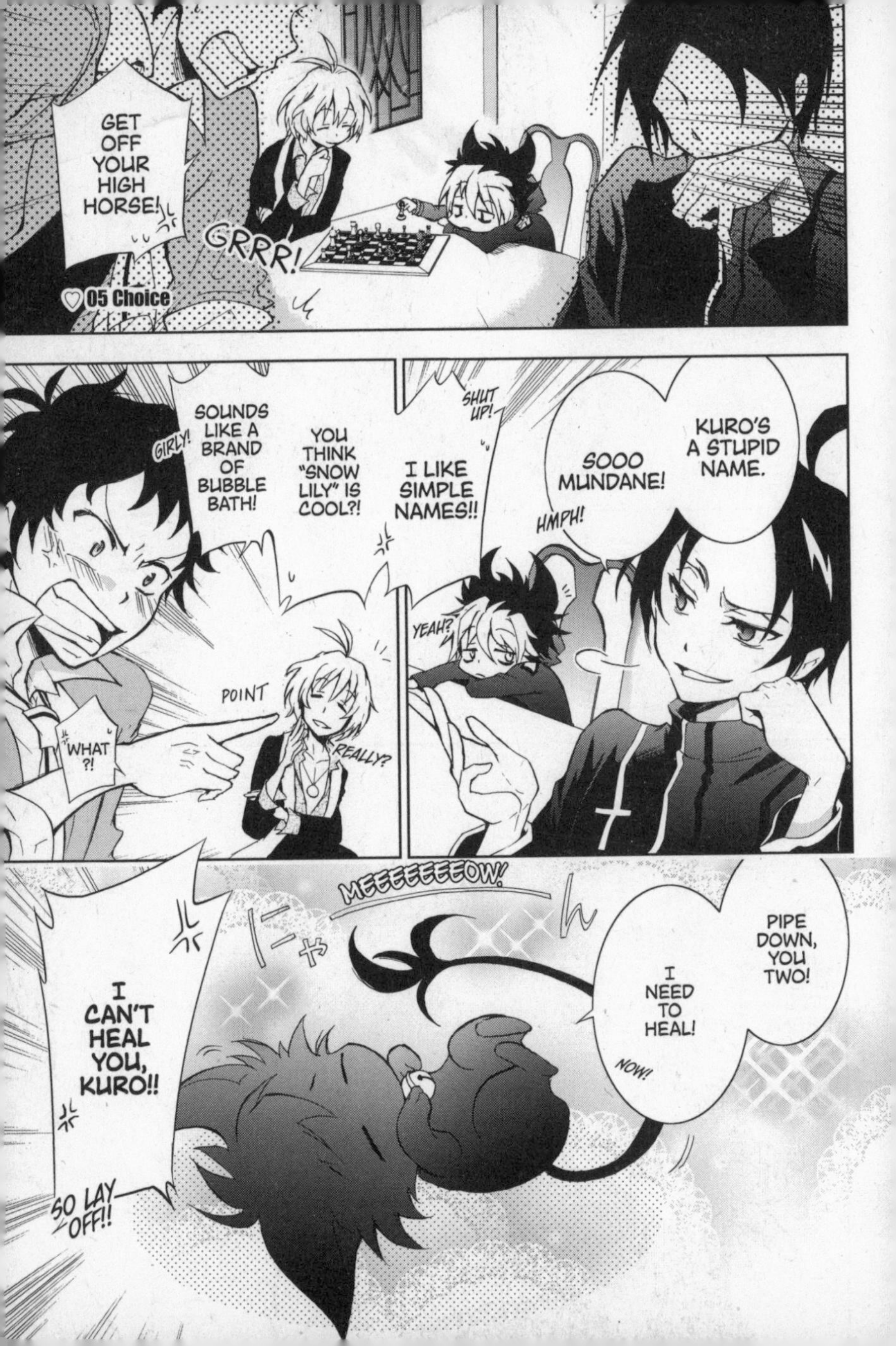
GET OFF YOUR HIGH HORSE!
GRRR!
05 Choice
KURO'S A STUPID NAME.
SOOO MUNDANE!
HMPH!
SHUT UP!
YEAH?
I LIKE SIMPLE NAMES!!
YOU THINK "SNOW LILY" IS COOL?!
SOUNDS LIKE A BRAND OF BUBBLE BATH!
GIRLY!
REALLY?
POINT
WHAT?!
PIPE DOWN, YOU TWO!
I NEED TO HEAL!
NOW!
MEEEEEEEOW!
I CAN'T HEAL YOU, KURO!!
SO LAY OFF!!

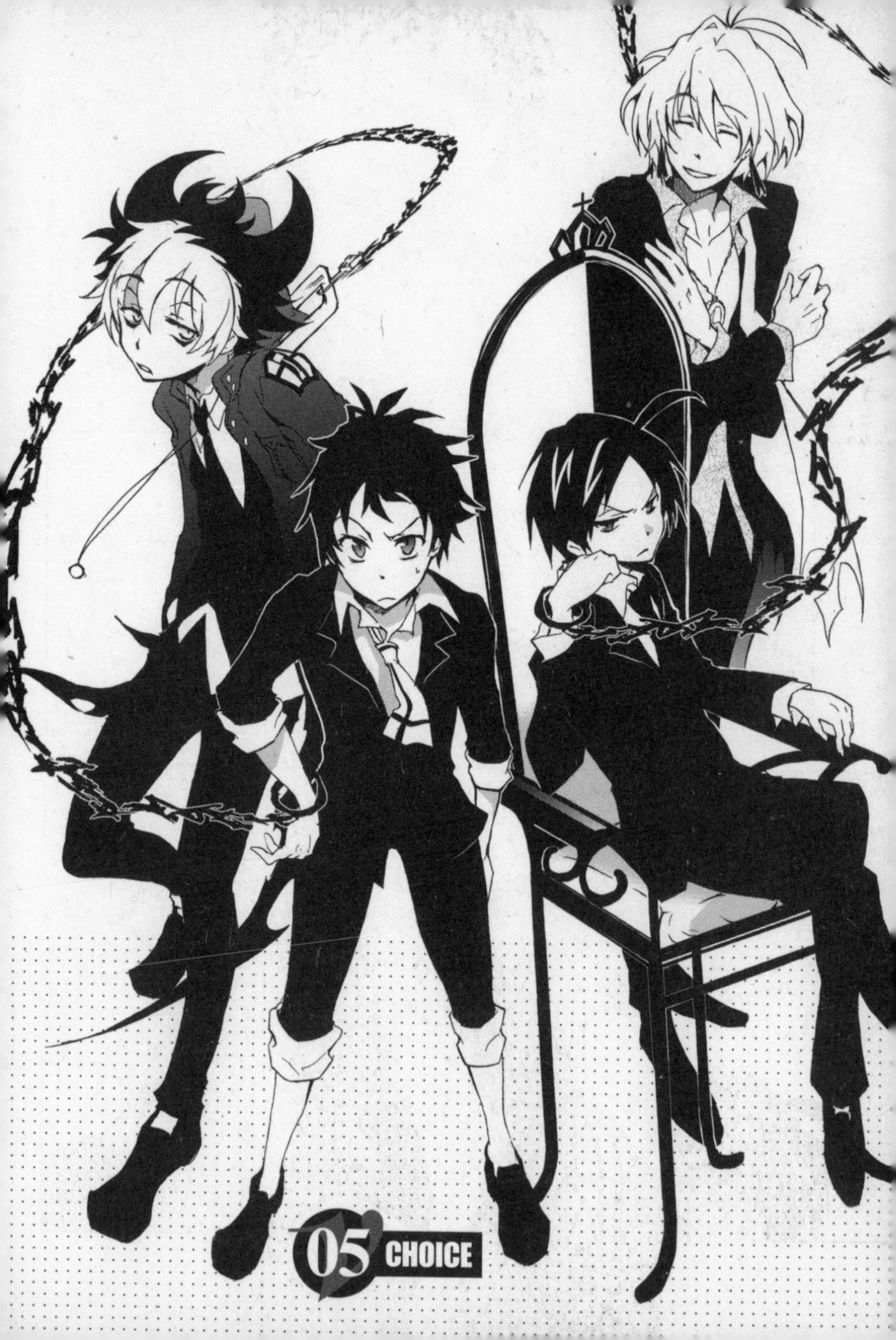
05 CHOICE

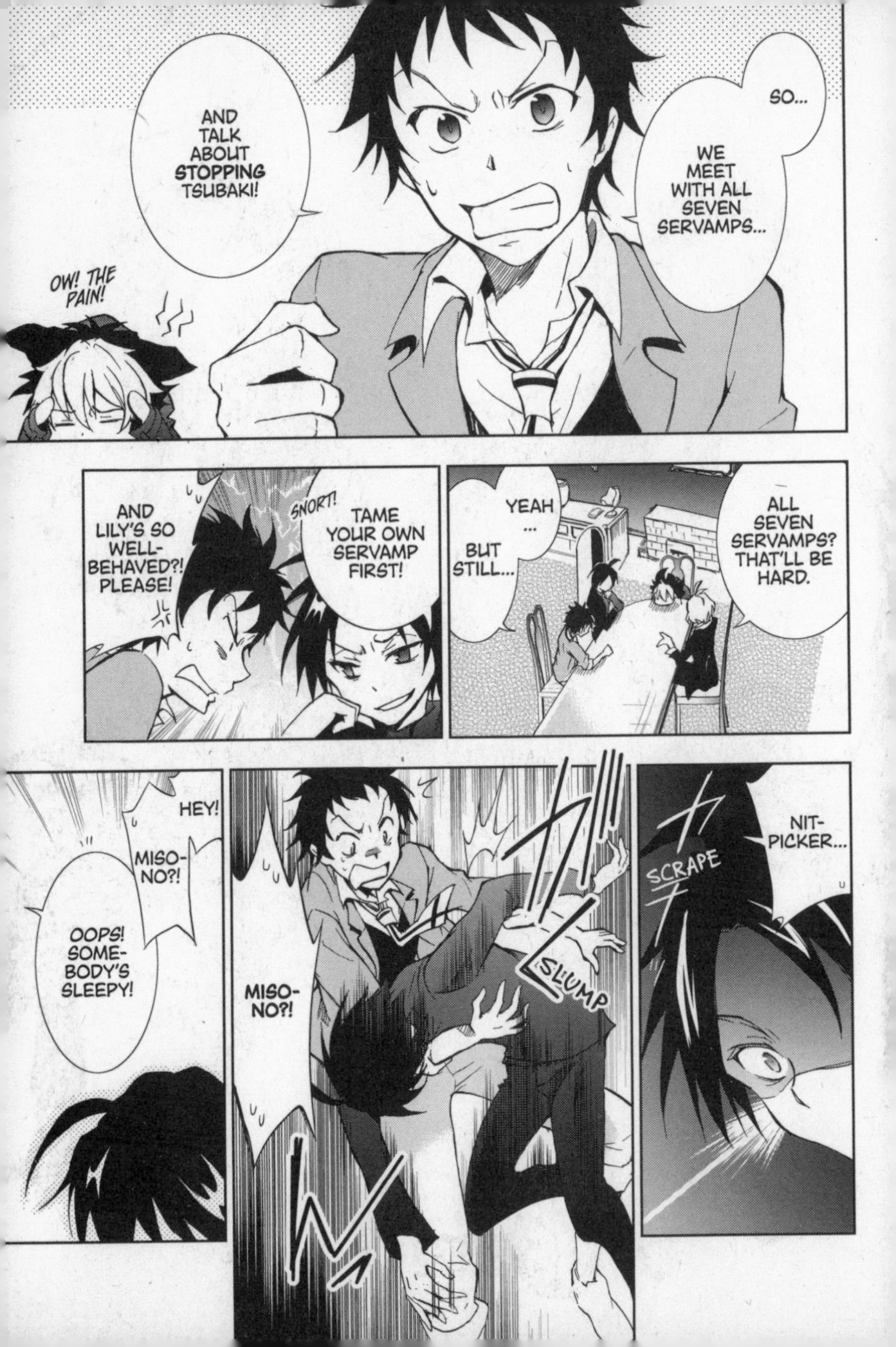
SO...
WE MEET WITH ALL SEVEN SERVAMPS...
AND TALK ABOUT STOPPING TSUBAKI!
OW! THE PAIN!
ALL SEVEN SERVAMPS? THAT'LL BE HARD.
YEAH ... BUT STILL...
TAME YOUR OWN SERVAMP FIRST!
SNORT!
AND LILY'S SO WELL-BEHAVED?! PLEASE!
NIT-PICKER...
SCRAPE
SLUMP
MISO-NO?!
HEY!
MISO-NO?!
OOPS! SOMEBODY'S SLEEPY!

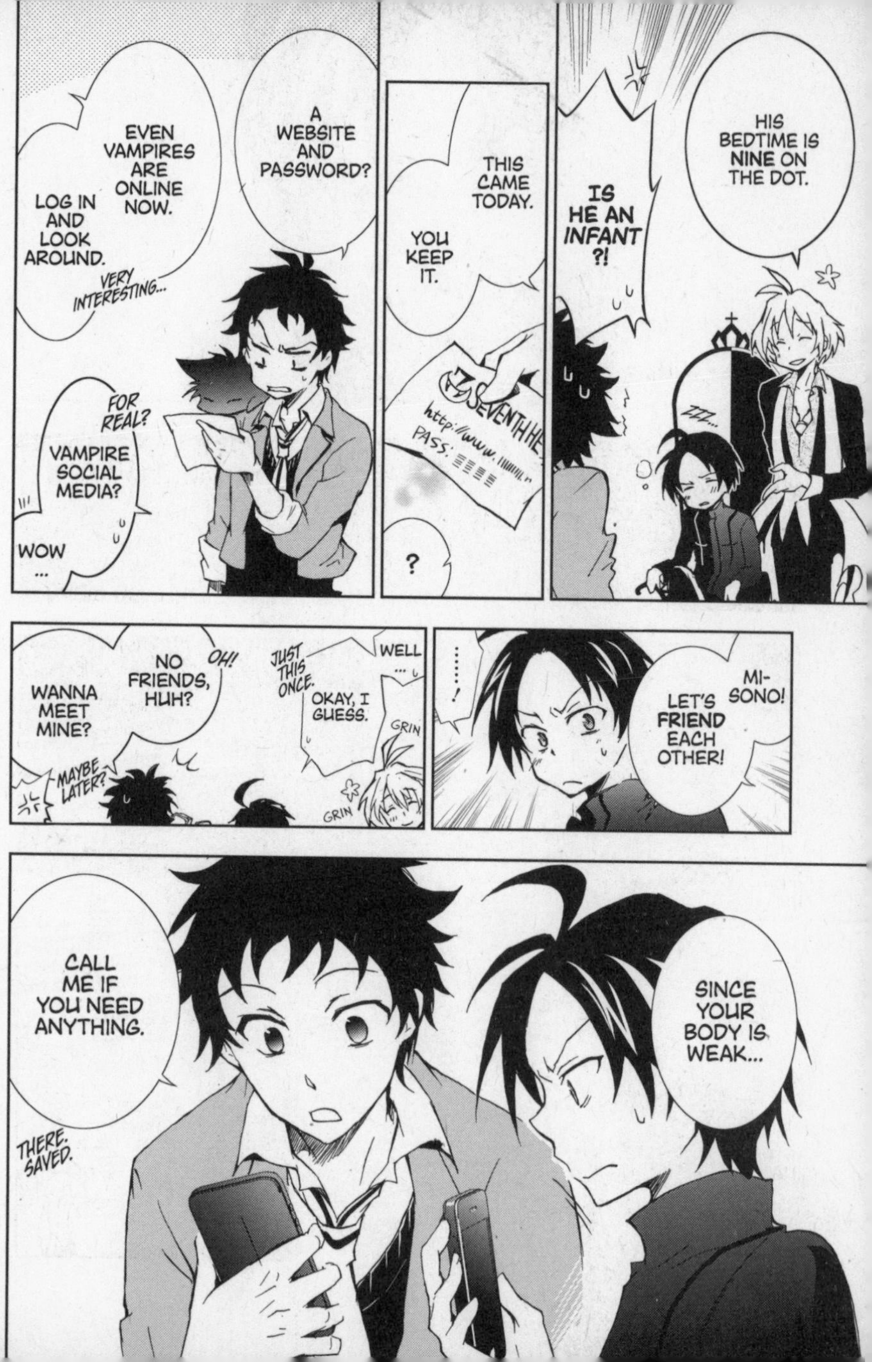
HIS BEDTIME IS NINE ON THE DOT.
IS HE AN INFANT?!
ZZZ...
THIS CAME TODAY.
YOU KEEP IT.
?
A WEBSITE AND PASSWORD?
EVEN VAMPIRES ARE ONLINE NOW.
LOG IN AND LOOK AROUND.
VERY INTERESTING...
FOR REAL? VAMPIRE SOCIAL MEDIA?
WOW ...
MI-SONO!
LET'S FRIEND EACH OTHER!
......!
WELL ...
OKAY, I GUESS.
JUST THIS ONCE.
GRIN
GRIN
OH!
NO FRIENDS, HUH?
WANNA MEET MINE?
MAYBE LATER?
SINCE YOUR BODY IS WEAK...
CALL ME IF YOU NEED ANYTHING.
THERE. SAVED.

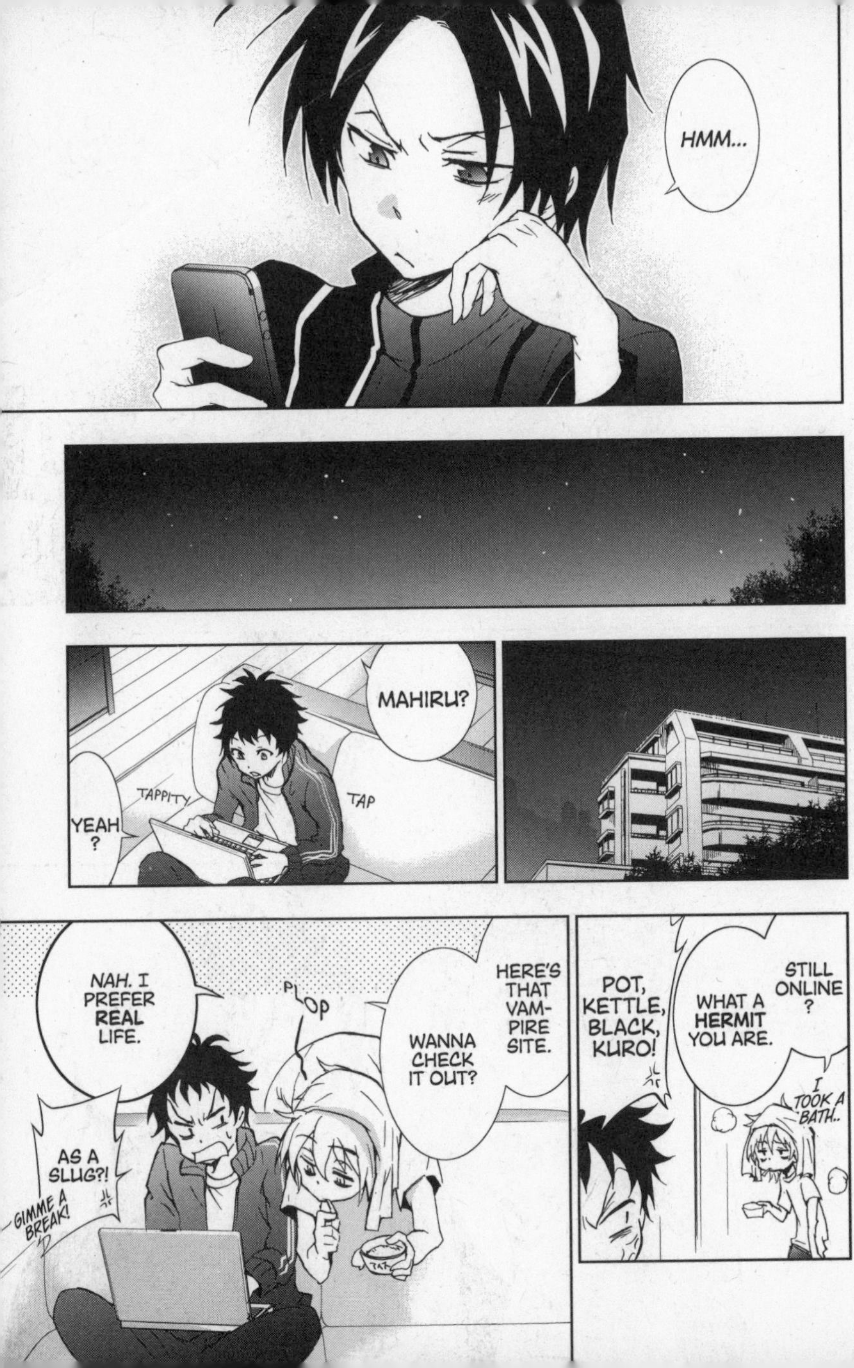
HMM...
MAHIRU?
TAPPITY
TAP
YEAH?
STILL ONLINE?
WHAT A HERMIT YOU ARE.
I TOOK A BATH..
POT, KETTLE, BLACK, KURO!
HERE'S THAT VAMPIRE SITE.
WANNA CHECK IT OUT?
PLOP
NAH. I PREFER REAL LIFE.
AS A SLUG?!
GIMME A BREAK!

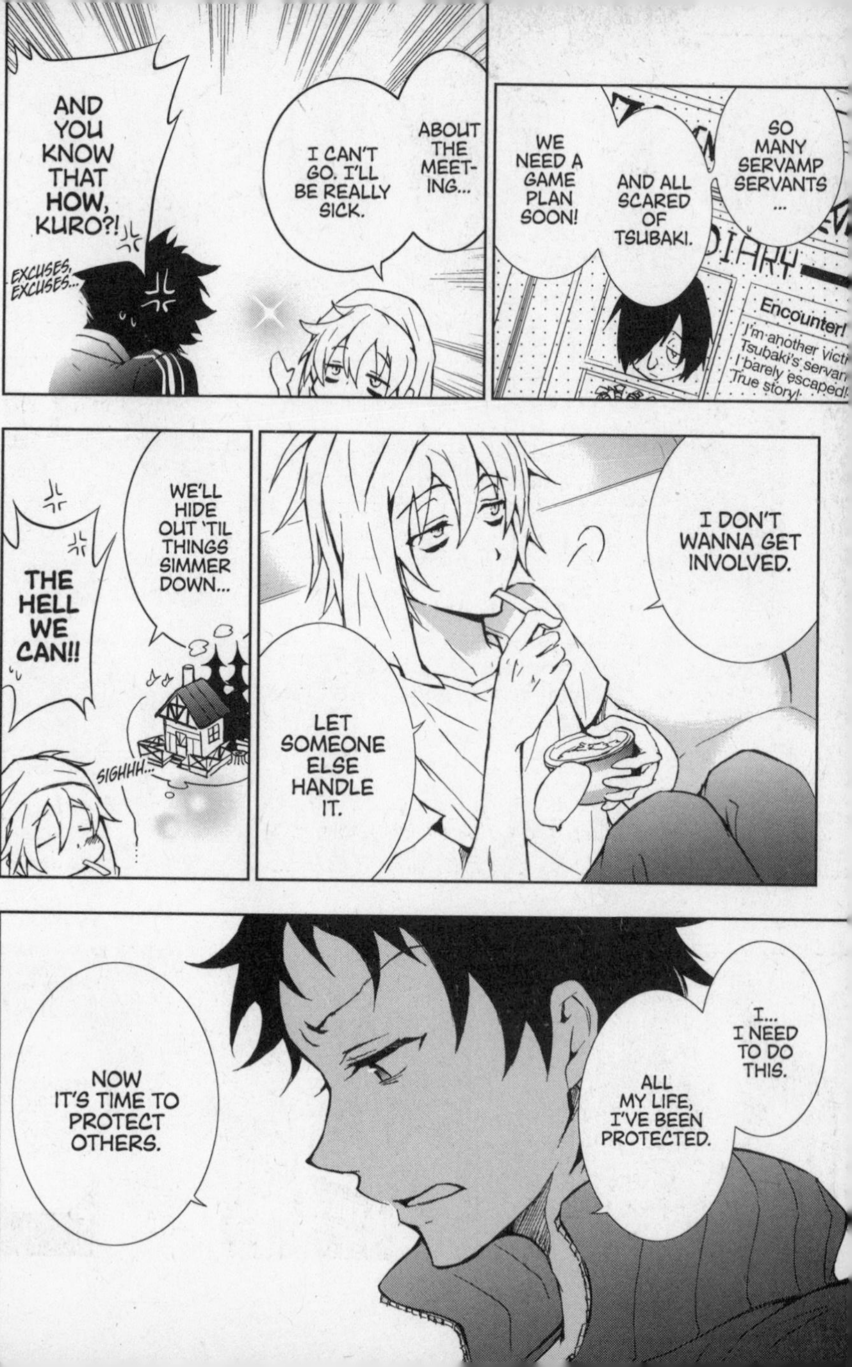
SO MANY SERVAMP SERVANTS ...
AND ALL SCARED OF TSUBAKI.
WE NEED A GAME PLAN SOON!
DIARY
Encounter!
I'm another victi
Tsubaki's servan
I barely escaped!
True story!
ABOUT THE MEET-ING...
I CAN'T GO. I'LL BE REALLY SICK.
AND YOU KNOW THAT HOW, KURO?!
EXCUSES, EXCUSES...
I DON'T WANNA GET INVOLVED.
LET SOMEONE ELSE HANDLE IT.
WE'LL HIDE OUT 'TIL THINGS SIMMER DOWN...
SIGHHH...
THE HELL WE CAN!!
I... I NEED TO DO THIS.
ALL MY LIFE, I'VE BEEN PROTECTED.
NOW IT'S TIME TO PROTECT OTHERS.

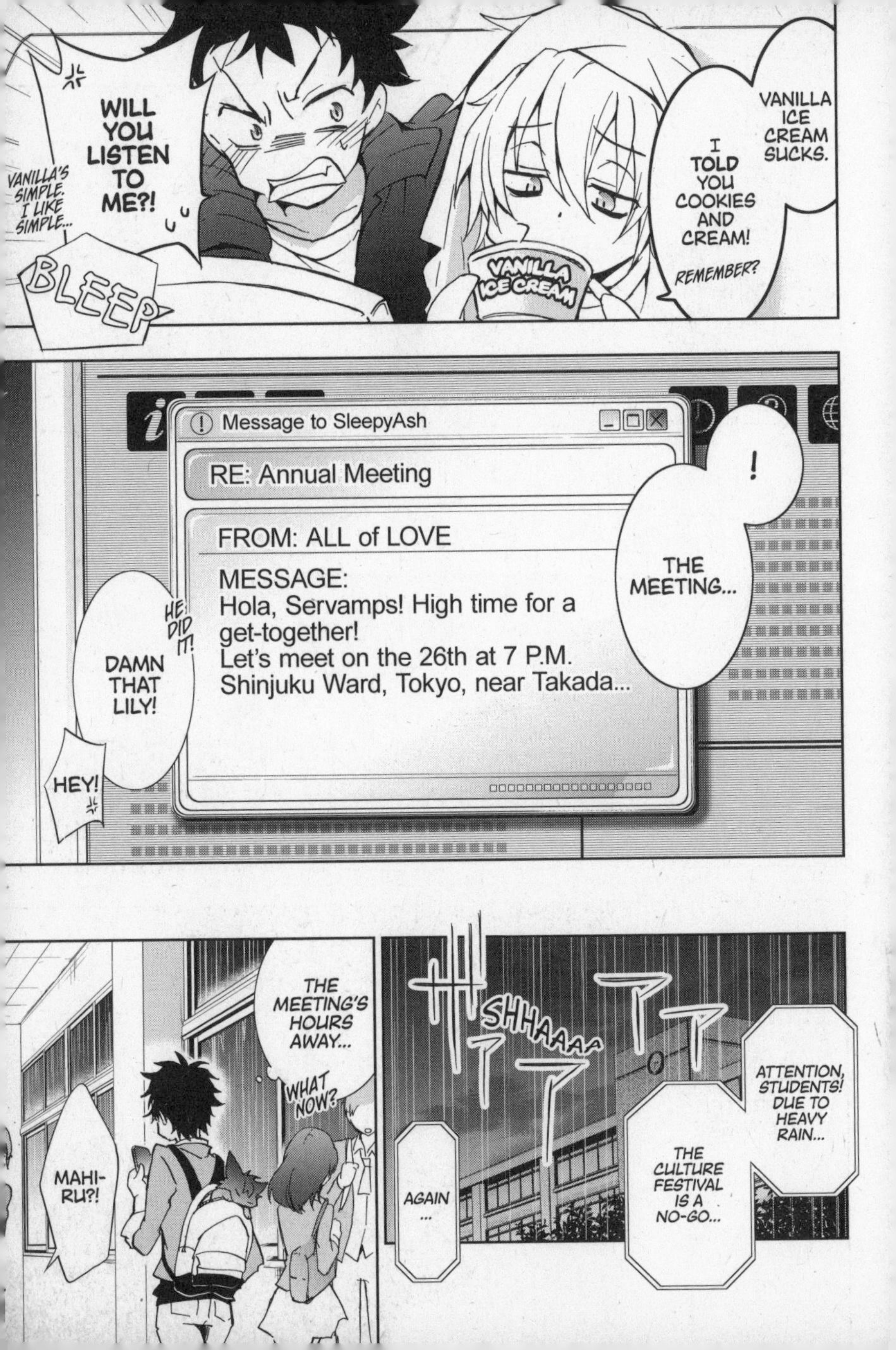
VANILLA ICE CREAM SUCKS.
I TOLD YOU COOKIES AND CREAM!
REMEMBER?
VANILLA ICE CREAM
WILL YOU LISTEN TO ME?!
VANILLA'S SIMPLE. I LIKE SIMPLE...
BLEEP
!
THE MEETING...
Message to SleepyAsh
RE: Annual Meeting
FROM: ALL of LOVE
MESSAGE:
Hola, Servamps! High time for a get-together!
Let's meet on the 26th at 7 P.M.
Shinjuku Ward, Tokyo, near Takada...
HE DID IT!
DAMN THAT LILY!
HEY!
SHHAAAAA
ATTENTION, STUDENTS! DUE TO HEAVY RAIN...
THE CULTURE FESTIVAL IS A NO-GO...
AGAIN...
THE MEETING'S HOURS AWAY...
WHAT NOW?
MAHIRU?!

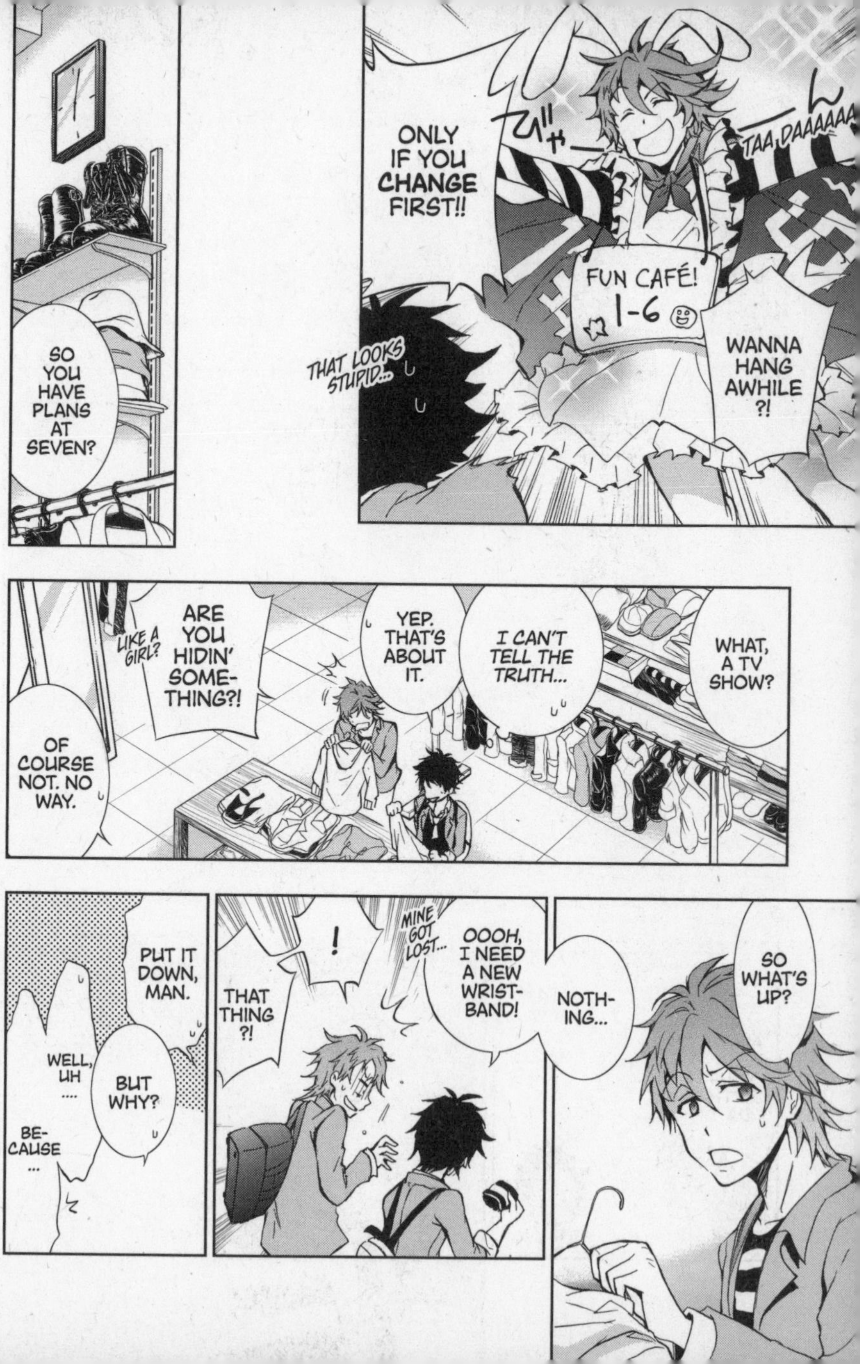
TAA DAAAAAA
FUN CAFÉ! 1-6
WANNA HANG AWHILE?!
THAT LOOKS STUPID...
ONLY IF YOU CHANGE FIRST!!
SO YOU HAVE PLANS AT SEVEN?
WHAT, A TV SHOW?
I CAN'T TELL THE TRUTH...
YEP. THAT'S ABOUT IT.
ARE YOU HIDIN' SOME-THING?!
LIKE A GIRL?
OF COURSE NOT. NO WAY.
SO WHAT'S UP?
NOTH-ING...
OOOH, I NEED A NEW WRIST-BAND!
MINE GOT LOST...
!
THAT THING?!
PUT IT DOWN, MAN.
BUT WHY?
WELL, UH ....
BE-CAUSE ...

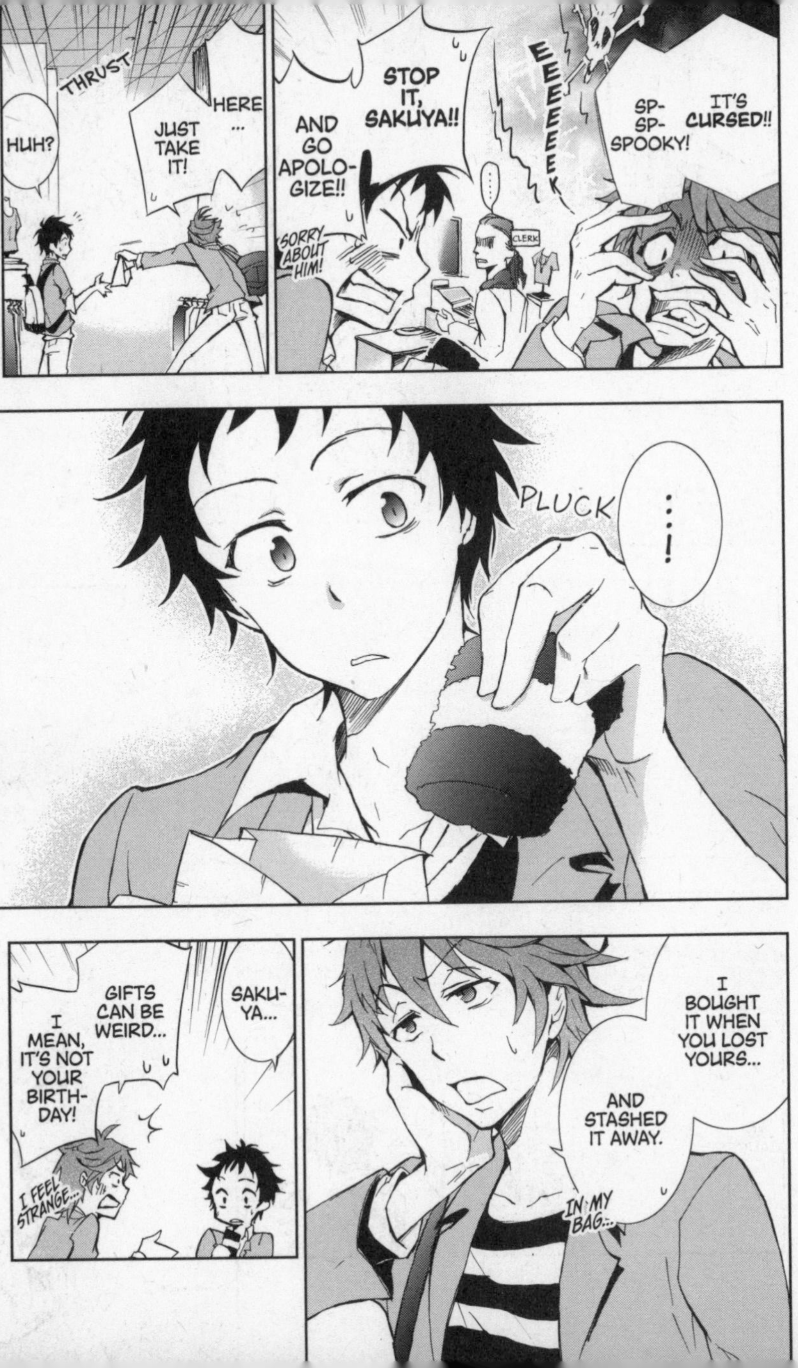
IT'S CURSED!!
SP- SP- SPOOKY!
EEEEEEEK
...
STOP IT, SAKUYA!!
AND GO APOLO-GIZE!!
SORRY ABOUT HIM!
CLERK
HERE...
JUST TAKE IT!
THRUST
HUH?
...!
PLUCK
I BOUGHT IT WHEN YOU LOST YOURS...
AND STASHED IT AWAY.
IN MY BAG...
SAKU-YA...
GIFTS CAN BE WEIRD...
I MEAN, IT'S NOT YOUR BIRTH-DAY!
I FEEL STRANGE...

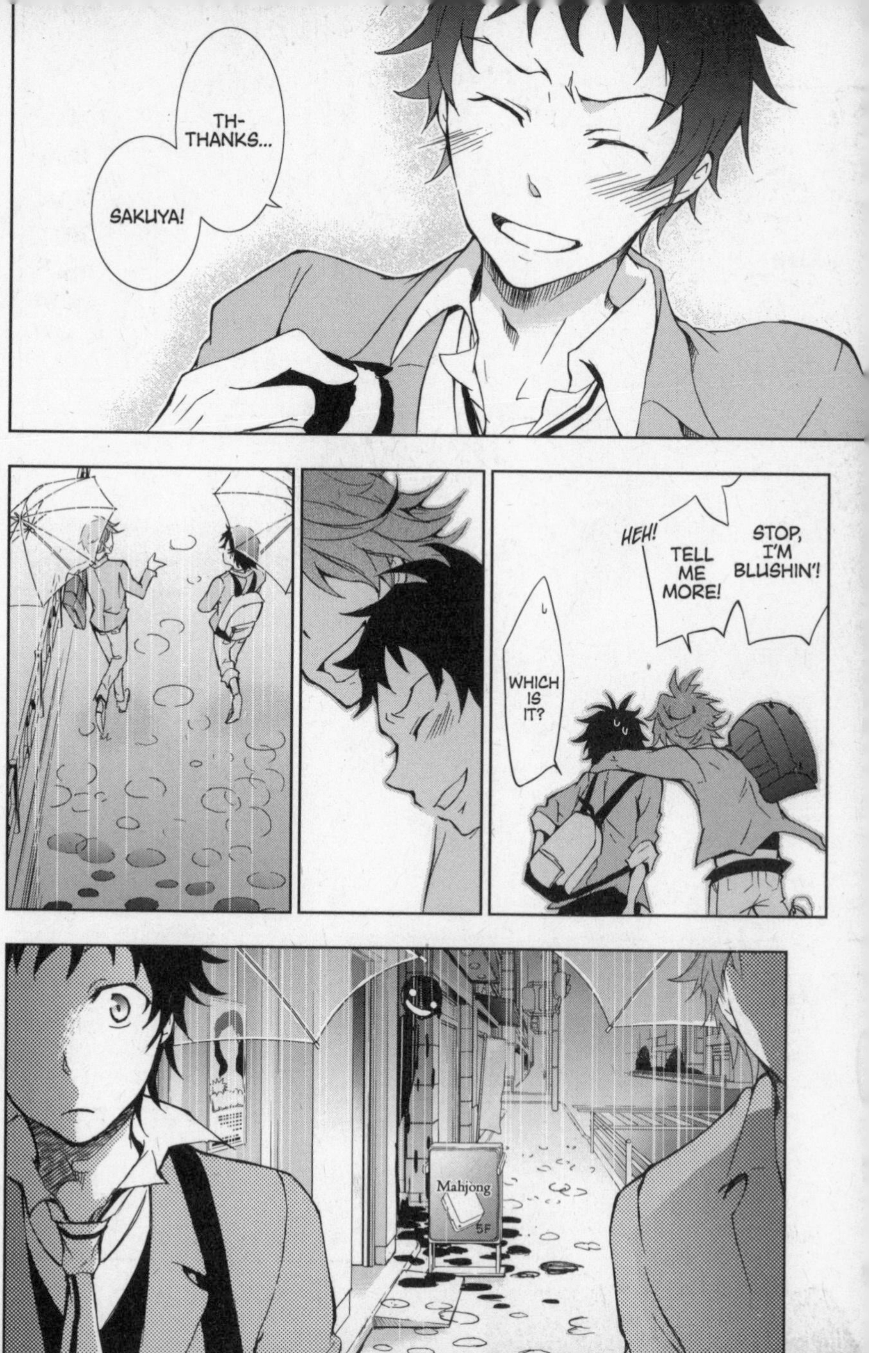
TH- THANKS...
SAKUYA!
STOP, I'M BLUSHIN'!
HEH! TELL ME MORE!
WHICH IS IT?
Mahjong
5F

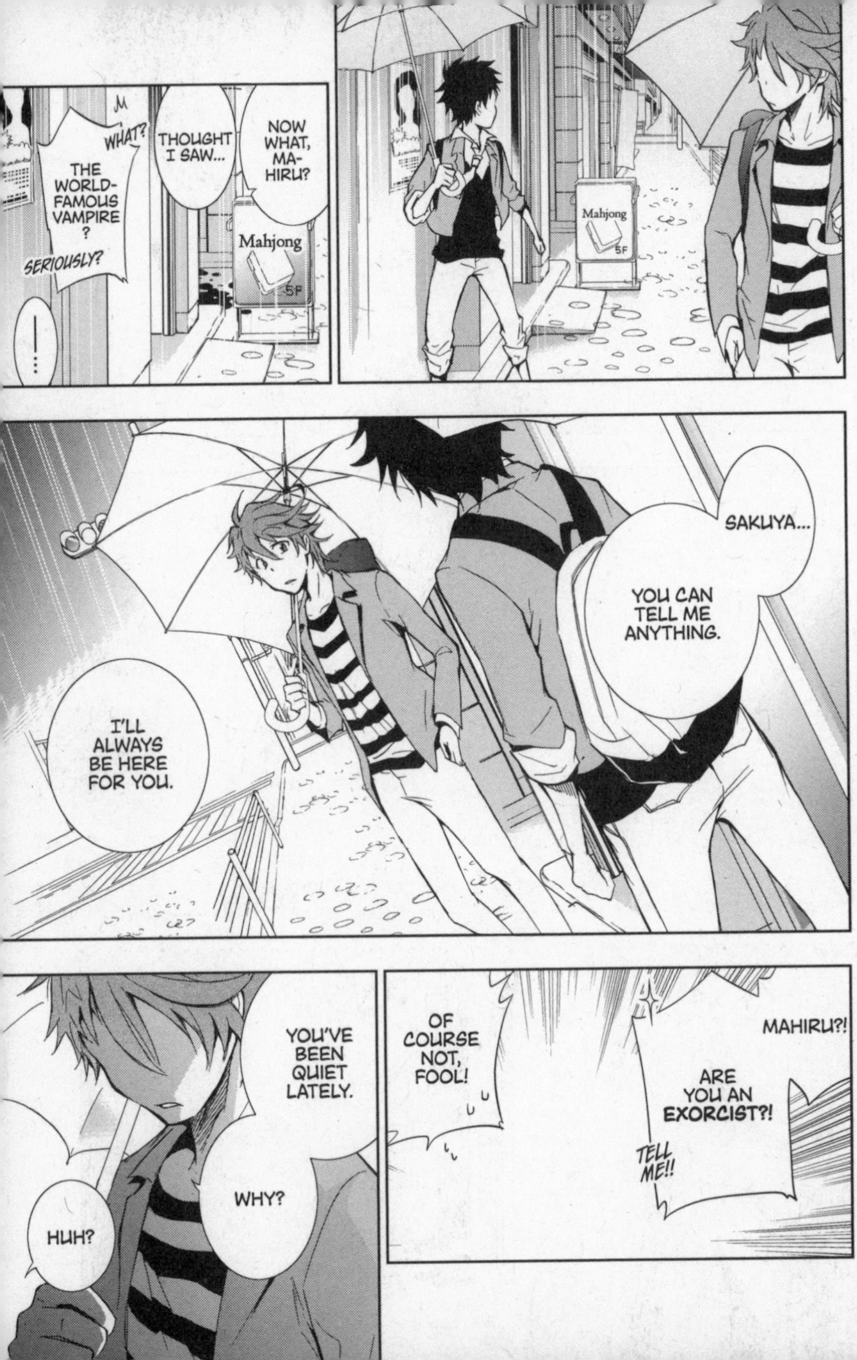
NOW WHAT, MA-HIRU?
THOUGHT I SAW...
WHAT? THE WORLD-FAMOUS VAMPIRE? SERIOUSLY?
!...
SAKUYA...
YOU CAN TELL ME ANYTHING.
I'LL ALWAYS BE HERE FOR YOU.
MAHIRU?!
ARE YOU AN EXORCIST?!
TELL ME!!
OF COURSE NOT, FOOL!
YOU'VE BEEN QUIET LATELY.
WHY?
HUH?

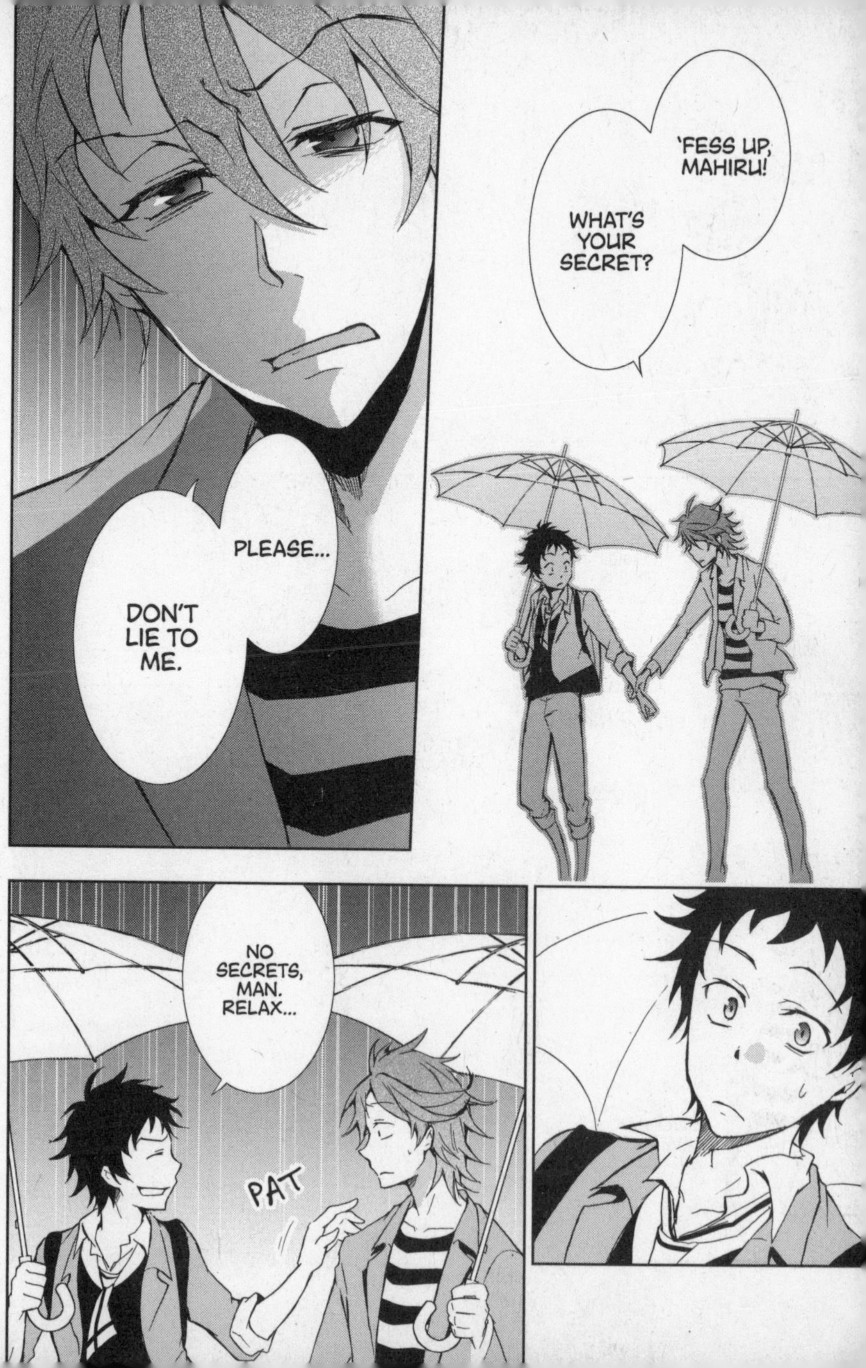
'FESS UP, MAHIRU! WHAT'S YOUR SECRET?
PLEASE... DON'T LIE TO ME.
NO SECRETS, MAN. RELAX...
PAT

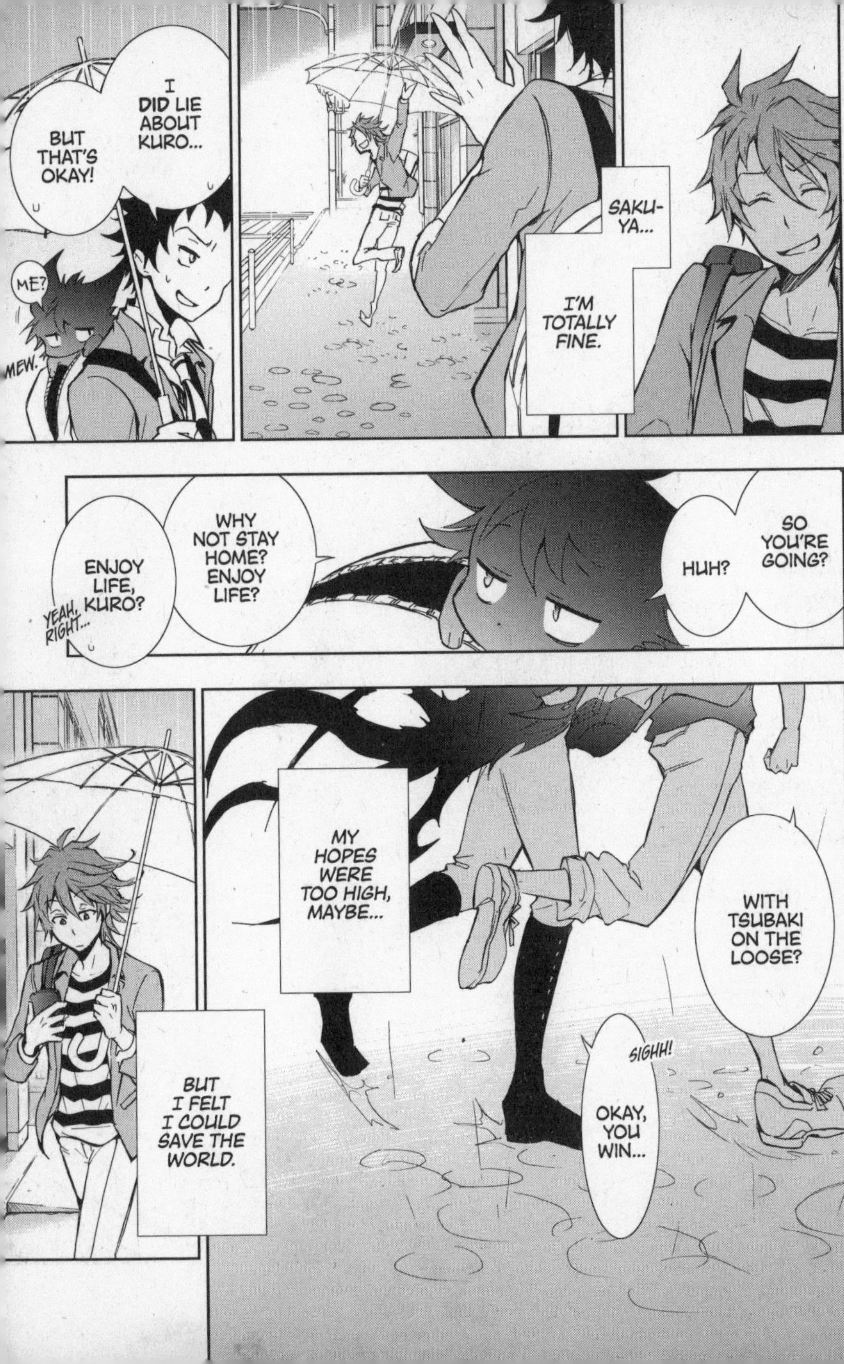
SAKU-YA...
I'M TOTALLY FINE.
I DID LIE ABOUT KURO...
BUT THAT'S OKAY!
ME?
MEW.
SO YOU'RE GOING?
HUH?
WHY NOT STAY HOME? ENJOY LIFE?
ENJOY LIFE, KURO?
YEAH, RIGHT...
WITH TSUBAKI ON THE LOOSE?
SIGHH!
OKAY, YOU WIN...
MY HOPES WERE TOO HIGH, MAYBE...
BUT I FELT I COULD SAVE THE WORLD.

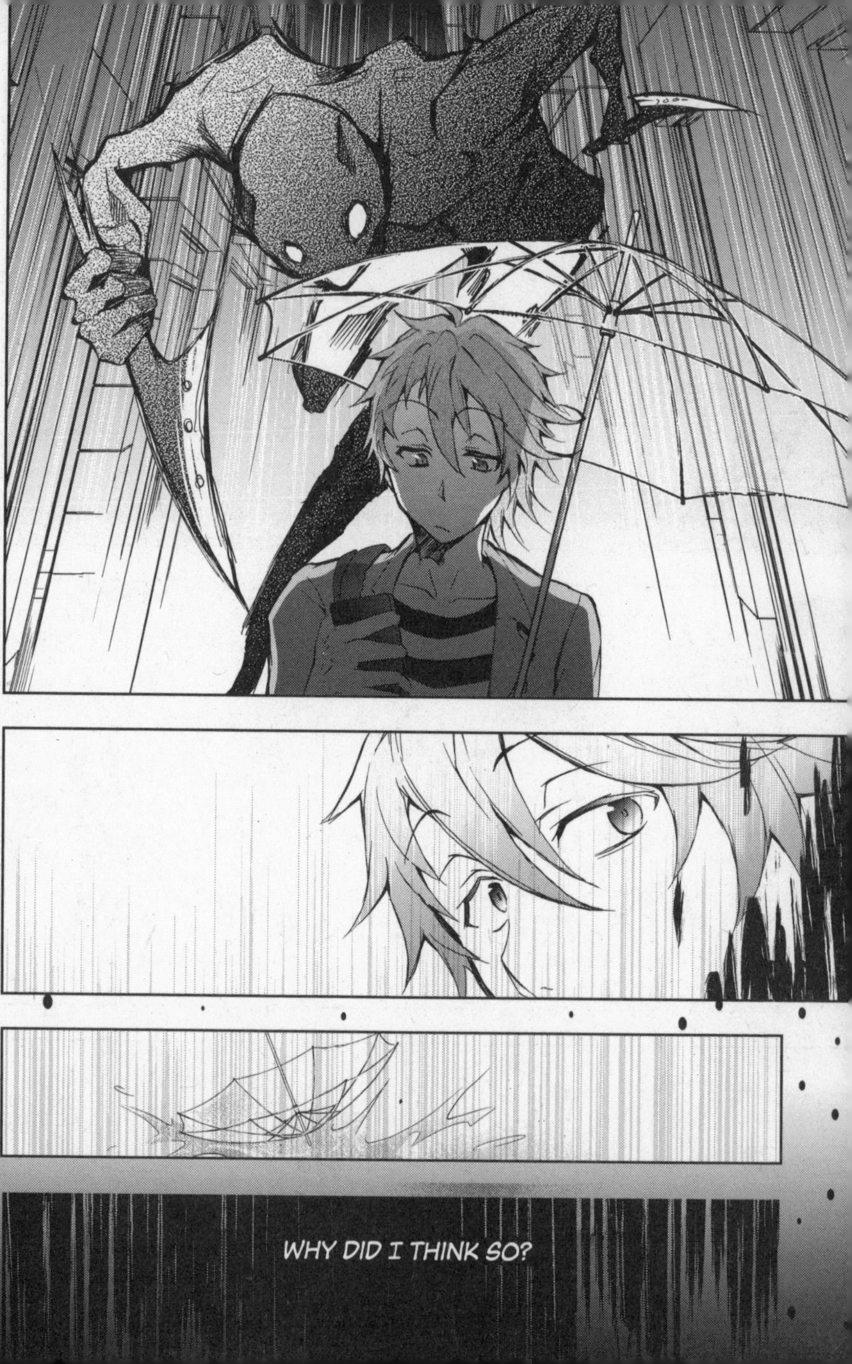
WHY DID I THINK SO?

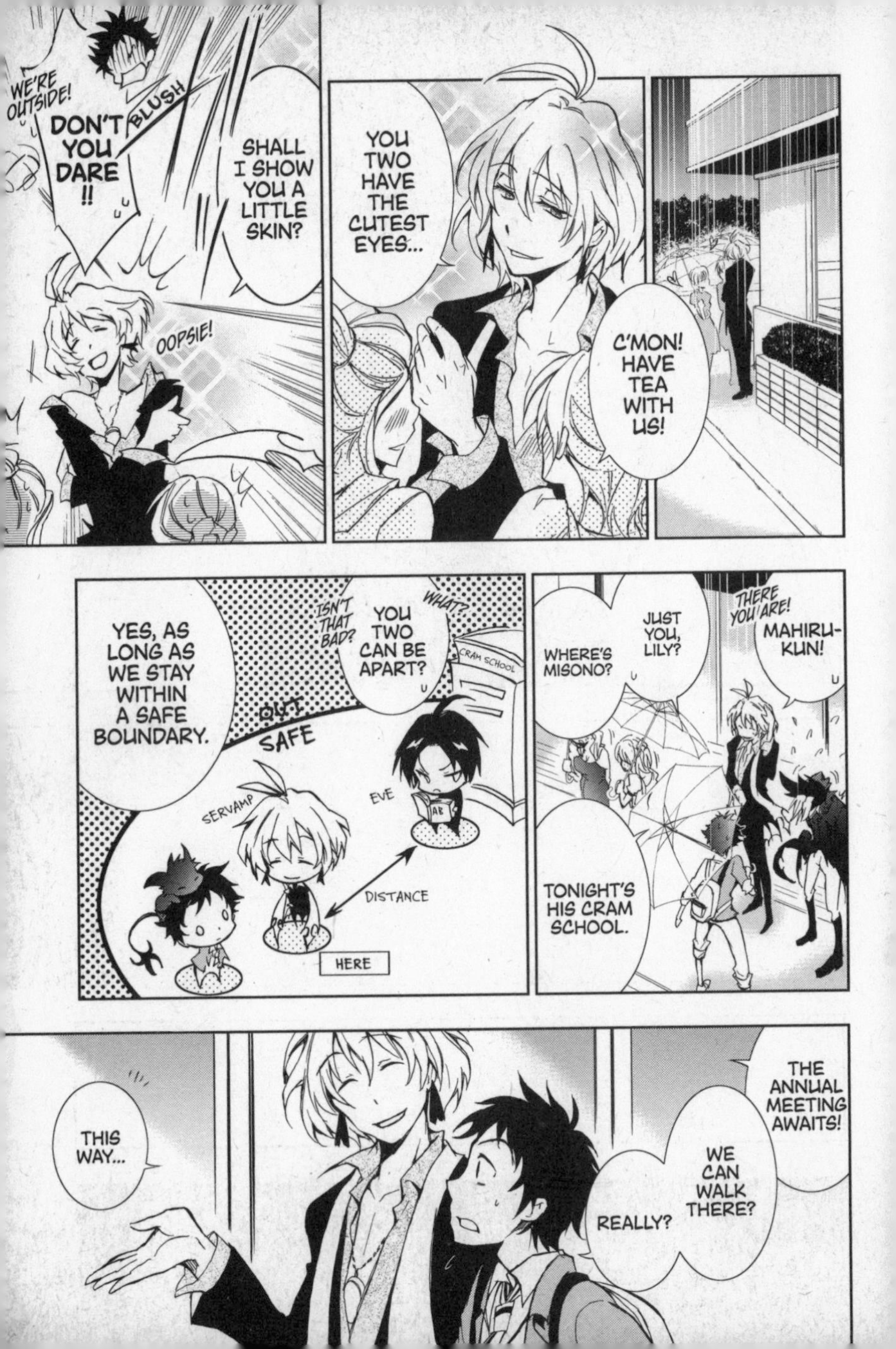
C'MON! HAVE TEA WITH US!
YOU TWO HAVE THE CUTEST EYES...
SHALL I SHOW YOU A LITTLE SKIN?
BLUSH
DON'T YOU DARE!!
WE'RE OUTSIDE!
OOPSIE!
THERE YOU ARE!
MAHIRU-KUN!
JUST YOU, LILY?
WHERE'S MISONO?
TONIGHT'S HIS CRAM SCHOOL.
WHAT?
YOU TWO CAN BE APART?
ISN'T THAT BAD?
YES, AS LONG AS WE STAY WITHIN A SAFE BOUNDARY.
CRAM SCHOOL
OUT
SAFE
EVE
SERVAMP
DISTANCE
HERE
THE ANNUAL MEETING AWAITS!
WE CAN WALK THERE?
REALLY?
THIS WAY...

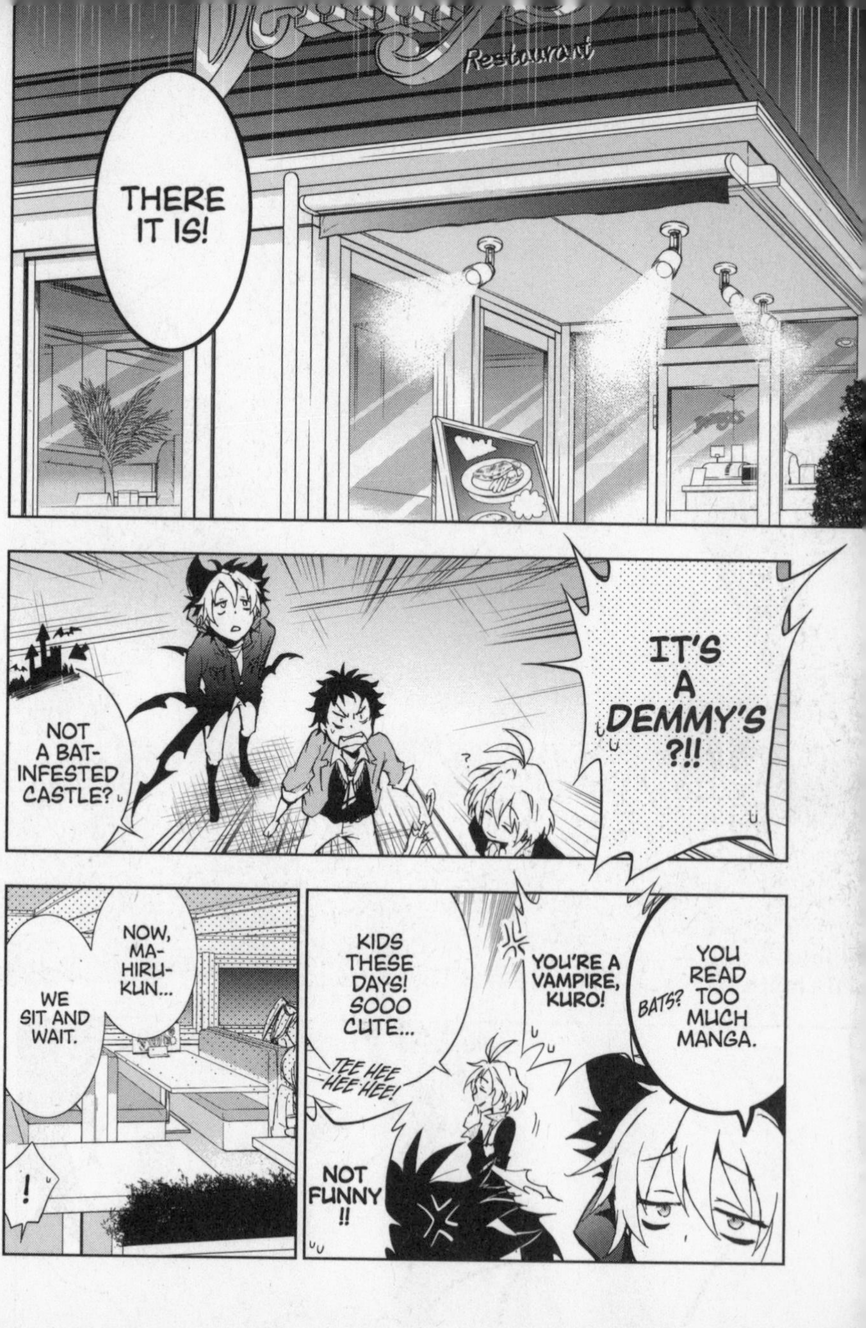
Restaurant
THERE IT IS!
IT'S A DEMMY'S ?!!
NOT A BAT-INFESTED CASTLE?
YOU READ TOO MUCH MANGA.
BATS?
YOU'RE A VAMPIRE, KURO!
KIDS THESE DAYS! SOOO CUTE...
TEE HEE HEE HEE!
NOT FUNNY !!
NOW, MA-HIRU-KUN...
WE SIT AND WAIT.
!

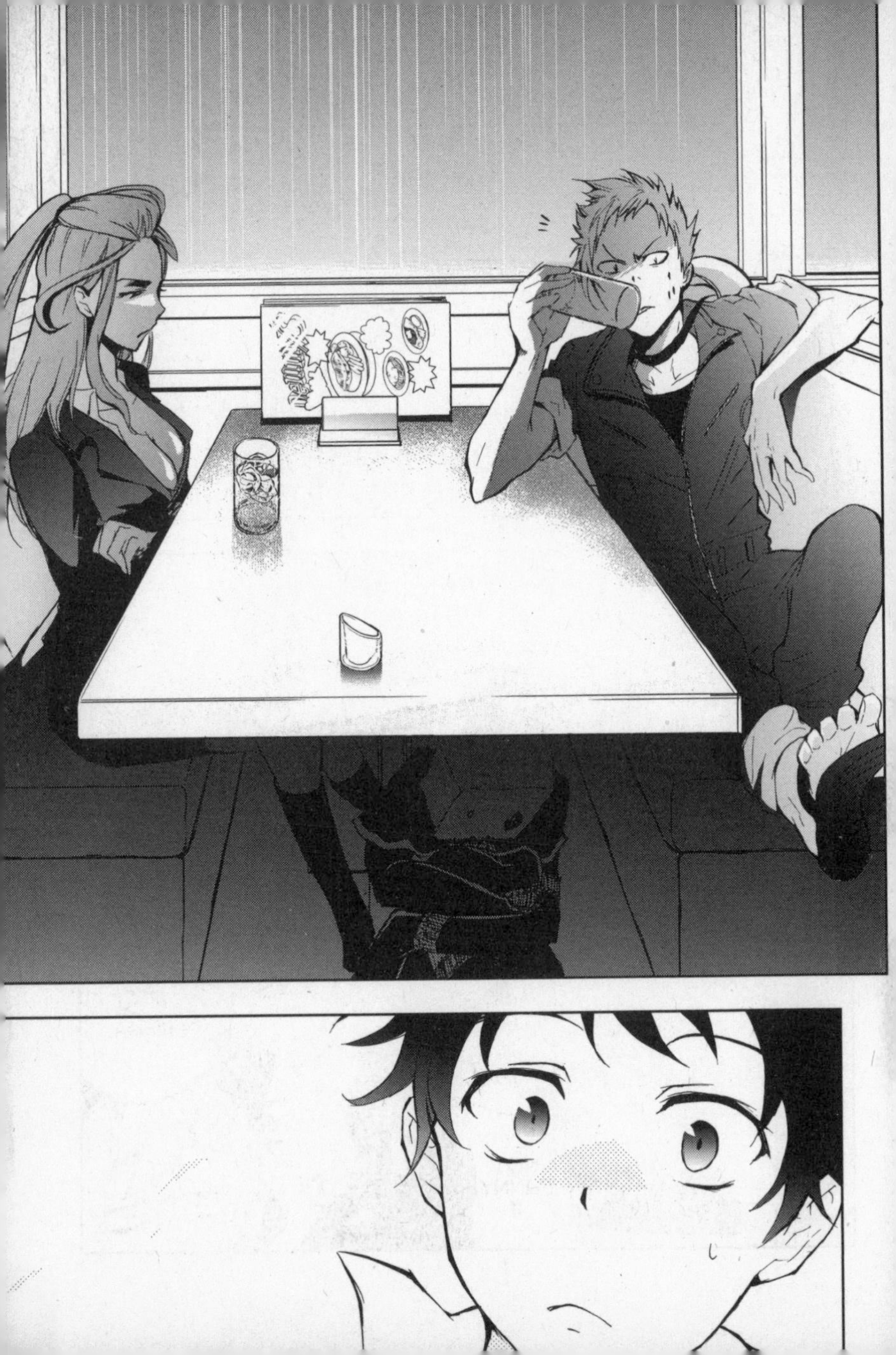

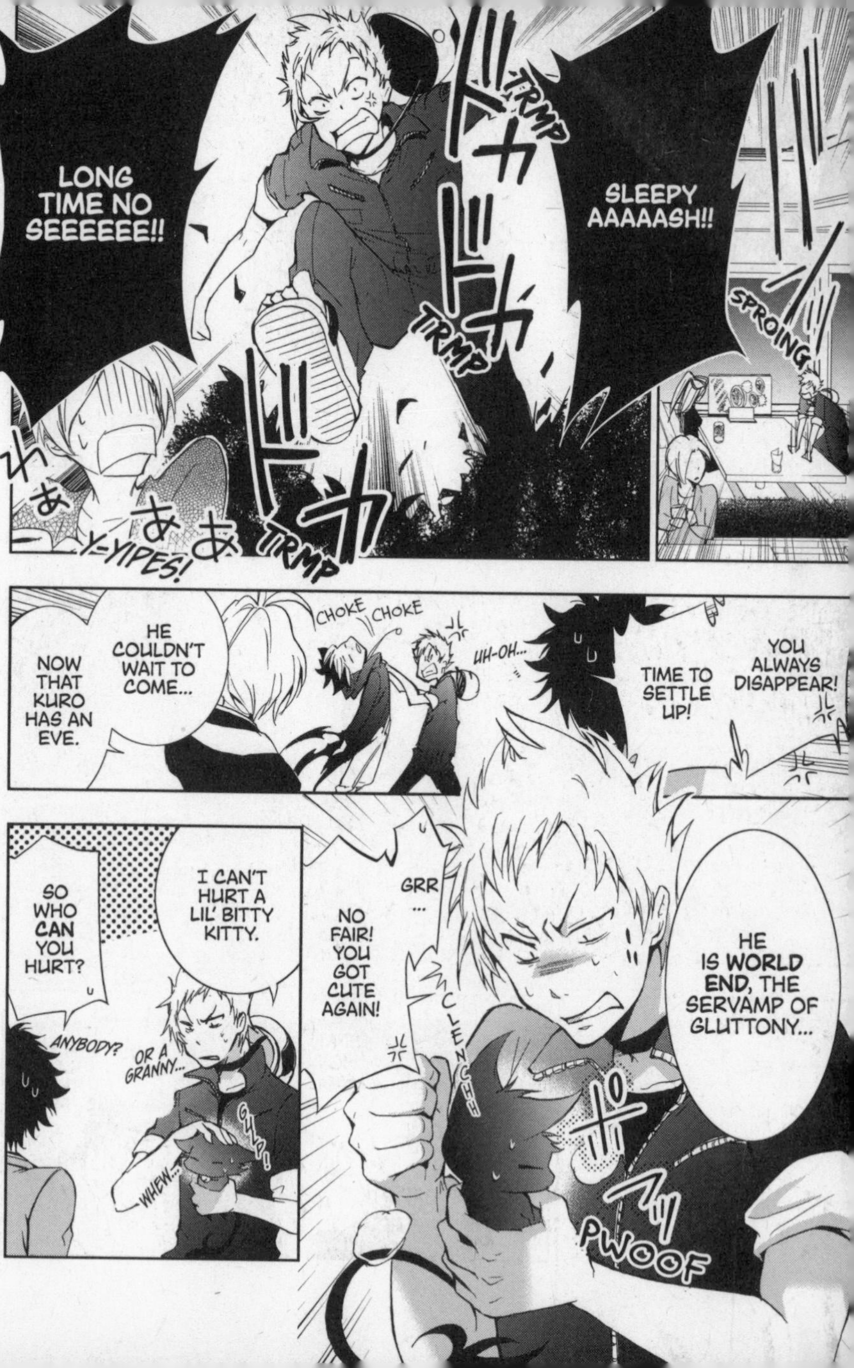
TRMP
SLEEPY AAAAASH!!
LONG TIME NO SEEEEEE!!
TRMP
TRMP
Y-YIPES!
SPROING
YOU ALWAYS DISAPPEAR!
TIME TO SETTLE UP!
UH-OH...
CHOKE
CHOKE
HE COULDN'T WAIT TO COME...
NOW THAT KURO HAS AN EVE.
HE IS WORLD END, THE SERVAMP OF GLUTTONY...
PWOOF
CLENCH!!
GRR...
NO FAIR! YOU GOT CUTE AGAIN!
I CAN'T HURT A LIL' BITTY KITTY.
SO WHO CAN YOU HURT?
ANYBODY?
OR A GRANNY...
WHEW...

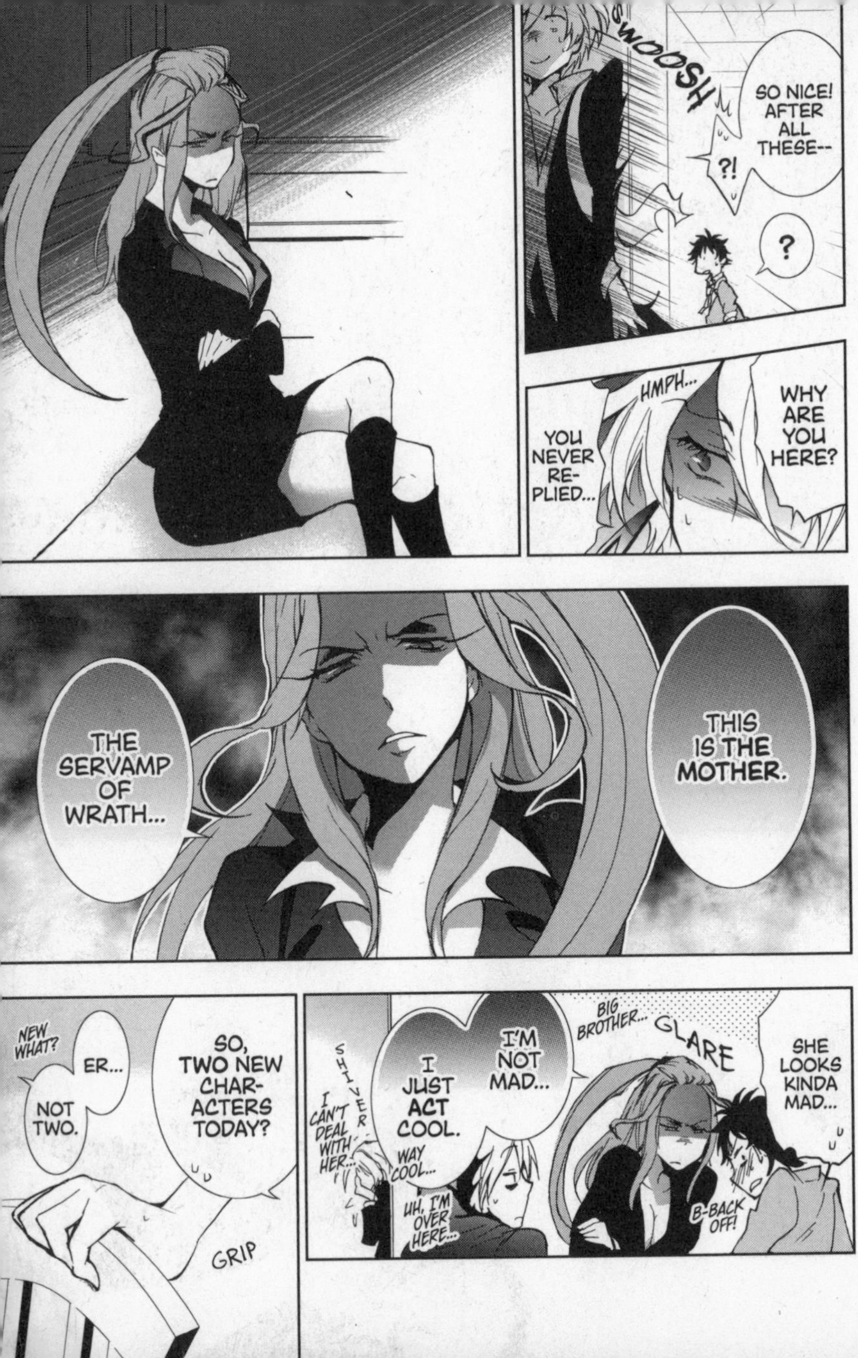
SWOOSH
SO NICE! AFTER ALL THESE--
?!
?
WHY ARE YOU HERE?
HMPH...
YOU NEVER RE-PLIED...
THIS IS THE MOTHER.
THE SERVAMP OF WRATH...
SHE LOOKS KINDA MAD...
GLARE
BIG BROTHER...
B-BACK OFF!
I'M NOT MAD...
I JUST ACT COOL.
WAY COOL...
SHIVER
I CAN'T DEAL WITH HER...
UH, I'M OVER HERE...
SO, TWO NEW CHAR-ACTERS TODAY?
ER...
NOT TWO.
NEW WHAT?
GRIP

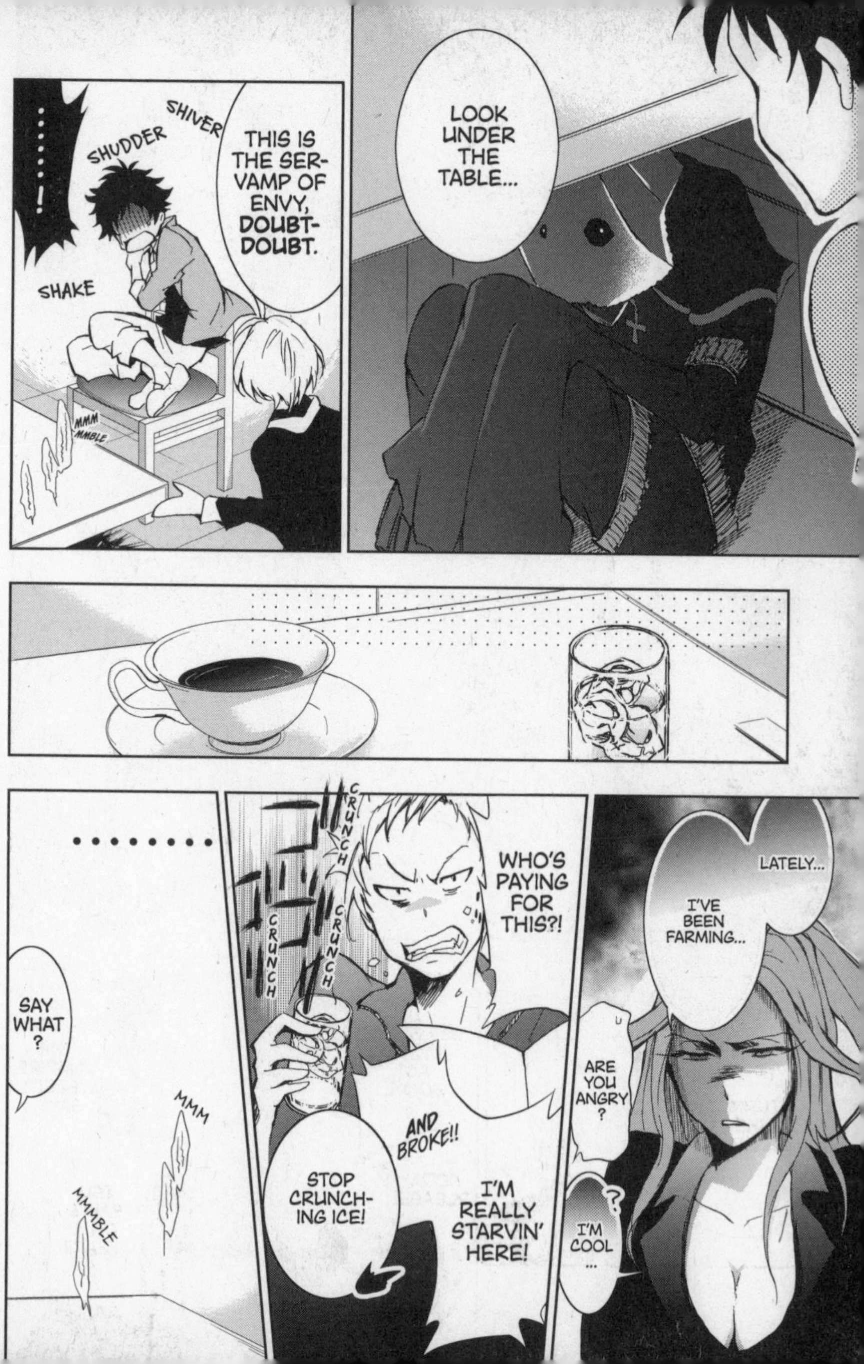
LOOK UNDER THE TABLE...
......!
SHIVER
THIS IS THE SERVAMP OF ENVY, DOUBT-DOUBT.
SHUDDER
SHAKE
MMM MMBLE
LATELY...
I'VE BEEN FARMING...
ARE YOU ANGRY?
?
I'M COOL...
CRUNCH
WHO'S PAYING FOR THIS?!
CRUNCH
CRUNCH
AND BROKE!!
I'M REALLY STARVIN' HERE!
STOP CRUNCHING ICE!
....
SAY WHAT?
MMM
MMMBLE

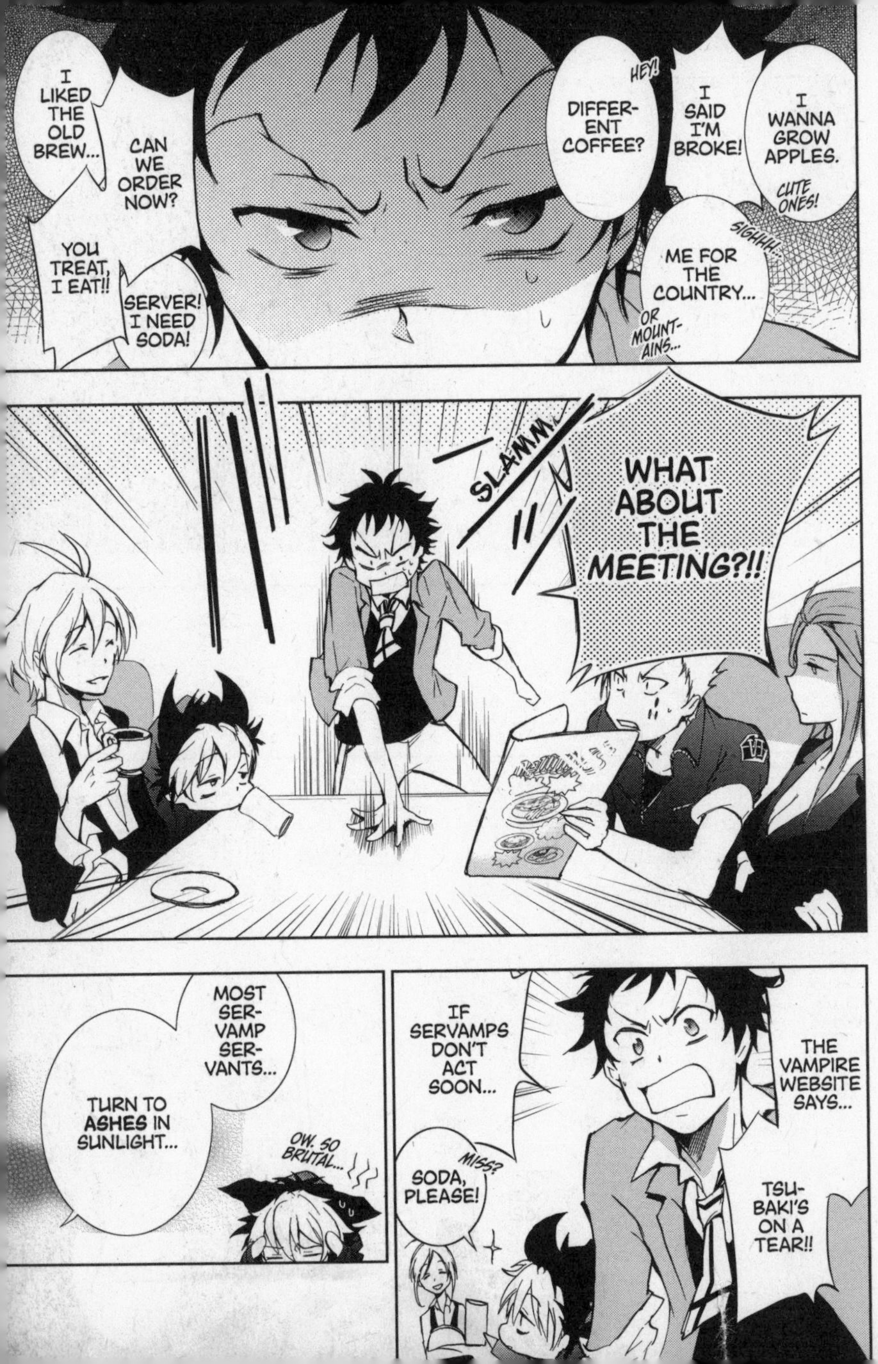
I WANNA GROW APPLES.
CUTE ONES!
I SAID I'M BROKE!
HEY!
DIFFERENT COFFEE?
SIGHHH...
ME FOR THE COUNTRY...
OR MOUNTAINS...
I LIKED THE OLD BREW...
CAN WE ORDER NOW?
YOU TREAT, I EAT!!
SERVER! I NEED SODA!
WHAT ABOUT THE MEETING?!!
SLAMM
THE VAMPIRE WEBSITE SAYS...
IF SERVAMPS DON'T ACT SOON...
TSUBAKI'S ON A TEAR!!
MISS?
SODA, PLEASE!
MOST SERVAMP SERVANTS...
TURN TO ASHES IN SUNLIGHT...
OW. SO BRUTAL...

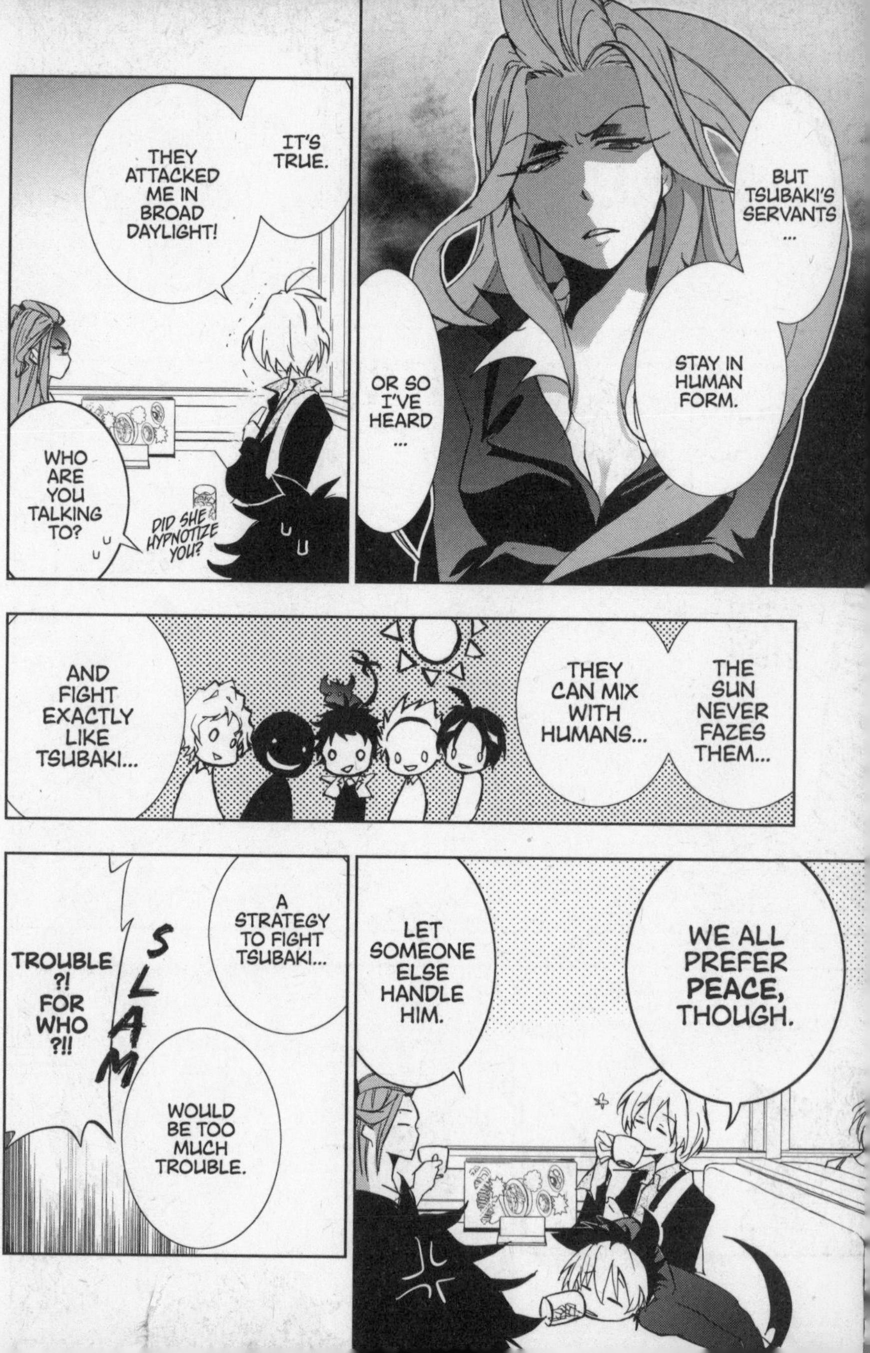
BUT TSUBAKI'S SERVANTS ...
STAY IN HUMAN FORM.
OR SO I'VE HEARD ...
IT'S TRUE.
THEY ATTACKED ME IN BROAD DAYLIGHT!
DID SHE HYPNOTIZE YOU?
WHO ARE YOU TALKING TO?
THE SUN NEVER FAZES THEM...
THEY CAN MIX WITH HUMANS...
AND FIGHT EXACTLY LIKE TSUBAKI...
WE ALL PREFER PEACE, THOUGH.
LET SOMEONE ELSE HANDLE HIM.
A STRATEGY TO FIGHT TSUBAKI...
WOULD BE TOO MUCH TROUBLE.
SLAM
TROUBLE?! FOR WHO?!!

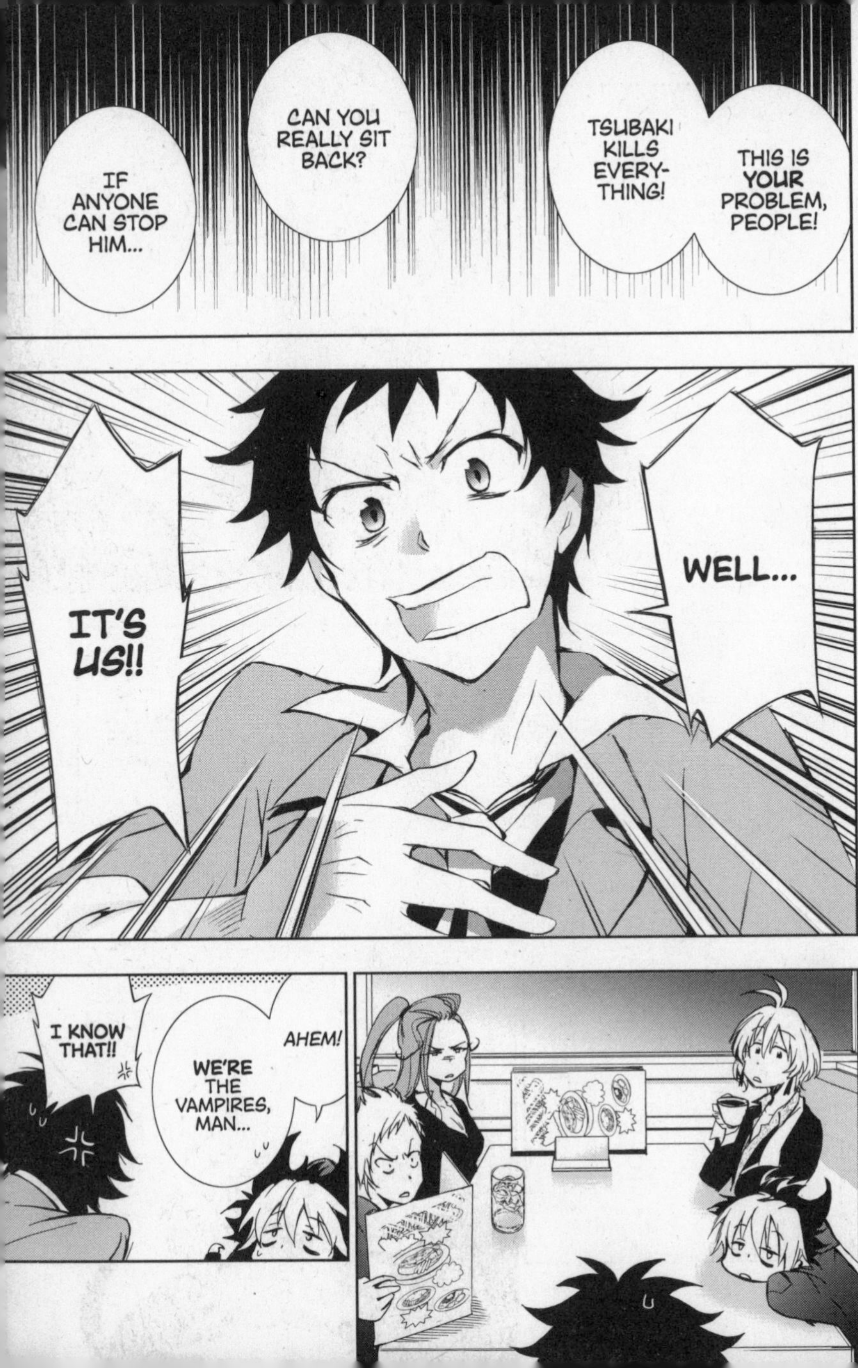
THIS IS YOUR PROBLEM, PEOPLE!
TSUBAKI KILLS EVERY-THING!
CAN YOU REALLY SIT BACK?
IF ANYONE CAN STOP HIM...
WELL...
IT'S US!!
AHEM!
WE'RE THE VAMPIRES, MAN...
I KNOW THAT!!

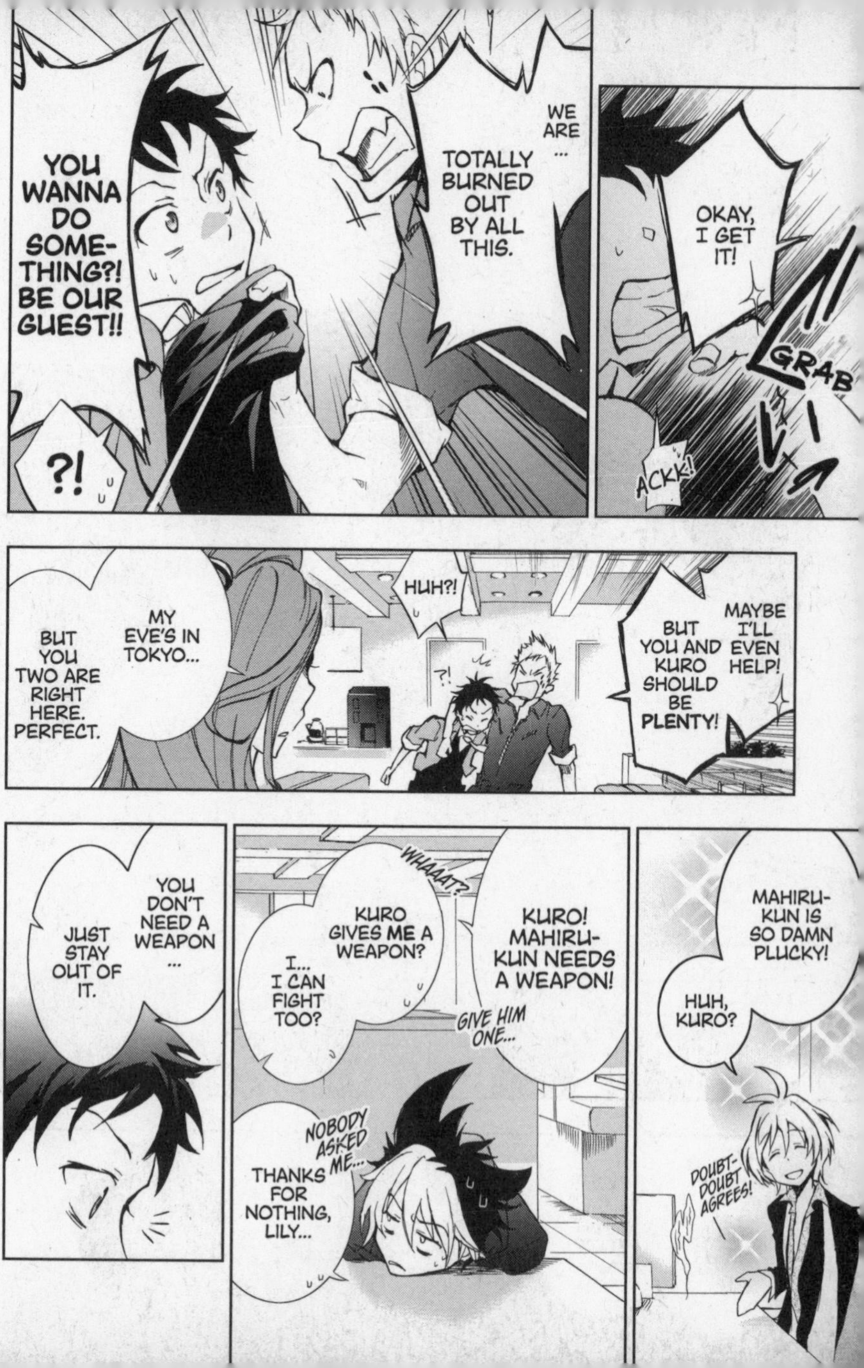
OKAY, I GET IT!
GRAB
ACKK!
WE ARE ...
TOTALLY BURNED OUT BY ALL THIS.
YOU WANNA DO SOME-THING?! BE OUR GUEST!!
?!
MAYBE I'LL EVEN HELP!
BUT YOU AND KURO SHOULD BE PLENTY!
HUH?!
?!
MY EVE'S IN TOKYO...
BUT YOU TWO ARE RIGHT HERE. PERFECT.
MAHIRU-KUN IS SO DAMN PLUCKY!
HUH, KURO?
DOUBT-DOUBT AGREES!
KURO! MAHIRU-KUN NEEDS A WEAPON!
WHAAAT?
KURO GIVES ME A WEAPON?
I... I CAN FIGHT TOO?
GIVE HIM ONE...
NOBODY ASKED ME...
THANKS FOR NOTHING, LILY...
YOU DON'T NEED A WEAPON ...
JUST STAY OUT OF IT.

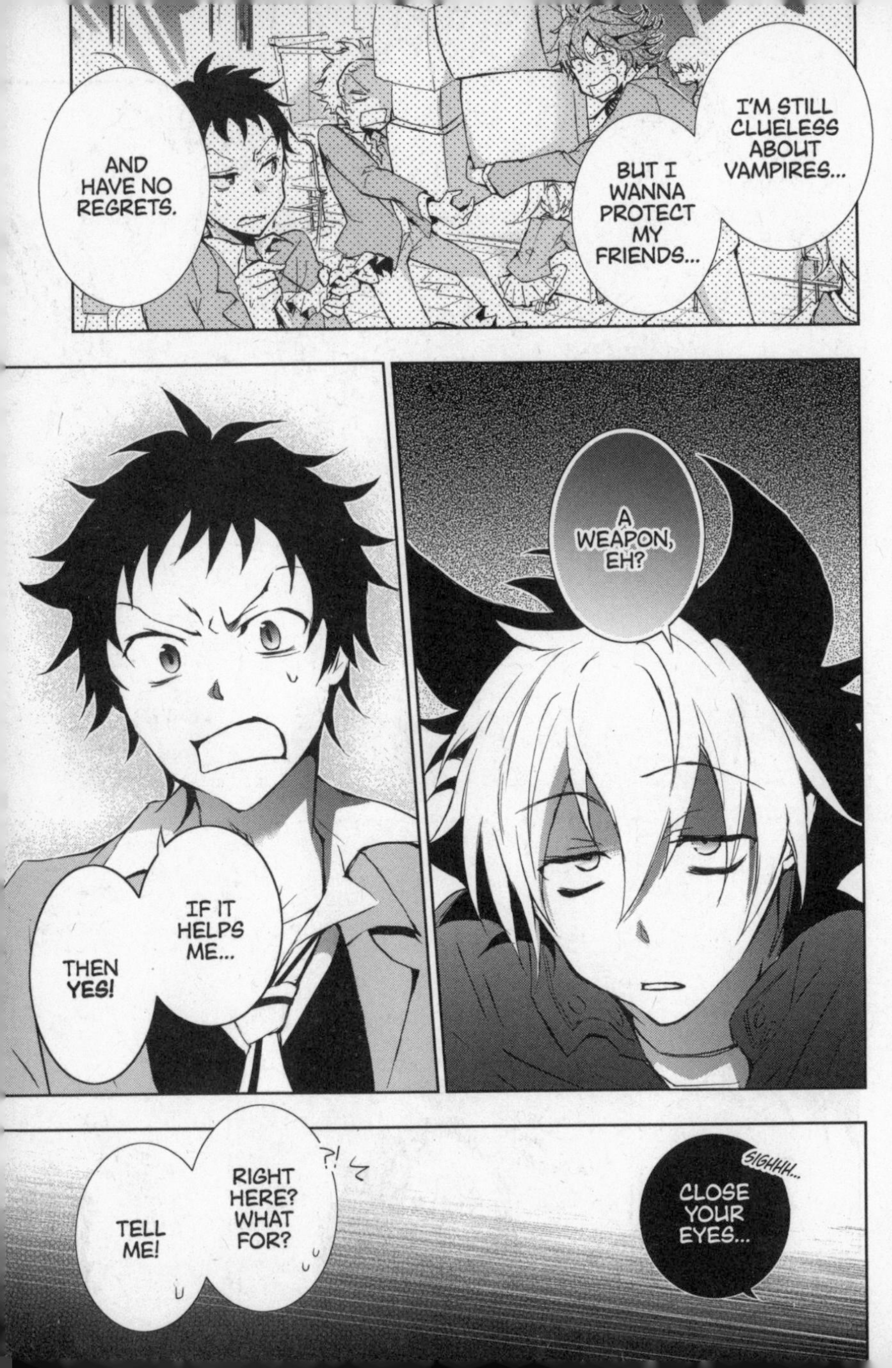
I'M STILL CLUELESS ABOUT VAMPIRES...
BUT I WANNA PROTECT MY FRIENDS...
AND HAVE NO REGRETS.
A WEAPON, EH?
IF IT HELPS ME...
THEN YES!
SIGHHH...
CLOSE YOUR EYES...
?!
RIGHT HERE? WHAT FOR?
TELL ME!

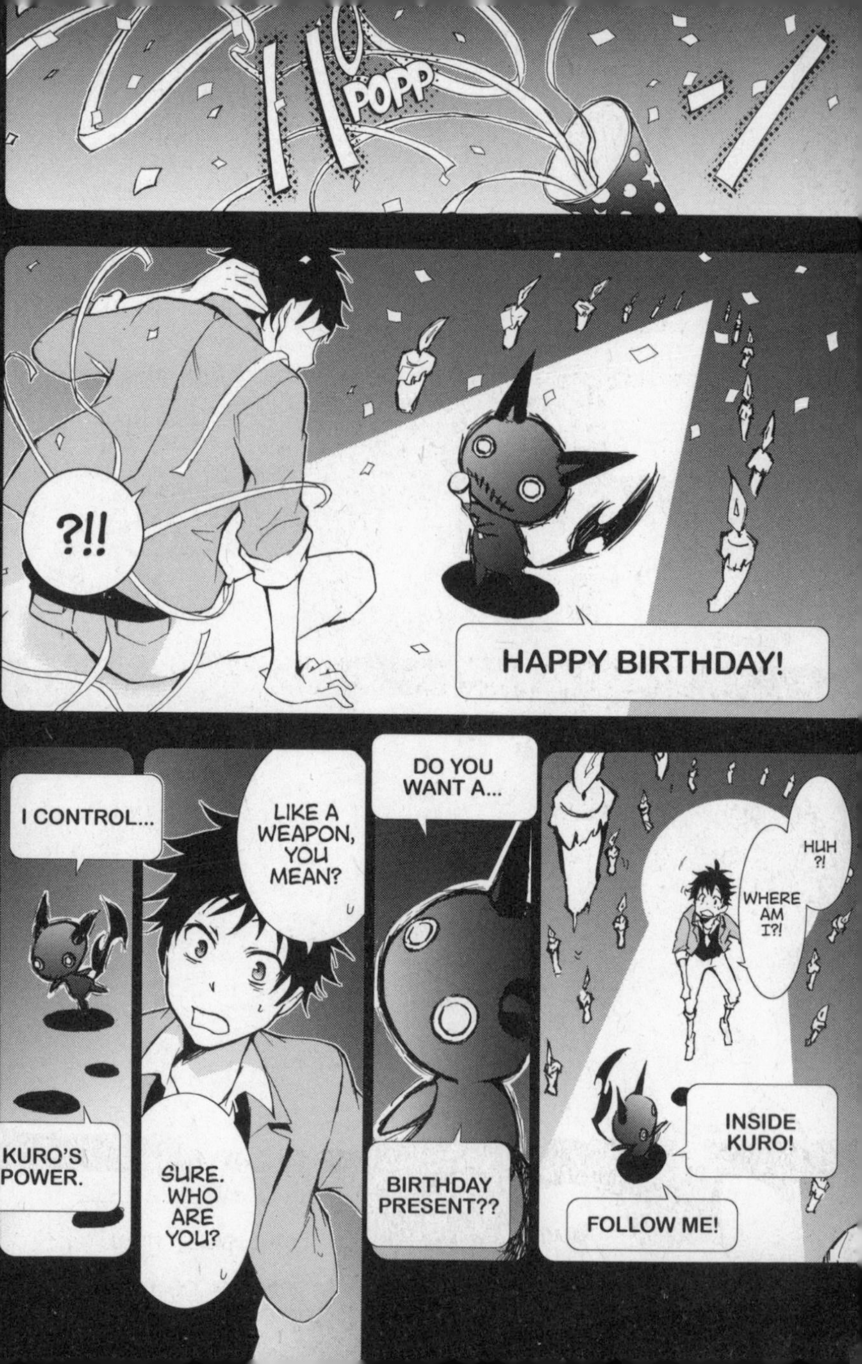
POPP
HAPPY BIRTHDAY!
?!!
HUH?! WHERE AM I?!
INSIDE KURO!
FOLLOW ME!
DO YOU WANT A...
BIRTHDAY PRESENT??
LIKE A WEAPON, YOU MEAN?
SURE. WHO ARE YOU?
I CONTROL...
KURO'S POWER.

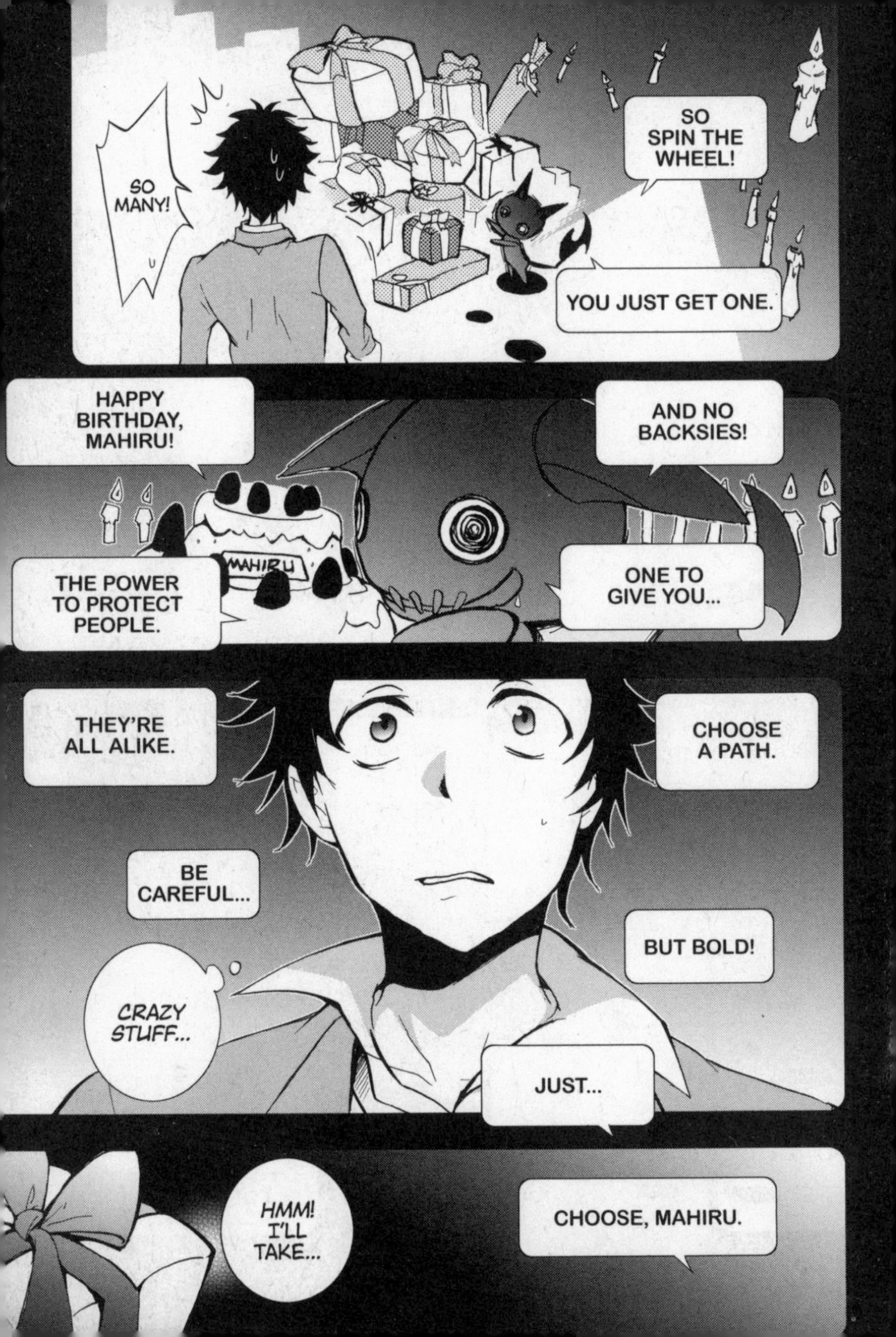
SO SPIN THE WHEEL!
YOU JUST GET ONE.
SO MANY!
AND NO BACKSIES!
HAPPY BIRTHDAY, MAHIRU!
ONE TO GIVE YOU...
MAHIRU
THE POWER TO PROTECT PEOPLE.
CHOOSE A PATH.
THEY'RE ALL ALIKE.
BE CAREFUL...
BUT BOLD!
CRAZY STUFF...
JUST...
CHOOSE, MAHIRU.
HMM! I'LL TAKE...

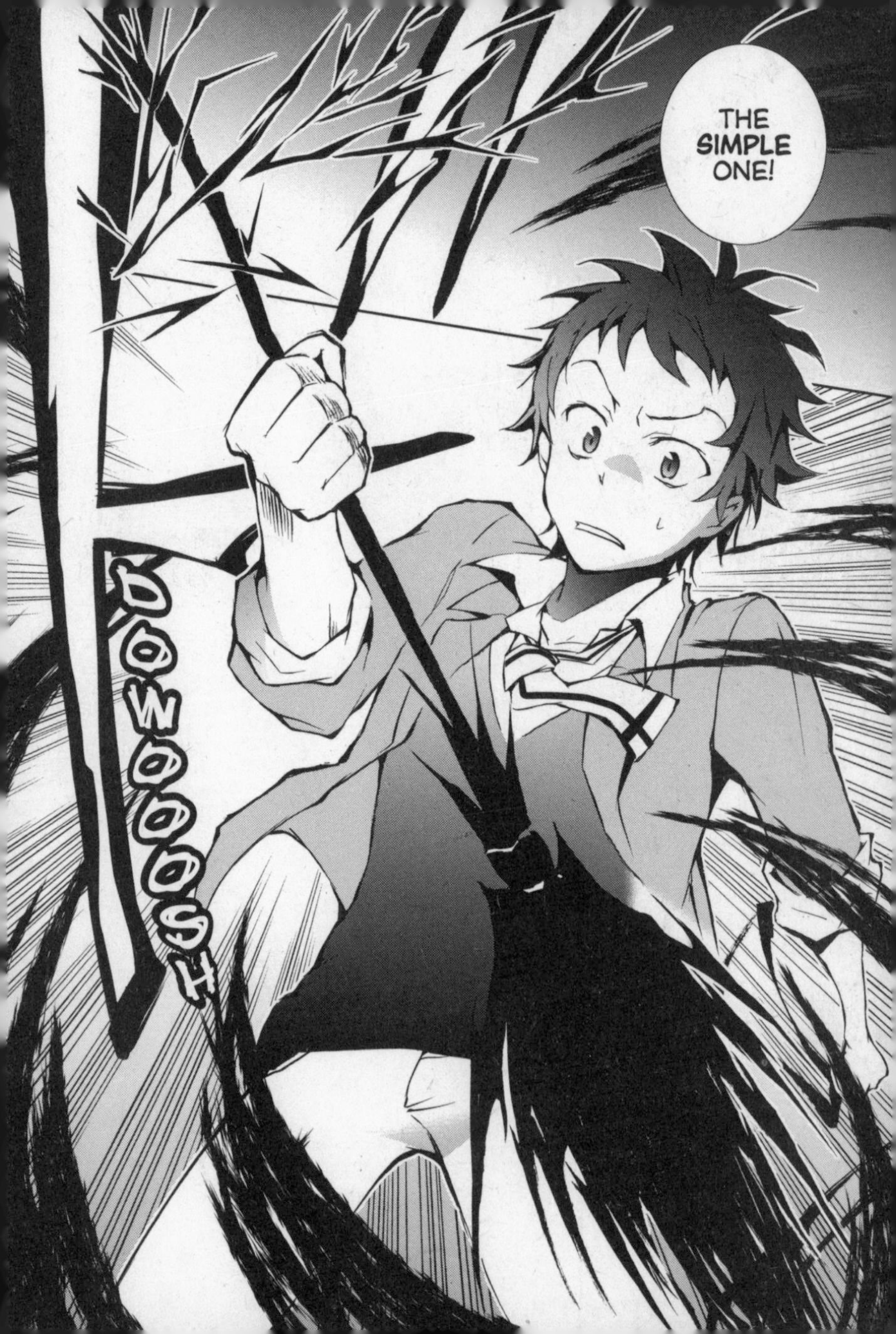
THE SIMPLE ONE!
DOWOOOSH

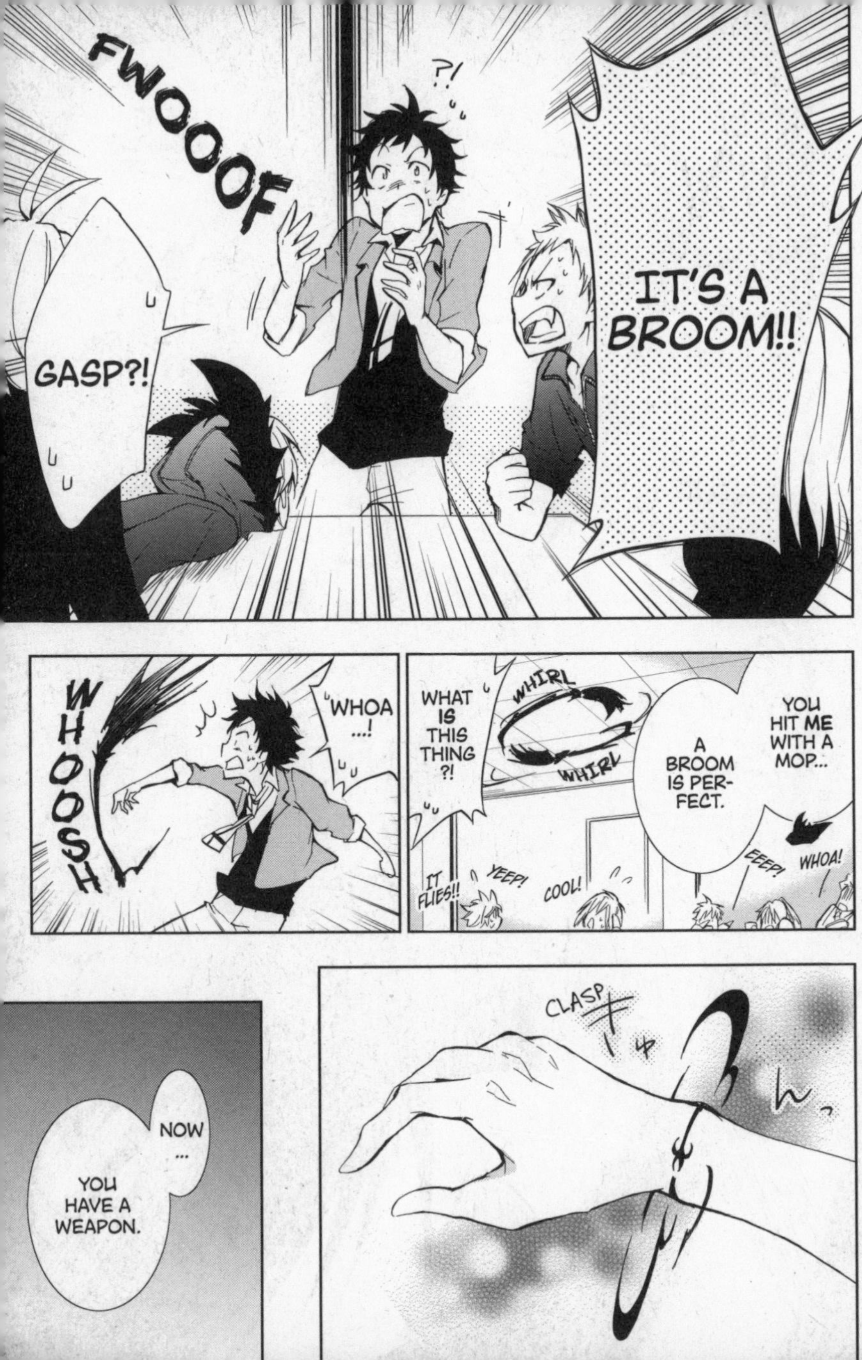
IT'S A BROOM!!
?!
FWOOOF
GASP?!
YOU HIT ME WITH A MOP...
A BROOM IS PERFECT.
WHIRL
WHAT IS THIS THING?!
WHIRL
WHOA!
EEEP!
COOL!
YEEP!
IT FLIES!!
WHOA...!
WHOOSH
CLASP
NOW... YOU HAVE A WEAPON.

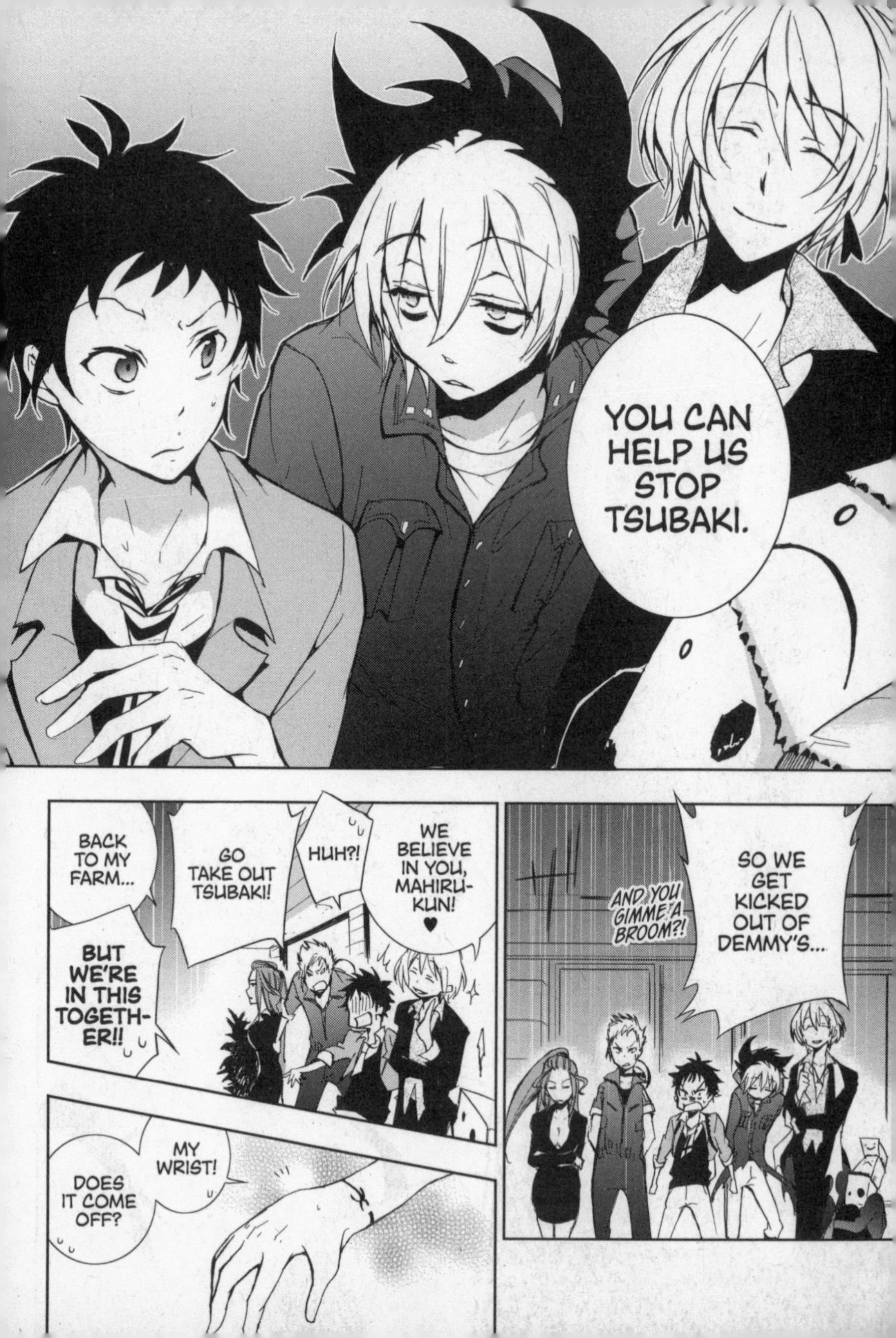
YOU CAN HELP US STOP TSUBAKI.
SO WE GET KICKED OUT OF DEMMY'S...
AND YOU GIMME A BROOM?!
WE BELIEVE IN YOU, MAHIRU-KUN! ♥
HUH?!
GO TAKE OUT TSUBAKI!
BACK TO MY FARM...
BUT WE'RE IN THIS TOGETHER!!
MY WRIST!
DOES IT COME OFF?

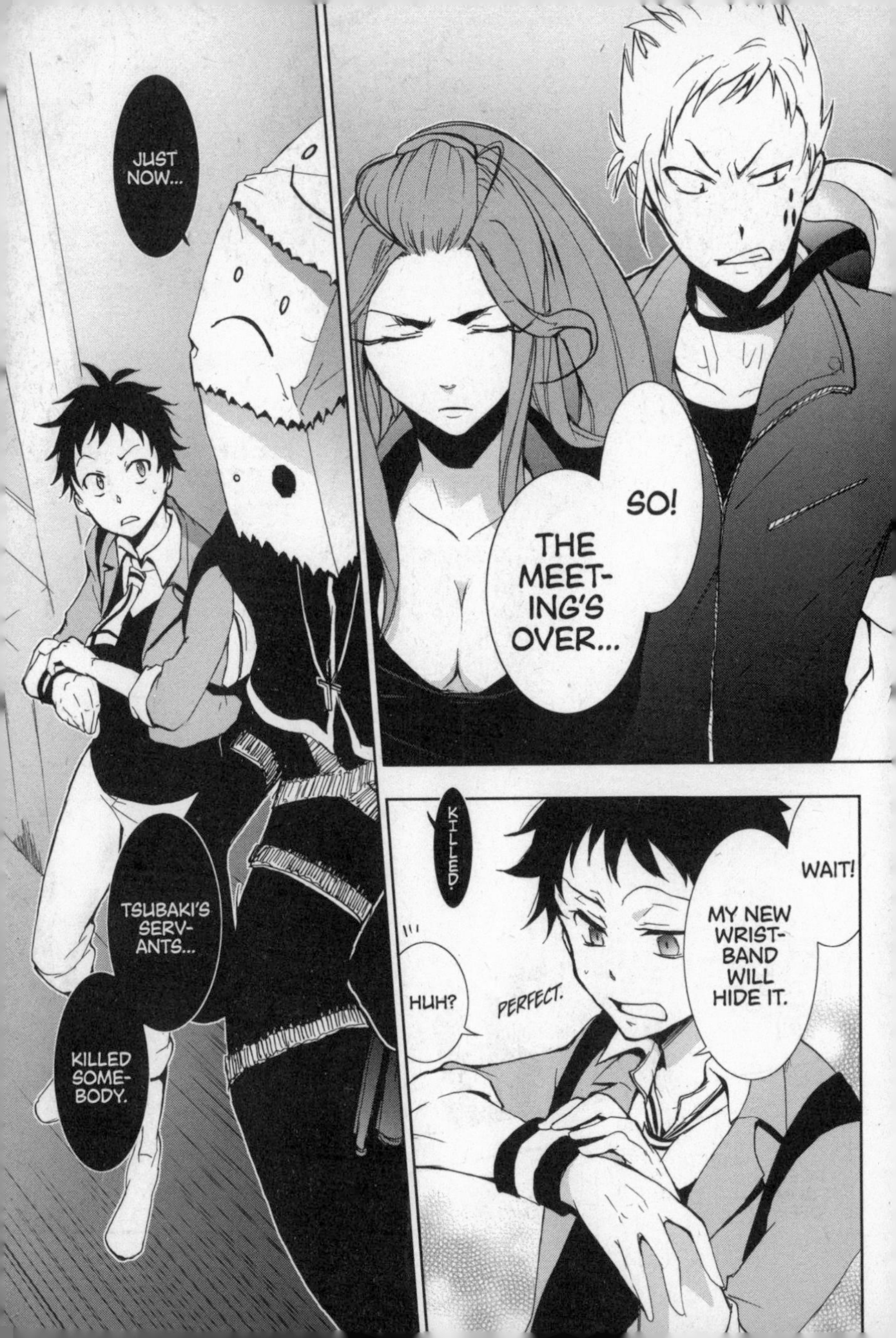
SO!
THE MEET-ING'S OVER...
WAIT!
MY NEW WRIST-BAND WILL HIDE IT.
PERFECT.
HUH?
KILLED.
JUST NOW...
TSUBAKI'S SERV-ANTS...
KILLED SOME-BODY.

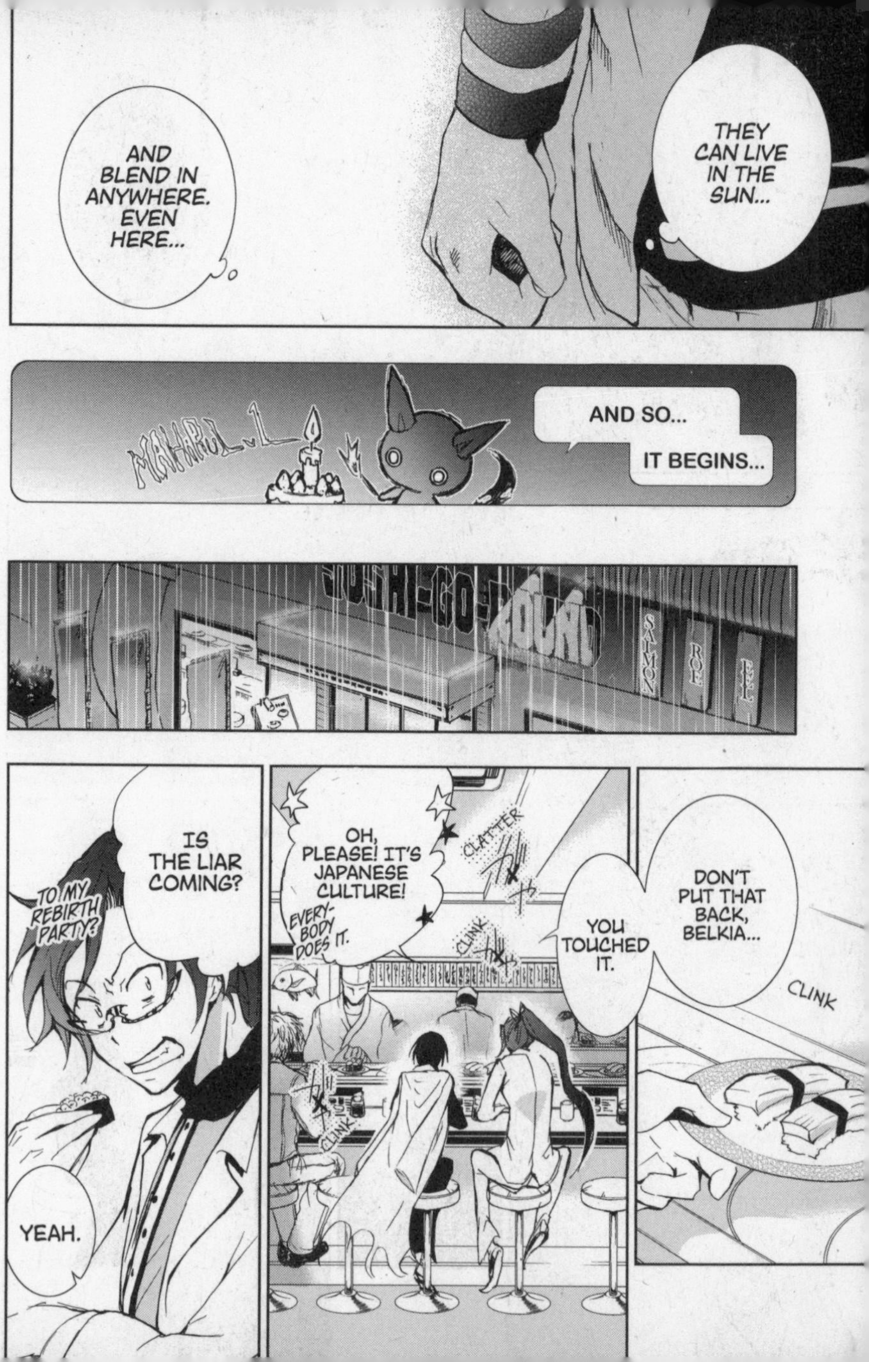
THEY CAN LIVE IN THE SUN...
AND BLEND IN ANYWHERE. EVEN HERE...
AND SO...
IT BEGINS...
EEL
ROE
SALMON
DON'T PUT THAT BACK, BELKIA...
CLINK
YOU TOUCHED IT.
CLATTER
OH, PLEASE! IT'S JAPANESE CULTURE!
EVERYBODY DOES IT.
CLINK
CLINK
IS THE LIAR COMING?
TO MY REBIRTH PARTY?
YEAH.

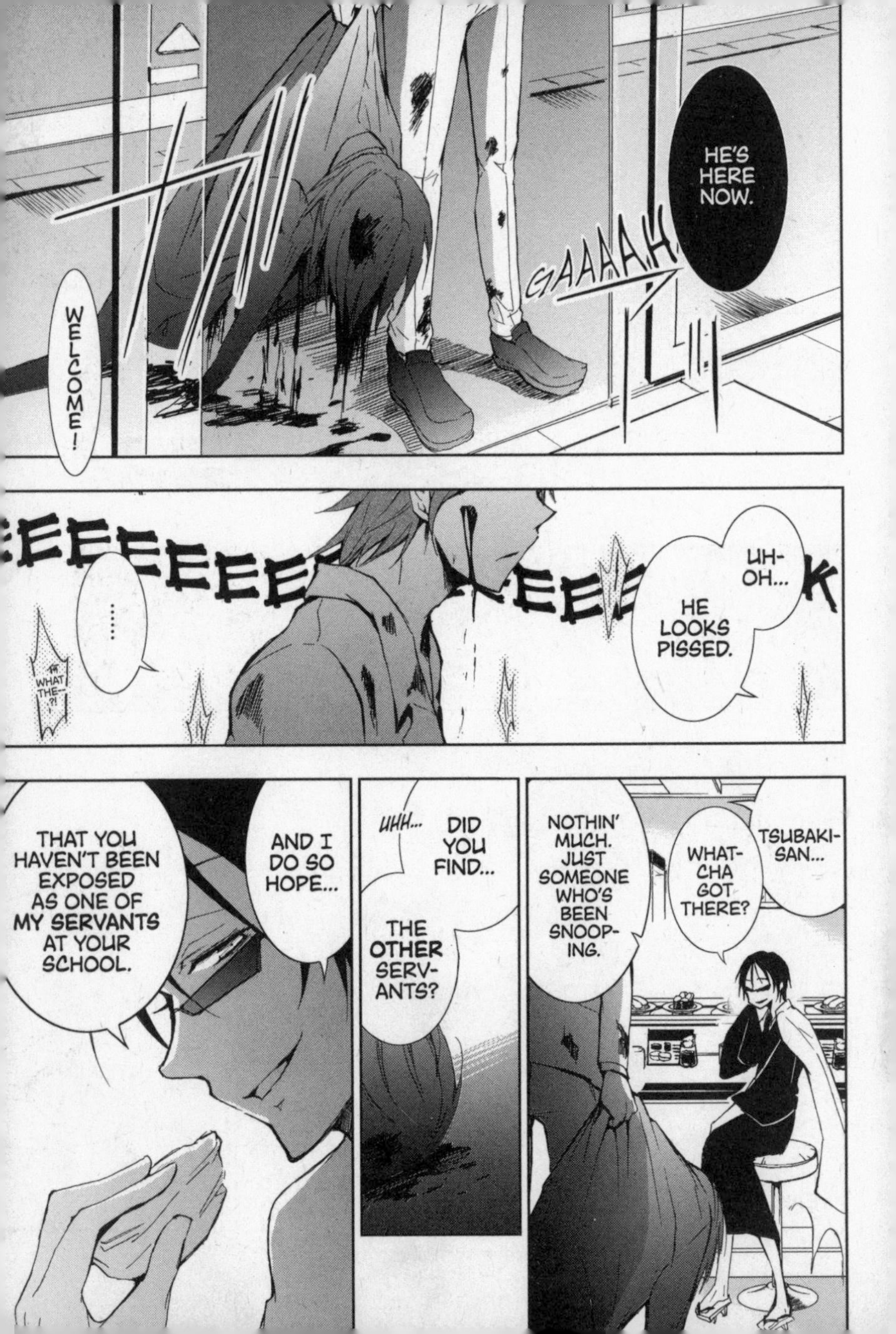

HE'S HERE NOW.
GAAAAH
WELCOME!
UH-OH... HE LOOKS PISSED.
EEEEEEEEEEEEK
......
WHAT THE--?!
TSUBAKI-SAN...
WHAT-CHA GOT THERE?
NOTHIN' MUCH. JUST SOMEONE WHO'S BEEN SNOOP-ING.
UHH...
DID YOU FIND...
THE OTHER SERV-ANTS?
AND I DO SO HOPE...
THAT YOU HAVEN'T BEEN EXPOSED AS ONE OF MY SERVANTS AT YOUR SCHOOL.

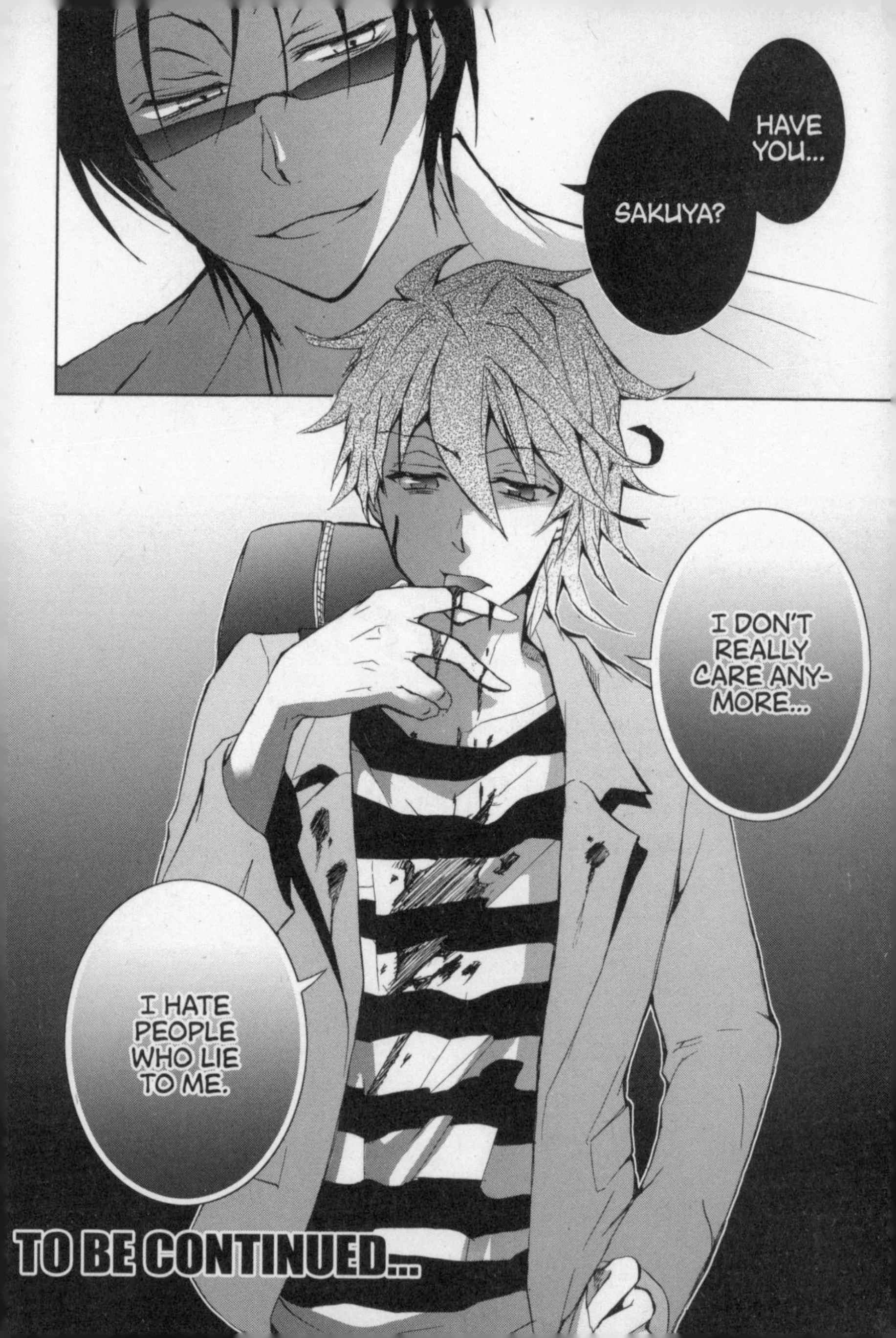
HAVE YOU...
SAKUYA?
I DON'T REALLY CARE ANY-MORE...
I HATE PEOPLE WHO LIE TO ME.
TO BE CONTINUED...

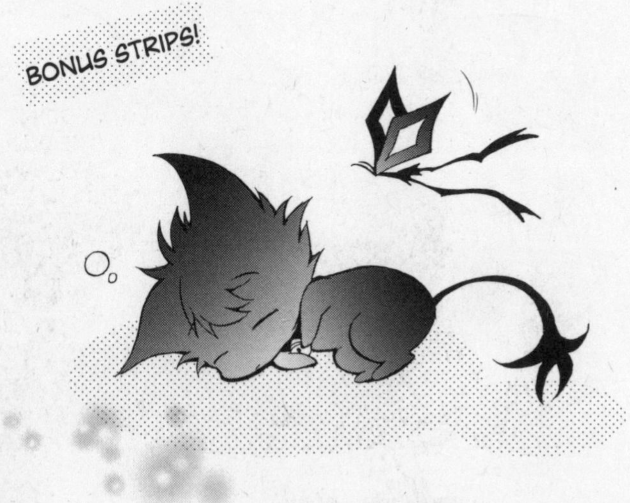
BONUS STRIPS!

TRASH DAY!

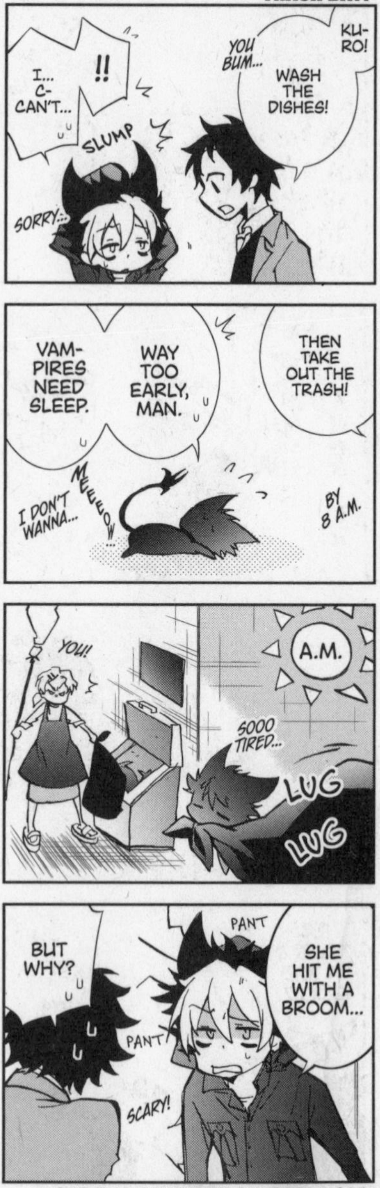
KU-RO!
WASH THE DISHES!
YOU BUM...
!!
I... C-CAN'T...
SLUMP
SORRY...
THEN TAKE OUT THE TRASH!
BY 8 A.M.
WAY TOO EARLY, MAN.
VAM-PIRES NEED SLEEP.
MEEEOW...
I DON'T WANNA...
A.M.
YOU!
SOOO TIRED...
LUG
LUG
SHE HIT ME WITH A BROOM...
PANT
BUT WHY?
PANT
SCARY!

SHE THOUGHT I WAS A STRAY CAT.

DISCIPLINE

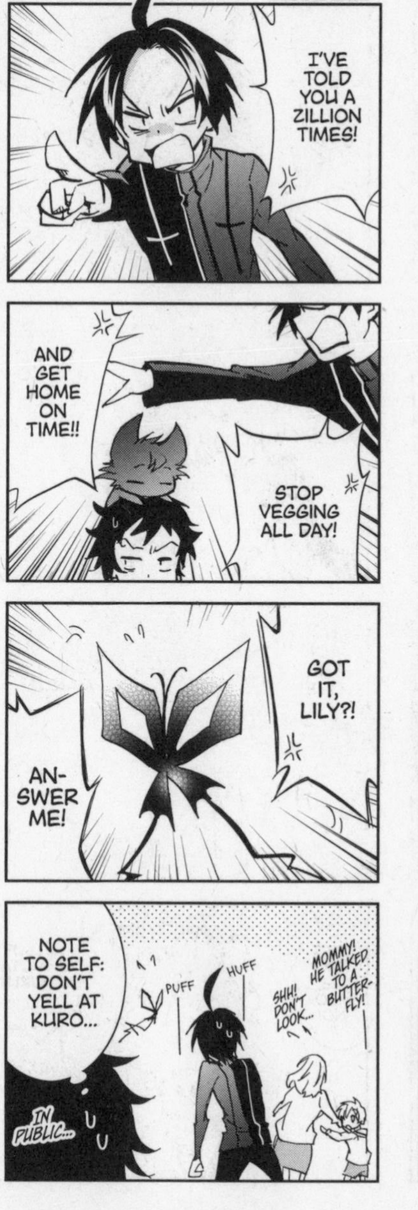
I'VE TOLD YOU A ZILLION TIMES!
STOP VEGGING ALL DAY!
AND GET HOME ON TIME!!
GOT IT, LILY?!
AN-SWER ME!
MOMMY! HE TALKED TO A BUTTER-FLY!
SHH! DON'T LOOK...
HUFF
PUFF
NOTE TO SELF: DON'T YELL AT KURO...
IN PUBLIC...

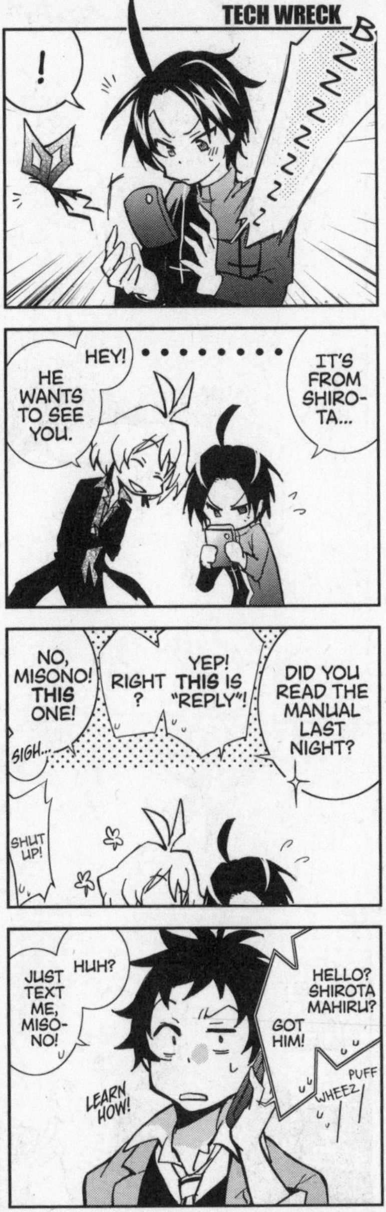
TECH WRECK
BZZZZZZZ
!
IT'S FROM SHIROTA...
....
HEY!
HE WANTS TO SEE YOU.
DID YOU READ THE MANUAL LAST NIGHT?
YEP! THIS IS "REPLY"!
RIGHT ?
NO, MISONO! THIS ONE!
SIGH...
SHUT UP!
HELLO? SHIROTA MAHIRU?
GOT HIM!
PUFF
WHEEZ
HUH?
JUST TEXT ME, MISO-NO!
LEARN HOW!

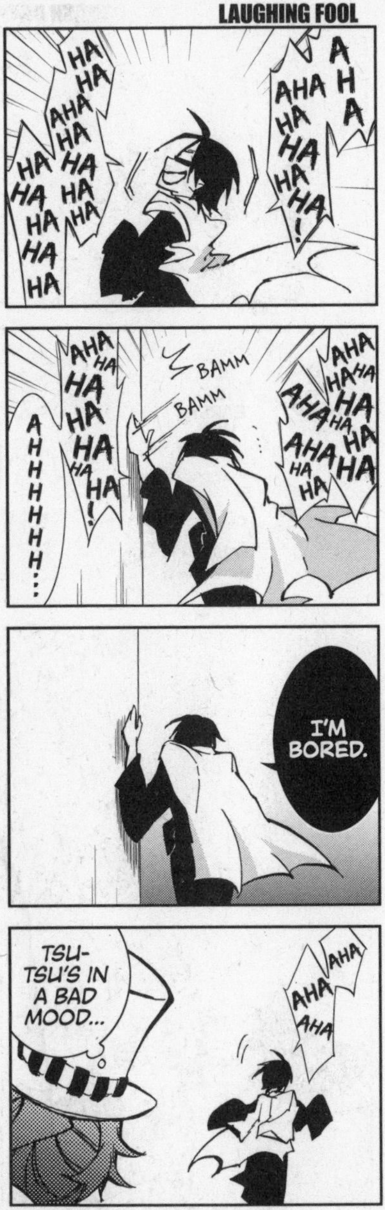
LAUGHING FOOL
A H A
AHA HA HA HA HA HA!
HA HA AHA HA HA HA HA HA
HA HA HA HA HA
AHA HA HA HA AHA HA HA AHA HA HA HA HA
BAMM
BAMM
AHA HA HA HA HA HA HA HA!
AHHHHHHHH...
I'M BORED.
AHA AHA AHA
TSU-TSU'S IN A BAD MOOD...

LAUGHING FOOL 2

BEL-KIA!
WANNA HEAR SOMETHIN' GOOD?
SURE!
TELL ME ALL!
HOLD ON...
AHA
AHA HA HA HA HA HA!
AHA!!
AHA HA HA HA!
AAAAAAAAH...
I'M BORED.
ANOTHER BAD MOOD...
SIGH...
HOO BOY...

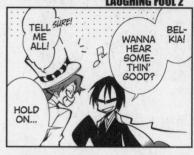

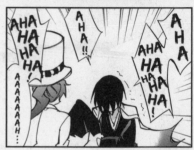

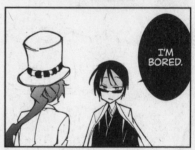

THANKS, EVERYBODY!
SEE YA NEXT ISSUE!
STRIKE TANAKA

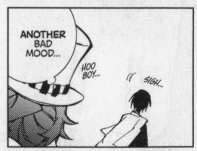

Experience all that SEVEN SEAS has to offer!

Visit us Online and follow us on Twitter!
WWW.GOMANGA.COM
WWW.TWITTER.COM/GOMANGA

SEVEN SEAS ENTERTAINMENT PRESENTS

SERVAMP

story by and art by STRIKE TANAKA — VOLUME 1

TRANSLATION
Wesley Bridges

ADAPTATION
Janet Gilbert

LETTERING AND LAYOUT
Jaedison Yui

COVER DESIGN
Nicky Lim

PROOFREADER
Janet Houck
Katherine Bell
Lee Otter

ASSISTANT EDITOR
Lissa Pattillo

MANAGING EDITOR
Adam Arnold

PUBLISHER
Jason DeAngelis

SERVAMP VOL. 1
© STRIKE TANAKA 2011
Edited by MEDIA FACTORY.
First published in Japan in 2011 by KADOKAWA CORPORATION, Tokyo.
English translation rights reserved by Seven Seas Entertainment, LLC.
under the license from KADOKAWA CORPORATION, Tokyo.

No portion of this book may be reproduced or transmitted in any form without
written permission from the copyright holders. This is a work of fiction. Names,
characters, places, and incidents are the products of the author's imagination
or are used fictitiously. Any resemblance to actual events, locals, or persons,
living or dead, is entirely coincidental.

Seven Seas books may be purchased in bulk for educational, business, or
promotional use. For information on bulk purchases, please contact Macmillan
Corporate & Premium Sales Department at 1-800-221-7945 (ext 5442)
or write specialmarkets@macmillan.com.

Seven Seas and the Seven Seas logo are trademarks of
Seven Seas Entertainment, LLC. All rights reserved.

ISBN: 978-1-626921-75-7

Printed in Canada

Second Printing: September 2015

10 9 8 7 6 5 4 3 2

FOLLOW US ONLINE: *www.gomanga.com*

READING DIRECTIONS

This book reads from *right to left*, Japanese style.
If this is your first time reading manga, you start
reading from the top right panel on each page and
take it from there. If you get lost, just follow the
numbered diagram here. It may seem backwards at
first, but you'll get the hang of it! Have fun!!

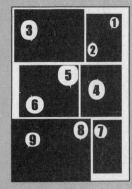